D1617019

Heaven's Harsh Tableland

AMERICAN WESTS
sponsored by West Texas A&M University
Alex Hunt, General Editor

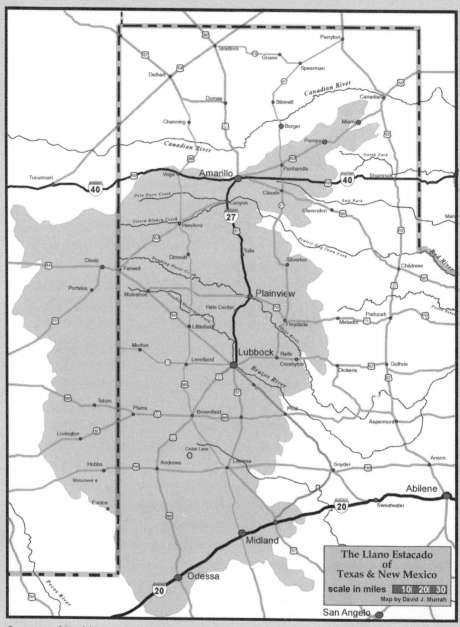

Courtesy of David J. Murrah

Heaven's Harsh Tableland

A New History of the Llano Estacado

Paul H. Carlson

TEXAS A&M UNIVERSITY PRESS
COLLEGE STATION

∞ This paper meets the requirements of ANSI/NISO Z39.48-1992
(Permanence of Paper).
Binding materials have been chosen for durability.

Library of Congress Cataloging-in-Publication Data
Names: Carlson, Paul Howard, author.
Title: Heaven's harsh tableland : a new history of the Llano Estacado /
    Paul H. Carlson.
Other titles: New history of the Llano Estacado | American Wests.
Description: First edition. | College Station : Texas A & M University
    Press, [2023] | Series: American Wests | Includes bibliographical
    references and index.
Identifiers: LCCN 2023019139 | ISBN 9781648431548 (cloth) | ISBN
    9781648431555 (ebook)
Subjects: LCSH: Human settlements—Texas, West. | Human settlements—New
    Mexico. | Llano Estacado—History.
Classification: LCC F392.L62 C39 2023 | DDC 976.4/8—dc23/eng/20230425
LC record available at https://lccn.loc.gov/2023019139

Cover photo taken on the John Roley Ranch adjoining Casas Amarillas. Courtesy
Monte L. Monroe

For my brother and sisters and their spouses

Karen and Floyd Bouley
David and Judy Carlson
Jean Forrest and the memory of her husband Ralph
JoAnn and Steve Shaw

And for Ellen's sister, brothers, and their spouses

Harlan and Darlene Opperman
Patsy and Harold Burkinshaw
Don and Joanne Opperman

Contents

Foreword

In the 1920s, on the Llano Estacado as elsewhere in the United States, the economy boomed and population grew. On that flat, treeless expanse, more development meant, among other things, the planting of trees around dwellings and amidst communities. As a result, the region experienced the arrival of new bird species common in America but unknown on the Llano—mockingbirds and other thrashers, wrens, and robins. Human activity changed the natural habitat, which in turn led to a change in species that have since become familiar. A few years later, people were again planting trees on the Llano, but this time the changes were signs not of prosperity but of an ominous new reality. Workers in federal labor programs planted trees around farmland to create "shelter belts," groves established at the public expense in hopes of holding down the earth that was otherwise blowing away in the teeth of Dust Bowl winds. Once again, human activity profoundly altered the environment.

Paul Carlson's *Heaven's Harsh Tableland*, while a modestly sized volume, is rich and full with such evocative stories. The reader of this new history of the Llano Estacado will be enlightened, and even the most devoted scholar of the region will find here new stories and insights. The central theme of Carlson's work is change, and indeed the region has seen transformational change due to climatic cycles and human activity over millennia. The reader is engaged by a dynamic quality of the region that is out of keeping with its reputation for flat monotony and staid culture.

It is quite a thrill to write the foreword to what will be the benchmark work on the Llano Estacado region of Texas and New Mexico. As a resident of the Llano Estacado, located near the junction of the Tierra Blanca and Palo Duro creeks, I welcome Carlson's book, the latest work in an impressive body of work. I have benefitted more than I can measure from books like *The Cowboy Way, Empire Builder in the Texas Panhandle, The Plains Indians, Pecos Bill, The Buffalo Soldier Tragedy of 1877, Comanche Jack Stilwell, Myth, Memory, and Massacre*, and *Amarillo: The Story of a Western Town*. Drawing on his well-earned expertise, *Heaven's Harsh Tableland* is a much needed and welcome synthesis of classic and recent historical, geographical, and anthropological scholarship.

As a brief overview, the book moves from the geological formation of the Llano Estacado, land masses moving and rising "at about the speed fingernails grow," as well as its early climate, ecology, and human cultures. Carlson then takes us from the end of the Pleistocene, as glaciers retreated and human cultures changed with the climate, through the Comanche era. We then learn of the Spanish and Mexican periods of the Llano Estacado before moving into the complex cultural interactions during the shifting powers of the 19th century. After a consideration of US federal presence and military conquest, the final few chapters present the modern Llano Estacado, emphasizing land use in its economic regimes, from commercial buffalo hunting, ranching and farming, community growth and mechanized agriculture, to the Dust Bowl and World War II era. The final chapter takes us to the present, covering agribusiness and urbanization, and the epilogue looks into the future, emphasizing the finite waters of the Ogallala Aquifer and the trends of a warming climate.

Carlson's book conjures for the reader great scenes, not the "successive waves" of progress described by Frederick Jackson Turner, but nevertheless a sense of momentous encounters in an awesome landscape. Here Clovis people hunted the mammoths and bison in a lush llano we would not recognize. Here Comanches dominated a vast empire defined by the southern plains bison herd, controlling trade on eastern and western frontiers. Here thousands of cattle were grazed and driven north to market under the care of the iconic cowboy. Here steel plows broke and turned under thousands of square miles of grassland to produce wheat and cotton. Here rose the most populous cities of the southern plains, underwritten by the precious Ogallala aquifer. Though organized chronologically, as historians are wont to proceed, the trajectory from terra incognita to the Trump presidency does not imply a march of progress so much as a succession of human endeavor based on what it took to survive or what could be taken to thrive.

Carlson's awareness of audience interest struck me as impressive as he held my interest even through chapters I would not have expected to thrill me, for example the importance of the Graham-Hoeme Plow or the founding of Texas Tech University. As further evidence of his engaging style, take his use of sidebars, exploring matters such as the murky origins of the name "Llano Estacado," the evolution of dinosaurs and humans as related to the region, the route of the Coronado expedition, estimates of southern plains bison population, the sad history of treaties between the US government and indigenous peoples, and too-often overlooked important women of the region.

Carlson says that his is not an environmental history, but the book comes pretty close, demonstrating the degree to which human history and change are essentially connected to the bioregional realities of a place, particularly when a place is so difficult for human endeavor—high, dry, treeless, remote, and given to climatic extremes. The book starts as Pleistocene glaciers retreated, and brings us forward to the Anthropocene and its already palpable dangers—heat, drought, and dropping water tables. While, as he says, his work is a broadly drawn economic, social, cultural, political, and military history, underlying all of this is a sense that climate change and natural limits have been determining factors, and will continue to be so.

One intriguing aspect of Carlson's book is its subtle treatment of regional uniqueness. Certainly the Llano Estacado has long been shaped by its connections to the larger elsewhere, and Carlson acknowledges the importance of outside forces that shape it, from the Spanish conquistadores to the globalized investments of agribusiness. Yet at the same time the region does seem markedly different from other areas of the United States, American West, Texas, and even Great Plains contexts that enclose it. Where else, we might ask, have people relied so profoundly on water and petroleum pumped from beneath our feet to sustain their economy? Where else is the combination of wind and sun quite so powerful, so rich in potential energy? Where else can we find such a distinctive alchemy of ethnicities, religions, and political ideologies that give our identity its wonderful and odd tincture? While Carlson's book harbors some mysteries and silences—and given its scope, how could it not?—this is the new standard history to the Llano Estacado and an essential work of synthetic bioregional history.

Heaven's Harsh Tableland is an important new work for the American Wests series at Texas A&M University Press. I feel fortunate to have it on my bookshelf and rest confident that its readers will find it of great value. The Llano Estacado, an often overlooked but fascinating region, deserves no less than this great effort by Paul Carlson.

—Alex Hunt, General Editor

Preface

The Llano Estacado is a big, broad Southern Great Plains region in western Texas and eastern New Mexico. A stark, sunbaked mesa, it extends from Amarillo and the Canadian River Valley southward some 250 miles to Midland, Odessa, and the oil-rich Permian Basin. Its east-west axis reaches from its dramatic, serrated eastern escarpment, which separates it from the Texas Rolling Plains country, nearly 200 miles west to its long, curved, less-dramatic western escarpment and the Pecos River Valley in New Mexico. The Llano is a level territory, and its extensive flatness is apparent to all who travel across it. If one flies over the semiarid, horizontal-looking land and views the ground below with its scores of oil pump jacks near Midland and Odessa, its cotton-based center-pivot irrigation systems near Lubbock, its seemingly empty rangeland in New Mexico, and its feed lots, dairy operations, and wheat fields near Amarillo, one sees the essential life patterns that characterized the Llano in 2022.

The Llano Estacado is a unique geographic region, but it embodies more than its celebrated environment and physiography. Its history, for example, remains fascinating and, although dominated by the last two centuries, reaches back more than twelve thousand years. The region's long past and historical record deserve chronicling. Hence, the principal aim of the book is to review the Llano's historic contours from its earliest foundations to its energetic present and manage it all in a short, sharply drawn volume designed for an educated reading public. It attempts to inform and engage readers, such as my Upper Midwest relatives, who might live far beyond the distinctive area with its novel Spanish name. As a secondary purpose it seeks to place the Llano's regional story in a broad perspective.

The book is not environmental history, but an important theme stresses the role of the environment. Not a static place, the Llano Estacado through time has witnessed significant natural, demographic, cultural, biological, physical, and climatic transformations and sometimes seemingly all at once. Those transformations, both minor and major, became set marks for explaining the region's dynamic nature, thus making the idea of flux another important theme in the narrative. Although it focuses mainly on economic pursuits, the book neglects neither social and cultural events nor significant political and military activities.

Such a conventional study seems warranted. Many exceptional older works cover the Llano's natural history, canyonlands, rivers, geology, archaeology, indigenous peoples, explorers, early settlers, and such economic pursuits as ranching, cotton and wheat growing, and petroleum mining. And over the past dozen or so years several competent edited works touching on the region's past have appeared, as have histories of Amarillo and Lubbock, the Llano Estacado's largest cities. New archaeological and geoarchaeological surveys have enhanced our understanding of the Llano's prehistory and its environmental and geophysical makeup. Likewise, some fresh studies of area ranches and cattle raisers and a pictorial history of the area's prominent cotton industry have become available, as have book-length accounts of its natural history, its music, its churches, its bison hunters, and its major universities. Nor have women and other minorities been neglected in the latest studies. A recent book featuring breathtaking aerial views of the Llano, its historic sites, and its spectacular canyonlands adds to the growing list of specialized works.

In short, although many excellent histories touch on it, no broad synthesis embracing the entirety of the Llano Estacado experience remains available. Accordingly, the work presented here represents a modest effort to identify and describe with interpretive notions essential components of the Llano's history. All chroniclers make judgments about topics to embrace. In that sense, the book is a personal history, for it contains only material, stories, personalities, and events and episodes I chose to include. I gave the selections my best shot.

As the notes and sources make clear, I have relied heavily on the works of others. The Llano Estacado has had no shortage of chroniclers, journal and diary keepers, memorialists, and personal record keepers. Its professional agronomists, archaeologists, climatologists, demographers, environmentalists, geoarchaeologists, geologists, historians, literati, naturalists, social scientists, and related scholars plus countless amateur sleuths have examined the Llano with its soils, minerals, animals, plants, and humans from one end of the region to the other and from deep in its geologic past to its very present, including careful assessments of Llano citizens' 2020 presidential voting records. The brief history presented here, then, represents a subjective synthesis of the work and views of many others as well as over forty years of my own research on the region. Using such studies, I have tried to bring some chronological order and a larger understanding to the Llano's past and on occasion to offer my own interpretations. I trust the result is more than jabberwocky.

Acknowledgments

Of the many people who provided assistance during research and writing, two were particularly influential: David J. Murrah and Monte L. Monroe. Murrah, a close friend since graduate school days, provided suggestions and ideas, shared information and material, reviewed portions of the manuscript, prepared several maps, and gave unstinting support. A native son of the region, Murrah comprehends the Llano Estacado and its colorful saga as well as anyone and better than most. In fact, for him the Llano's history has been something of a lifelong pursuit, and his critical studies of its cities, churches, ranches, historians, natural history, music, and leading figures have informed my own research and understanding of the so-called greatest of mesas. Without him the book would not have been possible.

Monroe, archivist of Texas Tech University's magnificent Southwest Collection/Special Collections Library and the Texas state historian, offered endless amounts of advice, counsel, ideas, and notions—most of them helpful. He read and commented deeply on the entire manuscript, noted questionable issues, suggested illustrations, offered information, and provided photos. Moreover, he got me going again on this project, one I had started many years ago and then for various reasons put off until, when deep into the COVID-19 pandemic in mid-2020, he insisted that I resume the work. Pandemic fatigue had set in, but with health advisers at the time still telling us to stay home, coupled with Monroe's enthusiastic doggedness, I turned again to my little history of the Llano Estacado. Without him there would be no book.

Other associates and colleagues at the Southwest Collection/Special Collections Library likewise proved essential. In the archive's reading room Randy Vance, J. Weston Marshall, and their assistants, particularly Kristen Britz, Whitney Johns, Shelby Newman, Jennifer Perea, and Roshini Yuvarajan, retrieved materials, located photos, asked questions, and offered help of all kinds. Southwest Collection/Special Collections Library director Jennifer Spurrier and many staff members, including Connie Aguilar, Austin Allison, H. Allen Anderson, Katelin Dixon, Zach Hernandez, Nicci Hester, Rob King, Tai Kreidler, Curtis Peoples, John Perrin, Elisa Stroman, Robert Weaver, and Lynn Whitfield, extended courtesies and aided in many ways.

Several friends and colleagues read portions of the manuscript. They offered opinions about what data to include (or not), suggested changes in style, corrected some problems of fact and interpretation, and focused my thinking on what material constitutes a good, representative portrayal of the Llano Estacado through time. In particular, this helpful group included former Texas Tech librarian, historian, and writing partner John T. "Jack" Becker, the "editor from hell," who reviewed several chapters, traveled with me to historic sites, provided photographs, and assisted in truly major ways; and John Wolf, a bibliophile, who offered ideas, corrections, and approaches and who also provided important bibliographical materials. Susan Karina Dickey, a hospital administrator and writer-historian, provided critical analysis. Thomas A. Britten, whose study of the Lipan Apaches represents a model of Native American scholarship, was thorough in his evaluations. Don and Sally Abbe, superb historians of the Llano Estacado, offered much good advice. Judge Tom Crum, lawyer-historian and thoughtful writing partner, questioned many of my assumptions and set me straight on others as we discussed the project during our semiannual Big Bend National Park hiking trips.

Plenty of others helped. Deborah Liles read an early draft of the manuscript and offered good advice. M. Scott Sosebee, professor of history at Stephen F. Austin State University and director of the East Texas Historical Association, during his many research visits to Tech's Southwest Collection took time over coffee and dinner to discuss the project. Alwyn Barr, a splendid Texas Tech University history department colleague, discussed the evolving manuscript at weekly coffee sessions with me and several friends mentioned above. Warren Stricker of the Panhandle-Plains Historical Museum research center and archive once again competently and enthusiastically assisted with information, ideas, photos, and research materials. He was generously accommodating. Amy McVay Tellez and John LeMay at the Historical Society of Southeast New Mexico and its archives were helpful with information, photos, and research materials, as was Donna Blake Birchell of Carlsbad. Cynthia Olivarez at the Slaton, Texas, Public Library; Sarah Harris at the American Windmill Museum; Lacee Holting at the FiberMax Center for Discovery; and Dolores Mosser and Sammie Simpson, whose big manuscript on the ancient Portales River Valley deserves publication, provided information. Matthew Tippens supplied important material on German "colonies." Ruby Nell Hardin near Portales and painter Gayle Walker provided information, photos, and paintings of several towns in New Mexico. Patsy and Harold Burkinshaw, my sister- and brother-in-law, from their ranch located deep in the Sand Hills of Nebraska, furnished important information on raising sheep and cattle on native, unbroken grassland. My neighbor and Portales, New Mexico, rancher–farmer–commercial operator Wayne Hardin discussed the problems and joys of modern agriculture on the Llano Estacado. In 2022, the Burkinshaws and Hardins, like most people in Great Plains agriculture, struggled with the same issues farmers and ranchers faced 130 years ago: drought and water, predators and livestock diseases, feed and market fluctuations, fencing, and winter storms among them.

Others who provided aid, pictures, information, or advice included Brendon Asher, Ute Becton, John Beusterien, Darryl Birkenfeld, Clint E. Chambers, Don Enger, Pat Ginn, Aaron Lynskey, Gene Lynskey, Jessica Mallard, Laura Monroe, Shannon Marie Pierce, James Pipkin, Steve Porter, Gene Preuss, Bob Reitz, John and Stephanie Roley, Joe W. Specht, Leland Turner, KJ Waters, Andy Wilkinson, and Lynette Wilson. My son, Kevin Carlson; my daughter, Diane McLaurin; and my grandson Tim McLaurin helped in numerous ways, as did staff members of the *Lubbock Avalanche-Journal*, particularly Adam D. Young and now-retired associate editor Karen Boehm.

Managers and editors at Texas A&M University Press were superb. Peer reviewers offered ideas, made suggestions, and helped a lot. Jay Dew, director of the press, and Thom Lemmons, editor in chief, gave encouragement and kept me centered. Christine Brown, Nicole DuPlessis, and especially Patricia A. Clabaugh also aided the book's publication, and copyeditor Cynthia Lindlof made improvements, strengthened the narrative, and sharpened its focus. I am grateful.

And, once again, I owe a huge debt of gratitude to my lifelong partner, Ellen Joyce Opperman Carlson. Through the long pandemic and afterward, she encouraged my work, tolerated the long hours I spent in front of my computer, traveled with me to visit historic sites and distant archives, took several photographs used in the book, and, by reading portions of the manuscript and commenting wryly on them, kept me measured and humbled. Professionally and personally, I am deeply thankful for her unlimited support and effervescent spirit. To Ellen, fortunately for me, the glass is always half full.

Finally, I alone am responsible for any errors, misinterpretations, or lamentable issues that may remain. For them I apologize. In the end, if the story as presented here did not happen the way I have described it, well, darn, it should have. *Bon lecture!*

Heaven's Harsh Tableland

1

Land and First Peoples

**Lord, lift me up and let me stand, By Faith,
on heaven's table-land.**[1]

Twelve thousand years ago in a wet, frigid climate, huge Columbian mammoths sauntered across a marshy Llano Estacado. Monstrous armadillos and giant ground sloths the size of old Volkswagen Beetles walked through the Llano's tall, coarse grasses. Saber-tooth cats hunted small, three-toed horses, tiny camels, and four-horned antelope. Giant bison, a third larger than modern species, ranged over the grassy tableland. Aggressive, short-faced bears, powerful dire wolves, and elephant-like mastodons shared the Llano's uplands and canyonlands. They are gone from the Llano now, as are the Clovis people who lived among them.

Today, in a dry, warm climate the Llano Estacado is different. In the absence of Ice Age animals and Clovis hunters, it is dominated by us— we moderns. It is now a varied territory of huge cotton and wheat fields; of concrete and asphalt cities; of large, steel, oil pump jacks; of white, towering wind turbines with endless miles of wire stretched between massive, lace-like metal towers. In place of aggressive carnivores, timid, often hornless, beef cattle graze the Llano's short-grass rangeland. How the long, grand shift occurred is in part the subject of this little book about the Llano Estacado—heaven's harsh tableland.

Shallow and saline Cedar Lake in Gaines County, Texas, is the largest playa on the Llano Estacado. Except for its extensive size, it is typical of most playa lakes. Courtesy of John T. "Jack" Becker

The Llano Estacado, or Staked Plains, is North America's largest mesa. A huge, elevated upland located in western Texas and eastern New Mexico, it appears horizontal, uniform, and ruler straight. Encompassing nearly fifty thousand square miles of territory under a big "blue bowl of sky," it exceeds the land area of nineteen states, including the combined size of all New England. Covering all or portions of thirty-seven counties in Texas and seven in New Mexico, it is a windswept, semiarid, and sunburnt plateau. It contains few water-running streams, and its largest body of natural water, Cedar Lake in Gaines County, Texas, appears as a shallow, shimmery prairie tarn. Until well after Euro-American settlers arrived in the late nineteenth century, few trees or large shrubs, excepting such cactus species as tall-stalked sotol and yucca, graced the dry flatness of this giant mesa.[2]

The "Llano," if you will, is a stunning, beguiling place, attractive in many ways with a mystic quality about it. Its brilliant sunrises and sunsets; its big, blue, open, often cloudless sky; its cool summer evenings; its spectacular canyonlands; its wide-open, enormous stretches of grassy rangeland; its long, multiplex past; and its friendly, passionate, purposeful people with varied racial, ethnic, and cultural backgrounds all speak to life and living on this level Southern High Plains country with its traditional American values, rural character, and western personality. It is a region where residents think what other Texans and New Mexicans call "the center of nowhere" is in fact someplace special.

The Llano Estacado's Name

The Spanish name El Llano Estacado for the southern High Plains in western Texas and eastern New Mexico enjoys a varied and sometimes strange history and evolution. In translation, the name is most often interpreted as "Staked Plains"—sometimes pronounced "Stay-ked Plains." If the late geographer and historian of the Llano John Miller Morris is correct, the term "Llano Estacado" was "widely familiar when American Travelers arrived in New Mexico in the 1830s." If so, comancheros and ciboleros, the Spanish and Pueblo villagers from New Mexico who had traded and hunted on the High Plains for decades, may have been the first people to use the term. Josiah Gregg may have been the first person to put the term in print when he placed it on a map for his 1844 book Commerce on the Prairies.

The "Llano" in the name represents no problem; it means "plain" or "plains," or a few times in the nineteenth century, "prairie." The "Estacado" component, on the other hand, finds little agreement on its meaning, origin, or use. In 1891, W. F. Cummins in the Third Annual Report of the Geological Survey of Texas summarized its etymology. In a long footnote to his report, he wrote that some people suggested the name came from the tall yucca and sotol plants on the Llano that resemble stakes. Others, perhaps with more solid arguments, Cummins noted, cited various handmade vertical objects: piles of bison ordure or arrows stuck in the ground or wooden stakes Indians and/or explorers placed to designate water holes. Perhaps the most-often-cited translations have Estacado as "Palisaded" or "Stockaded," referring to the steep walls of the Llano's escarpments—both the western and the more dramatic eastern inclines.

Historian H. Bailey Carroll, who thought deeply about the term, suggested that "Estacado" was corrupted from "Destacado," a term that meant "Elevated Plain." More recently, Morris wrote that perhaps the name should be attributed to Native Americans on the Llano Estacado. The Apaches and Comanches, he noted, staked—pinned with ropes and bridles—their horses to the ground.

In 2020, language scholar Meredith McClain suggested a much different interpretation for "Llano Estacado." She argues that the name comes from the Llano's playas, "those shallow, circular ponds" so prominently found in the region. There are over twenty-six thousand of them on the Llano, and they were full in 1541 when Francisco Coronado crossed the region. Coronado's chief chronicler "studied and described them." Coronado complained about traveling around them. McClain writes: "The noun in Spanish for a still or stagnant pool is estanque. The adjectival form used to describe the playa/estanque formations on the Llano is estancado. Clearly, then," she concludes, "El Llano Estancado (the pooled plain) is surely the original and explicit Mexican ciboleros' description of [the Llano], according to its definitive, ecological, and most important two features, flat land of still pools."

Historian Sandy Hoover summed up the many conjectures about the name's origin: "It might even be possible that the most lasting significance of the term 'Llano Estacado' lies in its mystery." It is indeed an enigmatic title for a region that juxtaposes harsh and heaven.

Although in most ways a grand corner of the world, the Llano Estacado is not always an easy place in which to live. Climatologically, aridity and scarce water supplies, periodic drought, ceaseless winds, frequent dust storms, tornados, and hail bursts all contribute to its spartan environment. In 2022, farmers and ranchers, like agricultural societies here thousands of years ago, were no strangers to its harshness. A two-thousand-year-long drought with massive sandstorms, beginning some 6,500 years ago, speaks to the past's unforgiving conditions. More recently, Llano residents during the Dust Bowl days of the 1930s faced catastrophic crop and livestock losses and then endured several years of devastating drought in the 1950s. In 2011, extreme drought led to range fires in the Texas Panhandle, including parts of the Llano Estacado, and even larger Panhandle fires occurred in 2006 and 2017.[3]

Current occupants of the Llano, like people elsewhere on the Great Plains, confront typical continental weather conditions with cold winters and hot summers. Their life here is complicated by a boom-and-bust economy in the oil patch, an inability of cattle raisers to establish a stable price for their beef, and nearly seven months of empty ground with brownish-red, blowing dirt and dust in the cotton fields. Moreover, some climate modelers suggest that the region, having just left a twelve-hundred-year cycle of relatively cool and wet weather (really?), has now entered a long megadrought with high temperatures.[4]

Such news and harshness aside, in 2022, the Llano Estacado, although a rural and agrarian place, found 80 percent of its 1.4 million residents living in urban or small-town settings. The region enjoyed a limited, if growing, population. Lubbock, Amarillo, and the large oil towns of Midland and Odessa, all in Texas, represented its major cities. Politically, the Llano was conservative and right-wing leaning. Economically, petroleum mining, cotton and wheat growing, cattle feeding and raising, and dairy production represented major influences driving the region's wealth and marketplace.

Educationally, many colleges and universities spread across the Llano Estacado: Texas Tech University, the University of Texas Permian Basin, West Texas A&M University, Eastern New Mexico University, University of the Southwest, Lubbock Christian University, and Wayland Baptist University. Several community institutions, including Midland College, Odessa College, Clovis Community College, South Plains College, New Mexico Junior College, Amarillo College, and several technical institutions and business colleges supported them. In 2021, Texas Tech opened a veterinary school in Amarillo where it operated a nursing school, and the Texas Tech University Health Sciences Center with the University Medical Center in Lubbock represented a major teaching hospital.

In 2022, the Llano Estacado was culturally diverse and generally divided into four subregions, each marked by economic distinctions and the rise of larger trade cities within it. The central Llano—the South

Plains—centered at Lubbock, was Southern in background, settled by people who practiced some form of evangelical Southern Protestant Christianity. Although diversified agriculture expanded in the twenty-first century, the South Plains was still cotton country in 2022. Many groups and families in the area traced their agricultural-based societies back through East Texas to the American South and its former cotton civilization.[5]

The upper Llano, or lower Panhandle below the Canadian River, centered at Amarillo. It was cattle country in 2022, characterized by range-cattle operations and cattle feeding with crop agriculture to support the feedlots. Wheat growing also served as an important agricultural commodity, and in recent years large dairy operations appeared. Many settlers of this region and the larger Panhandle came from the American Midwest, bringing with them a northern, traditional brand of Protestantism. In the early years of settlement, they looked to the Midwest, especially Kansas City and Chicago, as their marketplace. Moreover, Amarillo, the region's dominant city, lies closer to state capitals in Colorado, New Mexico, Oklahoma, and Kansas than to the Texas political center in Austin.[6]

A third subregion, the lower Llano, edging into the Permian Basin along both sides of modern Interstate Highway 20, was oil country in 2022 with an alternating boom-and-bust economy dependent on global petroleum markets. Its rural territory contained livestock, but it was also dust-filled, mesquite and scrub brush country where oil pump jacks stood like giant chess pieces on the distinctively square-graded terrain. Its largest cities, Midland and Odessa, were young and modern and full of growth.

The fourth subregion lies in New Mexico. Here in 2022, the Llano Estacado, still influenced by Hispano-Indian traditions, remained open and empty rangeland with long, straight highways that stretch through a distant, grassy horizon. In the Portales area, however, dairy farming with feed-crop agriculture to provide requisite support, assumed a significant role in the rural economy, and some farming existed elsewhere, especially in Curry and Roosevelt Counties. Clovis with a population of forty thousand and its Cannon Air Force Base and Hobbs with a population of thirty-nine thousand and its large Zia Park Casino Hotel & Racetrack were its largest cities, but the high, mostly vacant rangeland was cattle country, open, expansive, and sun-dried tan in appearance.

Geographically, in its far-northwestern sections in New Mexico, the Llano Estacado lies five thousand feet above sea level. It slips imperceptibly in elevation toward the south and east in Texas, where it measures just under three thousand feet above the seas. Although scarred by several deep and magnificent canyons and broken by occasional sand dunes and hillocks, its otherwise high, horizontal surface extends on three sides (north, east, west) between fifty and three hundred or more feet above surrounding physiographic sections. On the southern flank of this once-grassy plain, the terrain simply melts into the Edwards Plateau and Permian Basin.

Across its surface, the Llano Estacado appears infinitely level. Indeed, musician and area native Butch Hancock suggested—fictitiously—that in "Lubbock you can see fifty miles in any direction. And if you stand on a tuna fish can, you can see a hundred miles." The land is flat, obviously, although not as flat as a Swedish pancake. Partly as a result, until well into the twentieth century, the Llano Estacado appeared as a monotonous grassy steppe dominated by blue grama, buffalo grass, and other short grasses with a sprinkling of taller side oats grama, wheat grass, and little bluestem. An ocean of grass some of the first European visitors, early explorers, and initial settlers called it. In an October 1541 letter to his king Carlos I, for example, thirty-one-year-old Spaniard Francisco Vázquez de Coronado, the great explorer of New Mexico, wrote that the Llano held "not a stone, nor a bit of rising ground, nor a tree, nor a shrub, nor anything to go by." The place seemed "as bare of landmarks as if we were surrounded by the sea."[7]

Some three hundred years later, little had changed. Having to lead a large party of California-bound gold seekers out of Fort Smith, Arkansas, in 1849, army officer Captain Randolph B. Marcy encountered the Llano. He wrote: "[When] we were upon the high table land, a view presented itself as boundless as the ocean. Not a tree, shrub, or any other object. . . relieved the dreary monotony of the prospect; it was a vast, illimitable expanse of desert prairie—the dreaded 'Llano Estacado' . . . or in other words, the great Zahara of North America." Three years later, the forty-year-old Marcy led an exploring expedition in the same area, one aimed at finding the headwaters of the Red and Canadian Rivers. This time, the army captain reported the land "is much elevated . . . very smooth and level . . . without a tree, shrub, or any other herbage to intercept the vision." Clearly, the hilly, woodland-reared military commander from Massachusetts did not like the level, grassy, treeless Llano Estacado of Texas and New Mexico. Clearly, too, he believed it to be a dreary, dreaded, and harsh tableland.[8]

The ocean-desert image did not go away. In 1877, a quarter century after Marcy, Dallas-based surveyor C. U. Connellee visited the Llano. He wrote: "[The] plains was covered with a thick coat of grass and extended as far as the eye could see, and [it] was the broadest country I have ever seen." And about two dozen years after Connellee, a pioneer woman, upon climbing onto the Llano Estacado for the first time said, "Good Heavens! An ocean of land!"[9]

To many such early arrivals on the high plateau, the Llano Estacado not only appeared as broad as the ocean, but also it presented a foreboding quality, one that clung to the empty, horizontal-looking, grassy plain. In the seventeenth century, for example, Spanish missionaries from New Mexico with plans to bring Christianity to Native Americans (Jumanos) east of the High Plains in Texas skirted the Llano's southern reaches. Some Spanish explorers, ordered in the eighteenth century to find more direct routes between Santa Fe and San Antonio, avoided the Llano for a route along the Canadian River. Some of the first American explorers in the Southwest, likewise, steered away from the sometimes-formidable land, and West Texas cattle drovers Charles Goodnight and Oliver Loving in 1866 led their herds south around the high, mystic, and oftentimes water-scarce terrain. In 1877, US soldiers got lost on it.[10]

This huge, flat, mysterious terra incognita, although geologically very young, developed over a period of ten million or more years. It grew from outwash materials of the Rocky Mountains in New Mexico. Geologists and other earth scientists explain the process beginning with tectonic plates that underlie the globe's surface. The southern Rockies formed, they suggest, as two very large, deep plates—the Pacific and the

North American—moving only an inch or two a year (about the speed fingernails grow), collided some 70 million years ago. Bolstered by the subduction of other, smaller tectonic masses, the plates with relentless force mashed and heaved and pressed against one another. They wrinkled and folded under the intense pressure and for some 50 million years thrust upward to create the mountains. But as time passed, the mountains, aided by volcanic and other diastrophic activity, fell back on themselves only to rise again. The last major upthrust occurred about 10 million years ago—although some of the southern mountain ranges, such as the Sangre de Cristos, are a mere 5 million years in age.[11]

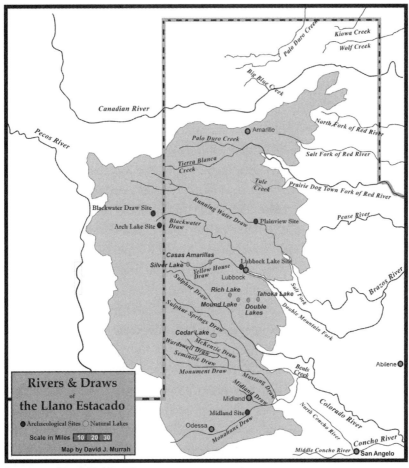

Courtesy of David J. Murrah

But even as they inched skyward, the New Mexico mountains eroded. Natural forces, such as wind, rain, snow, and flood, ate away at the elevated terrain, driving displaced material in the form of sand, silt, mud, and gravel away from the expanding highlands. Despite such erosion, in time the mountains became towering landmasses: Wheeler Peak in the Taos Mountains reached upward to over thirteen thousand feet. Congruently, as the mountains grew, a swelling volume of outwash matter escaped the giants. On the southeastern slopes where the Llano Estacado emerged, countless tons of debris roared down the mountainsides and sped away in rushing streams and roiling rivers.

During spring snow melts or after heavy rains, the ancient rivers carried even larger amounts of waterborne debris down from the uplands and out across the plains. They emptied their sand and gravel loads in fan-like formations, filling their channels before spilling over to create a new course. The rivers repeated the process countless times, and the plains pushed east and southeastward toward the Gulf of Mexico. In effect, the Llano Estacado arose in much the same way river deltas form.

Even as it formed, the Llano Estacado, like the southern Rockies, came under assault. Between 1 and 2 million years ago the Pecos River began carving a channel away from its mouth at the Rio Grande in present Val Verde County. It cut northward and perhaps 100,000 years ago, the Pecos cut through, "beheaded," one after another the upper Concho, Colorado, Brazos, and Red Rivers, the once-massive water systems that moved mountain rubble over the plains. The Pecos "stole" their water and the loads of sand, silt, mud, and gravel the rivers carried. Deprived of its building blocks, the Llano's expansion halted. And complicating the story, for millions of years the lower Brazos and Colorado Rivers had, like the Pecos, carved channels and valleys up from their mouths at the Gulf of Mexico. In the process they and eventually the Red River cut away the sand and dirt and rocks that composed the plains, moving its eastern edge west some two hundred miles to its present location.[12]

At least two critical phenomena grew from the Llano's creation and in fact still remain part of it: the Ogallala Aquifer and the Caprock. The aquifer exists as a large underground reservoir that extends eight hundred miles through the western High Plains from Texas to South Dakota.

The Ogallala Aquifer underlies the Llano Estacado and much of the Great Plains. Its water supplies farmers, ranchers, and cities and towns of the Great Plains. Courtesy of David J. Murrah

It underlies most of the Llano Estacado and, through irrigation, supplies in 2022 most of the water needs of the Llano's towns and indispensable agricultural economy. The aquifer occurs in the Ogallala Formation, the unconsolidated geologic remnant created, as noted previously, when huge deposits of sand, silt, and gravel washed eastward from the Rocky Mountains. Water in the aquifer survives within voids (pore spaces) between sedimentary particles that compose the formation.[13]

The Caprock, which rests on the Ogallala Formation near the Llano's surface, represents a band of sandy limestones and calcium carbonate (caliche) originating from the evaporation of calcium-rich water that percolated up from the aquifer's underground sources. Often whitish in color, it remains harder than the eolian soils above it and the sedimentary

The Caprock Escarpment represents the steep walls that on three sides of the Llano Estacado mark an edge of the high mesa and separate it from landforms below it. The Caprock, the narrow band of calcified limestone prominent in this photo, is harder than the sandy soils of the Llano's surface (or Blackwater Draw Formation) above it and the water-rich Ogallala Formation below it, thus helping keep the Llano Estacado from wearing away. Courtesy of Ellen Carlson

materials of the Ogallala Formation below it. Consequently, it slows erosion along the Llano's edges, or escarpments, where the Caprock has become one of the more conspicuous elements of the Llano Estacado. The Llano's current surface, mostly eolian created, rests on the Caprock and ranges from a few to several feet thick.

Several canyons and draws slice deep into the Llano Estacado. The major ones, located along the region's northeastern rim, include Palo Duro and Tule in the upper Red River drainage system, Quitaque in the upper Pease River, and Blanco and Yellow House in the upper Brazos River. The late social geographer John Miller Morris wrote of them: "Sculpted by rainfall and runoff, blasted by wind and ice, and eaten away at their bases by groundwater erosion, the [canyons] provide a vivid and colorful spectacle." The canyon walls—some six hundred to eight hundred feet high in Palo Duro—display magnificent stratigraphic banding in their rocks with such colors as orange-red, white, lavender, gray, brown, and yellow.[14]

Several additional rifts augment the allure of the eastern canyonlands. North of the majestic twelve-mile-wide and forty-five-mile-long Palo Duro Canyon, North Fork Draw and McClellan Creek and Mulberry

Canyons add to the serrated beauty of the Llano's eastern escarpment. Little Sunday and Cita Canyons cut into the southern wall of lower Palo Duro. Below the deep, narrow, and spectacular Tule Canyon, other marvelous canyons attract a growing number of visitors: Caprock Canyons (Caprock Canyons State Park and Trailway) plus Los Lingos and Quitaque Canyons. South of them are Blanco Canyon, created by Running Water Draw, and Yellow House Canyon, cut by Blackwater and Yellow House Draws. Below the mesquite-filled Yellow House, Double Mountain Fork Canyon (the upper end of the South Fork [Main Fork] of the Double Mountain Fork of the Brazos River) provides a major portion of water in Lake Allan Henry reservoir near Justiceburg. Near the southern end of the eastern escarpment, Muchaque Valley and Tobacco Creek mark the upper Colorado River drainage system, as do several other draws farther south that 12,000 years also ago carried water to the Colorado. Of varying sizes and depths, the latter include Sulphur, Lost, Sulphur Springs, Mackenzie, Wardswell, Seminole, Monument, Mustang, Midland, and Monahans Draws.

Along the Llano Estacado's less dramatic western rim, few canyons notch the long curve of the Mescalero Escarpment. Near present-day Portales, the uninspiring Canon Blanco, really a small ravine, enters the Llano. But here in a primeval past the once-mighty upper Brazos River carried tons of mountain gravel, rocks, and even rugged boulders across the ancient Portales River Valley, the landmass between Running Water and Yellow House Draws. Above there, near the northwestern corner of the Llano, curly Alamosa Canyon verges into the plains. North of the little canyon, in the vicinity of Redondo and Tucumcari Mesas, the Pecos and Canadian River Valleys mesh or almost so. East of there, along the Llano's Canadian River Valley escarpment, at Arroyo del Puerto (Puerto de los Rivajenos) in modern Quay County, New Mexico, the nearly eighteen hundred members of Coronado's entrada in 1541 ascended the Llano.[15]

The entry point, a wide break in the low-lying plains escarpment, proved an easy climb for the expedition. Coronado's native guides knew of its existence, apparently, and led entrada members to the location. Although in 2022 most people refer to the entryway as the "ramp," neither Coronado nor his several chroniclers mention the gentle incline up which they pulled their carts, drove their livestock, and walked themselves. Rather, once on the High Plains the Llano's sweeping flatness and the huge bison—the "cows"—immediately grabbed their attention. And yet, from the air today, nearly five hundred years later, the modest grade of the ramp appears vivid and striking. Located about fifteen miles south of Glenrio, writes Paul V. Chaplo, and "secluded on private land," the ramp faces north and with escarpments on either side helps create a "dramatic edge [to] the Llano."[16]

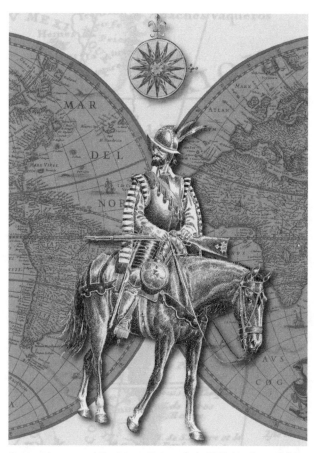

Coronado crossed the Llano Estacado in 1541, leading a large "army" of nearly eighteen hundred people with horses, cattle, sheep, goats, and loaded carts. Courtesy of Southwest Collection/Special Collections Library

Among Coronado's chroniclers, the northeastern canyons (*barrancas profundas*) more immediately captured their excitement. Understandable, of course, for they had just walked about a hundred miles across incredibly level land when suddenly they came upon deep gulfs with their vertical walls and tree-lined rivers far down below. Pedro de Castaneda, the chief chronicler for Coronado, suggested that the canyons remained "so concealed that until you are standing at the edge of them, they are not seen."[17]

Away from the spectacular canyons and their dramatic rims, the Llano's otherwise smooth surface contains several sand-dune fields. Two of the larger sand dunes reach like narrow fingers across the land: the Muleshoe Sandhills between Blackwater and Yellow House Draws and the Lea-Yoakum Sand Dunes between upper Sulphur and Sulphur Springs Draws. Also, just off the Llano's western edge, the huge Mescalero Sands trend south to north and cover an enormous stretch of empty rangeland. On the sandy southwestern edge of the Llano Estacado, the amazing Monahans Sandhills hunch up their sandy mounds in the oil-rich Permian Basin country and reach a hundred miles northwest into the Mescalero Sands.

The two finger-like dunes—Muleshoe and Lea-Yoakum—that trend west to east on the Llano Estacado represent an eastern extension of the huge Mescalero Sands. Each of the dune fields, including Monahans, originated from sands of the Pecos River Valley. Vance T. Holliday suggests "the sands accumulated in the late Quaternary," starting perhaps 11,000 years ago, with "sand deposition" occurring in several "episodes."[18] The Pecos River Valley sands, one suspects, came originally from the desiccating mountains after the Pecos beheaded the ancient streams that helped create the Llano.

Playa lakes—shallow, temporary, rainy-weather ponds—also interrupt the Llano Estacado's tableland. They abound on the Llano; perhaps twenty-six thousand exist. The playas, although located throughout the flat region, seem concentrated in its north-central sections in Texas, including such present-day counties as Floyd, Hale, Lamb, and Fisher. About forty of them remain permanent, including previously mentioned Cedar Lake; the long, narrow Tahoka Lake in Lynn County; and Shafter

Lake in Andrews County. With a few exceptions, including a couple of lakes in eastern New Mexico, water in the permanent "lakes" remains saline, brackish, and unfit to drink. Although they might drain an isolated watershed of approximately 140 acres, playa basins average less than 30 acres in size and the playa lakes themselves when full of water average only 15 or so acres. Rain fills them, and during exceptionally high rainfall, the playas grow well beyond their normal boundaries.

For the most part, the playas appear circular in shape. Chronicler Pedro de Castaneda in 1541 described them as "round ponds . . . like plates." During wet weather—as when Castaneda saw them—the playas seem blue and fresh and alive. From the air, they compare to modern center-pivot irrigation system fields. During dry weather the playas appear as low empty sinks, and during droughty seasons in our modern times many Llano Estacado farmers plow through the basins and plant crops in the low-lying soil.[19]

When they crossed the Llano Estacado in 1541, Coronado and his party encountered a large number of water-filled playas. As noted, the year—in the middle of the Little Ice Age—had been unseasonably wet and cold, and in fact at the Tiguex pueblos, near present-day Albuquerque, the Rio Grande froze over. Expedition members had spent the winter of 1540–41 there, and the cold weather had in part delayed the entrada's spring start. The wet weather had also filled the playas. In any case, once on the Llano, Coronado's grand company found playas galore. Coronado complained of having to march his great force of people, horses, cows, goats, sheep, carts, and supplies around the many lakes (*lagunas redondas*), a circumstance that slowed his progress.[20]

Associated with thousands of playas occur lunettes—crescent-shaped sand dunes. Found usually on the east or southeast side, the normally low-slung dunes might reach thirty feet or more high. Created by eolian-deposited playa sediments and soils, the lunettes apparently built over a period of twenty thousand or thirty thousand years. Plants of various kinds grow in the dunes and stabilize the sandy ridges, keeping them in place. Several lunettes hold evidence of Paleoindian activity, including camp and butcher sites.[21]

Lunettes, playas, and sand dunes aside, the Llano Estacado has been home to countless plants and thousands of animals. No dinosaurs, however, occupied the Llano. Nonetheless, geoarchaeologists, geologists, archaeologists, paleontologists, and others, led most recently by Sankar Chatterjee and Vance T. Holliday, have found fossil evidence of dinosaur species dating to the Triassic period (252 to 201 million years ago) long before the Llano came into existence. Most of the fossil material lies buried in the red bed sands and silt and mud of the Triassic's Dockum Group deep below the Llano's current surface and in its lower scarped edges. Moreover, scientists have found relatively little evidence of rocks and sand being deposited during the Jurassic and Cretaceous periods (195 to 66 million years ago)—the classic age of dinosaurs—that followed. The absence, with exceptions on southwestern parts of the Llano and the Lubbock Lake Landmark, of such material suggests an unconformity—a buried zone where either no deposition of soils occurred or erosion had removed the soils—existed between the Triassic period and the Llano's Ogallala Formation. In other words, the Llano Estacado's ancient and modern base, the Ogallala Formation, rests with some exceptions on Triassic rocks and clays.[22]

From the late Triassic through the Jurassic and Cretaceous, dinosaurs of one order or another lived on Earth for perhaps 180 million years. They did not all live at once through the long time span, of course, for some species died out and new genera evolved. The iconic *Tyrannosaurus rex*, for example, did not appear until the Cretaceous, the last of the geologic periods in which dinosaurs lived. With a few exceptions, such as birds and crocodiles, dinosaurs disappeared at the end of the Cretaceous—at the Cretaceous-Tertiary (Paleogene) or K-T boundary some 66 million years ago. In a cataclysmic mass extinction, they vanished—abruptly—as did many plants.[23]

The mass extinctions at the K-T boundary created a niche for the proliferation of birds and the rise of mammals—hair-covered, warm-blooded, breast-feeding fauna. In time birds and mammals evolved into an exceptional variety of creatures, large and small. Millions of years later, as the Llano Estacado slowly developed into its distinctive

The Llano and Dinosaurs

Dinosaurs did not live on the Llano Estacado. The high mesa did not exist until long after the last of the dinosaurs disappeared in a cataclysmic crash of an asteroid on earth some 66 million years ago. Delineated into eras, periods, and epochs (plus sub-eras and sub-periods), the deep geologic time scale can be confusing. Dinosaurs began to appear after a time of great global warming during the late Permian period, about 250 million years ago. They existed roughly between 248 million and 66 million years ago, or during the Mesozoic era, and they characterize much of the long era's three periods: Triassic, Jurassic, and Cretaceous.

Dinosaurs represent a diverse group of animals. They were of separate orders, genera, and species, and although the tendency is to emphasize the largest of them, they enjoyed an abundance of different shapes and sizes. Some were warm-blooded. Through their 180 million years of life on Earth, they evolved and changed, and because they did not all live at the same time, some species became extinct as others began to develop. Amphibians, lizards, beetles, insects, and other animal species, including the first mammals, existed at the same time, of course, and birds were beginning to evolve, particularly in the Jurassic period.

Dinosaur hunters working in eastern New Mexico and western Texas have found bone fragments and other remains of the fantastic creatures, but not on the Llano Estacado. They have found such vestiges below the region's current surface, buried deep in the red bed sands and silt and mud of the Triassic period's Dockum Group. In the 1890s geologists excavated dinosaur bones in Dockum soils near Big Spring. Similarly, Triassic rocks with fossils of various kinds can be found along the Canadian River breaks and west of the Llano Estacado in New Mexico. Sankar Chatterjee of Texas Tech University in Lubbock has discovered fossils of the Dockum near Post, deep in the Llano's eastern escarpment. Archaeologists and paleontologists at West Texas A&M University in Canyon have located dinosaur fossils from the Dockum Group in Palo Duro Canyon.

The fossil and geologic records reveal much about this pre–Llano Estacado area. In the late Permian, some 250 million years ago, the surface of the region mirrored that of the modern Amazon delta. Long-vanished rivers, floodplains, swamps, and a jungle-like environment intermixed with seawater. Over tens of millions of years, the advance and retreat of the seas alternately destroyed and fostered swamps and plant life. And through millions and millions of years, action associated with plate tectonics moved the deep Dockum landmasses around the globe. Finally, millions of years after dinosaurs had perished, those same plate actions created the southern Rocky Mountains and eventually, through natural mountain erosion, the current Llano Estacado surface.

construct, some ancient and prehistoric fauna inhabited the region. By the late Pleistocene epoch, about 15,000 to 10,000 years ago, they included such Ice Age quadrupeds as *Bison antiquus*, woolly mammoths, dire wolves, saber-tooth cats, camels and horses no larger than llamas, giant armadillos, huge ground sloths, tapirs, short-faced bears, and others that, like dinosaurs, disappeared. But many species, including pronghorns, coyotes, deer, elk, rabbits, wolves, prairie dogs, and countless additional animals, survived to the present.

Plants likewise spread over the Llano Estacado. Tall, coarse grasses predominated during the late Pleistocene. A scattering of trees existed, especially in the canyonlands and draws, but no forests on the uplands. Because a wetter and colder climate existed at the time, firs, pines, and spruces might have been part of the flora mass, but unlikely. Many palynologists argue that pollen counts on the Llano from the late Pleistocene are too small for a forest conclusion, and modern analyses of the ancient pollen suggest that a wooded landscape on the Llano existed only in its draws and canyonlands. Nonetheless, the climate during the period, regulated by powerful forces of Ice Age glaciers that reached southward into present Montana and South Dakota, remained generally uniform with relatively mild temperatures, moderate rainfall, and no seasonal extremes. In this humid, as opposed to today's semiarid, environment, freshwater ponds, lakes, swamps, marshy grass-lined sloughs, and beaver meadows dotted the landscape. In short, the Llano became a premium grassland-grazer habitat.[24]

Humans also reached onto the Llano Estacado. Most authorities suggest the first human occupants of the Llano arrived about 12,000 years ago—perhaps earlier. Mainly, the early arrivals lived in hunting and foraging societies whose ancestors over a long stretch of time had worked their way into North America from Asia. Those ancestors varied in ethnic, racial, and cultural makeup and entered the Western Hemisphere at different times and by different routes. While some people probably traveled from Asia by boat along the Aleutian Islands and down the North Pacific coast, most of the new arrivals came by way of Beringia, a one-thousand-mile-wide—about the distance from New York City to Omaha—stretch of land connecting modern Siberia and Alaska.

Beringia existed as a result of global ice ages. Over the past million years, writes Brian Fagan, perhaps "eight major glacial cycles have enveloped the world . . . at intervals of about one hundred thousand years." During long stretches of extreme cold, the weather locked up water in giant ice sheets and lowered the water table, thus creating the "land bridge" of Beringia and a route for both animals and humans to and from the Western Hemisphere. Think about it: some 50,000 to 70,000 years ago *Homo sapiens sapiens* (modern humans) walked out of Africa. For thousands of years, they spread through Europe and Asia and sometime about 15,000 years ago, after the last (Wurm/Wisconsin) glaciation, entered North America. They probably did not know they entered a new land, but over time followed the animals they hunted and collected the plants, nuts, and berries they found.[25]

On the North American plains, including the Llano Estacado, the new arrivals—Paleoindians we call them—encountered the lush environment as described previously. They lived by hunting and gathering. On the northern Great Plains, the Paleoindians preferred to chase down or catch the young of woolly mammoths. On the Llano, they sought other species of mammoths, particularly the Columbian, or smooth-skinned, mammoth. On the eastern edge of the plains, including the Llano, they pursued mastodons—the stocky, straight-tusked, elephant-like animals that had become extinct in Europe and Asia. Their movable commissary also included such extinct herbivores as large, slow-moving ground sloths, three- and four-toed horses, giant beavers, four-horned antelopes, several kinds of bears, musk oxen, and several species of camels. They sought ancient, straight-horned bison (*Bison antiquus*), which were about 30 percent larger than present-day bison. In addition, they hunted such contemporary animals as rabbits, caribou, bighorn sheep, elk, foxes, prairie dogs, pronghorns, and birds.

Carnivores—modern-day gray wolves and coyotes among them— sought many of the same animals. Such extinct meat-eating quadrupeds as dire wolves and large cats also preyed on the herbivores. Dire wolves (*Canis dirus*), unlike gray wolves that arose in Europe, evolved in North America. They looked much like gray wolves but with larger and heavier bodies and more massive jaws and teeth. These powerful canines hunted in packs with the small Ice Age horses their favorite prey. They also took bison, mastodons, camels, and giant ground sloths when available and convenient.

The so-called American lion (*Panthera atrox*) must have been rare on the Llano Estacado. Pantherine-looking, as some scholars describe it, the giant cats had important jaguar-like features. They hunted singularly or in pairs, seeking out many of the now-extinct herbivores of the late Pleistocene.

Saber-tooth cats (*Smilodon fatalis*), the iconic symbol of Ice Age predators, appeared more numerous on the Llano Estacado. In North America during the late Pleistocene these killing machines possessed seven-inch-long, curved canine-like teeth that protruded from the mouth, thick muscled necks, and short, powerful legs. They preferred to hunt in woodland areas, but they took such High Plains herbivores as mammoths, mastodons, and ancient bison as well as smaller animals. They hunted alone or in pairs. Often when hunting, they jumped on the backs of their prey and sank their long teeth through the skin, twisting and tearing until they had opened a fatal wound.[26]

Animal carnivores faced competition from early humans on the Llano Estacado. Paleoindians hunted, but they also gathered seeds, nuts, plants, and tubers. On the Llano, they harvested prairie turnips, a nutritious starchy ground plant, and mesquite beans. The highly nourishing pigweed and giant ragweed with its seeds and tubers became part of the food supply. In the draws, canyons, and valleys, they picked hackberry seeds, grapes, and plums, and in New Mexico piñon nuts served the early arrivals well. Paleoindians also collected such xerophytic plant foods as sotol, prickly pear cacti with their rich-purple "apples," and yucca pods when available.[27]

On the Llano Estacado, the most characteristic Paleoindians included people of the Clovis and Folsom traditions. Clovis represent the first humans to occupy the Llano, and their occupation of the region lasted about five hundred years (a good, long time, actually), from roughly 11,500 years ago to about 11,000 years ago. The Folsom tradition, which followed, lasted equally as long but from 10,800 years ago to 10,300 years ago. While some important data exist for pre-Clovis traditions in North America, Clovis people nonetheless stood among the first humans to push below the ancient glacial ice sheets. Once below the ice, their cultural patterns spread rapidly over much of the continent, producing something of a continent-wide way of life.[28]

This continent-wide Clovis tradition takes its name from an archaeological site near Portales, New Mexico. Although first discovered in 1929, in the summer of 1932, A. W. Anderson and George O. Roberts, area residents, found several fossil bones and artifacts in the area's Blackwater Draw. The men carried their finds to Edgar B. Howard, an archaeologist from the University of Pennsylvania who worked a cave site west of Carlsbad in southeastern New Mexico. Before heading east at the end of the summer field season, Howard stopped at Blackwater Draw. After viewing the site, he determined to come back in the spring. But in the fall a road-construction company digging for gravel in the draw saw additional fossilized animal bones. Thereupon, Howard returned in

This view at Blackwater Draw shows human and animal occupation through perhaps twelve thousand or more years. Courtesy of John T. "Jack" Becker

November to inspect the new finds. Several months later, in the summer of 1933, he and a team of scientists began systematic excavations. They found, among much other fossil evidence, several human-made projectile points embedded in animal remains. They had discovered the Clovis culture.[29]

Clovis people became highly effective hunters and foragers. Their technology, based on sharpened stone knives and projectile points, proved far more efficient than tools of earlier societies and cultures. As skillful stone workers and artisans, they produced beautiful weapon and tool points with fluted bifaces. For the business ends of their spears and lances, most Clovis-tradition groups on the Llano favored Alibates flint, an agatized dolomite from the Canadian River area northeast of modern Amarillo. Some groups used stones and rocks from other local sources, and such fine-grained rocks as chalcedony and obsidian located at places far from the Llano served as well. A significant part of the Clovis toolkit was the atlatl, a short stick with a notch on one end and used to throw short spears and darts with greater velocity and accuracy. On the Llano

Estacado, Clovis hunters sought a large variety of Ice Age megafauna. They took a wide range of smaller animals as well, and archaeological evidence suggests that on the Llano they ate Canada geese, snow geese, teal and pintail ducks, and turkeys. They gathered vegetable foods, including plants, seeds, fruits, and nuts.[30]

Still, the elephant-like, smooth-skinned Columbian mammoths may have been their most important prey. Indeed, some paleontologists argue that Clovis hunters lived by following mammoth herds through the annual seasons from water hole to water hole, hoping to catch one off guard or trap one in a marshy bog. A downed mammoth might provide meat

The spear and dart points shown here represent at the top, Folsom (5), all of which exhibit secondary chipping; at the bottom, Clovis (2); at left, Plainview (3); and at right, Midland (2). The American dime is added for perspective. Courtesy of Gene Lynskey

for several weeks, as well as cooking fat, bones and tusks for tools and weapons, and skins for clothing. During their pursuits from one downed animal food source to another, the people camped along rivers, streams, lakes, and other water sources where game animals came to drink. On the Llano they stopped at canyon caves and rock shelters, places where they may have spent the winter. They developed a successful, highly mobile hunting society on the Llano Estacado, one that extended over half a millennium.

For all that, the Clovis hunting culture did not last. Over most of North America it closed rather suddenly. On the Llano Estacado it concluded about 11,000 years ago as features that identify Clovis faded into other cultural traditions. People adapted to new conditions as their lifeways evolved and their societies changed. Reasons for the Clovis decline remain complicated. In part, they relate to a mass global extinction event at the end of the Pleistocene when a huge number of large animal species died out. In South America, for example, the large-size species suffered an 80 percent death rate. In North America the loss of large fauna that Clovis people hunted reached over 66 percent. Obviously, the extinction event negatively impacted Clovis populations.

There seems much to consider here. Among paleontologists, archaeologists, biologists, historians, and other scholar-scientists causes for the Pleistocene extinctions provide ongoing controversy. Some bioarchaeologists include such influences as disease epidemics, accidental change of sex ratios, astronomical agents, and the beginning of agriculture in their theories.

Many specialists suggest overhunting of the large fauna. According to this view, the imaginative Clovis hunters with their creative hunting kit killed animals at a rate that could not sustain the species. Below the ice sheets 15,000 years ago, the argument goes, Clovis folks found a lush environment, huge numbers of giant ungulates that had not devised an adequate defense against humans, and plenty of food. Clovis populations increased significantly, and they rapidly spread southward through North America, into Mexico, and over South America. Paul Martin and his team say the Clovis society within a mere one thousand years reached the extreme southern points of South America—Tierra del Fuego and

Cape Horn. As human populations rapidly increased and expanded, according to this theory, Clovis people needed to take more and more of the late Pleistocene megafauna. The Ice Age animals had no chance.

Another popular theory emphasizes a shifting global climate. As glaciers retreated in the late Pleistocene, weather patterns warmed, ecosystems changed, vegetation types shifted. On the Llano Estacado, tall, coarse grass savannas that supported the megafauna disappeared in favor of such short grasses as buffalo grass and blue grama. Streams, water holes, marshes, and swamps dried up. Over time, the humid, lush environment that Clovis-era people first encountered on the Llano became a dry, semiarid landscape. Mammoths, giant ground sloths and beavers, horses, and other Ice Age herbivores could not and did not adjust to smaller and smaller grazing and foraging zones. The larger carnivores who fed on the grazers also succumbed.[31]

Whatever the cause, as the Clovis tradition faded on the Llano Estacado, the Folsom culture emerged. Evidence of Folsom has been found over much of the Llano but especially at archaeological sites in Lubbock (Lubbock Lake Landmark) and near Portales, New Mexico (Blackwater Draw). In many ways Folsom cultural patterns mirrored Clovis lifeways: big-game hunters and gatherers who traveled in seasonal circuits in pursuit of sustenance. But there remain differences, particularly in the Folsom's beautifully made, fine-grooved—fluted—projectile points and in their heavy exploitation of now-extinct large, straight-horned bison. Mammoths, ancient camels and horses, four-horned antelope, and other large Ice Age animals had disappeared.

The Folsom tradition takes its name from an archaeological site near Folsom in far-northwestern Union County, New Mexico. George W. McJunkin, an African American foreman of a cattle operation in the area, and a cowboy companion in the early 1920s stumbled onto the location. McJunkin realized the bones they found came from an extinct animal, and he informed interested people in Raton, a mountain town not far away. In turn, one of the curious folks, Charles Schwachevin, contacted authorities at the Colorado Museum of Natural History. From there in 1926, Jesse D. Figgins and the museum sponsored excavations at Folsom, and Figgins published a description of what they found. After seeing the report, the famed paleontologist Barnum Brown of the American Museum of Natural History in New York got involved, and by the end of 1927 Brown and other scientists, including Frank H. H. Roberts Jr. from the Smithsonian's Bureau of American Ethnology, had visited the site. Their subsequent excavations produced nineteen Folsom-style projectile points and bones from some twenty-three *Bison antiquus*, the large straight-horned species that had become extinct.[32]

Folsom-tradition people lived during the retreat of the glacial ice sheets, a time when the globe changed. Climatic patterns shifted, for example, resulting in great ecological alterations. Grass cover on the Llano changed. Mammoths, mastodons, and other Ice Age fauna vanished. In effect, temperatures warmed and modern climate models emerged. Streams, lakes, swamps, and marshy bogs disappeared. Straight-horned bison, the Folsom's favorite prey, steadily declined. As these biological and environmental transformations occurred—however slowly—the Folsom tradition declined.

As Folsom faded on the Llano Estacado, several regional traditions emerged. Archaeologists, anthropologists, and other scientists give several names to the new groups: Plainview, Midland, Firstview, and Plano among them. These late Pleistocene cultures sometimes overlapped and intruded on one another, and some arose and then faded after a relatively brief time span. In terms of sustenance, the people remained broad-spectrum generalists more than big-game hunters. Evidence for one or another of them can be found at several sites across the Llano, but especially along four draws: Running Water, Blackwater, Yellow House, and Monahans.[33]

Each represents a prehistoric tradition associated with the Llano's late Paleoindian period, 10,000 years ago to 8,500 years ago. The Midland complex, named for a site on Monahans Draw in present Midland County, remains renowned in archaeology. The site yielded some well-preserved human bones. Originally dated to 20,000 or more years ago, the bones belonged to a man (now called Midland Man). Recent investigations and analyses show the bones date to the Paleoindian's Folsom stage. Nonetheless, stone tips found at the site, which has been worked repeatedly, show relationships to points elsewhere on the

Llano, suggesting a Midland complex separate from but nearly parallel to the Folsom.

The Firstview complex dates to a time after Folsom. It ranges from about 9,500 to 8,500 years ago. Its materials have been found only at a few sites on the Llano Estacado: Blackwater Draw, Lubbock Lake Landmark, and a few surface collections elsewhere. As with the Midland people, the Firstview people adopted an economy that emphasized wide-spectrum foraging with a subsistence life pattern.

The Plainview tradition (ca. 9,800 to 7,100 years ago) seems worthy of special note. It represents the fundamental biological, climatological, environmental, and population transformations occurring as the Pleistocene epoch gave way to the Holocene (modern) epoch. Although Plainview lifeways mirrored those of their Clovis and Folsom ancestors in some ways, their hunting schemes suggest that they possessed more complex sociopolitical organizations. They moved across the Llano in larger bands, for example, and the scattered groups probably came together more frequently for interband gatherings. Their dependence more on seed, nut, and plant collecting and root digging than earlier Pleistocene cultures indicates the development of varied diets and a precursor to agriculture.

Moreover, Plainview people may have worked out an important new way to preserve meat. The innovative method foreshadowed modern Native Americans' production of pemmican. In it, women dried small strips of meat in the sun, pounded the dried meat into small bits, mixed it with animal fat and berries, and packed the concoction in skin bags they sealed with fat. When carefully sealed, pemmican might last for years.

In a major Plainview-phase discovery, several members of a Portales, New Mexico, archaeology society found the remains of Arch Lake Woman. A fully intact human skeleton, the bones suggested a teenage woman about five feet, six inches in height and about eighteen years old. Buried with her, society members unearthed stone scraping tools, utensils, a knife, and talc necklace beads. They uncovered the skeleton at Arch Lake, a dry, saline playa in Roosevelt County, New Mexico, just across the state line from Texas. Another Plainview-culture site exists just thirty-two miles northwest of Arch Lake, suggesting a possible home for Arch Lake Woman. Dated to about 10,000 years ago, Arch Lake Woman represents perhaps the third-oldest set of human bones found in North America.[34]

The Plainview tradition name came from a site in Plainview, Texas. Discovery of the site dates to the late 1930s when a local company began mining caliche from Running Water Draw, a headstream of the White River. In 1939 and 1940, Plainview residents, including teenagers Val Keene Whitacre, Billy Weeks, and J. B. Roberts, found and collected some very large teeth, projectile points, and related artifacts in the resulting quarry and its tailings. News of such findings brought professional archaeologists to the site in 1944 and 1945, and they located a large bone bed that contained partial skeletons of more than one hundred animals: a species of *Bison antiquus*. The archaeologists, like the teenagers, also found projectile points—the consequential Plainview point—and some flaked stone tools. The professionals, led by E. A. Sellards of the Texas Memorial Museum in Austin, his chief assistant Glen L. Evans, and Grayson E. Meade of Texas Technological College (Texas Tech University), returned in 1949.

The site, some sixty-two feet long and ten feet wide, is now buried below at least nine feet of silt, trash, garbage, and other fill. It has not been worked in forty-five years—not since Eddie Guffee of Wayland Baptist University dug through the debris in 1977. And yet, because of what it reveals about shifting life patterns, bison evolution, and environmental transformations, the Plainview bison kill site remains significant. The bones, projectile points, and other lithic material suggest a Plainview culture that represents the divide between Paleoindian times and the Archaic period that followed.[35]

Summary

The Llano Estacado began forming between 10 and 5 million or more years ago as pebbles, gravels, silt, and dirt washed out of the Rocky Mountains. About 100,000 years ago, the Pecos River cut off the outwash material, and when a drier and warmer climate appeared about 10,000 years ago, the Llano's current surface soil developed as windblown material picked up in the sandy Pecos River Valley became deposited on the plains. The early, grassy Llano appeared as something of an isotopic plain—as when in the middle of the ocean, it looked the same in every direction. Never static, however, it and its paleoenvironment changed over time.

Humans entered the Llano Estacado sometime after 12,000 years ago as the Wurm/Wisconsin glaciers began to withdraw. The retreating glaciers made possible the appearance of humans on the Llano and began a long period of climate transformation, particularly from wetter and colder weather to drier and warmer temperatures. The climate changes profoundly influenced plant, animal, and human evolution and history.

Clovis people, the first humans to occupy the Llano, lived as hunters who followed large, migratory mammals. The Clovis complex on the Llano gave way to the Folsom tradition, also a hunting culture but one in which ancient bison became the major food source. And after the Folsom complex faded, several concurrent Paleoindian cultures appeared under such names as Plainview, Midland, Firstview, and Plano. These traditions depended far more on floral food sources than on big-game hunting.

During the 3,000 years between the arrival of Clovis people about 11,500 years ago and the decline of the last Paleoindian groups about 8,500 years ago, major changes occurred on the Llano Estacado: the Ice Age ended, warmer weather patterns with less rainfall developed, Pleistocene megafauna disappeared, hunting technology and tools improved, and people began turning to growing some of the foods that for thirty centuries they and their predecessors had been gathering. Nonetheless, as suggested by the Plainview tradition, several features of the late Pleistocene epoch continued into the Holocene epoch that followed.

Post–Ice Age to Premodern Era

As the Pleistocene epoch on the Llano Estacado slowly closed 8,500 or more years ago, the Holocene (or Modern) epoch began. During the long transition from Pleistocene to Holocene major transformations occurred. The Ice Age ended. Glaciers retreated northward. The climate changed, and on the Llano a characteristic continental weather pattern

Yellow House Draw, especially near the horseshoe-shaped Lubbock Lake site, was a favorite camping and hunting location for early humans on the Llano Estacado. Courtesy of Southwest Collection/Special Collections Library

developed with such seasonal temperatures as hot summers and cold winters. Also on the Llano, semiaridity appeared where once there had been a lush, mesic ecosystem. Flora increased in number of species. Major grasses shifted and adjusted with the fluid weather patterns and fluctuating rainfall amounts. Modern bison came to dominate the Llano's fauna. The Paleoindian period closed, and different people occupied the region.[1]

Patterns of change in human occupation of the Llano Estacado and, similarly, weather and environmental alterations have continued on the Llano to the present day—through all eighty-five centuries of the Holocene epoch. The Llano has never been static, of course, and in 2022 it remained dynamic as modifications occurred on a regular basis. To illustrate the dynamism, if oversimplifying the argument, the Ogallala Aquifer diminishes. New crops (hemp, for example) get planted. Innovative technology (irrigation improvements) and scientific breakthroughs (hybrid seeds and feed) impact farming and ranching. Population demographics and composites change. Ghost towns appear.

Transformations aside, for analytical clarity geologists, archaeologists, anthropologists, historians, and others divide the Llano's Holocene epoch into various and general cultural periods: Archaic (8,500 to 2,000 years ago), Ceramic (2,000 to 500 years ago [to AD 1450]), and Protohistoric (AD 1450–1650) among them. For the past few decades, Eileen Johnson and Vance T. Holliday have led archaeological and geoarchaeological research and reporting on the Llano Estacado. Thus, accepting their well-informed dates and phases for identifying and reporting the Llano's Holocene periods of Archaic, Ceramic, and Protohistoric seems reasonable.[2]

For nonscientists, dealing with archaeological and related studies sometimes remains confusing. The often highly technical archaeological reports remain jargon-rich, and too often such scientists use different date-times and calibrations for similar periods—even in the same publications. Thus, making one's way through the maze and confusion of the often-contradictory dates and data becomes an exercise in patience, for it seems the practitioners, despite the careful review of literature their reports suggest, pass over information that conflicts with their own interpretation of the evidence. One hopes not. But the impression remains that no contemporary, satisfactory synthesis exists.[3]

Nonetheless, those variant reports suggest that like the late Pleistocene epoch the Holocene over time experienced continual change. Fluctuating meteorological conditions occurred, ranging from drier and warmer (xeric) weather to wetter and colder (mesic and hydric) conditions and back again. When significant in length or breadth, this climatic waxing and waning produced swings in animal populations, shifts in human occupation, and for the Llano Estacado modifications in the grassland environment, suggesting again the dynamic nature of the Llano's environment and ecosystem.[4]

On the Llano Estacado, as reported by Johnson and Holliday, the longest archaeological-anthropological-cultural phase of the Holocene proved to be its first, the Archaic. The Archaic did not begin suddenly 8,500 years ago. People living at the time did not see that one epoch was ending and another beginning. In fact, several features of the late Pleistocene continued into the Holocene, or, as Bryan Fagan has written, the Archaic culture evolved from Paleoindian lifeways "to the point that the boundary between the two is often impossible to draw." The demarcation of 8,500 years ago, then, belongs to modern scholars, and they use it to analyze both long- and short-term changes in zoological, biological, botanical, and human life patterns.[5]

In their economic pursuits, early Archaic people on the Llano Estacado remained like their predecessor hunter-gatherers. They continued to harvest plants, seeds, nuts, tubers, and berries in season and, in fact, increased their focus on plant collecting. On the Llano and in its canyon areas, several dozen edible plants grew. As hunters, rather than pursue megafauna, which except for Ice Age bison appeared nearly extinct, they sought smaller, more varied animals than the groups that preceded them, and they developed a toolkit for hunting and processing such animals. An important development in the early Archaic tool package proved to be a shift in weapon and hunting points. From the innovative Clovis and beautifully fluted Folsom lance points, people in the Archaic fashioned smaller side-notched points that worked better for spears and darts used with the atlatl (and later with the bow and arrow as they began to appear after the end of the Archaic).[6]

Besides new toolkit adoptions, two events surely characterize the Archaic age on the Llano Estacado. These include the trend toward drying and warming weather and the slow extinction of the large *Bison antiquus* together with the evolution of a smaller modern bison species. The shifting weather occurred for perhaps many reasons, but clearly the retreat of glacier ice sheets and a concomitant decrease in moisture as Pacific air masses shifted position meant that fewer and fewer cooler and wetter air flows reached the Llano. Water sources dried up, streams ceased to run, and dusty weather increased.[7]

Also, as the weather warmed and conditions dried, grasses changed. On the Llano Estacado, the tall, coarse grasses, including switch grass, side oats grama, and bluestem, gave way to buffalo grass and blue grama, both of which grew only five to six inches tall—although the stems of the blue grama in seed time might reach higher. Tall grasses thinned on the Llano but could be found near playas and water sources, such as Lubbock Lake. The taller grasses possess little nutrient value after they mature and die, but for the Llano's grazers the short grasses retained their food value after dormancy, thus providing excellent winter feed, especially for pronghorns and bison.[8]

Modern bison, having evolved from and by mixing with a subspecies (*Bison antiquus occidentalis*) of *Bison antiquus*, thrived in North America and on the Llano Estacado. Although smaller than their Ice Age predecessors, they still remained large animals, with bulls weighing up to twenty-four hundred pounds, standing six feet tall at the shoulders, and reaching up to eleven feet in length. The modern species developed longer estrus (breeding) seasons, and females gave birth to smaller calves. The magnificent brown ungulates adapted well to the shortgrass plains and as both grazers and browsers became less selective in their food choices. Also, partly because of the spread of new grasses and partly because of warmer winters, their cold-weather mortality rates declined.[9]

Early Humans

Planet Earth has been around for 4.6 billon years. Humans, however, or more correctly perhaps hominins, reach back only a few million years to when a new lineage of great apes, as Andrew H. Knoll writes, slowly diverged from its closest relatives. Over time, these hominins, as they have been designated, differed from other great apes in that they could walk erect. Only humans walk upright.

A well-defined skeleton of a young woman, found preserved in 4.4-million-year-old rocks in Ethiopia, provides solid evidence of an ancestor of humans. Ardi, the specialists call her. She walked upright, thus freeing her hands for other functions, and, writes Knoll, her bipedalism "set Ardi and her relatives on the road to us."

Time passed, and a new group of hominins, called australopithecines, arose. They resembled earlier hominins but clearly existed farther along the evolutionary path tread by Ardi and her folks. Among the many australopithecines' genus, and perhaps the most famous of all prehuman hominins, is Lucy, discovered in 3.2-million-year-old rocks—like Ardi—in Ethiopia. She was about the size of Ardi but possessed a larger brain, and her physical characteristics suggest she walked upright with greater ease and, because of her large molars, had turned to eating nuts, seeds, tubers, and other products associated with savannas or open woodland, but she was small in stature and could still move among the trees.

By about 2 million years ago, hominins had further evolved, and the Homo genus had emerged, the only still-living hominin. Among them was Homo erectus. Characterized by a larger brain than Lucy's people and with a body type between that of australopithecines and modern humans, Homo erectus people moved out of Africa and spread through much of Europe and Asia. Having existed from about 1.9 million years ago to about 250,000 years ago, they walked erect, remained on the ground, made tools, and for subsistence hunted and employed wide-spectrum foraging.

Then came us—Homo sapiens. First appearing about 300,000 years ago in Africa, Homo sapiens were not the same as but close to modern humans. Other Homo species existed about the same time, including the Neanderthals, who were sophisticated hunter-gathers; Homo florensiensis, discovered recently in Indonesia; and Denisovians, whose fragments were found in caves in Siberia. Genomes from fossils suggest that Neanderthals, Denisovians, and modern humans are closely related and may have occasionally interbred. Finally, writes Professor Knoll, "50,000–70,000 years ago, our species spread rapidly throughout Asia and Europe." They came to North America about 15,000 (perhaps more) years ago and to the Llano Estacado no later than 12,000 years ago.

During the Archaic, bison herd sizes on the Llano Estacado may have been smaller, fewer, and more mobile than on northern parts of the Great Plains where weather conditions stayed more mesic. Bison movements may have been less predictable as well. Archaeological localities on the Llano containing bison evidence from the Archaic period suggest that most of the locations served as human camping areas rather than kill sites. If so, Archaic folks probably spent much of the year as mobile hunters and gatherers, following the plants in season and patiently pursuing bison and other game.

Bison procurement practices on the Llano Estacado changed a bit. Of course, single animals still might be caught. But now hunters preferred either the older method of driving animals over cliffs—as at the older Plainview locality, which contains no evidence that it was used in the Archaic—or the newer technique of entrapping them in a surround of some sort or perhaps a corral-like structure in a draw or canyon. Neither method proved easy, for on the Llano little evidence for such sites exists, suggesting that driving bison to such killing spots often remained a matter of chance. Bison grazing practices added to the difficulty. Bison instinctively grazed the most abundant rangeland before moving to another rich field of grass. They left behind a depleted, grazed-over area and did not return to it until, relative to other sections, it again had become the most abundant range. Thus, a good bison harvesting site might be available only sporadically.[10]

Although bison herd sizes may have been smaller and fewer, the total number of bison on the Llano Estacado may have increased in the early Archaic. The same may have been true for pronghorns and, at least in the draws and woody areas, deer and elk. The big Pleistocene predators that fed on these herbivores had disappeared. But then in the early middle years of the long Archaic period bison numbers on the Llano decreased—as did the numbers of many other larger animals, all of them seeking more mesic conditions. As animal populations shrank on the Llano, human populations likewise declined, although evidence at the Lubbock Lake site suggests humans inhabited the region through most of the Archaic.[11]

This view on the John Roley Ranch of the Llano near Casas Amarillas in northern Hockley County, Texas, shows the extensive nature of the far-reaching level land of the big region. Courtesy of Monte L. Monroe

Reasons for the sizeable declines in animal and human populations related to a long, hard, and deep drought. For the Llano Estacado, Johnson and Holliday argue that it occurred between 6,500 and 4,500 years ago—two thousand years of dry and windy conditions with major sand- and dust storms. Some 70 years ago, Swedish-born geologist Ernst V. Antevs, while working at the Gila Pueblo Archaeological Foundation in Arizona, wrote about the severe drought, which had been recognized by paleobotanists in the nineteenth century, as an "altithermal." Later paleoclimatologists adopted such terms as "climate optimum" and "thermal maximum" for the drought, and more recently scholars use the terms "hypsithermal" and "mid-Holocene warm period" to identify the long, severely dry period.

The altithermal—as we will call it here—touched the entire Great Plains. On the Llano Estacado its dry conditions and high temperatures

Some two hundred yards southeast of this spot in a large, now-covered-over caliche pit along Running Water Draw near downtown Plainview, Texas, several young people and later archaeologists discovered stone points, bones, bison teeth, and lithic material that represent a transition in point construction and cultural life on the Llano Estacado from Paleoindian forms to Archaic traditions. Courtesy of Paul Carlson

reached maximum limits. As at other times when the climate warmed, tallgrass prairie gave way to shortgrass steppe, and in the most severe instances the short grasses tended to give way to desert shrubs and near-desert conditions. Some places became nearly bare of vegetation. Water tables dropped, many springs quit flowing, and bison and other large mammals declined in number as they sought drought refugia elsewhere. Many humans left the Llano. Because some places on the Llano held water throughout the altithermal, other people diversified their subsistence strategies, turning more and more to vegetable acquisition and small animal hunting. Thus, parts of the Llano supported a human population throughout the long drought.[12]

On the Llano Estacado, during the altithermal huge wind-, dust-, and sandstorms became frequent. They began modestly enough more than 10,000 years ago, during Folsom occupation when the climate began changing and, as glaciers retreated northward, the weather began warming. Temperatures continued their upward trend through the Pleistocene-Holocene changeover, and by the mid-Archaic the Llano's weather measured hot, dry, and dusty. Dental records from bison show poor and worn teeth as a result of the animals having to eat grass and weeds loaded with dirt, sand, and grit. Very little rain fell.[13]

With the dirt and sandstorms came the development of dune fields. Sand dunes started tentatively during the Folsom years but expanded in length and mass as the climate continued to warm into the early Holocene. By the mid-Holocene's altithermal period wind- and dust storms had become massive, increasing in strength and frequency. In response, dune building became significant. Think about it: the long and large Lea-Yoakum Dunes and Muleshoe Sandhills date back to only about 10,000 years ago.[14]

In addition, the eolian depositions of dust and dirt added to playa lunettes and filled in such once-deep upper streams and water courses as Blackwater, Yellow House, and Running Water Draws. The enormous accumulations of sand and dirt, as an example, hid the steep walls of lower Running Water Draw. The former "dean" of West Texas historians, William Curry Holden, pointed out that the amount of dirt and sand that wind deposited in the upper Yellow House and Blackwater Draws "is evidenced by the fact that when the Santa Fe [Railroad] built [south] from Plainview to Lubbock, bridge pilings were driven down nearly a hundred feet . . . without reaching the old river bottom." The upper Colorado River draws also filled in with sand and dirt. Shallow Sulphur Draw, for instance, was once part of New Mexico's Hondo River, and Seminole Draw formed a part of the Penasco River. Both the Hondo and Penasco now empty into the Pecos, that "riverine thief" that 100,000 years ago blocked Rocky Mountain runoff from reaching the plains.[15]

About 4,500 years ago, as global warming ended, the altithermal on the Llano Estacado gradually decreased in severity. Cooler and wetter conditions replaced the long drought. As Johnson and Holliday write, "Sedimentation ceased, little wind erosion occurred, and a stable vegetation cover returned." Moreover, these important scholars of the Llano's prehistory write that the alterations produced "landscape stability and environmental changes that have generally persisted into modern times." While something of a semiarid landscape remained, marshlands returned to some of the deeper valleys, and trees, especially the ubiquitous cottonwoods and junipers, appeared in draws, suggesting the presence of greater moisture.[16]

As the Archaic period on the Llano Estacado approached its end between 4,500 and 2,000 years ago, the changes became significant. Bison numbers increased sharply, and a greater reliance on bison by humans for subsistence returned. Procurement methods turned more to large community affairs that seemed needed for successful jump-kill and trapping strategies. People who had been employing bison hides for clothes and other material began using the hides for tents as housing. Stone drills and bone and stone awls, useful in sewing hides together, appeared in the archaeological record. Projectile-point innovations saw the development of a corner-notched point, one a bit larger than the side-notched weapon so characteristic of the Archaic period. Of course, vegetable collecting, or, as archaeologists write, "wide-spectrum foraging," continued to be an essential part of the Archaic economy.

Another important part of late Archaic life was the use of dogs. As indicated by mitochondrial DNA, all dogs are descendants of gray wolves.

Blackwater Draw Archaeological Site

Located a few miles north/northeast of Portales, New Mexico, the Blackwater Draw National Historic Landmark archaeological site contains physical and life-related evidence that dates to some 12,000 to 13,000 or more years ago. Archaeologists, earth scientists, anthropologists, paleontologists, and others have discovered lithic material, animal bones, and other data suggesting that many animals, both large and small, visited the place to drink and eat. Early humans in North America, Clovis people we call them, also used the once well-watered site to chase down smooth-skinned mammoths, an ancient species of bison, and other animals. Michael Stark called the site a cornucopia of food sources for early humans in the area.

A broad, shallow valley without through-flowing water, Blackwater Draw extends southeastward through the Llano Estacado and joins Yellow House Draw at Mackenzie Park in Lubbock to form Yellow House Canyon. Geologically and hydrologically, it was once part of the large and ancient Portales River Valley that carried water and debris from the Rocky Mountains out across the Llano Estacado. In 2022, at least three important archaeological sites exist over a twelve-mile stretch where the draw runs through the western Muleshoe Sandhills in upper Roosevelt County. Those sites include Anderson Basin #1 and #2 and Blackwater Draw Locality 1 (or the Clovis site).

The Clovis site is located in a gravel pit on the draw's north rim where Blackwater Draw is two miles wide and about forty feet deep. A shallow ravine leads southward from the site (an ancient basin) to the main draw. Discovered by Ridgley Whiteman in 1929 and first visited by archaeologist Edgar Howard in 1932, the site reveals important information on the Paleoindian period and Pleistocene epoch and gives its name to the Clovis culture, something of a nationwide way of life. Mining for gravel destroyed much of the site before scholarly investigations began there.

Anderson Basin refers to a stretch of Blackwater Draw about six to eight miles downstream from the Clovis site. Sand blown from the valley floor exposed old bones and mammoth tusks, and subsequent investigations revealed fossils of late Pleistocene megafauna, such as mammoths and ancient, straight-horned bison. Significant lithic debris has been documented by private collectors at the two Anderson Basin sites.

In 2022, Eastern New Mexico University in Portales safeguards the sites and controls most of the fieldwork and scholarly excavations. The university maintains a Blackwater Draw archaeological museum on campus and at the Clovis site a few miles away has erected elaborate housing to protect the physical and intellectual integrity of the important archaeological discoveries.

Such wolves and dogs crossed the Beringia land bridge with humans 12,000 or more years ago. Dogs served as pets, as guards, as transportation vehicles, sometimes as food, and sometimes as sacrificial subjects in religious services. A larger dog might carry a load of forty pounds on its back. Some evidence implies that the first people in North America employed dogs to drag a travois, a wood-frame structure without wheels designed to move gear and other property over land. A dog might pull a travois with a sixty-pound load on it. With the growing utilization of skin tents for housing at the end of the Archaic, dogs took on greater economic value: big, hide tents needed to be moved in an expeditious way from campsite to campsite, and dogs proved effective in the job.

Around 2,000 years ago on the Llano Estacado, the Archaic time gave way to the Ceramic. The Ceramic period, named for its people's adoption of pottery and characterized by long, episodic droughts, saw life and economic activities evolve over time. As one important example, archaeological evidence indicates that the often-absent prairie vole, a little rodent, reestablished itself on the northern Llano. The short-tailed, large mouse-looking creature with grayish-brown fur on the upper portion of its body and yellowish fur on the lower portion preferred the more mesic conditions that prevailed at the crossover from late Archaic to Ceramic.

After about AD 800, as periodic drought returned, the vole disappeared again and no longer ranges on the Llano Estacado.[17]

As the prairie vole reestablished itself in the early Ceramic, a highly developed bison culture also emerged on the Llano Estacado. By 300, some people living on the High Plains had begun pursuing bison as their chief economic activity. Like their Archaic ancestors, they collected vegetable fare, of course, but bison dominated their lives. They followed the herds on foot, lured them into traps, or drove them off cliffs. They used all manner of bison products for food, housing, fuel, tools, and weapons. People from east of the Llano, who may have been semisedentary horticulturists, climbed the steep escarpment to hunt Llano animals in season.

Another development during the Ceramic period was the widespread adoption of the bow and arrow. Bow and arrow technology dates to some 11,000 or more years ago in South Africa. No consensus among scholars exists about its adoption in North America, with dates ranging between about 200 and 700. Often archaeologists associate early adoption of the bow and arrow with small, side-notched points manufactured first for use with small spears and darts. Once adopted, bow and arrow use spread quickly and over a wide area. On the Llano Estacado, by 300 or afterward, the bow and arrow had become a major part of a person's hunting or weapon kit.

Ceramic-age people on the Llano did not exist in isolation. They left and returned in relationship to food supplies, including bison numbers. They made contact with groups of people off the Llano, and such contacts led to exchanges in ideas and beliefs, technology and practices, and data and understandings. From the east during the Ceramic, people on the Llano learned about grit-tempered, cord-roughened pottery. Indeed, the adoption of pottery not only provided a name for the period, but also it implied a more settled lifestyle. From southwestern groups, Ceramic folks on the Llano Estacado received samples of and help with various forms of smooth pottery as well as architectural ideas about housing forms.

At least one important cultural focus, the Lake Creek phase, illustrates the interconnectedness of Ceramic-age life. Lake Creek dates between

200 and 800 or so, maybe to 900. Located on the northern boundary of the Llano Estacado along Canadian River tributaries on both sides of the river, Lake Creek archaeological sites show connections with people living elsewhere. Archaeologists found both eastern-based, cord-roughened and southwestern-based, smooth-surfaced pottery. They also found corner-notched projectile points made from local lithic materials, such as Alibates flint (agate/dolomite) found along the Canadian River escarpments northeast of present-day Amarillo. Lake Creek residents developed an economy based on wide-spectrum collecting, including acorns, mesquite beans, such fruits as grapes and plums, and such xerophytes as cactus "apples," sotol, and yucca. Bison hunting played a secondary role in the economy and culture, but the people hunted smaller animals of several kinds. The cord-roughened pottery found at Lake Creek sites suggests an eastern manifestation. Although the smooth-surfaced ware implied a southwestern influence—an association with Jornada Mogollon, a culture from the Llano's southwestern Mescalero escarpment—some troubling conclusions exist. The earliest manifestation of Jornada Mogollon in the area, according to Timothy G. Baugh, dates to between 950 and 1100, or after people of the Lake Creek phase had abandoned their villages. Whatever the discrepancies in dating may be, Baugh writes, "Mogollon interaction with Plains groups is . . . apparent."[18]

The development of the Medieval Warm Period, about 900 to 1350, also occurred. A global warming trend, it extended across western Europe and North America, including Texas and the Llano Estacado. A drier and warmer era, the 450-year period witnessed profound changes. In Europe, for example, during the Medieval Warm something of an agricultural revolution set in. Fields and crops expanded in acreage and number, horsepower with the adoption of the horse collar improved by a multiple of three, and populations increased. Cities grew, universities expanded, commerce revived, the western Christian Church reformed itself, and architects (master masons) designed and supervised construction of Europe's great Gothic cathedrals with their flying buttresses, pointed arches, and open interiors, including those at Paris, Chartres, Reims, and Amiens in France and at Canterbury and Lincoln in England.[19]

In the Western Hemisphere during the Medieval Warm some of the pyramids of Central America appeared. In North America, populations increased and horticultural settlements emerged. Along the Mississippi River, towns associated with the great Cahokia, a city in present southern Illinois in which ten thousand or more people lived, dominated a huge agricultural area. In the Southwest, Casas Grandes with its seven-story-high adobe structures arose in present northern Mexico, and people living around the massive stone masonry structure at Pueblo Bonito at Chaco Canyon in modern-day New Mexico controlled a large region.

On the Llano Estacado during the long warming trend, the Palo Duro and Antelope Creek communities developed. Palo Duro archaeological sites can be found from the upper Red River tributaries southward toward the upper Brazos River tributaries. Although in territory it may overlap a bit with the Lake Creek focus, Palo Duro clearly extends farther south and began some years later. The people of Palo Duro preferred deer and pronghorn to bison, for bison had become scarce in the Panhandle. Rather than hunters, they became horticulturists who processed many wild plants plus acorns, mesquite beans, berries, grapes, and such xerophytes as yucca and sotol. The people used such stone tools as drills, scrapers, knives, and corner-notched arrow points. They also fashioned awls and other implements from bones. They possessed a variety of southwestern pottery, probably some of the brown stoneware of the Jornada Mogollon. But eventually, the Palo Duro complex with its cultural affiliations with both the Southwest and the East disappeared—sometime between 1000 and 1200.[20]

As the Palo Duro complex withered around 1200, the Antelope Creek focus arose. Although most of the best-preserved sites for the important and relatively well-known Antelope Creek complex are north of the Canadian River and not technically on the Llano Estacado, its cultural reach extended south into present-day Briscoe, Swisher, and Castro Counties and up Tule Canyon and upper Tule Draw. Camping sites have been found in Palo Duro and Tule Canyons, suggesting these places served as favorite hunting grounds. Archaeologists and anthropologists have also excavated a permanent village site in Tule Canyon. Antelope Creek village homes with their stone-slab foundations and adobe and masonry walls, plus many of their trade items, show an intriguing relationship with Puebloan cultures in New Mexico. Their homes varied in size with some single-room dwellings, but often they built elaborate structures with adjoining quarters and sometimes the buildings contained semi-subterranean rooms.

The Antelope Creek culture flourished between about 1200 and 1450—during a climate shift when the Medieval Warm Period was giving way to colder weather conditions. The people lived by hunting deer, pronghorns, smaller animals, and sometimes bison. They gathered nuts, fruits, and edible plants, and they practiced maize horticulture that included corn, beans, squash, and sunflowers. They controlled the important Alibates flint quarries along the Canadian River and used the flint to develop trade patterns with people who needed Alibates for weapon and tool points. Antelope Creek folks mined the flint and traded quarry blanks, and perhaps some finished points, over considerable distances. They exchanged with Pueblo folks to the southwest, for archaeologists have found shell ornaments, obsidian, and turquoise among the villages. Jack T. Hughes, who has reported extensively on Antelope Creek ruins, writes that the "culture is characterized not only by its slab houses but also by several kinds of small triangular arrow points, a distinctive kind of cordmarked pottery, and various other traits."[21]

Perhaps because bison numbers had declined on the Llano Estacado during the Medieval Warm Period, the Palo Duro and Antelope Creek villagers turned toward horticulture and plant, seed, fruit, and nut collection. They also looked to hunt deer, pronghorns, and smaller animals. Housing in Antelope Creek villages included large stone and adobe structures, although, obviously, they did not rival Casas Grandes or Pueblo Bonito. Trade with pueblos in the Southwest increased. Corn and beans to meet carbohydrate needs moved to the Llano area while meat products for protein went to the southwest. In addition, archaeologists have found turquoise, shell beads, and southwestern-style pottery at the sites. In short, during the Medieval Warm a close relationship developed between Antelope Creek people and people of the Southwest, and both cultures profited.[22]

After 1400, major changes came to the Llano Estacado and indeed to the entire Great Plains. First, the Medieval Warm had given way to the Little Ice Age, 1300 to 1850, a long, generally cold period that happened on a global scale. In Europe, for some five hundred years crop failure and famine occurred often as frost sometimes came late in the spring or early in the fall, killing food plants. In response, people turned to growing potatoes (from Incas of South America after 1500), rutabagas, and other ground crops, but for centuries they struggled with subsistence living. In North America, during the Little Ice Age, average temperatures also dropped over long periods of time. William C. Foster has written that the "climate change to colder weather and shorter growing seasons threatened marginal horticultural communities," such as Antelope Creek on the Llano Estacado. Moreover, as weather turned colder, a more mesic climate returned and with it more traditional plains grasses, especially little blue stem and buffalo grass, those protein- and calorie-rich plants. A colder, wetter climate with sometimes deep snow on the Great Plains encouraged bison to drift south, and for a time they could be found as far south as the Gulf Coast in Texas and in northern Mexico.[23]

Second, strong groups of Athapaskan-speaking people, dominated by proto-Apaches, migrated south from a northern homeland and advanced with devastating results. By 1400, or well into the Little Ice Age, some of the Apaches had moved along the east face of the Rockies, progressed deep onto the Southern Plains, and raided plains villagers, including people living in the Antelope Creek complex. The Apache advance forced villagers to abandon their homes. Among scholars, little agreement exists about the Antelope Creek exodus. The villagers may have gone north toward the upper Arkansas River and become part of the ancestral Pawnees of that region. They may have moved east down the Canadian and Red Rivers and merged with village groups, descendants of a Washita River phase, along the present Oklahoma-Texas border. Or perhaps they abandoned agriculture for hunting. Their disappearance remains a puzzle.[24]

Third, Europeans arrived, starting in 1536 with the intrepid Álvar Núñez Cabeza de Vaca. Although Cabeza de Vaca did not reach the

Llano Estacado, he may have come near its southern edge. He visited people at the La Junta de los Rios villages, located at the junction of the Conchos River and the Rio Grande (near present-day Ojinaga and Presidio). He and his three companions, all survivors of a Gulf Coast shipwreck some eight years earlier, pursued bison with a La Junta hunting party, Jumanos probably, before turning south toward Spanish provinces below the Rio Grande and home.

By this time on the Llano Estacado—the early to mid-sixteenth century—the Johnson and Holliday–identified Protohistoric archaeological period had begun. The Protohistoric, Johnson and Holliday write, "covers the time when Europeans were in the region, but their influence was manifested in neither the aboriginal material culture nor in the archeological record." Cabeza de Vaca and others among the first Spaniards, such as Francisco Vázquez de Coronado, who climbed onto the Llano, represent such Europeans in the region. While they did not leave much in the way of influencing the archaeological record, they left written records that help historians comprehend the Llano's past.[25]

Coronado and his chroniclers proved particularly important for understanding the Protohistoric Llano Estacado and its human inhabitants. After climbing onto the Llano in 1541, during the peak years of the Little Ice Age, Coronado met a people he called Querechos—probably an early Apache group. About fifty of them resided in a temporary camp (*ranchería*) and lived "like Arabs" in hide tents. Mobile bison hunters, they used dogs with travois to carry loads of meat, hides, poles, and personal possessions. The Querechos organized large communal hunts in the fall and spring, killing bison, deer, pronghorns, and other animals. They did not grow crops but utilized bison meat, viscera, bones, horns, hoofs, hair, and hides to live. Most anthropologists believe them to be ancestral Lipan Apaches who had entered the Panhandle's Tierra Blanca Creek area sometime after 1400.[26]

Several days later Coronado and his huge entourage met a different group of people. This coalition, living in a series of *rancherías* possibly in the Red River drainage system in present Briscoe County near lower Tule Canyon or thereabouts, Coronado called Teyas. A tattooed people, the Teyas proved to be part-time bison hunters who camped near the plains to pursue game before returning to their more permanent villages and the crops they had, of necessity, temporarily neglected. Concerning the Teyas, anthropologists and historians cannot reach a consensus on two counts: the specific location of the *ranchería* canyon and the general location of their permanent villages. Some argue for an eastern setting, suggesting the Teyas remained a part of the Caddoan complex in East-Central Texas and visited the plains for their semiannual bison hunt. Others insist that as speakers of an Uto-Aztecan dialect the Teyas must be a branch of the Jumanos, relatives perhaps of the same folks Cabeza de Vaca met at La Junta de los Rios only five years earlier. Sadly, the Teyas and Querechos, both prairie-plains people, remained enemies.[27]

After Coronado, when they climbed onto the Llano Estacado, other Spaniards encountered people they called Vaqueros. Nomadic, bison-hunting early Apaches, the Vaqueros, who may have been of the same affiliation as Querechos, settled into a place Jack T. Hughes called the Tierra Blanca complex surrounding upper Tierra Blanca Creek—the area near but southeast of where Coronado's expedition climbed onto the Llano and probably near where Coronado met the Querechos. The Vaqueros at Tierra Blanca reflect a hunting-and-gathering economy with important trade relations with Puebloan groups in the Southwest.[28]

With little doubt, Querechos and Vaqueros of the Llano Estacado were early Apaches. They lived in bison-hide tipis and relied on large dogs for transport. In their Tierra Blanca complex, they came to control some of the Alibates flint quarries and traded with Indian groups both in the Southwest and East. Their ceramics included southwestern trade wares, and a few others they fashioned themselves. Some stone circles associated with the complex may represent tipi rings.

Below the Red River but reaching into the Llano Estacado's upper Brazos River tributaries spread the Garza complex, perhaps the most extensively identified cultural assemblages of the Protohistoric period. Dating from about 1450 to 1750 (during the Little Ice Age), Garza evidence in stone points, hearths, and butchering sites extended westward to the Pecos River Valley and eastward down the Brazos. Garza people relied on bison hunting as the basis of their economy. Throughout the widely identified complex area one might find a concentration of camping sites, processing stations, and semisedentary villages, particularly along the White River in Blanco Canyon. The important Garza complex shows intriguing associations with Southern Plains Caddoans, suggesting an eastern orientation. Not all anthropologists or other scholars agree, for some suggest the Teyas-Garza folks appeared as proto-Jumanos. Among them, social geographer John Miller Morris argues that the Teyas spoke an ancient Uto-Aztecan language variant with associations to people of the Salinas Pueblos in New Mexico. Over time descendants pushed eastward onto the Llano, became bison hunters and excellent traders, and eventually moved into the lush eastern canyons, especially Blanco Canyon, of the Llano Estacado. Coronado met them as Teyas, but a half century later writes Morris, "they became the well-known Jumanos of later history." In any case, people of the Garza complex seem to have been related to the Teyas people Coronado saw in the lower Tule Canyon–present Briscoe County area. Indeed, their villages in Blanco Canyon may have represented Coronado's important "Cona" location where in the summer of 1541 the Spaniards rested for nearly three weeks and reevaluated their situation.[29]

Obviously, whether it was a Caddoan or proto-Jumano population, the final answer remains in question. In either case, they were a tattooed people who hunted bison and other game, gathered such wild crops as grapes and nuts, practiced some gardening, and traded widely with both Caddoans in the East and Puebloan people in the Southwest. They visited the Llano mainly on a temporary basis to procure meat, hides, bones, and horns, but perhaps as well to gather flint for dart and arrow points.

About the time that Europeans such as Coronado arrived on the Llano Estacado in the early sixteenth century, at least three important developments occurred—or were about to. First, the population of the Southern Plains, including the Llano, expanded: an "explosive increase in total population," writes Donald J. Lehmer. Much of the increase, he notes, came "from the immigration of migrating hunting groups from the west, northeast, and east." Such groups, of course, included the Querechos and Teyas (whether Caddoan or Jumano). The growing population continued to increase until the late eighteenth century.

Second, people on the Southern Great Plains, including the Llano Estacado, acquired horses and European trade goods. Such items produced a profound effect on human inhabitants of the plains—materially and culturally. Horse technology allowed for larger loads, larger tipis, larger collections of personal possessions, and larger concerns for the grassland environment and the grazing requirements of their animals. With horses, humans could travel faster and farther and seek bison or deer or antelope over greater distances. For the first time, hunting could be done other than on foot. European trade goods, such as metal and cloth, replaced stone and bone weapons and tools and skins for dress. Although the use of bone tools continued for a very long time, soon enough Indians received in trade iron axes, hatchets, heavy knives, weapon points, and many other handy goods, such as cloth, blankets, and tobacco. The acquisition of horses also expanded and accelerated intertribal warfare.

Third, European-borne diseases struck. As early as the Spanish conquest of the highly organized and compact Aztec people of Mexico in the 1520s, disease pandemics decimated Native American inhabitants. Smallpox proved the worst, but yellow fever, cholera, measles, malaria, whooping cough, and influenza also wasted populations. In the greater Llano Estacado area, disease pandemics came later than in most other places, in part perhaps because on the plains the population was less dense. Nonetheless, even while the population increased, outbreaks of cholera occurred, probably some even before Coronado arrived in 1541.[30]

Amid such swirling trends, Lipan Apaches took over the Llano Estacado. One of several eastern Apache divisions that had emerged from the Querechos and Vaqueros, the Lipans, in the early seventeenth century and not long after Spaniards had colonized New Mexico in 1598, acquired horses. Once mounted and armed with lances, they hunted bison on horseback and pushed either Caddoan-speaking horticulturalists east away from the Llano or the proto-Jumanos south and west out of the Llano canyons. Or they removed both Protohistoric groups from the High Plains. By the end of the seventeenth century the Lipan, Jicarilla, Mescalero, Natages, and other eastern Apaches had split from one another with the Lipans taking over the Llano Estacado.

Unlike their Apache relatives, the Lipans adopted a plains-oriented economy and lifestyle: male-dominated, mobile, horse-mounted, hunting society and culture. Soon enough, they came to control a lucrative bison hide and meat trade with Spaniards in New Mexico and with other indigenous groups in the Southwest, including Texas. But after the 1680 Pueblo Revolt against Spanish oversight along the upper Rio Grande, Lipans turned away from Santa Fe and New Mexico and looked more southeastward into Texas. During the seventeenth and early eighteenth centuries, Lipan Apaches represented the dominant power on the Llano Estacado and, indeed, perhaps all of Spanish Colonial Texas. They were superb horsemen and horsewomen and formidable warriors, "adaptive, brave, and resilient," as Thomas A. Britten calls them.[31]

Lipan men, as described by Britten, "were tall and well proportioned" with "no beards or mustaches," and warriors "pierced their ears . . . and "wore at least one earring in each ear." On the left side of their faces, men "cut their hair off even with their left ear while allowing the hair on their right side to grow long." They used tattoos, painted their faces and bodies, and decorated their hair with such items as trinkets and feathers. On formal occasions they wore colorful clothing. In battle, they went nearly naked.[32]

Lipan women wore their hair long in braids or let it hang loose. They used earrings, necklaces, and on formal occasions colorful clothes. They worked hard, took charge of the tipi, prepared meals, and oversaw family life. As craftswomen, they produced soft, beautiful robes from deer and bison hides and, with their products, became excellent traders. They enjoyed respect and equality. They participated in hunts, and when men were gone—sometimes for weeks—they handled daily decision-making. In 1828, according to Jose Maria Sanchez, Lipan women, especially maidens, were "as a general rule, [judged] good-looking." Englishman William Bollaert visiting Texas in 1826 suggested that Comanches "have often made war upon the Lipans so as to become possessors of their women."[33]

Lipan boys learned to become hunters and warriors. A grandfather often watched over his grandson's training, and as the boy became proficient with a bow and arrow, the elder gave ritualistic instructions and, according to Britten, performed "a ceremony over the boy's first kill." Part of "the young hunter's training was his recognition of, and adherence to, elaborate and complex rules regarding the compact that existed between hunters, and between man and animal:" share in the kill, respect the animal's carcass.[34]

Girls learned domestic duties and prepared their way toward adulthood. With their mothers they gathered a wide variety of plants, nuts, berries, and tubers. After Lipans began some proto-horticulture, they tended to "gardens," and some of them acquired skills in the use of wild plants for medicinal purposes. Mothers and grandmothers taught them the difficult work of butchering game and preparing hides. They also participated in communal pronghorn hunts.

The Lipan population was never large. Contemporary estimates are often low because Lipans scattered over a big, broad area, but, according to Morris E. Opler, a "judicious estimate of all Lipan Apache in 1700, including those living in Mexico, would be 6,000." At that time Lipans lived on, hunted on, and dominated the Llano Estacado. Half a century later, about four thousand lived in Central Texas, and in 1840, after a long series of wars with Spaniards and Americans, a reasonable estimate suggests two thousand Lipan individuals living in Texas below the Colorado River. While their declining numbers might suggest otherwise, in warfare Lipans often gave as good as they got, defeating Comanches, Spaniards, Texans, and others.[35]

Hunting was a key to Lipan Apache livelihood. Lipans hunted bison, deer, pronghorns, and many other animals, large and small. The hunts might be individual, but many were communal affairs. Sometimes, as noted, women might take part, especially if the group was after pronghorns or rabbits, considered less dangerous prey. Women, when they participated, used a rope and could claim any animal they had lassoed or touched with the rope. The annual autumn bison hunt was particularly important. It lasted about three weeks, with shamans praying for a successful hunt and leaders carefully supervising the whole affair. In most such hunts a division of labor existed. Men hunted and helped skin the dead prey. Women expertly and quickly butchered the carcass, leaving for spiritual reasons some offal to crows and thanking the spirits for a good hunt.

Lipans controlled the Llano Estacado for nearly two hundred years, but their hegemony did not last. Sometime around 1718, Comanches, who had showed up at the Taos Pueblo as early as 1706, struck eastward onto the southern Great Plains and the Llano Estacado. They carried guns. Horse-mounted and armed with the horrifying weapons, Comanches, after heavy raiding and much fighting over a long time span, removed Lipans from the High Plains. Lipans in turn invaded Central Texas, where they crushed other tribes who had been decimated by European diseases and whose lives had been disrupted by the Spanish presence. In their new homeland the Lipans, writes Henry F. Dobyns, "rustled horses from Spanish San Antonio and [secured] a living as hunters and gatherers." Their southeastern migrations, however, did not stop Comanche attacks on their *rancherías* in the Edwards Plateau and Texas Hill Country.[36]

Comanches from the northwestern deserts and mountains pushed onto the Great Plains much like the Apaches had before them. They shoved others aside. Aggressive, horse-mounted, and seeking bison for sustenance, the Comanches by the 1740s had taken over much of the Southern Plains, including the Llano. Like nearly all human groups on the Llano Estacado before them, they adopted an economy based on bison hunting, trade, and collection of wild fruits, nuts, tubers, and plants. They traded animal products, especially hides and meat, with neighboring people for agricultural products and, as European contact increased, acquired manufactured goods of all kinds.

The Comanche hold on the Southern Plains lasted for well over a century after 1740. Indeed, through alternating hostility and peaceful agreement, the grip expanded until Comanches controlled a huge territory Euro-Americans called "Comancheria," and what some recent scholars have referred to as the "Comanche Empire." Although the Llano Estacado stood at the geographic center of this Comanche heartland, the economic and commercial hub spread along the upper Arkansas River basin in eastern Colorado. Comanches developed a major trade center there, particularly for the dispersion of horses, animals in significant demand among Indians of the central and northern plains. Interestingly enough, several archaeologists speculate that the same Arkansas River basin served sometime between 500 and 1000 as a horticultural center supplying maize through trade to outlying regions. The basin area had represented a major route for the movement of new varieties of maize between the Southwest and Central Plains.[37]

Although united by language, history, and customs, Comanches divided into several separate and highly independent political branches. As occurred among Apaches and a few other tribal groups, no single, cohesive entity characterized Comanche social organization. In the eighteenth century three major divisions existed: Yamparika, Jupe, and Kotsotika. A century or so later, as coalitions came and went, six politically independent divisions lived and hunted on the Southern Plains: Yamparika, Kotsotika, Penaticka, Nokoni, Kwahada, and Tenawa.[38]

The Comanche population expanded as their territory increased in size. In 1700, for example, about the time they showed up in New Mexico, their population counted something like seven thousand. A century later, in spite of disease, war, and alien intrusions, their population may have stood at fourteen thousand or more people. Indeed, one historian suggests a population of forty thousand people. Their home country covered a lot of ground, at times allowing them to ride deep into Mexico. Until the early 1830s bison roamed thickly across much of Comancheria, thus providing ample support for a population nearly as large as the higher figures suggest.[39]

In many ways, Comanches represent the characteristic Indians of the Llano Estacado. They dominated the tableland for a century or more. Their plains lifestyle as mounted bison hunters appealed to all who spent time with it. They held the area against Spanish and other early encroachers. They fought a long, bitter war against Texans and Americans, including the military, who sought to remove them from the big, blue-sky country they lived on and loved for generations. Then, slowly, like the Lipan Apaches a century before them, they lost it—or most of it—moving onto reservation land in Indian Territory (present Oklahoma). But the larger Comanche story comes later, as Spanish, French, and American traders, explorers, and soldiers sought wealth and trade and succor on the Llano Estacado.

Summary

During the ten thousand years of the Holocene, or modern, epoch, life and history on the Llano Estacado remain understood best by assessing climate shifts and changing weather patterns. The two-thousand-year-long drought of the altithermal, for example, and the four-hundred-year-long Medieval Warm Period followed by the five-hundred-year-long Little Ice Age existed as environmental/ecological events with major long-term consequences for plant, animal, and human existence on the high tableland. Shorter swings in meteorological conditions might be a few years in length or decades long or longer, but they also impacted the comings and goings of flora and fauna and ultimately humans. Throughout such changes the Llano remained a dynamic place with technological innovations and lifeway adjustments. The human population increased over time, but one might argue that such an increase began with the first Paleoindians in North America and did not end until smallpox came to the Western Hemisphere with some of the first Spaniards in the sixteenth century.

The Archaic period, despite its long altithermal or maybe because of it, showed many and varied tools being adopted for many and varied purposes. On the Llano Estacado flora controlled the subsistence economic base. Because several life patterns of the period continued through the Ceramic and afterward, one might argue, as Robert F. Spencer and others do, that the cultural economy in the Archaic stage, while adaptable and subsistence-based, proved "universal and generalized." Some of its elements continued until well into the nineteenth century.[40]

During the Ceramic, improved technology—bow and arrow, ceramics, horticulture—characterized the period. There also occurred more cooperative production by larger and more complex human aggregations. Contact with people from the East and Southwest influenced human endeavors on the Llano Estacado, but a Plains village culture influenced Llano activities only indirectly. Nonetheless, the Llano's little-known Lake Creek village focus existed for six hundred years—lasting as long as or longer than the famous Clovis and Folsom cultures of the Paleoindian period. Alien invasions from the north and west in the Protohistoric period proved particularly life changing for people on the Llano, as did the slow swing from the Medieval Warm Period to the Little Ice Age.

The arrival of Spanish Europeans in the sixteenth century and afterward brought further changes in population dynamics and hunting-and-gathering applications. Indeed, as Euro-Americans approached the Llano Estacado, far-reaching alterations occurred over a very short time. Those changes began with the earliest Spanish explorers and American traders.

3

Coronado and Spanish Entradas to Comanches

For over two hundred years, 1540–1740 and afterward, early Spanish and Mexican activities in the New Mexico's upper Rio Grande area impacted the Llano Estacado. During that long stretch of time, as Englishmen and Frenchmen built up colonies along the Atlantic Coast and up the St. Lawrence River, Spanish conquistadors, missionaries, soldiers, traders, and adventurers moved across the Llano. They explored it, traveled across and around it, hunted and traded on it, proselytized among its indigenous people, and in the process brought back a startling amount of information on its Native Americans, climate, geography, topographical structure, and fauna and flora. By the end of the seventeenth century, they had named nearly every prominent river, creek, and place on the Llano. Indeed, they had provided its very name: El Llano Estacado.

Although Native Americans had traveled the area for several millennia, the first European explorers and traders to reach the Llano Estacado appeared in the sixteenth century. Francisco Vázquez de Coronado and his agents led the way by crossing the Llano in 1541—more than half a century before Englishmen settled Virginia. Coronado and his chroniclers commented on the astonishing flatness of the vast region, wrote about indigenous groups they met and the water-filled playas they

needed to march around, ate incredible numbers of bison on their journey, and experienced some of the vagaries of the Llano's weather. Plenty
of other explorers, adventurers, missionaries, and traders followed.
Some, such as the travels of Juan de Oñate, have been thoroughly studied
and widely reported. Others, such as the missionary efforts to find the
mysterious and enigmatic "Lady in Blue," remain far less well-known
and only recently have received greater scholarly attention.

The story of European exploration on the Llano Estacado begins with
the spectacular Coronado expedition. Perhaps no other Spanish exploring or military foray into New Mexico or Texas remains as carefully and
thoroughly chronicled. Nor has any been subject to as much learned
difference of opinion, at least as to the route Coronado took. For some
of the first Coronado researchers, the itinerary became important, for
by following it, they might determine where expedition members met
American Indians and what native groups the Spaniards encountered
and thus understand perhaps something of the indigenous background
and the Llano's geography and biodiversity.

As early as the 1850s, Coronado scholars began working through
Spanish documents trying to determine where members of the grand
entrada crossed the Llano Estacado. The most important of these early
scholars proved to be George Parker Winship, a librarian, author, and
1893 Harvard graduate. Winship in the 1890s became the first American
to examine thoroughly Pedro de Castaneda's narrative of the expedition.
In doing so, Winship took Coronado from the Pecos River at Pecos
Pueblo (Cicuye) southeastward down the Pecos and across the Llano
along upper tributaries of the Colorado River to a point near the mouth
of the Concho River east of modern San Angelo. From there he carried
Coronado north and into Kansas.[1]

Half a century later, about the time people in Spain, Mexico, and the
United States considered celebrating the quadricentennial of Coronado's
entrada, Herbert Eugene Bolton started work on an expedition manuscript. Among the most accomplished of southwestern borderlands
scholars, Bolton published his grand biography in 1949—too late for
the four-hundred-year anniversary. Nonetheless, in the celebrated book,
Coronado: Knight of Pueblos and Plains, he marked out a trail across the

Coronado's Cona

Cona is the canyon area where Francisco Vázquez de Coronado spent nearly three weeks resting his men and horses after having crossed the Llano Estacado in the summer of 1541. With his large entourage, Coronado, who had started from the Rio Grande near modern Albuquerque, arrived at the eastern side of the high tableland, probably near Tule Canyon in the area of modern Swisher and Briscoe Counties. Members of the expedition were tired and hungry, and they were missing a few members who had wandered off to hunt across the Llano and got lost. They needed to rest, gather supplies, and let their horses recuperate.

Teyas people met them in the canyon—the first barranca, as expedition chroniclers called it—and provided some food and information. But the deep canyon with its steep walls and inadequate grazing land was not sufficient to house the nearly eighteen hundred people plus livestock with Coronado. Then, a fierce storm with heavy rain, high winds, and large hailstones struck. The summer tempest damaged tents, equipment, and supplies; injured livestock; and caused Coronado and his assistants to look elsewhere, and the Teyas natives suggested another barranca, one off to the south.

The second barranca, Coronado's Cona, was Blanco Canyon in modern Floyd and Crosby Counties. The expedition made its way south and four days later entered the long (26 miles) and wide (2.6 miles) gulf with a stream of running water and plenty of trees for firewood. Wild game was within easy reach, and plums, grapes, nuts, and tubers were plentiful. The canyon walls helped hold the livestock.

Here, members of the entrada rested, refitted their equipment, and took stock of their situation. Here also, Coronado determined to divide his command, send the larger portion home under his chief lieutenant, and select thirty men and head for Quivira, the land of wealth and fortune he was seeking. About two weeks later, rested and decisions made, Coronado headed north and east. Captain Tristan de Arellano took the main force (about seventeen hundred people) back to New Mexico by way of modern Lubbock and Yellow House Draw.

Supporting the Blanco Canyon location for Cona, writes John T. "Jack" Becker, plenty of Spanish material has turned up in recent years. People have discovered bits and pieces of armor, chainmail, crossbow points, horseshoes, and fragments of horse tack, all of which buttresses the idea that Europeans spent time there nearly 500 years ago. Moreover, letters and other documents dating to the 1540s describe the canyon campsite, as well as the first barranca near Tule Canyon.

This William K. Hartman painting depicts Coronado's 1541 camp in Blanco Canyon. Here after two weeks, Coronado divided his huge force, sending the larger portion home by way of Silver Falls and Blackwater Draw and leading a smaller group in search of Cibola in modern Kansas. Courtesy of William K. Hartman, the Floyd County Museum, and the Southwest Collection/Special Collections Library

Llano Estacado that took Coronado to Tule Canyon (first *barranca*, as Coronado's chroniclers called it) with Teyas campsites and then north to Palo Duro Canyon (second *barranca*)—his (Bolton's) Cona, the important second valley in which they found Teyas *rancherías*, plenty of water, and lush vegetation. Here, writes Bolton, Coronado rested his army and its supporters. Here also he determined to take thirty men with him to

Quivira and send the larger part of this entrada back to Tiguex on the Rio Grande. Bolton, it seemed, had put the final stamp on the Coronado route and the location of Cona.[2]

But no. In nearly a dozen books or journal articles others have challenged the Bolton arguments. They disagree with either his route for Coronado's passage across the Llano or his location of Cona, or both. Those disputing some of Bolton's route claims include West Texas scholars William Curry Holden and J. W. Williams. Williams, a mathematician, used a highly ecological argument that places the route, like Winship, far to the southeast before turning north. Holden's proposed route took Coronado from Pecos Pueblo, down the Pecos River with a river crossing near modern Colonias, and then onto the Llano in the upper Yellow House Draw area. From there, Holden has the expedition members work down the draw area to near modern Lubbock, perhaps at the Lubbock Lake Landmark, and Lower Yellow House Canyon (first *barranca*), and finally north to Blanco Canyon (second *barranca*).[3]

More recently, John Miller Morris and Richard Flint and Shirley Cushing Flint have proposed still other passageways across the plains, and not long ago archaeologist Donald Blakeslee identified beyond doubt the elusive location of Coronado's Cona, the second *barranca*, in Blanco Canyon. Their important studies show nearly similar routes. In a general sense, they take Coronado and his nearly eighteen-hundred-member entrada onto the Llano Estacado near Arroyo del Puerto (Puerto de los Rivajenos) in Quay County, New Mexico, over to upper Tierra Blanca and Frio Draws, and southeastward from the draws overland to near modern-day Plainview and Running Water Draw. From there they have the expedition heading in a northeast direction to arrive at the dramatic edge of lower Tule Canyon somewhere in the Briscoe-Swisher Counties region. After climbing down into the canyon to a Teyas *ranchería*, a violent wind-, rain-, and hailstorm struck, damaging tents, carts, and equipment and greatly alarming them, their horses, and their remaining livestock.[4]

Needing rest and better food-gathering opportunities, Coronado turned his large troop south. The expedition entered Blanco Canyon. Here, its members found additional Teyas *rancherías*; a wide, lush, grassy valley; steep canyon walls to help contain their livestock; and plenty of water in the now-labeled White River. Here also, the expedition rested and Coronado reconsidered his entrada's logistical situation, its large size, and its purpose. After two weeks, he determined to take thirty men and head again for Quivira and send the bulk of his large assemblage back to Tiguex.

Decisions made, Coronado in early June started north with his small group. He soon left the Llano Estacado on his way to Quivira and the wealth he hoped to find. After about a month spent among Caddoan-speaking people (Wichita) living along the Arkansas River in central Kansas, he began his return to the Rio Grande and its Pueblo villages. On his return, he rode over a small portion of the Llano in its far-northwestern corner. Unable to find wealth or golden cities in either New Mexico or Kansas, Coronado spent a troubled winter back in Tiguex, and in the spring with most of his followers he headed south toward Mexico City and home.

At the time Coronado left Blanco Canyon for Quivira, his chief lieutenant, Captain Tristan de Arellano, took charge of those left behind—about 1,750 soldiers, servants, civilians, Indians, and other auxiliaries.

Located in Crosby County, Silver Falls attracted indigenous peoples, explorers, soldiers, ranchers, and early settlers to its refreshing waters on White River in Blanco Canyon. Courtesy of Southwest Collection/Special Collections Library

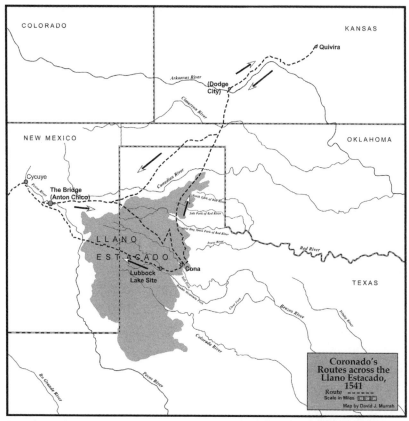

Francisco Vázquez de Coronado and his expedition members followed these
general routes on the Llano Estacado in 1541. Tristan de Arellano used a bit
different route to lead most members back to New Mexico. Courtesy of David J.
Murrah

After mid-June, having collected supplies for the return journey, Arellano's large "army," following its Pueblo guides, left for Tiguex. It moved
down the canyon to Silver Falls, today hidden beneath State Highway 114
in Crosby County. From there, it traveled westward to reach Blackwater
Draw in the northern reaches of the current city of Lubbock. The draw,
about where it ambles through present-day Lubbock Country Club,
contained in 1541 plenty of water and afforded a fine camping place for
Arellano's multitude. It provided a good supply of agaritas, squash, hackberry seeds, wild onions, mesquite pods, plums, streamside mints, cactus
fruit, sunflowers, and other edible plants. Bison grazed in the area, and
mesquite roots and bison ordure served for cooking fires.

On their journey back, Arellano's force needed to butcher about sixty bison each day. It proved a major operation. Hunters moved ahead of the main group, which in fact strung out over a considerable distance, killed animals as they found them, and left markers for the downed bison or elk or other wildlife they had dispatched. Skinners stripped hides from the dead beasts, and older women, who were experts at butchering, processed the animals and cut out the choice parts: the tongue, backstrap, and hindquarters. Younger women tended to fires over which they cooked the meat by roasting it or, perhaps like their indigenous guides, boiling it in water in a skin container into which they placed red-hot rocks until the water cooked the meat.

From the Lubbock-area resting spot, Arellano either continued up Blackwater Draw or led his army over to the spring-fed lake in Yellow House Draw. There, in a horseshoe bend of the draw a plentiful supply of fresh water served the returning army. Indeed, it became a place Spaniards called Punta de Agua (Point of Water), present Lubbock Lake Landmark. From the lake, if in fact that is where he stopped briefly, Arellano followed Yellow House Draw to the Casas Amarillas (Yellow Houses) basin with its Illusion and Yellow Lakes. A day's march from the basin and still following Yellow House Draw brought them to water at Silver Lake (Laguna Plata) on the northern edge of the Cochran-Hockley County line. From there, they traveled to Coyote Lake and the numerous water sources in present Bailey County, continued through the Arch Lake salt flats where water could be found, to Portales Springs, and off the Llano's eastern escarpment near Taiban Springs. They made for the Pecos River and followed their outbound trail back to their headquarters at Tiguex.

For Coronado and his fellow wealth seekers the underachieving summer of 1541 proved a major disappointment. Unlike Hernán Córtes in Mexico twenty years earlier, they found neither great cities, nor gold, silver, or other precious metals. On the Llano Estacado they found a mobile people living in tents, living from the products of bison, "cows," and living with dogs as their beasts of burden. They found other people residing on a temporary basis in the eastern canyonlands—people who provided the Spanish entourage with food, advice, and important geographic information. They also found a land as horizontal as the oceans,

Spanish soldiers (a conquistador pictured here) and explorers on horseback with missionaries (often Franciscans on the Llano) on foot crossed and recrossed the Llano Estacado. They sought wealth, adventure, or converts to Christianity. Courtesy of Southwest Collection/Special Collections Library

a land filled with playa lakes (*lagunas redondas*), and in this wet-weather summer a land with plenty of water. Such meager results for nearly half a century discouraged further exploration of the Llano Estacado.

Then in the 1580s two issues in particular rekindled interest in the north and by extension the Llano Estacado. One included startling news that reached Spain and Mexico. The daring Englishman Francis Drake, Spaniards heard, had between 1577 and 1580 circumnavigated the globe. From Spain's point of view, Drake must have found the semi-mythical Strait of Anian or Northwest Passage, the fabled transcontinental water route north of Mexico. The strait must be found, fortified, and held against English claims to it.

The second development related to the passionate efforts of Franciscan missionaries in northern Mexico. Franciscans had been proselytizing among Native Americans living at Santa Barbara, the old mining town established in 1567 near the headwaters of the Concho River. The missionaries soon moved downriver to labor among Jumano villages at the junction of the Concho and Rio Grande (La Junta de los Rios, present-day Ojinaga and Presidio). There they heard of similar communities far up the larger river. Some Franciscans visited many of the several dozen pueblos, and soon word spread about the northern towns. In turn, the news reawakened the so-called glory, God, and gold phenomenon that had driven Hernán Cortés, Francisco Coronado, and others, including the religious and adventurous figures with them, on their quests. In any case, a series of missionary, military, and unauthorized expeditions followed.

In one of them in 1581, Fray Augustín Rodríguez, slave-hunter Hernán Gallegos (looking to enslave indigenous people), and a soldier named Francisco Sánchez Chamuscado led the way. A small entrada, it consisted of twenty-eight people: missionaries, soldiers, and servants. Known as the Rodríguez-Chamuscado expedition, it traveled in the early summer from Santa Barbara to the upper Rio Grande, and on September 28 most of its members, including Franciscan Fray Francisco Lopez, headed for the Llano Estacado. They left from a pueblo north of Albuquerque and reached the upper Canadian River, where they may have climbed onto the bison country near the ramp (Puerto de los Rivajenos in present Quay County) Coronado had used. The region's utter flatness and the "cows" inspired the missionaries, and later they talked of good pastureland, of plenty of water holes, and of sunny days. But little chance existed for them in doing God's work among the mobile hunting bands (Vaquero Apaches), for the Indians did not stay put. Soldiers in the meanwhile hunted bison and for the return journey, which began on October 19, "jerked" some of the meat. The little expedition remains "noteworthy," according to John Miller Morris, "for its role in re-opening Spanish awareness of New Mexico."[5]

The Rodríguez-Chamuscado expedition also renewed interest in the Llano. Partly as a result, two or three times afterward others sought to check the upper Rio Grande pueblos and the neighboring Llano Estacado. Some of them, such as the unauthorized and little-known Francisco Leyva de Bonilla–Antonio Gutiérrez de Humana entrada of 1593–94, covered the same ground as Fray Augustín Rodríguez and his colleagues. Some, such as the Antonio de Espejo–Fray Bernardino Beltran entrada, did not spend much time on the Llano. Then, beginning in 1598, about the time that William Shakespeare was building the Globe Theatre in north London and nine years before English colonists founded Jamestown in Virginia, Don Juan de Oñate established permanent Spanish settlements in New Mexico's upper Rio Grande region.

Juan Perez de Oñate y Salazar, the son of a Zacatecas silver baron, married the granddaughter of Hernán Cortés and the great-granddaughter of Moctezuma, the Aztec emperor whom Cortés had dethroned. The wealthy, forty-eight-year-old Oñate, a Spanish-Mexican conquistador, too often given to brutality, proved relentless and unforgiving. He established a temporary capital at a pueblo on the Rio Grande and renamed the village San Juan. Not long afterward, Oñate and his lieutenants explored some of the northern edges of the Llano Estacado.

Of these lieutenants, Oñate's nephew Vincente de Zaldivar led the way. With some fifty men in the fall of 1599, he traveled to the Llano going by way of the Pecos and Canadian Rivers to the area of Coronado's ramp. The men met some friendly Vaquero-Apaches, visited their Canadian River Valley *rancherías*, and built a large corral from trees and driftwood in which to trap bison. The trap failed miserably. On the Llano, Zaldivar noted in his report to Oñate, the "cattle" graze "on some very level mesas which extended over many leagues." The mesa, he wrote, was "continuously covered with an infinite number of cattle, and the end of them was not reached." Zaldivar's men rode among the bison herds and participated in the Vaquero-Apaches' fall bison hunt. They returned to Oñate's headquarters in November. Oñate, it turns out, was more interested in finding Coronado's Quivira along the Arkansas River in modern Kansas than in examining the Llano.[6]

Thus, two years later, in the summer of 1601, Oñate directed a large entrada to the Canadian River and the Llano Estacado before heading to Quivira. His expedition included two Franciscans, seventy men, and hundreds of horses and mules with eight carts to carry supplies. Once in the Canadian River Valley, it stayed on the south side of the river, camping along some of the Llano tributaries to the river, hunting bison, and gathering plums, berries, seeds, and other plants. Oñate and his missionary companions, driven by the elusive and mystic (and medieval?) glory, God, and gold manifestation, climbed the Caprock onto the Llano in its far northeastern reaches and then turned north toward the Arkansas. He found no riches, of course, but the Llano impressed Oñate with its flatness, its ease of transport, and its bison with their large size and—to him—their unusual shape and huge numbers. Bison, in his view, appeared to be a continuous rolling ball of black hair.[7]

For nearly three decades after Oñate's return, Spanish leaders showed little interest in the Llano Estacado. For Christian missionaries, however, the desire to seek converts among Native Americans on and beyond the Llano remained high. Indeed, it may have increased. Reports and rumors out of Spain, from Mexico City, and at Pueblo communities along the upper Rio Grande suggested that a Franciscan nun named María de Jesús de Ágreda after 1620—about the time Pilgrims from England landed in New England—made spiritual journeys from her convent in Ágreda, Spain, to North America. The beautiful young woman who soon became abbess, evangelized, so the rumors said, among Jumanos, Apaches, and others, most of whom lived just east of the Llano. About the same time, Jumanos from Texas showed up in New Mexico claiming that a woman dressed in blue similar to a painting of Mother Luisa de Carrión at Tompiro Pueblo had come among them, preaching and speaking to them in their own language.[8]

To check the rumors and seek the mysterious "Lady in Blue," Franciscans Juan de Salas and Diego López (or Diego León, sources differ) in 1629 headed for Jumano country. Their goal was to reach the upper Colorado River region east of the Llano in the modern Ballinger–San Angelo area. Their route across the Llano Estacado remains debatable. One group of scholars suggests that from their Isleta mission a few

miles below Albuquerque the missionaries with Jumano guides and
accompanied by three soldiers went east, climbed the escarpment—like
others—near Coronado's ramp, moved over to upper Frio Draw and
Tierra Blanca Creek, and then traveled southeastward along one of the
routes of La Pista de Agua Viva (Trail of Living Water). Running Water,
Blackwater, Yellow House, Sulphur, Sulphur Springs, Mackenzie, Seminole, and Monument Draws all represent routes of La Pista de Agua
Viva. If, in fact, as some historians have suggested, they followed Yellow
House Draw, Salas and López went through the site of modern Lubbock
and continued down Yellow House Canyon before turning south to
reach one of the headstreams of the Colorado River. Others, including
Llano scholar William Curry Holden, suggest a different route, at least
in its early stages. This one followed closely some of Captain Tristan de
Arellano's return route from Cona in 1541. That is, according to Holden,
Fathers Salas and López, the soldiers, and their guides went "from Santa
Fe, by Pecos Pueblo, down the Pecos River to the Portales Draw, along it
until it becomes [Blackwater] and continued down the draw to its junc-
tion with the Yellow House." And, from there, of course, to the Concho
River area of the upper Colorado. Still others have argued for a route
that took the men down the Pecos and then east to climb the escarpment
near modern Lovington, New Mexico, and from there down Seminole
Draw to the Concho River.[9]

Salas and López, while looking for their mysterious Lady in Blue,
proselytized among Jumanos for several weeks, even building a crude
jacal-like mission. Other Indian groups, including Apaches, came to their
little mission station and asked for instruction in Christian teachings.
They, too, said the blue-coated woman had visited with them in their
own language. The woman, María de Jesús de Ágreda, was a mystic who
went into deep trances. The episodes had started when she was eighteen
years old in 1620 and continued for eleven years. She told Spanish and
New Mexican authorities who met with her in Ágreda, Spain, that while
in the trances she had transmigrated to North America some five hundred times. Later, she disavowed her mystic crossings, but nonetheless
she became for a time the most famous woman in Spain, even becoming
something of a spiritual adviser and confidant to Spain's King Philip IV.[10]

Salas and López or León did not find the Lady in Blue in 1629. But Fray Salas with another missionary and some soldiers for escort tried a second time in 1632—about when María de Ágreda had disavowed her spiritual bilocations. Salas again did not find her among the Jumanos, but he found in the Middle Concho River near modern San Angelo a handful of freshwater pearls. When Salas returned to the Rio Grande, his missionary companion, Fray Juan de Ortega, "stayed behind for six peaceful months, getting to know the Jumano lifeway quite well."[11]

The handful of pearls Fray Salas brought back to his mission along the Rio Grande may have inspired a new round of expeditions to and across the Llano Estacado. In the best known of them Captains Hernán Martín and Diego del Castillo in 1650 traveled two hundred leagues from Santa Fe to the Concho River country, crossing the Llano along one of the draws in its lower reaches. They spent six months among the Jumanos, explored about fifty leagues eastward from the Jumano *rancherías*, and established friendly relations with the Indians. Like Fray Salas, they also found a huge number of pearls—of an indifferent quality—in the Concho Rivers.

Suffice it here to say that other expeditions followed. Some went along the Canadian River with the intent to check once again on Quivira and Indian nations to the north. A few went east to establish contact with indigenous groups beyond the Jumano country. Probably several, mainly commercial, expeditions entered the Llano Estacado to trade with Jumanos and their enemies the Apaches, gather bison meat and hides, and check on the possibility of mineral wealth and more pearls. Missionaries traveled with some of the expeditions, especially those designed to increase trade and improve diplomatic relations between the Spanish communities along the Rio Grande and Indians of the Llano Estacado and beyond.

Then, rather suddenly in the 1680s three developments ended—at least temporarily—official Spanish connection with the Llano Estacado. First, Franciscan enthusiasm for preaching among the mobile Indians of the Llano and its environments waned. The work was hard and their labors had not produced significant accomplishments. Franciscans found their efforts at Rio Grande pueblos and mission stations far more successful and rewarding. Second, in 1680 Pueblo people in the upper Rio Grande region revolted against Spanish dominion. Many Spanish settlers, soldiers, administrators, and missionaries died in the bitter uprising, and during it Pueblos drove the Spaniards out of the region to as far south as modern El Paso. Spaniards did not launch a "reconquest" until the 1690s. And, third, in 1685 Frenchmen, led by René Robert Cavalier, Sieur de La Salle, landed on the Texas Gulf Coast. Because the French threat to Spanish Texas needed to be removed, officials turned their attention away from the western plains and toward East Texas.

As Spain turned its attention elsewhere at the beginning of the eighteenth century, Comanches arrived on the Llano Estacado. As we have seen, various Apache divisions had come to dominate indigenous life on the Llano. They had swept in from the north long before Francisco Coronado visited the plains, drove away such settled groups as the Antelope Creek people, and over time began alternately to trade with or fight Wichitas and Jumanos east of the Llano and Pueblos west of the high tableland. Largely a mobile hunting culture, eastern Apaches pursued bison, deer, pronghorns, and other animals; collected various plants from the Llano; and traded for other food and necessities. Most of the eastern Apache divisions lived in tipis, used dogs as beasts of burden, and pretty much took over the Llano Estacado.

Then Comanches arrived. A Shoshonean-speaking people, Comanches appeared from the west and north, showing up in New Mexico about 1705. Aggressive and powerful and growing ever more so, they moved east onto the Southern Great Plains and the Llano Estacado and quickly adopted a Plains Indians life style: tipi dwelling, bison hunting, dog employing, horse-mounted, and mobile, plus certain nonmaterial cultural affinities and social organizations. They pushed the Apaches from the Llano, in turn fought and traded with Spaniards, expanded their range of territory, and carefully increased the size of their individual horse herds, which became an important measure of wealth and prestige.

For more than a century afterward, Comanches represented the dominant power over much of the Southern Great Plains, including the Llano Estacado. Although, as we have seen, they divided into several independent divisions, Comanches, connected by language, history, and family and cultural affinities, ranged across a huge territory that included large portions of Texas, New Mexico, Oklahoma, Kansas, and Colorado—Comancheria it came to be called. On the Llano, Comanches camped and hunted its canyons, breaks, lakes, and draws, and sometime during the mid-eighteenth century began spending cold winter seasons in such protective canyons as Palo Duro, Tule, Quitaque, Blanco, and Yellow House. They traded at Pecos Pueblo (Cicuye), Taos, and other pueblos in New Mexico and established a large trading and horse-distribution center along the upper Arkansas River. They defended their bison range against challengers, and, through diplomacy

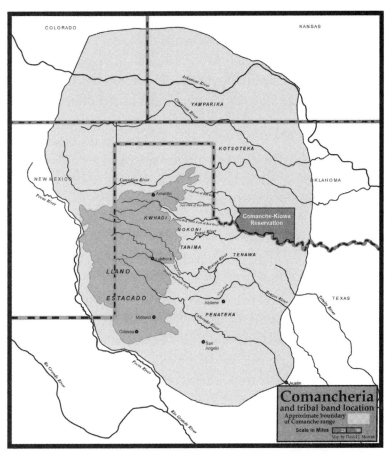

The map indicates the approximate range and boundary of Comancheria about 1780 and Comanche divisional locations about 1850. Courtesy of David J. Murrah

and alliances and treaties with other tribal groups and Spanish authorities, they maintained their hegemony for generations.[12]

But not all proved ideal for the Llano's Comanches. Frenchmen sometime after the turn of the eighteenth century brought trade goods to the
plains, providing many of the Comanches' sometimes enemies, such
as the Wichitas, with guns and other Euro-American-manufactured
goods. For the Llano and the Comanches, perhaps the trading brothers
Pierre and Paul Mallet represented the most influential of the several
early French interlopers. Born in Canada, the brothers had made their
way down the Mississippi River and worked out of a trading base along
the river, perhaps at a place called Arkansas Post or maybe New Orleans, which other Frenchmen had established in 1718. In the late 1730s,
the Mallets made their luckless way—they lost a lot of trade goods—to
Santa Fe by a northern route across Nebraska, Kansas, and Colorado.
By happenstance on their return to New Orleans they stumbled onto the
Canadian River and followed it to the Arkansas and ultimately back to
New Orleans—a very good water route between the cities. They headed
back to Santa Fe in 1742 or 1743, contacting eastern Comanches and
suffering once again the loss through an overturned canoe of many trade
goods. In mostly skirting the Llano Estacado, the Mallets spent little
time on the great mesa, but by again reaching Santa Fe, they encouraged
other Frenchmen, including unauthorized traders, or *contrabandistas*, to
approach the plains. At least one of the Mississippi-based traders infected
with smallpox carried the deadly pathogen to Comanches, resulting in
a significant loss in the Llano's Comanche population.

Other changes occurred. In one, Spanish authorities in the 1750s
moved to stop the French intrusions. They arrested Frenchmen and other
foreigners who arrived in the upper Rio Grande, including in 1751 Pierre
Mallet and several companions. In response, French traders pulled back
to the middle Red River from where they conducted a lively trade with
Wichitas and other Caddoan speakers in the Texas-Oklahoma borderland, particularly at a place called Spanish Fort in modern Montague
County, Texas. Comanches also showed up there.

In a second change, the Seven Years' War (French and Indian War),
the last of the four great "Wars for Empire" between France and England,

broke out in 1754. Fighting in North America drained much of the Mississippi River Valley of Frenchmen and reduced the flow of European goods to Comanches and other Indians in the West. At the close of the war in 1763 the huge French territory of Louisiana, including parts of Texas and much of the Great Plains north of the Red River, suddenly passed into Spanish hands. Spain, now under its remarkable Bourbon king Carlos III, ordered a reevaluation of its hold on the far-northern frontier, of its difficulties in maintaining settlements in the region, and of its military and diplomatic relationships with Indian nations of the north.

Reforms followed—as did new Comanche-Spanish diplomatic understandings. Among such agreements the erstwhile antagonists negotiated the Pecos Treaty of 1786, which proved significant for activity on the Llano Estacado. Brokered between Ecueracapa (Leathercloak), a Comanche headman "distinguished as much by his skill and valor in war as by his adroitness and intelligence," and Juan Bautista de Anza, an able military leader and governor of New Mexico, the far-reaching military and commercial alliance established peace between Comanches and the New Mexican settlements. It called for a joint war against Apaches (Lipan Apaches, mainly), allowed New Mexican bison hunters (ciboleros) and traders (comancheros) access to the Llano, and permitted Spaniards the right to explore a short and passable route between Santa Fe, Nacogdoches, and San Antonio.[13]

The road came first. From the Spanish view, Americans, who in 1783 had secured their independence from England, seemed to have aggressive designs on the West and by extension Spanish land in Florida and the Great Plains. A good, short road connecting New Spain's far-northern cities might help protect the north country. Accordingly, Pierre ("Pedro") Vial, a former *contrabandista* now in the employ of Spanish Texas officials, traveled in late 1786 from San Antonio north and west to establish a good trail to Santa Fe. After spending the winter along the Red River, he reached the Llano Estacado's eastern escarpment and followed mainly the Canadian River Valley, eventually reaching Santa Fe. It was not the short route that authorities wanted. But in these days of the wet and frigid Little Ice Age, Vial and his lone companion

noted a good number of "bluff springs" along the wide valley's southern escarpment, plenty of other water sources, and a large number of
Comanches—perhaps "several thousand of these Comanches [ranged]
the immense mesa and its environs."[14]

Although he welcomed Vial to Santa Fe, New Mexico's governor,
Fernando de la Concha, realized the talented explorer had not paved
a short, useful route between Santa Fe and San Antonio. Thereupon,
at the end of July 1787 he dispatched José Mares, a retired corporal, to
find a more direct route. Mares and his two companions, one of whom,
Cristobal de los Santos, had accompanied Vial to Santa Fe, headed east,
and in doing so perhaps became the first official Spanish sojourners to
navigate the Llano Estacado in more than 130 years—since, writes John
Miller Morris, "the pearling expeditions of the 1650s." The three bold
pathfinders rode onto the Llano Estacado at Coronado's ramp, moved
over to upper Tierra Blanca Creek, and then traveled to Frio Draw.
They traveled "across a very wide plain," wrote Mares, "which contains
no landmark." From Frio Draw, they followed a well-worn bison and
Comanche trail that led them to upper Tule Creek. Here, near modern
Tulia, they found permanent water in the creek and cottonwoods and
reeds (tules) in the wet, marshy land lining its banks. They continued
east and two days later suddenly found themselves at a precipitous drop,
the Llano's eastern escarpment, probably in the vicinity of present-day
Caprock Canyonlands State Park and Trailway with its red sandstone
surroundings. Once down off the bison mesa, the Mares party rode east
and then due south to San Antonio. After three months in the South
Texas town, Mares started back to Santa Fe, this time cutting northwest
from San Antonio, and in late March 1788 he reached the Llano near his
outbound route. He retraced his former course across the tableland.[15]

Mares found an abundance of trees—junipers, chinaberries, and cottonwoods especially—and water along lower Tierra Blanca Creek and in
the Tule Creek marshlands. Perhaps in the relatively mesic weather conditions—think of Coronado's experience on the plains—of the previous
two hundred or more years something of a forest environment began
encroaching on the Llano. Mares writes that the plains looked flat and
featureless, but he found travel easy, and although water existed in the

draws and creeks, he reported during his second crossing of seeing only one playa with water. The Llano suffered from a drought at the time, one that lasted about three years.

After meeting with Mares in Santa Fe, energetic and competent Governor Concha in the summer of 1788 again sent Pedro Vial eastward. Concha wanted the erstwhile Frenchman to find a road to Nacogdoches and the French settlement at Natchitoches, Louisiana. With six companions Vial left Santa Fe in June and moved over the familiar route past Tucumcari Mesa to Arroyo del Puerto, the wide, easy "ramp" onto the Llano Estacado. Once on the Llano, Vial and his party saw land "so extensive that one sees only sky and plain." Unlike Mares a few months earlier and despite the drought, they found some thirteen playas in the northern Llano, each with considerable water. They followed upper Tierra Blanca Creek downstream to Palo Duro Canyon and the Prairie Dog Town Fork of the Red River, passed through the area where Mares's "Tule River" joined the larger Red, and continued east. On his return, Vial struck the Brazos River near the junction of the Salt Fork and Double Mountain Fork of the Brazos in modern Stonewall County and from there headed west to strike White River, an upper branch of the Brazos. He followed White River into Blanco Canyon and up Running Water Draw before crossing over to Tierra Blanca Creek and his outbound trail.[16]

On their crossings of the Llano, both Mares and Vial visited several Comanche *rancherías*, especially in upper Palo Duro Creek, Tierra Blanco Creek, and Palo Duro Canyon. The Comanches in nearly every case remained friendly and helpful, sometimes providing guides for the Spanish explorers. Among the many Indians he met on his second crossing, Vial visited Ecueracapa, the skillful Comanche headman and negotiator during the Pecos Treaty discussions with Juan Bautista de Anza two years earlier. Clearly, the treaty's important pledges of friendship and brotherhood still prevailed within Comancheria, including the Llano Estacado. To further the peace and prevent starvation during a 1786–89 drought that had caused bison to drift from the Llano, Governor Concha twice—in 1787 and 1788—sent supplies of corn to Comanches. And the next year, 1789 (the year George Washington was inaugurated as president of the United States), Ecueracapa showed up in Santa Fe with 180 people from the Llano seeking help because they had no hides to trade for corn or other foodstuffs.[17]

By this time, 1780s and afterward, comancheros and ciboleros had made their way onto the Llano Estacado. Indeed, Pueblo hunters on occasion had been pursuing bison for generations, probably since the days of the Antelope Creek culture in the fifteenth century. Trading to, from, and at villages of the upper Rio Grande also dated to a very early period. In the seventeenth century Spanish settlers and mixed-blood Hispanic-Pueblo residents joined the commerce. After Comanches arrived in the Llano area, Spanish and Pueblo bison hunts, and even exchange efforts, became dangerous and declined a bit. But the Pecos Treaty of 1786 gave Hispanic-Pueblo hunting and trading efforts, when licensed, official approval, and both groups took advantage of the new conditions.

Comancheros with trade goods on their ox-drawn, two large-wheeled *carretas* (carts) or on pack animals covered the Llano Estacado. They stopped annually at such places as Quitaque, Blanco, and Yellow House Canyons, where they set up small "trade fairs" that mirrored the much larger events held in Taos, Pecos, and other Rio Grande pueblos. They established semipermanent camps in Casas Amarillas, at Lubbock Lake, along lower Tule Creek, and elsewhere. East of the Llano, they conducted substantial trading at Muchaque Peak (Mushaway Peak) south of modern Post in Garza County and at the junction of Duck Creek and the Salt Fork of the Brazos River in modern Kent County, where a substantial comanchero trade center existed as late as 1870. Many comancheros followed the Canadian River and set up trade stations along creeks and draws coming out of the Llano's north-facing escarpment. In the mid-nineteenth century old and worn horse and cart trails in the river valley stretched twenty-four tracks wide. Other New Mexican traders followed routes through the center of the Llano, and some peeled south to follow the upper reaches of the Colorado River. A comanchero journey from New Mexico took at least four weeks followed by trading activities lasting a month or two, after which the comancheros started home, another trek of four or five weeks, unless they drove livestock they had acquired in trade, a circumstance that lengthened the trip.[18]

Ciboleros, like comancheros, and sometimes with them, ventured from their Rio Grande villages onto the plains to pursue bison meat and hides. Often women and children accompanied the hunters, for bison needed skinning, meat needed preservation (pemmican and jerky), and hides needed work. Ciboleros headed for the plains, especially the Llano Estacado, in the fall: crops harvested, weather cool, bison nearby, and hides in good condition. Whole caravans in gorgeous colors moved to the level bison plains with their carts, searched for a herd, and upon finding one set up a temporary camp. Hunters on horseback set out with bow and arrow or, in the case of many experienced huntsmen, a lance to dispatch the prey. To them, hunting was as much an exciting sport as it was an effort to procure winter supplies. Quickly, others cut the throats of downed animals to bleed them out properly, and skinning began with women and children participating. To acquire enough meat, hides, and other bison products for the extended family or families, the cibolero caravan might be at the task for a month to six weeks or more, and, as it did for comancheros the journey to the bison grounds and back took several weeks.[19]

Ciboleros and comancheros remained active for nearly a century. They appeared as a lively, family-oriented collection of Hispanics, Indians, and mixed-blood villagers who grew crops, who as skillful handymen and women found work at a variety of occupations, and who used the Llano Estacado and its environs to sustain their village lives in the upper Rio Grande. Comancheros carried craft goods, foodstuffs, and other articles to the plains and exchanged them with Comanches, Apaches, and other native peoples for bison robes and hides, meat, and lard. Tobacco, sugar, flour, corn, bread, cloth, guns, lead, iron arrow and spear points, and liquor became part of the commerce. Some trade in humans also existed. That is, comancheros traded goods to Indians in exchange for Anglos and Mexicans taken in raids at ranches near San Antonio or in northern Mexico. They exchanged the captives in Santa Fe, Taos, and other villages along the upper Rio Grande, from where some of the hostages eventually returned to their families. Toward the height of the comanchero era, cattle became an important part of the trade, as comancheros contracted with New Mexican businessmen whom Texans identified as "German Jews." Two of them, Charles Probst and August Kirchner, were "immigrant beef contractors from Prussia" who bought cattle from comancheros. The businessmen, in turn, sold the cattle in gold- and silver-mining markets in Colorado, Nevada, and elsewhere or to the federal government to be distributed at Indian reservations.[20]

The careful chronicler and western traveler Josiah Gregg, who in the 1830s hunted with ciboleros and dwelt with comancheros, suggested that some of them came from "indigent and rude classes" but some represented "avid traders from time immemorial." As time passed, perceptions of them changed, and myths grew about them. Their competent historian Charles L. Kenner, for example, wrote that Americans viewed the "striking and picturesque" New Mexicans at first as "harmless rovers" but later as "notorious villains." Their enterprises on the Llano also evolved over time as relationships with Comanches and newly arriving Americans ebbed and flowed, soured and improved.[21]

In the meanwhile, major events far from the Llano Estacado impacted life and human activity on the bison plains. First, Spain, which had acquired French Louisiana in 1762, returned it to France in 1800, and three years later France sold it to the newly aggressive United States. Second, Spanish authorities worried about their former lands above the Red River, especially after word reached them that their soldiers in 1806 had captured American military officer Lieutenant Zebulon M. Pike and his exploring party in the Colorado mountains. Third, they also worried about threats to Texas in the form of a supposed "invasion" of the province led by an American spy Philip Nolan. And, fourth, the powerful French leader Napoleon Bonaparte in 1808 deposed the Spanish king Ferdinand VII and set up Joseph Bonaparte on the throne of Spain. Many Spaniards objected to Napoleon's action, and in Mexico creole and mestizo leaders began thinking of an independent state. Because of these worrisome activities, officials in Mexico City determined to impress Americans with the power and mobility of the Spanish-Mexican military.

To ensure such a result, officials in Mexico City wanted again to find a shorter route between Santa Fe and San Antonio. They also wanted to impress the Comanches with their strength. Francisco Amangual, a nearly seventy-year-old Spanish cavalry soldier and officer of some distinction, accepted the responsibility. On March 30, 1808, he led some two hundred men with carts and eight hundred animals out of San Antonio and headed for the Llano Estacado. Most historians suggest that Amangual and his troopers, upon reaching the Llano's eastern escarpment in May, turned north according to Comanche advice to go to the Canadian River. But, perhaps in the vicinity of Quitaque Canyon, they climbed onto the Llano rather than continue east of the escarpment toward the Canadian and found a "plains so immense that the eye could not see their end." Amangual's diary reported: "There was nothing but grass and a few small pools of rain water, with very little water . . . on these plains." Traveling north, Amangual crossed Tierra Blanca Creek, followed Amarillo Creek with its cottonwood trees and spring-fed pools northward, climbed down into the Canadian River Valley, and turned toward Santa Fe, reaching the town on June 19. Importantly, during his eighty-day sojourn through West Texas, Amangual met at different times with a large number of Comanches, including three of their principal chiefs: Somiquaso, Cordero, and Quegue.[22]

Amangual's passage across the Llano Estacado seems instructive. In his diary, Amangual recorded that he and his men experienced a fierce windstorm, for example, one that carried hats away and nearly blew men off their horses, but because of the extensive Llano grasses little dust accompanied the intense winds. He did not mention whether strong gusts turned over any carts. Later, perhaps because they lacked headgear, many men became badly sunburned, and three men out hunting did not return—even though the main party set fires to signal their whereabouts. Amangual wrote that heavy rains delayed his journey for two days, and one evening, he noted, they camped where "there were buffaloes as far as the eye could see." He also noted that on occasion at night the men needed to drive stakes or spikes to tie and hold their horses, a practice Comanches had been using for years. John Miller Morris in his superb work *El Llano Estacado* wonders if the word *estaca* became "gradually and casually linked to the word *llano*—the staked plain." If so, he suggests, "the name *Llano Estacado* owes as much to Comanche practice as

Hispano." Finally, while in the Canadian River Valley, Amangual and his men encountered a party of ciboleros, one of whom gave them good advice about the best trail to take with their carts to Santa Fe.[23]

Summary

Francisco Amangual's 1808 journey was among the last of the official Spanish-Mexican activities on the Llano Estacado. For the giant mesa, it ended nearly 250 years of Hispanic exploration, wealth seeking, missionary activity, Indian diplomacy, foreign challenges to the land, and general discovery. While no permanent Spanish settlements appeared on the Llano, soldiers, entrepreneurs, adventurers, and others covered the region from one end of the Staked Plains to the other. In doing so, they named nearly every stream, lake, canyon, and other place of interest on the high tableland—Spanish toponyms abound on the Llano Estacado.

As we have seen, nearly all who rode onto or across the Llano commented on its flatness, its playas, and its huge numbers of bison, which many, like Coronado, called "cows" (*vacas*) in the sixteenth century but before the end of the eighteenth century, like Amangual, called "buffaloes." Many Spaniards on the Llano Estacado noted its short grassy landscape; its lack of trees except in the draws, creeks, and canyons; its occasional mystic qualities; and its high winds, which blow nearly constantly as along an ocean's shore. Indeed, Francisco Coronado, at the very beginning of Spanish activity in the area, experienced a terribly difficult rain-, wind-, and hailstorm while just off the Llano's edge in the Briscoe County area in 1541. Francisco Amangual, at the very end of Spanish activity in the area, witnessed gale-force winds whipping up a vicious sand- and dust storm that frightened men and horses just off the Llano's eastern edge in the rough, broken, thin-grass country of perhaps lower Briscoe County in 1808—some 347 years later.

Between such set points, Apaches and Comanches struggled to hold the land and make a living on it. They adopted mobile, bison-hunting cultures that after acquisition of horses increased their mobility and their ability to prey on bison for sustenance and for a meat and hide trade that grew as their own and the Spanish populations increased. But they also struggled bitterly and desperately with one another until at the time of Amangual's crossing of the Llano, Comanches dominated the High Plains and the larger area called Comancheria. By that time, however, Americans had become interested in the Llano Estacado.

4

Comanches, Traders, and Anglo Explorers

At the beginning of the nineteenth century, Comanches dominated the Llano Estacado. Except for comancheros (traders) and ciboleros (bison hunters), few foreign traders or hunters climbed onto the Llano and few other indigenous groups challenged Comanches for the high tableland. Powerful, aggressive, and diplomatically nimble, they stood near the peak of their influence in the greater Southwest. Comanche men were proud leaders willing to risk all for the safety of the village, but they needed success in hunting and martial pursuits to gain social position and political prestige. Comanche women, who dominated tipi life, proved effective as negotiators in trade, skilled at essential life crafts (including bison-hide tanning), and protective of their families. Comanche villages, or *rancherías*, in 1800 were generally prosperous, often containing very large numbers of horses, a circumstance that as a result of their ponies' grazing needs required Comanches to maintain a mobile lifestyle.

Part of the Comanche success related to their large population. Pekka Hamalainen in his revisionist study *The Comanche Empire* argues for a population in 1800 at nearly 40,000 people, a number at the time larger than the Euro-American populations of New Mexico and Texas combined. In New Mexico, for example, the Spanish, creole, mestizo, and *genízaro* (Indians who were indentured servants of the Spaniards and whose release placed them in cultural limbo) population stood at 23,769. The Texas population of similar Spaniards plus Americans, enslaved and free blacks, Germans, and other foreigners numbered less than 4,000. But whatever the numbers might have been, the Comanche population was large.[1]

For the Llano Estacado, Comanche population numbers remain uncertain. But just before 1800, Comanches in their three original divisions—Yamparika, Jupe (Yupe, Hupe, Hois), and Kotsotika (Cuchanec)—experienced rapid population growth, causing many Kotsotikas to split from their brethren and moved south and east. They became the "Eastern (Oriental) Comanches," and in the mid-nineteenth century such new divisions as Tenawa and Penaticka formed. The Penatickas came to represent Comanches who raided and fought Lipan Apaches in South Texas and who swooped in on ranches and settlements in the San Antonio area. The Yamparikas occupied the region north of the Canadian River stretching into Kansas and the upper Arkansas River Valley. The Kotsotikas occupied most of the Llano as their homeland until the mid-nineteenth century, when the new Kwahada division began co-occupying the western tableland. About that time, too, the Nokoni division started hunting the Llano's northeastern corner. The Jupes covered the plains north and east of Santa Fe but often hunted the western Llano. Such dispersion served as an effective means for Comanche coexistence.

In the mid- to late eighteenth century, Jupe headman Cuerno Verde (Green Horn) attained prominence as an influential Comanche spokesman. A brilliant and powerful leader, Cuerno Verde, who, according to Elizabeth A. H. John, "employed all the panoply and ceremony of a king," attended Rio Grande trade fairs at Taos, Pecos, and elsewhere. His entrances (what we would now call "photo opportunities") received startling attention from Spanish chroniclers, and the Jupe warriors who accompanied him adopted something of an arrogant gang culture. At the time, the Comanche "nation" represented a considerable force with a large population that looked to Cuerno Verde's counsel and direction. Less than a century later the Jupe division had disappeared from the historical record. Clearly, through much of the Comanche experience on the Southern Plains, division names, makeup, and locations shifted.[2]

Population numbers, at least according to contemporary sources, also shifted. If we consider that if eight to ten or twelve persons resided in each lodge (tipi) and that eight Kotsotika *rancherías* or bands in 1800 held seven hundred lodges, the Kotsotika population totaled about eighty-four hundred people, perhaps two thousand of them warriors. The Jupes and Yamparikas counted about four thousand warriors in the late eighteenth century. If the four thousand Jupe and Yamparika warriors represent half the male population and there existed a similar number of women and girls, the Jupe and Yamparika population about 1800 numbered perhaps sixteen thousand people. Combined with the Kotsotika figures, the numbers do not reach the dizzy heights proclaimed by some modern observers, but they are substantial.[3]

Not all went in favor of Comanches. Smallpox and other diseases, including a yellow fever outbreak in 1787 (an eastern US plague as well) and another pox epidemic in 1799, cut into the growing Comanche population, reducing the number of warriors and hunters available for fighting and for procuring bison for food and hides for trade. As the long, mesic Little Ice Age began to wane after 1800, recurring drought struck the western plains, thus acerbating the Comanche milieu. Moreover, Comancheria expansion halted. Utes, for example, counterattacked in the Great Basin area and pushed the Comanches back to the east. Cheyenne and Arapaho war parties struck the Yamparikas in the north and drove them below the Arkansas River. Kiowas and the small, but affiliated, Plains Apache (Naisha, Kiowa Apache) group likewise assailed Comanche positions north of the Canadian River. The long-standing wars, raids, and counterraids against Lipan and other Apaches slowed, with a resulting slowdown in Comanche expansion to the south and east. Consequently, as a result of disease, shifting weather patterns, constant struggles with foreigners, including other indigenous groups, and the arrival of aggressive Americans, a general population decline set in, and it did not reverse itself until the early to mid-twentieth century.

Still, as the nineteenth century opened, the Comanche position vis-à-vis the Llano Estacado did not seem threatened. Because, for example, both national groups in the 1790s and afterward wanted peace and, with it, stability, Kiowas and Comanches sought an accommodation and in 1806 took an important step in that direction. They arranged a truce of sorts when a Kiowa leader, El Ronco, married the daughter of Somiquaso, a Yamparika leader, and moved into Somiquaso's village. In addition, other Native American groups, perhaps like modern-day migrants trying to reach the United States, wanted to participate in Comancheria largesse. As they did so, they made Comancheria, and by extension the Llano Estacado, a multiethnic, multinational region whose members found themselves united by bison economics, custom, desire, sign language, and trade and exchange.[4]

Nonetheless, changes came. Once again, French traders approached the region from the east, moving up the Red River, establishing trading sites, and seeking diplomatic contact and economic relations with Comanches, Kiowas, and other Native American groups on and around the Llano Estacado. Partly as a result, eastern Comanche groups turned away from Spanish sources at San Antonio and toward French suppliers of manufactured goods, particularly along the Red River. Further, the Mexican effort at independence beginning in 1810 cut the amount of trade goods moving to New Mexico and the comanchero staging areas in the upper Rio Grande. In turn, except for foodstuffs, fewer goods—such as iron knives, iron arrow and spear points, iron strike-a-lights, cloth and blankets, and tobacco—from Mexico reached the Llano and its Comanche inhabitants. And after the huge Louisiana Territory in 1803 passed from French to American hands, more explorers and traders from the United States began to press into the Southwest.

Indeed, Americans boldly entered Texas and reached toward New Mexico. As noted in chapter 3, Zebulon Pike and Phillip Nolan became the first Americans to arouse Spanish and Mexican leaders about the new foreign threat to their far-northern territory. Others followed, and the reasons seem complicated. For one thing, in 1819 the United States and Spain signed a treaty—the Adams-Onís or Transcontinental Treaty—that set the boundary between Spanish Texas and New Mexico and America's Louisiana Purchase territory. That boundary ran along the Sabine River and then, in stairstep fashion, up to the Red River, along the

Comancheros

Comancheros were Spanish and mixed-blood New Mexican and Pueblo traders, some, suggested Josiah Gregg, from "indigent and rude classes" and some "avid traders from time immemorial." From New Mexico, they worked the Llano Estacado, its draws, canyons, and watercourses to trade with indigenous people, especially Comanches. At first, many Americans saw them as colorful, picturesque, and inoffensive traders but later believed them to be thugs and dishonorable highwaymen intent on robbing everyone, Indians included.

Comancheros carried their New Mexico village products on packhorses or pack mules or in large, ox-drawn, two-wheeled carts (carretas) to the southern Great Plains, including the Llano Estacado and its canyonlands. The village wares included craft goods, foodstuffs, blankets, cloth, tobacco, perhaps watered-down liquor, knives, gunpowder, and other articles (sugar, flour, corn, bread, guns, lead, iron arrow and spear points). They exchanged such items for bison robes and hides, deer skins, cattle, dried meat, and on occasion humans.

Trade and exchange on the Llano Estacado were ancient. They dated from a time when humans first occupied the high tableland. The early Llaneros traded with people living on both the east and west sides of the flatland, but after Spaniards pushed into the upper Rio Grande country and married into Pueblo families, the nature of the commerce changed. European goods now entered the exchange strategies.

After about 1706, when Comanches first showed up in New Mexico, trade between the tribe's members and New Mexico's villagers increased. Over time, however, New Mexicans suffered from increasingly frequent Comanche raids, for the Comanches alternately traded at and attacked the Rio Grande villages. In 1779, Juan Bautista de Anza, the governor of New Mexico, with a huge force attacked a principal Comanche ranchería, killed a powerful

Comancheros and Indians engaged in trade on the Llano Estacado during the eighteenth and nineteenth centuries as depicted in this mural of exchange activities in Palo Duro Canyon. Courtesy of Panhandle-Plains Historical Museum

chief, and got the dead man's people to accept peace. Over the next few years, other Comanche groups and New Mexicans accepted peace.

Then, in 1786, at Pecos Pueblo in eastern New Mexico, Governor Anza and Ecueracapa, another important Comanche leader, agreed to a broad treaty of peace and friendship. The Pecos Treaty, as it is called, opened the way for full development of what became known as the comanchero trade. Prior to the treaty, commerce had been limited mainly to trade fairs at Santa Fe, Taos, Pecos Pueblo, and various Spanish settlements.

After the Pecos Treaty, comanchero trading grew and flourished. It lasted until the 1880s, until well after most Comanches had gone to live on a reservation in Indian Territory (Oklahoma). A couple of times a year, such as after crops had been harvested in the fall, comancheros traveled to a favorite spot on the Llano Estacado and waited for their native trade partners. "Favorite spots" included the Canadian River Valley, the upper Red River with its various tributaries, Running Water Draw and Blanco Canyon, Blackwater and Yellow House Draws, and several tributaries of the upper Colorado River. One trading site existed as far east as the juncture of Duck Creek and the Brazos River in modern Kent County.

The comanchero trade lasted for a century, but it was always in flux. American traders entered the business and impacted the commerce. Indian populations declined. Cattle became a major focus of the enterprise. Gunrunning and alcohol use increased in volume. And, once Comanches moved onto government-run reservations, it came to an end.

Some former comancheros, such as Polonio Ortiz, became guides for the US Army. Some, such as Casimero Romero, became sheepherders (pastores) and freighters. Others became cattlemen, teamsters, or businessmen. Some, especially the younger ones, became cowboys on ranches of the Llano Estacado.

Red, and up to the Arkansas River. From the source of the Arkansas, it ran north to the 42nd parallel and west to the Pacific coast. For another thing, in the aftermath of the economic panic of 1819, a gigantic folk movement westward occurred with most of the migrants heading to Texas. Then, after Mexico secured its independence from Spain in 1821, virtual hordes of Americans overran the Mexican state of Coahuila y Tejas. The "Father of Texas," Stephen F. Austin, determined to carry out his father's wishes, led the way when he received a grant of land to settle some three hundred people in the Mexican state. From the Mexican point of view, the liberal gift to Austin and subsequent land grants to additional *empresarios* (land agents) aimed to protect its northeastern territory by establishing something of a buffer zone to block American land grabs and general aggression.

Three of the land grants included the Llano Estacado. In 1826, John L. Woodbury, an agent for a German merchant in Mexico City, accepted a grant from the Mexican government for land in present Southeast Texas, and a Woodbury & Co., either at the same time or later, received a large grant that covered territory in the upper Concho River region, including land in what was called the "Llano Prairies." Woodbury & Co. made no permanent settlement. In 1827, John Cameron, a shrewd and well-informed Scot and early Texas settler, accepted a large grant along the upper Colorado River and extending onto the Llano in exchange for bringing one hundred families to the area. A year later he received a grant of land along the upper Red River that reached onto the Llano. He planned to settle two hundred families there. The Mexican government extended both grants in 1832, but it issued no land titles in either grant.[5]

Although the Llano-area land grants came to little, plenty of people pushed into Texas and others sought to reach New Mexico. Major Stephen H. Long and William Becknell were among them. Under military orders, Long, a thirty-six-year-old army veteran, in the spring of 1820 headed with nineteen soldiers southwest from the Missouri River at modern Council Bluffs to seek the source of the Red River, to check the Mexico-US boundary area, and to report on the land he traversed. Long missed the Red but found the upper Canadian River and followed it. On July 29, he and his men climbed onto the Llano Estacado in its far northeastern edges where for two days severe thunderstorms inhibited travel. Once back on the Canadian, they followed it to the Arkansas River and the military post at Fort Smith. Long's expedition in missing the important source of the Red proved a failure. Nonetheless, his report on the Great Plains, including what Long saw of the Llano, caused a sensation. It suggested the region could not support a civilization based on agriculture, thus challenging the "Myth of the Garden" about living and farming in the West. Moreover, an official map of the expedition labeled the whole of the western country the "Great American Desert." The negative reports did not stop westward migration.[6]

Although not the first American to reach Santa Fe, the thirty-three-year-old Becknell, often considered the "Father of the Santa Fe Trade," in 1821 succeeded in opening commerce between New Mexico and western Missouri. While transportation routes to and from Santa Fe avoided the Llano Estacado in its early years, in the 1860s a new route with two branches passed through the Texas Panhandle at the edge of the Llano. The Panhandle routes developed in response to the Civil War and the American need to supply food and other goods for Apaches at first and then for Navajos confined and starving at the Bosque Redondo Reservation along the Pecos River near Fort Sumner.

During the same time, other issues, including Rocky Mountain beaver trapping, impacted the Llano Estacado. In 1832, at the height of the western mountain fur trade, some forty-five trappers from Taos and Santa Fe headed across the Llano in search of beaver grounds in the upper Brazos River country and in the headstreams of nearby rivers. Led by Albert Pike, a poet, journalist, lawyer, and during the Civil War a Confederate officer; Bill Williams, usually a loner and one of the more successful mountain men of the West; and John Harris of Missouri, who sponsored the expedition, the beaver trappers headed east in September. They climbed the western escarpment near Taiban Springs, found the upper Blackwater Draw—shallow now due to eolian and alluvial depositions—and rode down it as they made their way across the Llano.

Pike reported on their experience, not always a pleasant one. He called the high tableland the "Staked Prairie," and some of the trappers, he noted, thought it "a place from which we could not escape alive." The late-September buffalo and grama grasses, having turned brown and curled in on themselves, made the land give off "the appearance always of having been scorched by fire." Nonetheless, they found well-worn paths to follow. Indeed, the "road" they traveled "was now broad and plain, consisting of fourteen or fifteen horse trails side by side." Clearly, before them plenty of people had taken Blackwater Draw, a major La Pista de Agua Viva trail across the Llano. Such recent trekkers included comancheros, ciboleros, and modern Native Americans such as Apaches and Comanches. The route had been used for centuries.[7]

The trappers quickly discovered that life on the Llano could be difficult. Although constantly short of water, they found small, shallow-dug wells in the Muleshoe Sandhills that paralleled the draw. Food in the form of wild game proved scarce: an occasional bison bull, a single pronghorn, a crane or two, but no deer. They found plenty of signs for wild horses (mustangs), but while most of the party at first did not want to eat horse flesh, they finally accepted it—and enjoyed it. Fuel with which to cook what game they killed proved hard to come by. On occasion, they found a bit of wood in the sands or dug roots, but more often they burned the ordure of horses and sometimes they lit a tightly twisted bunch of tall weeds, creating a fire that briefly burned hot and then went out. Moreover, the constant winds of the Llano blew hard, often filling the men's eyes with dirt and dust. In short, the trappers remained hungry, thirsty, and generally miserable.

Likewise, the trappers found some hungry Comanches. As they rode down Blackwater Draw, they met three separate Comanche *rancherías*. The first one, located in the draw but near the sandhills and perhaps in modern Lamb County, contained twenty lodges—about two hundred people. The village residents seemed "extremely poor," Pike noted. "They had no blankets—no buffalo robes—no meat—and were dressed shabbily." Although they controlled a herd of one thousand horses and mules, their lodges looked old and worn with very few dogs running about the camp. Many of the women had lashed themselves in lamentation for men who had been lost in a fight with comancheros.[8]

The trappers found a second camp in better condition. Located near present-day Mackenzie Park within the city limits of Lubbock or perhaps farther downstream at Buffalo Springs near Cañón del Resgate (Cañón de Rescate, Ransom or Traders Canyon), it stood in a grassy area. Most of the men were absent, and "as we approached," wrote Pike, "the women mounted their horses and took to the hills." Still, after a brief conversation with a Mexican boy the Comanches had kidnapped, the women returned and the beaver trappers exchanged some tobacco and knives for bison meat, dried meat, wood, and nuts. As the weather had changed to a wet, cold rain and one of the men appeared terribly incapacitated with rheumatism, old, long-haired, and grizzled Bill Williams rode over to the Indian camp and traded for a couple of lodge poles and some bison hides to provide some protection for his ill companion. Heavy rain continued through the night, making the trappers wretched.[9]

The third Comanche *ranchería* stood about thirty-five miles downstream from the second. The valley extended wider here, and it "was full of small hills interspersed with [mesquite] bushes." Pike counted fifty lodges, "much handsomer" than those in the other villages, and lots of horses. As in the previous camps, no warriors seemed present. They had left to hunt, or perhaps they continued to celebrate or mourn a fight with either American or New Mexican traders. Apparently, a major confrontation had occurred in which Comanches destroyed dozens of "wagons" that made up a caravan of comancheros with their big, ox-drawn, two-wheeled carts. Women in camp had cut and mangled their legs in mourning for lost loved ones, warriors who had died. Pike thought the fight occurred during "the attack on the wagons." The population of this large and prosperous village may have reached six hundred people. Pike noted the number of horses in the three *rancherías* totaled about five thousand.[10]

From the third village, the trappers rode down Yellow House Canyon before turning north toward the beaver meadows in the upper Wichita and Pease Rivers area. They did not find beaver, and the expedition broke up. Pike with some of the men headed for Arkansas. Others, led by Williams, returned to Santa Fe.

Several points related to the expedition warrant emphasis. First, it should be noted that Pike's report, as well as others, indicate that as early as 1832 some Comanches, although owning large horse herds, were otherwise destitute, suffering from food shortages, poor housing, and lack of essential bison hides. Second, Blackwater and Yellow House Draws in 1832 witnessed consistently heavy traffic. For at least forty years comancheros coming from New Mexico had been using the normally well-watered routes to reach trading sites in Casas Amarillas, Cañón de Rescate, Muchaque (Mushaway) Peak, Silver Falls, Los Lingos Canyon, and elsewhere in Comancheria. And third, horse breeding, raising, stealing, and trading throughout Comancheria, including the Llano Estacado, increased in importance.

In the 1830s an enormous demand for horses and mules existed, and it continued to increase in the years that followed. Americans, such as Phillip Nolan, had sought to capture or trade for horses in Texas as early as 1795. Northern Plains Indians wanted horses and in fact needed horses as they lost many to cold and snow and inadequate forage each winter. Eastern Plains tribes, such as Chickasaws, Cherokees, Osages,

Omahas, Delawares, and Shawnees, wanted horses. Demand for horses in Saint Louis, Fort Smith, and New Orleans, fueled by an insatiable American market, especially in the South, steadily increased. Comanches played a pivotal role in the trade. They acquired horses in New Mexico, raided Texas ranches for livestock, bred and raised their own animals, crossed into Mexico to gather horses and mules at northern haciendas, and like mustangers rounded up wild horses on the Llano Estacado. Indeed, Comanches became a model of supply-side economics in the horse and mule trade.[11]

The northern Mexico forays proved highly profitable. The raids had begun in the late eighteenth century and increased after the far-reaching Pecos Treaty in 1786 that, among other things, allowed comancheros to trade on the plains, and, as noted, their trading sites existed up and down the Llano's eastern escarpment and elsewhere. The raids increased further in the 1830s and 1840s as horse trading took on greater economic importance for Comanches, with the result that relations with Texans evolved into instability and after the war with Mexico beginning in 1846 eroded into chaos. Comanche incursions were often large and always destructive, and Kiowas and Apaches also attacked settlements and ranches in Mexico. Comanche warriors struck deep into Mexico and over a wide area. The historian and lively storyteller J. Evetts Haley, if we can believe him, described the Comanche raiding method as "a war of movement," bringing "terror, pillage and devastation" to towns, villages, ranches, and great haciendas across Durango, Zacatecas, and Chihuahua.[12]

Some of the Comanche raiding parties formed on the Llano Estacado. They often joined other parties coming from western Kansas or Indian Territory (Oklahoma) and rode with them. The route went south just off the eastern edge of the Llano, passing by Silver Falls and Muchaque Peak before turning a bit southwest to ride up the escarpment and across the lower Llano to Big Spring in modern Howard County. From there the Indians went to Sulphur Springs at the lower end of Sulphur Springs Draw. Here the riders and their trails divided to proceed in several directions. One of the trails went to nearby Mustang Spring on the upper reaches of the Concho River. In 1854, while crossing lower West Texas,

Comanche Trails to Mexico

Llano Estacado historian J. Evetts Haley called the trails the "Great Comanche War Trail." It was a "broad highway," he wrote, "that skirted the" Llano Estacado. Over it, Comanches rode south into northern Mexico, rounded up horses and cattle, stole goods and products of all kinds, and spread terror among citizens of Chihuahua, Coahuila, and Durango before returning with their spoils to Texas. The trail lasted for nearly a century (ca. 1770–1870), in time becoming a well-worn track. In 1854, US Army officer John Pope "was astonished by the heavy traffic" at Mustang Springs near modern Stanton "that had beaten out this great trail."

The trail had several branches. One arm began in Indian Territory; another, in Kansas. They met along the White River below where it emerged from Blanco Canyon. Remaining just east of the Llano's escarpment, the combined trail moved to Big Spring and then split at Sulphur Springs near the lower end of Sulphur Draw. From there, according to Haley, there were several arms or divisions. A "main" trail went southwest, crossed the Pecos at Horsehead Crossing, moved to Comanche Springs in modern Pecos County, continued south to enter the modern Big Bend National Park area, and crossed the Rio Grande near Lajitas. Another trail branched off near Horse Mountain, climbed through Persimmon Gap, and crossed into Mexico near present Boquillas, Mexico—the "Grand Indian Crossing," as it was called.

Over time, Comanches, Kiowas, and Apaches rode deep into Mexico and across a wide area. They carried their plunder and herded their livestock back by the way they had come, heading for trading rendezvous along the Llano Estacado's eastern escarpment or other sites, such as Casas Amarillas, well onto the Llano's vastness. On occasion, they carried hacienda residents with them and exchanged their human contraband with comancheros, who in turn sold the captives in Santa Fe or Taos. From there comanchero agents might ransom the captives back to their families in Mexico. Such was the complicated but effective commerce in captives. Canyon de Rescate, as it is spelled on an 1875 US Army map (Canyon of the Rescue or Ransom Canyon), in modern Lubbock County may have taken its name from the practice.

After the Civil War, traffic on the Comanche Trail dwindled rapidly and then ended. The US Army built forts along the trail; settlers pushed west to occupy the trail; "scalp hunters" in northern Mexico waylaid the northern interlopers; and Comanches, Kiowas, and Apaches moved onto reservations, where success in raiding and hunting became secondary to other paths to honor and stature. Still, the trail to Mexico along the Llano's eastern edge served Comanche people very well for a long time.

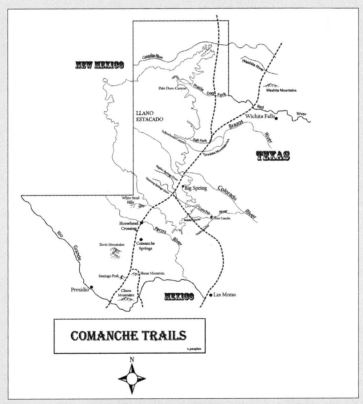

For about one hundred years, 1780–1880, Comanches and sometimes Apaches and other indigenous peoples rode south and crossed the Rio Grande to secure livestock and household items such as cloth, clothes, and perhaps guns and tools to bring home for trade or personal use. Courtesy of Curtis Peoples from base map by Jose Cisneros

US Army officer John Pope, writes Haley, "was astonished by the heavy traffic" near Mustang Spring "that had beaten out [a] great trail." The Indians, according to Pope, carried "into captivity hundreds of human beings, and thousands of horses and mules." Texas and Comanche historian Rupert R. Richardson wrote that Mexican citizens estimated 652 people were "killed, wounded, or captured in the state of Nuevo Leon from 1847 to 1857."[13]

Clearly, as early as the 1830s, Comanche assaults on Mexico from the Llano Estacado, from below the Arkansas River, and from the Wichita Mountains had become dangerous. They also became the subject of negotiations between the United States and Mexico. Then, in the 1840s and early 1850s, the raids finally reached a peak in number of strikes, harm to Mexican citizens, and destruction of property. In 1846, English adventurer George F. Ruxton, while passing through northern Mexico,

From left to right: Wild Horse, a headman; Isatai, a young spiritual guide; Black Horse, a headman; and Quanah Parker, an emerging political leader. Courtesy of Panhandle-Plains Historical Museum

stopped at Hacienda La Noria in Durango when vaqueros there spotted Comanches. They sounded a warning, Ruxton said, and everyone appeared "in greatest alarm and dismay." The women wept and flew "about in every direction, hiding their children and valuables, barricading the houses, and putting what few arms they could collect into the hands of the reluctant men." A year later, in 1847, during the US war with Mexico, the noted Comanche headman Buffalo Hump (Potsanaquahip) gathered about six hundred warriors to enter Mexico. He sought revenge for a failed earlier raid and planned to collect horses, captives, and perhaps cattle.[14]

Comanches and Kiowas usually carried their captives, stolen livestock, and other spoils back along the same route they had used to enter Mexico. Comancheros, especially, and perhaps other traders as well, awaited them at favorite sites, including Muchaque Peak in present Borden County or Yellow House, Blanco, Quitaque, Los Lingos, and Palo Duro Canyons. A multitude of trading sites existed. And in the 1850s and afterward, comancheros were often supported by American or German businessmen in Santa Fe and Las Vegas, New Mexico, who wanted cattle—large numbers of them to deliver to towns and gold- and silver-mining camps in the Rockies. Forays into Mexico declined after the 1850s as the US Army began to build forts along the trails worn deep by the countless horses, mules, and cattle; as an advancing Texas population moved into Comanche territory in West Texas; as Comanches began to settle onto reservations; and as "scalp hunters" spread across northern Mexico to intercept raiders from north of the Rio Grande. Nonetheless, for a century or so, the need for cattle and horses to enhance trade remained an important part of trail traffic.

At the same time bison hides for trade gained in importance. For decades hides and robes had been exchanged for various goods at Pueblo trade fairs. In the 1830s new markets, or at least, trade opportunities, opened. In 1830, for example, Plains Indians provided some five thousand hides to Saint Louis traders. The quantity increased annually, reaching one hundred thousand hides in 1840, a number sustained each season for many years. For Native Americans, including Comanches on the Llano Estacado, the tedious and laborious hide-tanning responsibilities fell to women, and as the need for more hides for trade increased,

In the temporary village pictured here, Comanches sit before a full rack of drying bison meat, which they will preserve by smoking or jerking (for pemmican) to provide a long-lasting source of protein. Courtesy of Southwest Collection/Special Collections Library

the work often required successful hunters to take a second or third wife—thus altering social dynamics and intraband relations. Moreover, bison populations came under greater pressure from humans, and bison numbers began a decline that would peak in the 1870s when white hide hunters entered the chase.

As horse and bison-hide trading expanded in the 1830s and 1840s, Comanche and Kiowa relations with Texas and Texans soured. In 1836, at the time that Texas secured its independence from Mexico, the population in Texas, including Americans and Mexicans, numbered about 34,400 with an additional 5,000 slaves. Ten years later the population stood at nearly 103,000 with some 38,000 slaves and perhaps 300 free African Americans. The increase seemed overwhelming. Moreover, Anglo-Americans among the growing citizenry proved as aggressive as the Comanches. Partly as a result of inevitable conflict concerning the two groups, a long and brutal free-for-all developed between Texans and

Comanches and their allies the Kiowas—a struggle that lasted nearly half a century. The Llano-based Comanches and Kiowas quickly made a clear distinction respecting Texans and Americans.

Josiah Gregg noticed the sharp dichotomy and its implications for trade. In 1840, the thirty-four-year-old American entrepreneur and trader determined to blaze a shorter trail between Santa Fe and the East. He also wanted a more southern route in order that he might start for Santa Fe as grasses greened in the southern region earlier in the year. To find such a route, Gregg left from Santa Fe, moved south and east, climbed onto the Llano Estacado near Coronado's now famous ramp, and proceeded east and then northeast to reach the Canadian River, which he followed to the Arkansas and Fort Smith. His Fort Smith–Santa Fe Trail gained great fame, mainly because, as Panhandle historian Frederick Rathjen has pointed out, Gregg gave it plenty of publicity in his widely circulated book *Commerce of the Prairies.* Nine years later, during the California gold rush, writes Rathjen, "at least twenty trains of California gold seekers used" the trail.[15]

During his 1840 crossing of the Llano Estacado, Gregg faced only a few difficulties. He and his party found water along creek beds, wood in the Canadian Valley, and generally smooth going while on the tableland. But not all went well. The party faced a nighttime Indian (Pawnee or Kiowa) attack while in present Oldham County, and after the three-hour fight, snow and cold rain fell. No one among the Gregg party died in the attack, but two received injuries—one in the hand and one in the head. As Rathjen describes the head wound, it occurred to an "indolent, corpulent" member nicknamed "Dutch," although he was of Italian descent. "The bullet," writes Rathjen, "glanced off his skull leaving a messy but not serious wound." Of the incident, Gregg observed, "Although teachers not [infrequently] have cause to deplore the thickness of their pupil's skulls, Dutch had every reason to congratulate himself upon possessing such a treasure."[16]

No additional encounters with Indians, Pawnees or Kiowas, occurred, and Gregg's party traveled eastward before dropping into the Canadian River Valley. Along the route they took, they camped at several springs or water sources that became important immigrant resting places on the way to Santa Fe or beyond to California. The stopping spots included Tecovas (Covering) Spring, which, located north of present-day Bushland, became the headquarters of the celebrated Frying Pan Ranch, and Wild Horse Lake in modern Amarillo.

By this time, the early 1840s, Comanches and Kiowas needed relief. In Texas, with bison numbers already in decline, Anglo-Americans pressing into their territory, and raids and counterraids exhausting their warriors and their women and children, southern Comanches, especially the Penatickas, sought peace. It proved a difficult undertaking. The Georgia-born, sometimes poet, and Republic of Texas president Mirabeau B. Lamar, in office 1838–41, changed Texas Indian policy. Unlike his Indian-friendly predecessor Sam Houston, Lamar saw Native Americans as tenants-at-will with no possessory rights to Texas land. Thus, Texas citizens could take territory whenever they wanted. Indians must conform to Texas law, leave, or be exterminated. As a result of Lamar's policies, Comanches sought an accommodation. Their peace overtures, however, blew up in 1840 after twelve Penaticka leaders with fifty-three warriors, women, and children under tall, old Muguara appeared in San Antonio for talks. Texas military officers double-crossed the Indians, killing Muguara and many others in the infamous Council House "massacre." In response, Comanches redoubled their revenge raids, some of which went sour, and western Texas became a troubled area.

At the same time, northern Comanches, particularly Yamparikas along with Kwahadas and Kotsotikas from the Llano Estacado, and Kiowas wanted peace. Kiowas and Cheyennes had been fighting a difficult war, and both groups needed to end the continuing conflict. Also, they both sought greater access to the trade at Bent's Fort, the castle-like, adobe structure Ceran St. Vrain and brothers William and Charles Bent had built in 1834 along the Arkansas River at modern La Junta, Colorado. The post had become an enormously successful commerce center, one Indian people, mountain men, Santa Fe traders, and others visited and used as a trade or rest area. Indeed, visitors to the place had used up all the timber for miles along the Arkansas, and, because of the heavy grazing requirements of their horses, mules, and oxen, grass had disappeared over a wide area around the post. With Cheyennes and sometimes their Arapaho friends fighting Kiowas and pressing into Comanche territory below the Arkansas River and Comanches with their Kiowa friends facing renewed problems with aggressive Texans, a general truce seemed beneficial to all. The result was a grand council of peace along the Arkansas River several miles downstream from Bent's Fort where timber and grass still existed. Perhaps five thousand Indians showed up. Leaders from each tribe exchanged gifts, feasted on various culinary delicacies, smoked the calumet of peace, and in general established a solid, but tenuous, friendship.

For Llano Estacado Comanches, unfortunately, trouble with Texans continued. Because he determined to exercise the financially strapped Republic of Texas claim to land stretching as far west as the upper Rio Grande, President Lamar organized an expedition to head to Santa Fe. It comprised independent merchants, government commissioners, correspondents, and others with a Republic of Texas military escort of 270 men under Colonel Hugh McLeod. In New Mexico, the commissioners expected to receive a grand welcome and to extend Texas political jurisdiction in the area. This Texan–Santa Fe expedition turned into a disaster. It left Austin on June 21, 1841, went north to present-day Wichita Falls, and then traveled west to near the edge of the Llano, making camp at the end of August near the junction of Los Lingos and Quitaque Creeks in the area where Motley, Briscoe, and Floyd Counties meet. Here, at Camp Resolution as they called it, the expedition, suffering from heat, hunger, thirst, and hostile Kiowas, disintegrated. McLeod divided the command, sending about one hundred men, mostly soldiers, ahead to Santa Fe to seek help. Mexican troops promptly arrested them. The others, still under McLeod's leadership, hunkered down for a few weeks, then, still suffering from Kiowa attacks, lost horses, food shortages, and other maladies, burned most of the wagons and left. About mid-September, they made a difficult climb up the four-hundred-foot eastern escarpment onto the Llano Estacado just below Tule Canyon. From there, McLeod's group crossed Tule Draw, moved northwest to Tierra Blanca Draw, followed it westward, and probably climbed off the

Llano near Puerto de los Rivajenos into the Canadian River Valley. In New Mexico on October 5, Santa Fe–directed soldiers arrested them. The ill-fated expedition thus accomplished little except to fuel animosity in both Mexico-ruled New Mexico and Texas.[17]

The Texan–Santa Fe expedition failure did not prevent others, especially traders, from entering the Llano Estacado. About 1843, the Bents and St. Vrain established a temporary trading factory along the Canadian River in present Hutchinson County with the aim of securing the Comanche-Kiowa trade in bison hides and horses. Because commerce there seemed at least marginally successful, three years later they built a large adobe structure (about eighty feet square with walls nine feet high) at the Canadian River site. The "Adobe Walls" post never fulfilled its early promise for the company, as Comanches and Kiowas alternately traded at and attacked the place. In 1849, after one last, but unsuccessful, effort to make a success of Adobe Walls, William Bent cleaned out its supplies and trade goods and blew it up.[18]

As the Bents and St. Vrain sought to build trade among Comanches and Kiowas of the Llano Estacado, Lieutenant James W. Abert entered the region. A West Point graduate, as well as an artist and scholar, the twenty-five-year-old Abert in the summer of 1845 led thirty-three men, mostly civilians guided by the famed mountain man Thomas Fitzpatrick, out of Bent's Fort. They planned to reconnoiter the Canadian River, contact Kiowas and Comanches, and generally make note of the country's plants and animals plus its water resources. After reaching the Canadian, Abert's party moved down the river, as instructed, making careful notes about flora and fauna, executing a number of drawings and maps, and reporting important water and fuel sources. Abert noted, as Josiah Gregg had a few years earlier, that Comanches and Kiowas of the Llano Estacado country made important distinctions between Texans and Americans, fighting the one group and maintaining friendly trade relations with the other. On September 16, the exploring company moved into Texas and climbed onto the Llano in modern Roberts County, moved south to strike the North Fork of the Red River in modern Gray County, and followed it for a time before turning north and east again to cross the Texas-Oklahoma border, from where it returned to the Canadian River and eventually to Fort Smith.

In his report of the expedition, a report that lay buried in the records for nearly a century, Abert wrote about the Llano Estacado. Not all of it was favorable. Once out of the Canadian River Valley, the party found little water and, as historian Frederick J. Rathjen has written, became "cooked by the sun, confused by mirages, and tormented by thirst." Abert wrote: "Our tongues seemed to cleave to the roofs of our mouths, and our throats were parched with dryness." The land played tricks on their minds. They began to think the Kiowa guides, who had left the expedition, had deceived them. Thoughts "of treachery, surprise, and massacre" revolved in their minds. When a lone, but mounted, Kiowa warrior appeared in the distance, the man "looked a very giant." Moments "of fearful forebodings" passed through the company until finally they sighted "some slight irregularities in the horizon," which meant they had succeeded in passing through what Abert called, "the great desert."[19]

Even as Abert led his little reconnaissance group through the Llano Estacado in the summer of 1845, events elsewhere transpired that led to the war with Mexico. The issues were numerous and complex, but the spark that ignited the war came shortly after the sixty-two-year-old Virginian general Zachary Taylor in March 1846 sent his troops to the extreme lower Rio Grande. In response, after some last-minute negotiations failed, Mexican general Mariano Arista sent his cavalry north over the Rio Grande and on April 25 defeated a small detachment of American dragoons. With that, war began. During the conflict, almost everywhere American troops succeeded—although sometimes, as in northern Mexico at the battle of Buena Vista, Americans got lucky. Military operations in the war with Mexico, which extended from 1846 to 1848, did not directly impact the Llano.

The war's end, however, produced important consequences for the Llano Estacado. Afterward, people poured into western regions of Texas, swelling the population many folds and pressing it up against the eastern and southern edges of Comancheria. Trade and travel routes below the Llano increased traffic between San Antonio and El Paso. Federal troops moved into the area, building forts and trying to keep peace between settlers and Indians, including Apaches and the Comanches and Kiowas in the Llano area. Government explorers arrived in significant numbers as they sought to identify the exact US-Mexican border and find a good route for a transcontinental railroad, as well as aid in the settlement of the New Mexico–Texas boundary dispute. In the end, the state boundary settlement became part of a much larger omnibus bill covering several issues, and in a plan written by James A. Pearce of Maryland the northern and western boundary of Texas—and thus the boundary between New Mexico and Texas—became set along its current borders. In other words, politicians divided the Llano Estacado between New Mexico and Texas along the 103rd degree of longitude.

While such debates waged for nearly two years, California mill-race builders in 1848 discovered gold in California. Word of the discovery soon leaked, and a year later the nation's great gold rush began. Gold seekers found that several routes to California existed. One of them came through the Texas Panhandle along Josiah Gregg's Fort Smith–Santa Fe Trail. In the summer of 1849 perhaps two thousand argonauts followed the trail, mainly along the south side of the Canadian River. Somewhere in Oldham County, because of a northward-extending spur of the plains, the route crawled up the northern escarpment onto the Llano Estacado. As noted earlier, army captain Randolph B. Marcy with eighty men provided escort service for nearly five hundred civilians—men, women, and children—headed for California through Santa Fe.

When on June 14 they climbed onto the Llano Estacado, expedition members saw a sight they could hardly believe. Marcy reported: "It is a region almost as vast and trackless as the ocean—a land where no man, either savage or civilized, permanently abides; it spreads forth into a treeless, desolate waste of uninhabited solitude." Such reporting represented some of his more favorable comments. Lieutenant J. H. Simpson of the Corps of Topographical Engineers accompanied Marcy and the expedition. He later noted: While on "the staked plains," the traveler *sees what he has not before seen during his whole route*—an uninterrupted expanse of *dead level prairie*, with not a tree anywhere upon it to vary the scene." Simpson also commented on what he called "the tantalizing and shifting *mirage*" where sheets "of water will appear to him, reflecting . . . the objects beyond them."[20]

Not all seemed bleak. On at least two points, the Llano Estacado held some advantages. In one point, Marcy reported that traveling proved easy. His large party followed a "road . . . perfectly hard and smooth, and our animals did not suffer much from the effect of the long drive of twenty-eight miles which we made." By late on June 14, they had crossed the Llano spur and again descended into the Canadian River Valley. They moved another two miles up the valley and made camp on "a creek with fine water, but little wood." As it turns out, the campground was an old comanchero resting and trading site.[21]

On a second point, Marcy wrote positively for a future railroad in the area. In addition to escorting civilians to Santa Fe, he held military and political instructions to evaluate the Fort Smith–Santa Fe Trail as a potential railway line. He made favorable notes on the matter: Few other "localities," he suggested, "could be found upon the continent which . . . would present as few obstacles to the construction of a railway as upon this route." Moreover, he suggested, "The surface of the ground is generally so perfectly even and level that but little labor would be required to grade the road." Finally, he said, "As there are but few hills or ravines, there would not be much excavation or embankment."[22]

Three years later Marcy returned to the Llano Estacado. This time he held orders to explore the Red River westward beginning at its junction with Cache Creek, which flows south through Cotton County, Oklahoma, into the Red northeast of present-day Wichita Falls. His instructions included finding the river's headwaters—a location that had eluded earlier explorers. Marcy arrived at Cache Creek on May 13, 1852, and with some thirty-three men began the long trek. At the mouth of the North Fork of the Red, across from Wilbarger County, he turned to follow it through modern Oklahoma and into Texas. On June 16, he climbed onto the Llano in present Carson County and went into camp. Knowing the Canadian River flowed not far away, he rode north while his men rested, located the river, and returned to his camp. Almost immediately, he took his men directly south, still on the Llano, across the Red's Salt Fork and into the broken country of Armstrong County to the Prairie Dog Town Fork. Leaving some of his party there, Marcy with horses and pack mules followed up this main fork of the Red for several miles, suffering from lack of potable water but later remarking notably of the eight-hundred-foot-high canyon walls. After returning downriver to the main camp, he gathered his men and, after celebrating Independence Day, began the long trip back to Fort Smith.

Upon his return, Marcy again wrote about the Llano Estacado. While traveling to and from the Canadian between June 16 and 19, he crossed the Staked Plains. He noted it was a place "where the eye rests upon no object of relief within the scope of vision." He expressed concerns about his water supply as he rode across the northern and eastern Llano, but he also indicated that near the draws and streams water, grass, and wood remained abundant. In the end, he determined that by exploring the three main branches of the Red and several of their tributaries on the Llano, he had at long last found the elusive headstreams of the important Southern Plains waterway that empties into the Mississippi River in Louisiana, some thirteen hundred miles away.[23]

As Marcy crossed portions of the Llano Estacado in the early 1850s, the federal government established a new Indian policy. The new plan aimed to concentrate Plains Indians away from main-traveled roads across the Great Plains. The government wanted such Indians in a place "where they can be controlled," in a permanent home in a country "of limited extent and well-defined boundaries."[24] To implement the policy, its officials called Comanche and Kiowa leaders to a conference at Fort Atkinson near modern Dodge City along the Arkansas River in Kansas. Hungry but faced with declining food supplies, beleaguered but faced with increasing white pressure, and dying but faced with mysterious maladies, the exasperated Comanches and Kiowas in 1853 showed up and spread their tipis over a wide area. Afterward, they sat down to discussions, smoked the calumet of peace, and negotiated a new treaty, the Treaty of Fort Atkinson. Indian delegates, led by Shaved Head and Rides on Clouds of the Comanches, Chief Little Mountain and war leader Satank of the Kiowas, and Poor Wolf of the Plains Apaches, made substantial concessions. They would allow peaceful transit along the

Santa Fe Trail, stop raiding in Mexico, and accept tribal limitations to their territory, such as staying below the Arkansas River. In exchange, the Indians received gifts and bounties, and the government promised to pay an annual annuity of eighteen thousand dollars for ten years.

Although the treaty was not effective and the funding failed to arrive, the Llano Estacado remained a Comanche domain—at least for a time. Five years later, the Butterfield (or Southern) Overland Mail crossed a portion of the Llano Estacado, but only for a brief time. The transcontinental mail service, established in 1858, ran from Saint Louis and Memphis through Texas, New Mexico, and Arizona to San Francisco. Through Texas, it generally followed the old California Trail, which had been established when "forty-niners" rushed to the Pacific gold fields. In the Llano region, the Butterfield route after reaching the area around present Carlsbad along the North Concho River in current Tom Green County (Texas) moved southwestward to the headwaters of the Middle Concho River. On the extreme southern edge of the Llano, it followed Centralia Draw west by southwest to climb through Castle Gap with its four-hundred-foot-high sides between Castle and Kings' Mountains and off the Llano to Horsehead Crossing twelve miles distant. In all, the route covered only about seventy miles on the Llano, and it lasted just over two years. The Butterfield Overland Mail ended in 1861 just after the Civil War began and the attention of America, North and South, turned in another direction.

Summary

During the first half of the nineteenth century the Llano Estacado became a busy place. Comanches and Kiowas claimed "right of ownership" by possession of the vast tableland, but they found that other Native American groups, especially Apaches, Cheyennes, and Arapahos, envied that occupation and sought to enjoy some of Llano's resources. Likewise, Anglo traders, including Frenchmen, worked their way toward the region in hope of commercial exchange with Comanches and Kiowas. The American and French merchants brought all kinds of manufactured goods plus various kinds of food and tobacco to exchange with Indians for hides, meat, and horses. The foreigners also brought European-borne diseases to the Llano-area Indians. In 1849, for example, argonauts passing through the Llano along the Fort Smith–Santa Fe Trail brought cholera, a deadly illness that cut significantly into Comanche population numbers.

The comanchero trade from New Mexico also remained busy and profitable. As time passed through the early part of the century, the trade evolved from Indians providing meat, hides, and robes to their providing horses and cattle, animals that Comanches and Kiowas had stolen from Texas ranches, from northern Mexico settlements and haciendas, and from other Native Americans. The number of cattle and horses in the trade became enormous.

Such activity combined with the Texas effort at independence and the subsequent war with Mexico brought additional traders to the area. It also brought government explorers to the Llano Estacado. Too often the merchants, such as Josiah Gregg, and the government agents, such as Stephen Long, James Abert, and Randolph Marcy, saw the Llano Estacado as flat, without water and trees, uninhabitable, dangerous, and in general an unworthy place. Drought, as when Marcy visited the Llano, sometimes occurred and did not improve their perceptions of the region. Comanches, on the other hand, viewed the same country in an entirely different way, and after the Civil War they fought desperately to hold on to the land they had inhabited for generations.

5

Federal Soldiers and Llano Indians

At the time of the Civil War, 1861–65, the western limit of settlement in Texas remained a good distance away from the Llano Estacado. In fact, during the war as a result of severe drought, Indian attacks, and many adult men having gone off to fight the United States, the front line of Anglo occupation in the northern Texas prairies moved back east from its leading edge, in some places perhaps a hundred miles. The four years of war represented something of a reprieve for bison in Texas and, until near the end of the conflict, also for Comanches and Kiowas. During the war the Llano Estacado–based Indian nations quickly realized that they had little to fear from either federal or Confederate troops, and they slowly at first but with increasing boldness stepped up their raiding. By the end of the war, their activities had become an important economic factor, for the Indians suffered food shortages and did not receive treaty-promised annuities and supplies. Hunger existed, but it was not new to Comanches. Penaticka leader Ketumsee as early as 1851 had talked about turning to agriculture and raising corn to cover food shortages.

Near and at the end of the Civil War, soldier-Indian fighting inten-sified. Local militia units and US government forces struck at Indians, and Comanches and Kiowas took a military beating. Those hit hardest included Kiowas, the Yamparika Comanche bands that had not slipped away to live for a several years in Mexico, Kotsotikas, and some of the recently formed Nokonis, Kwahadas, and Tenawas. Two major confrontations occurred. In November 1864, the mule-riding, indefatigable, cool-headed Kit Carson led some 335 military officers and enlisted men and 75 Utes and Apaches plus some cowboy-fighters from Lucien Maxwell's large ranch near Cimarron, New Mexico, down the Canadian River into Texas. They headed toward William Bent's long-abandoned and crumbling adobe trading post (Adobe Walls) in present Hutchinson County, Texas. Carson established a base camp about thirty-five miles above the old trade site, and after his scouts reported that an Indian camp lay ahead, Carson went after it. Although not everything went well for his force, the men managed to destroy the camp. When Kiowas, Comanches, Plains Apaches, and Arapahos struck back, Carson's force took refuge within the dilapidated adobe-mud walls of Bent's empty structure, and several hours later, after the Indians left the scene, the exhausted troopers retreated to New Mexico. Carson lost two soldiers and one Indian auxiliary killed plus fifteen others wounded. The Indians suffered sixty or more casualties, saw an entire village with all its winter supplies destroyed, and in a significant way suddenly lost any sense of security the depths of the Llano Estacado had previously given them.

In the second event, Comanches and Kiowas got caught up in struggles in Kansas and Colorado. As thousands of Anglo-Americans traveled through Cheyenne and Arapaho territory on their way to the Colorado gold fields in the early 1860s, trouble between Native Americans and whites occurred. Part of that antagonism led to the unnecessary but horrific Sand Creek massacre in November 1864 (about the same time that Kit Carson's men attacked Kiowas in the Canadian River Valley). In this ill-advised attack, militia troops under Colonel John Chivington, a barrel-chested elder in the Methodist Church, struck the quietly encamped Cheyenne village of Black Kettle, a sixty-year-old peace advocate, along Sand Creek in southeastern Colorado. Cheyennes suffered a bloodbath, losing at least 163 men, women, and children. In its aftermath, Plains Indians over much of the West, including Comanches and Kiowas, sought revenge through raiding but gained little except white animosity.

After hostilities settled somewhat, a series of government-Indian treaties ensued. For the Llano Estacado Indians the treaties of the Little Arkansas (1865) ended the fighting. The treaties resembled the earlier Treaty of Fort Atkinson (1853). Generally, the government got Indians to agree to limit their hunting and living range in exchange for gifts and annuities.[1]

In some ways, the treaties of the Little Arkansas appeared to be a set of strange agreements. According to the Comanche-Kiowa treaty, the two tribal units must stay below the Cheyennes (who must stay below the Arkansas River). The treaty gave the Kiowas and Comanches a large region in western Indian Territory (Oklahoma) and western Texas that included the Llano Estacado, all of the Texas Panhandle, and most of Indian Territory west of the 98th meridian. Although legally the Texas land was not federal property to give away, the federal government, according to treaty language, set it "apart for the absolute and undisturbed use and occupation of the" Kiowas and Comanches, and "no white person except officers, agents, and employees of the Government shall go upon or settle within the country." Much of the land in question Comanches had held in the form of possessory rights for generations. Moreover, as indicated, the US government did not own Texas lands, for the State of Texas retained its land titles when it entered the United States—although, granted, Texas was under a federally imposed Reconstruction government at the time of the Comanche-Kiowa treaty. Nonetheless, Kiowa leaders Stinking Saddle Horn, Satanta (White Bear), and Satank (Sitting Bear) accepted the treaty as did several Comanche representatives, including Buffalo Hump of the Penatickas, Paruasemena (Ten Bears) of the Yamparikas, and Quenahewi (Drinking Eagle) of the Nokonis. The Indians agreed to the treaty because they needed and wanted the gifts, food, and annuities the government dangled in front of them.[2]

Meanwhile, the end of the Civil War brought changes. The Texas population expanded again, reaching over eight hundred thousand in 1870, a 35 percent increase since the beginning of the Civil War. Ex-soldiers and westward-moving pioneers seeking ground on which to plant crops and raise a few cows moved into land where no nineteenth-century farmer should have been. A booming US beef market as a result of a Civil War–caused livestock shortage encouraged Texas cattlemen to push westward

Treaty Making

American Indian leaders and federal government representatives approached treaty making from significantly different social and cultural perspectives. As explained by Raymond J. DeMallie and others, both groups understood the meeting council as a diplomatic medium for open discussion, but they held different ideas about treaties. To such Plains Indians as the Comanches of the Llano Estacado the council—the coming together—was most important. To the federal government and its agents, the treaty, signed at the end of the council meeting, mattered above all else; the council served only as a preliminary to the written agreement.

Various treaty-making rituals, such as gift giving and pipe smoking, also differed. For the Comanches, pipe smoking was a pledge to truth and honor in the discussions to follow. Gift giving served as a prelude to bargaining. In addition, the Indians might hold feasts and dances, and younger men sometimes offered displays of horsemanship. For white negotiators, the gifts were awards—bribes—to be distributed at the end of the discussions, and the signing of the treaty document was important and necessary.

For Comanches of the Llano Estacado, three treaties with the US government proved particularly crucial: Fort Atkinson in 1853, Little Arkansas in 1865, and Medicine Lodge in 1867. At Fort Atkinson on the Arkansas River near present-day Dodge City, Comanches and some of the other Southern Plains Indians in a precedent-setting and highly significant concession agreed to broad limits on their range of territory. Comanches, led by Shaved Head and Rides on Clouds, promised to stay below the Arkansas River, thus surrendering former territory in the upper Arkansas River country of modern Colorado. There were other pledges, of course, some of which repeated assurances made in earlier treaties, and the federal government promised goods, gifts, and annual monetary payments (guarantees that proved difficult to maintain), but the land concession was vital.

The Little Arkansas agreements, made at the junction of the Little Arkansas and Arkansas Rivers (modern Wichita) also involved land concessions. Cheyennes and Arapahos at the conference agreed to a large reservation below the Arkansas River in southern Colorado, land that the government in 1853 had recognized as Comanche territory. In their Little Arkansas treaty, one separate from the Cheyenne-Arapaho accord, Comanches, led by Rising Sun, Buffalo Hump, and Ten Bears, gave up former claims to land below the Arkansas and promised to stay below the land assigned to Cheyennes and their Arapaho allies. All of the land, it should be noted, was once part of greater Comancheria. While they gave up a lot of land in this treaty, the Comanches retained the right to hunt in the Texas and Oklahoma Panhandles, including the Llano Estacado.

Two years later, after negotiations at Medicine Lodge Creek about seventy miles south of Fort Larned in Kansas, Comanches again signed away land. In return for buildings, agricultural equipment and farming instruction, clothes, cloth, hats, food, and a large annual annuity for thirty years, they accepted a reserve in present-day southwestern Oklahoma and were allowed the right to hunt south of the Arkansas River "so long as the buffalo ran."

From the Comanche and Kiowa point of view, there remained sadness and much melancholia about the discussions at Medicine Lodge. During the negotiations, Ten Bears, an elderly but powerful orator, brought tears to eyes of his listeners when he told the American peace commissioners, "I was born upon the prairie, where the wind blew free and there was nothing to break the light of sun." The sometimes-mulish Kiowa leader Satanta also spoke: "I love the land and the buffalo," he said. "I love to roam over the prairies," and when I do, "I feel free and happy." Such pleas notwithstanding, Indian leaders signed, thus ending the Comanches' and Kiowas' nearly two-centuries-old horse-mounted, mobile lifestyle on the Llano Estacado.

and increase their herd sizes. Comanches and Kiowas objected and sought to hold on to territory they had taken from Apaches a century earlier. Of economic necessity, and perhaps because of cultural heritage issues, they stole from encroaching cattle herds, hit isolated ranches for cows plus horses and mules, and raided farms and little communities in Texas. In response, the federal army moved back into Texas and reestablished and expanded a line of military posts that stretched from the Red River nearly to the Rio Grande. The army reasoned that the fortifications should safeguard pioneer settlers, stop Comanche raids in Texas, and block Indian use of the well-traveled Comanche trail to Mexico.

The federal garrisons represented a defensive, even passive, response to Indian raiding activities. Although they symbolized a show of force on the government side, they were not effective. Kiowas and Comanches, who usually organized raids during times when the moon was full and thus provided light through the night, quickly learned to strike in the wide area between military installations. Along the western edge of settlement in Texas after the Civil War, the monthly appearance of the "Comanche moon" became a time of unwelcomed worry and dread for

Plains Indians, government officials, and onlookers gathered at the 1867 meeting in southern Kansas that resulted in the important Treaty of Medicine Lodge in which Indians agreed to small reservations in exchange for government gifts of money, food, clothing, cloth, agricultural instruction, and additional help. Courtesy of Panhandle-Plains Historical Museum

pioneers along the "borderland." The long and violent fight between Comanches seeking to hold their territory and Texans seeking to push westward into it continued to boil and rage.

As the conflict intensified, efforts to secure a broad, general American-Indian peace emerged. The federal government, as well as Texas state officials, wanted peace with various Texas Indian groups. For the Llano Estacado's Comanches and Kiowas, the upshot was the Treaty of Medicine Lodge (1867). Treaty discussions occurred in October along Medicine Lodge Creek some seventy miles south of Fort Larned in southwestern Kansas. Here occurred a truly grand council of peace with several government commissioners and the principal southern Plains Indians—Comanches, Kiowas, Cheyennes, Arapahos, and Plains Apaches—present. Perhaps five thousand Indian people attended, and five hundred federal troops guarded scores of wagons loaded with supplies, food, and gifts to be distributed at the end of discussions. With their tipis ranging over a wide area, their camps noisy and busy, and their horses grazing across hundreds of acres, the Indian participants celebrated in the grassy valley.

The peace discussions became serious—and impassioned. Indian leaders did not want to give up land while government commissioners insisted that they would. Satanta, the witty but tempestuous Kiowa leader who in earlier days summoned dinner by blowing on a French horn, spoke fervently about the prairies and plains he loved and did not want to give them up. Ten Bears, the bespectacled but masterful Yamparika orator, said—among other things—that "Texans have taken away the places where the grass grew the thickest and the timber was the best . . . [but] the Great Father [in Washington] told me that all the Comanche land was ours and that no one should hinder us in living upon it. So, why do you ask us to leave?" The long speech brought tears to the eyes of those who listened to him talk. Indeed, it was an exceptional, moving address and one of the few Indian speeches recorded from any of the many past peace councils. As Thomas Kavanagh has written, nearly "every other sentence [in the presentation] was a figure of speech, a metaphor, simile, personification, or metonym, and each was appropriate to the context."[3]

The powerful Indian appeals notwithstanding, commissioners using threats, bribery, and coercion got several Comanche and Kiowa headmen to agree to terms. The Indians who put their signatures on the treaty must abandon as a living area nearly all the land their people had called home for nearly 160 years. In exchange, the Indians—horse pastoralists and former roving bison hunters—got a small reservation (three million acres) in western Indian Territory on which government agents would teach them to become settled farmers. The government promised in the treaty to provide instruction, buildings, farm equipment, tools, clothes, cloth, hats, food, and a twenty-five-thousand-dollar annuity for thirty years. For the most part the treaty stipulated that Comanches, Kiowas, and Plains Apaches must remain on the reservation, which extended between the Red and Washita Rivers, but with "passports" they could leave. It allowed them to hunt below the Arkansas River, including the Texas Panhandle and the Llano Estacado.[4]

Representatives of a third of the Comanches, including the Kwahada (Quahadachoko, Quahada) division, did not sign the Treaty of Medicine Lodge. Kwahadas traded in New Mexico at the time of the discussions and hence did not sign the treaty or go to the reservation. Because they did not sign the Medicine Lodge agreement, they had little access to the treaty's political and economic gifts. Most of the Kiowas went to the reservation, but Satanta took his small band onto the Texas plains. Raiding continued. Without treaty benefits, raiding had become an economic necessity for the Llano Estacado–based Kwahadas.

Elsewhere on the Great Plains similar problems existed. That is, treaties between the federal government and Indian nations had been signed, but fighting continued in the Dakotas and west of the Black Hills, in Kansas and Colorado, and elsewhere. In addition, mid-nineteenth-century reformers argued that too much fraud and corruption existed on America's reservations, which caused shortages in gifts, food, clothing, cloth, and other promised goods. Partly as a result, in 1869, after he became president of the United States, Ulysses S. Grant embarked on a major peace initiative. Grant's "Peace Policy" or the "Quaker Peace Policy" followed. It was a series of laws and executive actions aimed at establishing peace in the West, ending corruption on the reservations, and keeping the Indian Bureau within the Interior Department. The army became responsible for only those Indians off their reservations.

For Indian people of Comancheria—now essentially the Llano Estacado, the Texas Panhandle, and the reservation—the Peace Policy made little difference. Economic problems continued to mount and demographic issues proved shocking. Although population estimates are difficult, Comanche numbers continued to collapse, falling into something of a death spiral. In 1846, for example, contemporary observers estimated the population for all Comanche divisions at 14,300. In 1870, the Comanche agent Lawrie Tatum, "an unimaginative but courageous and sensible Quaker," noted a population of 3,742, a total that included an estimated 1,000 off-reservation Kwahadas—but the Kwahada number seems an exaggeration, for their bands were limited and each counted few in number of residents. For Kiowas and Plains Apaches, their combined population in 1870 or thereabout numbered perhaps 1,400 people, including non-Kiowa captives who had been assimilated into the tribe.[5]

Comanche and Kiowa economic plight remained complex. For one thing, the federal government cut Indian hunting territory. For another, even as church people under the Peace Policy came to head reservations, federal gifts still did not provide reservation people adequate, proper, and treaty-specified amounts of food, clothing, livestock, farming equipment and tools, and agricultural training. Also, the Indians suffered desperately from material shortages basic to sustaining life. Even reservation Kiowas and Comanches needed to steal food, cattle, horses, and other goods, and they did it from other Indians and from off-reservation sources, especially in Texas. Such activities did little to promote peaceful coexistence.

For the Kwahadas, particularly, theft proved indispensable. They stole horses, mules, and cattle and on occasion kidnapped humans from farms and ranches on the rim of settlement in Texas. Indeed, acquiring cattle for food and trade remained their principal economic resource. Accordingly, they continued to engage in comanchero trading and herded stolen animals as quickly as possible to old comanchero exchange sites on the Llano Estacado or just off the eastern escarpment in the Quitaque area, the Muchaque country, or elsewhere. As noted previously, one trading site existed as far east as the junction of Duck Creek and the Brazos River in modern Kent County. According to the report of a US Army recognizance officer, some six hundred Indian people (nations unknown) in 1870 camped there along what he called "an old Mexican cart road." At this and other rendezvous sites Kwahadas traded horses and cattle plus dried bison meat, hides, and on occasion humans to comancheros for hard bread and other food, blankets, equipment, tools, and sundry commodities otherwise unavailable to them.[6]

In 1870, Texas citizens, whose population stood at more than eight hundred thousand, saw Indian raiding as out of control. While Kiowa and Comanche bands struck Texas farms and ranches from the Llano Estacado and from their reservation, Lipan Apache and Kickapoo raiders crossed from Mexico to strike settlements above the Rio Grande. White outlaws, cattle rustlers, and horse thieves, sometimes dressed as Indians, raided both reservation herds and Texas villages, farms, and ranches. As thievery and depredations became more and more dangerous to them, Texas citizens began pulling back from the most-exposed points on the edge of settlement. Texas resources to deal with the Indian troubles were still evolving as the state struggled through a Reconstruction government controlled by federal mandates and regulations and that provided inadequate and ineffective measures to meet frontier needs.

Finally, at least from the Texans' point of view, General of the Army William T. Sherman, an officer who had used scorched-earth (total war) tactics during the Civil War, turned loose federal troops. In effect, the Peace Policy ended. With Grant's blessing, Sherman in May 1871 sent federal soldiers across the Plains. He did so in response to a vicious and deadly attack on a wagon train on Salt Creek Prairie in Young County, Texas, directed by Kiowa leaders Satanta, Satank, and others earlier in the month. Just days before, General Sherman had passed the very spot where the attack had occurred. After Sherman's new order, military units on the Southern Plains went in pursuit of Indians all over western Texas. In northwest Texas, led by Colonel Ranald S. Mackenzie, a highly competent and aggressive West Point graduate and Civil War veteran, soldiers struck at Kiowa and Comanche villages everywhere off the reservations. Off-reservation Indians in the Texas Panhandle or on the Llano found little rest.

Mackenzie began his operations on the Llano Estacado in the fall of 1871. He and his Fourth Cavalry Regiment moved out from Camp Cooper on the Clear Fork of the Brazos River in modern Throckmorton County and established a base camp at Duck Creek in Kent County. From there they rode west and a bit north along what later became known as the Mackenzie Trail to the mouth of Blanco Canyon in present Crosby County, a place where high walls of the Llano's escarpment opened wide and water from White River (Freshwater Fork of the Brazos) flowed. From here, Mackenzie and his troops planned to harass Kwahadas and other Comanches off the reservation. The plan failed. A small party of Kwahadas, perhaps led by the young (twentysomething) but brilliant Quanah, the son of Cynthia Ann Parker—Naduah her Comanche family and friends called her—whom warriors had taken in a raid on "Parker's Fort" in 1836, surprised the troopers. They rushed through Mackenzie's camp early in the morning of November 10, making as much noise as possible and scattering many of the horses before moving away. The troopers lost sixty-six animals. About daylight two scouting patrols went in search of the military ponies, and one of them ran into a large contingent of Kwahadas, who in turn went after the soldiers. A few of the troopers rallied but lost one of their men in the battle of Blanco Canyon. As Mackenzie brought up the main cavalry force, Indians fled. Mackenzie went in pursuit, but once on the Llano freezing weather, strong winds, and heavy snow in the area of Running Water Draw near present Plainview forced him to turn back. His men, who wore only summer uniforms, were exhausted, the horses jaded, and the supply base at Duck Creek over a hundred miles away.

By late November, Colonel Mackenzie and his Fourth Cavalry had returned to Fort Richardson, their headquarters post. Their expedition failed on most counts. They had lost one man dead and several wounded, including Mackenzie, who took an arrow deep in his thigh. They killed two warriors and captured no Indians. On the other hand, their efforts represented the first major American military operation to penetrate the Llano Estacado, where, one of the officers, Lieutenant Robert G. Carter, later wrote, "as far as the eye could reach, not a bush, or tree, or a twig or stone, not an object of any kind or a living thing was in sight." Perhaps more important, off-reservation Comanches could no longer feel safe in their once-private domain.[7]

In 1872, Mackenzie returned to the High Plains—this time leading a large, multicontingent operation. From Fort Richardson, he followed his old trail to the mouth of Blanco Canyon in present Crosby County, bringing with him several companies of his Fourth Cavalry, a score of six-mule team wagons and pack animals with supplies, and Tonkawa scouts. En route to the site, he met near the popular trading site at the mouth of Duck Creek other troops from Fort Concho with six 6-mule wagon teams and a comanchero prisoner, Polonio Ortiz. After initially splitting up, the two groups met again and established a supply camp at the mouth of White River in Blanco Canyon. There, coming from Fort McKavett in western Menard County, Mackenzie's trusted subaltern Lieutenant Colonel William R. Shafter, a big, burly but effective officer of the Twenty-Fourth Infantry (Buffalo Soldiers), planned to meet the others on July 1 with five 6-mule wagons, three companies of troopers, surgeons, and scouts. Mackenzie held orders to break up the comanchero trade, find and punish Kiowas who had attacked and burned a wagon train at Howard's Wells on the southern edge of the Llano earlier in the spring, and get Comanches to the reservation.

While awaiting Shafter's arrival, Mackenzie kept busy. He sent a small force to check Muchaque Valley, another long-popular comanchero trading site in Garza County. It found no comancheros but noticed a well-traveled cattle trail heading across the Llano Estacado. Mackenzie himself led a larger force up Blanco Canyon; then north across the Llano; down into the Quitaque Valley, another popular comanchero trading site; and up to the Red River before returning without finding comancheros or Comanches. Meanwhile, after Mackenzie had departed to the north, Shafter showed up at the mouth of Blanco Canyon and, as he waited for Mackenzie's return, sent his mounted-infantry troops in all directions, including some to Canyon de Rescate (Ransom Canyon) and up Yellow House Draw toward modern Lubbock. They found neither Comanches nor comancheros.[8]

Called by President Ulysses S. Grant "the most promising young man in the army," Ranald Mackenzie after the Civil War was active in West Texas and on the Llano Estacado, leading his Fourth Cavalry troops to try to get Comanches and Kiowas back to their reservation in modern Oklahoma. Courtesy of Southwest Collection/Special Collections Library

In 1875, Lieutenant Colonel William Shafter, or "Pecos Bill" as he was called by his troops, guided a four-month-long, thorough exploration of the Llano Estacado. Later, in 1898, he led American troops to Cuba during the Spanish-American War. Courtesy of Southwest Collection, Special Collections Library

Back at Blanco Canyon and convinced by Ortiz that comancheros traded cattle in New Mexico, Mackenzie determined to follow the big cattle trail from Muchaque. It was a daring venture. When he left, Mackenzie took with him eight officers and some 240 enlisted men of his Fourth Cavalry with wagons and pack mules to carry supplies, plus Tonkawa scouts and a few others, including Polonio Ortiz. Called "the first official United States expedition to cross the vast and unexplored" Llano Estacado, the men moved out of the supply camp at the end of July. They went up Blanco Canyon, turned a bit southwest, and struck Blackwater Draw (Double Mountain Fork of the Brazos, as Mackenzie called it) near modern Abernathy. Here he rested to let his horses and mules graze amid "Luxuriant and Nutritious grass." Then, following this watercourse but staying just to the south edge of the Muleshoe Sandhills, he again moved westward, crossing into New Mexico on the north side of "Salados" Lake—a place where settlers later gathered large amounts of salt—to Portales Springs.[9]

In New Mexico, Mackenzie continued to seek out cattle, comancheros, and cattle buyers. He and his men moved northwest past Tierra Blanca Lake and Lake Tule to the area near modern Melrose in western Curry County, thence to Las Canadinas and Taiban Springs near modern Tolar in northwestern Roosevelt County. Resting here, Mackenzie sent some men to Fort Sumner on the Pecos River for supplies, and upon their return he moved out, down off the Llano to follow the Pecos upstream to Puerto de Luna, an important outfitting point for cattle thieves and comancheros along the Pecos River. Finding neither thieves nor cattle, he returned downriver to Fort Sumner to rest his horses. Three or four days later he again planned to cross the Llano Estacado, this time going east toward the North Fork of the Red River and back to Texas in the Palo Duro area. He climbed onto the Llano near the much-used Puerto de los Rivajenos, followed the plainly visible wagon road past Lake Garcia to Tierra Blanca Creek, and then rode down it to its junction with the Palo Duro Creek near the present town of Canyon. After detachments scouted Palo Duro and Cita Canyons, Mackenzie turned his men toward his main camp at the mouth of Blanco Canyon, which they reached at the end of August. Of the upper Red River region he had covered, Mackenzie later reported, there existed "no country better adapted in winter to all the wants of the Indians than the headstreams at the eastern base of the Staked Plains."[10]

Although disappointed in not finding either Comanches or Kiowas, Mackenzie was not ready to quit. He decided to rest in camp, recuperate and reshod horses, obtain additional supplies from Fort Griffin, and then march north again toward McClellan Creek and the North Fork of the Red River where Polonio Ortiz suggested he might find Indians. All that done in a matter of three weeks, he pulled out on September 21 with twelve officers and 272 enlisted men plus scouts, an engineer officer, two surgeons, a guide, and Ortiz, the comanchero prisoner. Eight days later, on September 29, Mackenzie found a Kwahada and Kotsotika village of 175 large tipis and 87 smaller ones in a beautiful valley on the south side of the North Fork of the Red about five miles east of modern Lefors in present Gray County. He attacked. With residents busy with chores, the Comanche villagers had no chance. Mackenzie and his men stormed into the camp with guns blazing, and twenty minutes later the bloody fight ended.

The Battle of McClellan Creek, as many observers call it, became a great triumph for Mackenzie and his Fourth Cavalry. They killed or wounded many warriors (Mackenzie reported twenty-three dead) and some women and children, and perhaps an old white man. They captured 130 women and children and transported them all the way south to Fort Concho, although some died from wounds on the march. They seized the large horse herd, drove it off, and then stampeded it. Mackenzie's losses counted one soldier dead and three wounded plus ten horses dead or injured. They had ridden hard and successfully into the heart of Comancheria.

For Comanches and Kiowas, the battle marked a disaster. Warriors later reported fifty-two of their people killed. Some of the dead had been in the spring attack on the wagon train at Howard's Wells. Comanches lost the village and its stores of dried meat, pemmican, lodges, equipment, clothing, and robes, all of which the army destroyed. Their dogs went adrift. The captured women came from several Comanche divisions: thirty-four Kotsotikas, thirty Kwahadas, eighteen Yamparikas, eleven Nokonis, and nine Penatickas. Some were quite old. In the weeks and months afterward, many Comanches and Kiowas sought government protection. Several returned to the reservation, including Mowway of the Penatickas, and some went there for the first time, including Tebenanaka and Paruacoom (Bull Bear), band leaders of the Yamparikas and Kwahadas. Shortly afterward Tebenanaka took his people off the reservation to live (camp) close by. A few Comanches, including Terheryaquahip of the Nokonis, brought in white captives they wanted to exchange for the prisoners at Fort Concho, and later some Kwahadas brought in twenty-five horses for something of a down payment for fifty-three ponies taken from the Fort Sill quartermaster. But out on the Llano, a few Kwahadas and fewer Penatickas still continued to gather cattle to trade to comancheros. Raiding slowed considerably during the winter of 1872–73.[11]

Through much of 1873 a general peace prevailed on the Llano Estacado. Not all was serene. Kwahada cattle and horse stealing continued, and efforts at Fort Sill on the reservation to secure the release of the Fort Concho prisoners increased. Discussions over the release of Kiowa leaders Satanta and Big Tree, who also had been imprisoned over the 1871 wagon train massacre, complicated negotiations for permanent peace and the return of the Comanche women and children. By June, however, the prisoners had been sent back to the reservation.

In the fall of 1873, conditions on the reservation soured. The Comanches became nervous over the possibility of rations being cut and fighting with the army taking place. With President Grant's Peace Policy having broken down, horse and cattle stealing had increased. The government blamed peaceful Comanches—those on the reservation—for the raiding, theft, and murder committed by hostile Comanches—those off the reservation, the "wild" Comanches Texans called them. From the point of view of the reservation Indians, fighting seemed imminent. Some of them left for the Texas Panhandle and the Llano Estacado. In December, strong peace advocates, including Cheevers (a Yamparika), Terheryaquahip (a Nokoni), and Esitoya (a Penaticka), petitioned the new Comanche agent, James M. Haworth, a man filled with Quaker idealism, for peace. They asked him how the government could hold them—old, peace advocates—responsible for the acts of a few young men off the reservation. Although they admitted to being too old to fight, they would, if the government withheld rations, join Comanches on the Llano Estacado and die fighting. Such an act they preferred to death by starvation.[12]

In the spring of 1874 anxieties and alarms on the reservation mounted. Most of the worries, however, had little to do with the reservation itself. Rather, Anglo bison hunters had entered the Texas Panhandle and Llano Estacado. In the important 1867 treaty of Medicine Lodge, this land, indeed all land below the Arkansas River Valley, had been opened to, if not reserved for, the Comanches and Kiowas for hunting. The federal government kept troops at Forts Lyon, Dodge, and Larned in part to keep the reserved land for Indians. Bison hunters, seeking hides for a newly developed tanning process that had caused hide prices to skyrocket, had set up camps in 1873 along the Cimarron River and then the North Canadian. Federal troops took no action, and, as noted, in 1874 the bison hunters encamped along the Canadian River on the very edge of the Llano and deep in the Texas Panhandle.

Angry and disgusted, most Comanches, Kiowas, Cheyennes, and some Arapahos—both reservation and off-reservation warriors—went after the hunters. A few Yamparika, Penaticka, and Nokoni leaders as well as some Plains Apaches, refusing to participate in the violence, took their followers back to the reservation. Others, stirred into action by Isatai, a young Kwahada medicine man, and Quanah, the young Kwahada leader, on June 27 struck at bison hunters in the Canadian River Valley at their little stockade called Adobe Walls, named apparently for Bent's old post about a mile away. The sharp-shooting hunters, using their big buffalo guns, held off their attackers, but once the Indians veered away with heavy casualties, the hunters and hide buyers, about twenty-eight in number, pulled out north to Dodge City, which had become a center for hide buying and hunter outfitting.[13]

Comanches, especially, but a few Kiowas and many Cheyennes as well, expanded their attacks. They hit scattered and isolated white hunters and their camps and widened their assaults in Texas, killing or capturing settlers and stealing their horses and cattle. Cheyennes attacked in southern Kansas and southeastern Colorado. In response, the government issued orders for all Southern Plains Indians to go to, or return to, their reservations and register at their agency, an action they must complete by early August 1874. Some went in as ordered.

A majority stayed out—well past the deadline to register. Instead, they set up camps deep in the Llano Estacado's canyonlands, particularly the wild gulfs and rough breaks of the eastern escarpment in the upper Red River and its tributaries. From here, they pursued bison as needed, attacked bison-hunter camps on occasion, and, desperate for food, sought livestock in Texas along the edge of settlement. After the deadline to register passed, federal troops came after the off-reservation Indians—relentlessly. Troopers, well mounted, well armed, well provisioned, and led by officers well grounded in Indian fighting and tactics, chased the Indians. Moreover, the bloodhound-like qualities of the Tonkawa scouts allowed the army to trail them wherever they went: through the grassy prairies, over flowing streams, and across broken country.

The end came in the late summer and fall of 1874. Altogether, forty-six companies of federal troops, about three thousand men, the largest concentration of government troops on the Southern Great Plains to that time, rode into the eastern Panhandle of Texas from five directions. Their military sweeps, although not always well coordinated, converged on the headstreams of the Red River, where the "Tonks"—the Tonkawa scouts—had located Comanches, Kiowas, and Cheyennes in the heart of what was left of Comancheria.[14]

The Red River War followed. Led in the field by colonel of the Fifth Infantry Regiment Nelson A. Miles, a man who favored lavish military uniforms with embellishments, the troops included both infantry and cavalry regiments. Miles with 750 cavalrymen rode southwestward from Camp Supply in Indian Territory toward Palo Duro Canyon. He met about three hundred Cheyennes on the Washita River, and after pursuing them for a week, attacked them on August 30, 1874, before chasing them into Tule Canyon.

The other commanders enjoyed similar success. Forty-year-old, but insensitive Major William R. Price marched east from Fort Bascom in New Mexico. With four companies of the Eighth Cavalry, he moved down the Canadian River before turning due east across the Llano Estacado. Off the eastern escarpment he crossed Miles's path leading to the mouth of Tule Canyon. After a brief meeting with the colonel, Price turned northeast, sighted Indians in what today is eastern Wheeler County, went in pursuit, and on September 12 between the Dry Fork of the Washita River and Sweetwater Creek fought and defeated some 150 Indians apparently in flight from the reservation. His men killed two warriors, wounded six others, and captured twenty horses. They experienced several casualties themselves.

Lieutenant Colonel George P. Buell, an able but argumentative officer of the Eleventh Infantry, marched from Fort Griffin. He moved over to the Red River and scouted up that stream. On October 9, with five companies of his Eleventh Infantry, his men found and destroyed a small hastily abandoned Kiowa village located in southwestern Indian

During the Red River War, Colonel Nelson A. Miles led federal troops from Fort Dodge as part of the 1874–75 five-prong expedition against Southern Plains Indians in the Red River drainage system. Courtesy of Panhandle-Plains Historical Museum

Territory. Following a trail from the little camp, they pushed north and, on October 11, located another freshly deserted camp of seventy-five lodges and destroyed it. A day later Buell's men burned an empty but much larger Kiowa village. He continued to follow the trail of the fleeing Indians, reaching the Canadian River without catching them. Here Buell, his supply lines overextended, gave up the chase.

Lieutenant Colonel John W. "Black Jack" Davidson, a West Point graduate from Virginia, led a fourth column. He left Fort Sill on September 10 with six companies of his Tenth Cavalry (Buffalo Soldiers) and three from the Eleventh Infantry, plus guides, scouts, and interpreters and a mountain howitzer unit. He and his troopers moved north to the Washita River and followed it upstream, searching for Indians. They

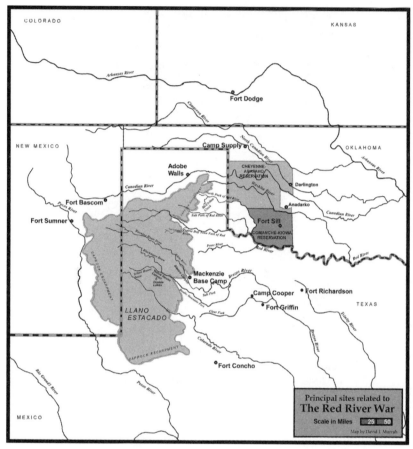

The map shows forts and the larger area where battles of the Red River War occurred. Courtesy of David J. Murrah

found none, ran short of supplies, and returned to Fort Sill to reprovision. That done, Davidson and his men reentered the chase. They examined the area from Fort Sill to the main fork of the Red River nearly to the Llano Estacado's escarpment without engaging Indians. Nonetheless, they operated from September to November, sometimes in freezing cold and snow, and succeeded in returning some three hundred Comanches who had surrendered to them to the reservation.

Perhaps the major blow delivered to Indians occurred on September 28, 1874, in Palo Duro Canyon. As part of the fifth column, Ranald S. Mackenzie, the courageous and unrelenting colonel of the Fourth

Cavalry, led his men out of his old supply camp at the mouth of Blanco Canyon in present Crosby County. With five hundred soldiers and a detachment of Tonkawa scouts, he rode north along the eastern escarpment of the Llano Estacado toward the headstreams of the Red River. Near Tule Canyon, Comanches harassed his expedition, but Mackenzie's men beat them back, after which they made an all-night ride to the edge of Palo Duro Canyon. Here, on September 28 in what has been called a daring, reckless maneuver, his Fourth Cavalry troopers climbed down a narrow twisting path along the high, sheer walls of the canyon. Once down, they attacked, defeating five villages of Comanches, Kiowas, and Cheyennes. They killed few Indians, but they burned tipis and destroyed tons of meat from recently butchered bison, equipment, and other supplies needed to get through the coming winter. The soldiers also rounded up fourteen hundred horses and mules. Mackenzie gave the Tonkawas a couple of hundred horses and directed his men to move the others to Tule Canyon. Here, in one of the most uncompromising and dramatic actions of the Red River campaign, he ordered all the remaining horses and mules shot.

The big campaign wound down. Indian people still on the Llano Estacado kept constantly on the move to avoid soldiers, but they struggled against hunger, cold, and deprivation. Nonetheless, from the soldier point of view, several mopping-up fights and skirmishes occurred in the upper Red River drainage system, Nelson Miles rode west with a force to seek Indians hiding on the northern Llano, and others scoured the rough and rock-strewn northeastern breaks of the High Plains. No place of safety for Indians existed on the eastern side of the Llano Estacado.

Knowing the Indian plight, Mackenzie with tired and worn horses returned to his supply camp along the White River (Freshwater Fork of the Brazos) near the mouth of Blanco Canyon. After resting the horses and refitting equipment, he headed once more onto the Staked Plains. He meant to chase down all Indian groups on the central and southern Llano (the South Plains). With such a plan in mind, he started on October 29 for the headwaters of the North Fork of the Double Mountain Fork of the Brazos River. Two days later he camped at Punta de Agua (the river's headwaters) within the limits of the present city of Lubbock amid a vicious cold "norther" and with no wood for fires. Two days later, his scouts having sighted Indians, he gave chase. He and his troopers moved southwest, checking such lakes and water holes as Laguna Rica (Rich Lake), Mound Lake, and Lagunas Quatras (Four Lakes), a place now called Double Lakes west of modern Tahoka in present Lynn County. Here he caught and defeated a band of Comanches, killing two warriors, capturing nineteen women and children, and rounding up 144 horses. Afterward, he moved eastward to Tahoka Lake, a long, shallow, and shimmery body of water that over the centuries had been used as an important Native American camping site. Meanwhile, others in his command had captured additional Comanches and their horses, and Mackenzie, now short of rations and forage, returned to his supply camp, where he prepared to return to his home station.

By this time, mid-November 1874, most of the so-called hostiles had returned to the reservation or seemed headed in that direction. As many of them were on foot and without tipis and adequate protection from the elements, the trip proved slow and painful for the horseless Kiowas, Comanches, and Cheyennes. Through the winter of 1874–75 several bands from the plains arrived at the reservation, one small group at a time, and finally, in February 1875, the influential Lone Wolf, a signer of the Treaty of Medicine Lodge in 1867, led his Kiowa followers back to the reservation. On March 6, old, peaceful Cheyenne leader Stone Calf surrendered 820 Indians at the Cheyenne reservation agency at Darlington, and shortly afterward, the influential Comanche leader Mowway brought in 170 of his Kotsotika followers. On the Llano, with rare exceptions, only a few Kwahadas under Wild Horse, Isatai, and Quanah, their young but fast-rising star, were still out.[15]

In effect, the Red River War was over. In it, the last major engagement on the Southern Plains, federal troops pressured Indians, attacked villages, destroyed supplies and lodges, ran off horses, and kept Indian men, women, and children on the move through fourteen pitched battles and many surprise encounters. Soldiers did not kill many Indians, but their destruction of homes, horses, and winter supplies produced economic catastrophe and social breakdown. Militarily the Indians fought back, killing or wounding a significant number of the blue-coated adversaries,

Lone Wolf (Guipago) was a Kiowa leader during
the Red River War of 1874–75. Courtesy of
Panhandle-Plains Historical Museum

but Indians who stayed on the Llano Estacado through the winter suffered
dearly from hunger, cold, and exposure. Some got by only on "roots and
rodents."[16]

As a post–Red River War operation, the US Army ordered a large,
sweeping campaign to clear the Llano Estacado of any Native American
holdouts, such as the Kwahada band with Isatai and Quanah. In addition, the army wanted the Llano thoroughly explored and mapped, water
holes marked, fuel supplies noted, and its resources as to flora and fauna
recorded. To lead the multifaceted expedition, military officials chose
Lieutenant Colonel William R. Shafter of the all-black Twenty-Fourth
Infantry Regiment. An overweight mountain of a man who later led
American troops to Cuba during the Spanish-American War, Shafter
gathered his men and supplies at Fort Concho, near modern San Angelo
in Tom Green County, and in mid-June waited to start.[17]

Then, on June 21, orders arrived suspending the operation, at least temporarily. Jacob J. Sturm, a physician, storekeeper, and interpreter at the Wichita agency, with orders from the new commander at Fort Sill, Ranald Mackenzie, had ridden in May with guides to the village of Wild Horse, Isatai, and Quanah, the determined holdouts from the recent Red River campaign. The Comanches were camped in the Muchaque Valley near modern Gail in Borden County. After two or three days of discussions, Wild Horse and the two young leaders with some noted Kwahada warriors agreed to return with their followers to the reservation near Fort Sill, in Indian Territory. A few weeks later, on June 2, with Quanah in the lead, over four hundred men, women, and children who had left the Llano Estacado, arrived at the reservation, laid down their arms, and surrendered. From the view point of some army officers, no need existed for Shafter's expedition.[18]

Still, three weeks after he received the suspending orders, Shafter, on July 11, got orders to move ahead. He commanded nearly 450 men of the Tenth Cavalry, Twenty-Fifth Infantry, and his own Twenty-Fourth Infantry, all black troops—Buffalo Soldiers. A company of Black-Seminole scouts under Lieutenant John L. Bullis, a handful of Tonkawa scouts under Lieutenant C. R. Ward, several medical officers, blacksmiths, packers, teamsters, and other civilian employees, mostly herders, supported the troopers. Twenty-five wagons drawn by six-mule teams and a pack train of approximately one hundred mules carried supplies for a four-month campaign, and civilian cowboys drove a herd of cattle to provide a ready supply of fresh meat. The long, striking column headed north for Blanco Canyon and White River 180 miles away.

Realizing the militant Kwahadas of Quanah, Isatai, and Wild Horse no longer lived and hunted on the Llano Estacado, Shafter changed his plans. He decided to break his command into smaller units, cover as much of the Llano as possible, and emphasize the nonmilitary purposes of the scout. Thus, on his way north, he sent Captain Nicholas Nolan, a bull-headed Irish immigrant who during the Civil War had served in the Union Army, with two companies of the Tenth to search westward before rejoining him in Blanco Canyon. Nolan's scouts found a fresh Indian trail and followed it to Cedar Lake, the largest playa on the Llano, in modern Gaines County where he attacked a party of Mescalero Apaches. The Mescaleros escaped, but Nolan burned their tipis and supplies and headed for Blanco Canyon.[19]

Upon receiving Nolan's report, Shafter again changed his plans. He determined now to strike out across the Llano and intercept the Apaches Nolan had jumped. Taking two hundred men, he rode up Blanco Canyon and camped at Silver Falls, where Captain Theodore Baldwin, one of his officers, complained that mosquitos hovered "10,000 to the inch." From this prominent and dramatic landmark, Shafter turned west, climbed out of the canyon, and headed for Punta de Agua on the North Fork of the Double Mountain Fork of the Brazos at modern Lubbock. From there, they moved forty miles west to Casas Amarillas basin with its Illusion and Yellow Lakes. Here, among small caves and a fort-like structure of rocks that comancheros must have built overlooking the basin, they rested and let the horses graze.[20]

On the morning of August 11, Shafter's command headed southwest into a torrid region absolutely unknown to black troops. They hoped to get beyond the Apaches that Nolan had surprised, but the plan did not work. The men did not return to their camp at Blanco Canyon until September 25, forty-five days after leaving Casas Amarillas and fifty-two days since leaving the base camp. They covered a lot of territory and rode more than 860 miles. In the first few days after leaving Casas Amarillas, they rode through several bison herds, each estimated to contain upward of one hundred thousand animals. In one of them, they found and caught a lone army horse. Enlisted men tended to old saddle galls on the captured steed, fed it some corn, and afterward Lieutenant Colonel Shafter rode the big mount every second day.

After leaving Casas Amarillas, the command found the going difficult. Playas with water were scarce, the Lea-Yoakum Dunes between Sulphur and Sulphur Springs Draws proved tough on horses, and the men ran out of water. On the last stretch of between forty and fifty miles before reaching the Pecos River near modern Carlsbad, they went forty hours without water. Pushed hard by Lieutenant Colonel Shafter during the late evening ride, they all made the river by midnight August 15 and subsequently called their commander "Pecos Bill," a name that stuck through the remainder of the officer's long military career. After resting here, Pecos Bill and his command pushed downriver to Horse Head Crossing in modern Crane County, where they again rested for several days. Then they moved back upriver, cut north through the Monahans Sandhills (White Sand on their maps), and northwest to a large water hole afterward called Monument Spring.[21]

Located in extreme southeastern New Mexico (near modern Monument in Lea County), the place, Shafter wrote, was a favorite "resort" for Indians. His men destroyed lodges, poles, supplies, and equipment Apaches had left behind. Several trails from different directions led to the large, spring-fed water hole. Because it seemed a busy place, Shafter sent some of his troopers to build a marker on a rise about a mile from the often-used spring. They built the monument of white stone (sandstone). It stood seven feet high on a rock base some eight feet in length and breadth. At the top it reached four feet on each side. The huge structure could be seen for miles. But now, with men fatigued, horses exhausted, and rations short, Shafter turned back to his supply camp in Blanco Canyon.

Twice more Shafter led men onto the Llano Estacado in search of holdouts from the Red River campaign. He found few, caught none, but made thorough notes about the land, its water sources, Indian trails, and comanchero roads. Subalterns, including Captains Nicholas Nolan, Theodore Baldwin, and Charles C. Viele; and Lieutenants C. R. Ward, Andrew Geddes, John L. Bullis, and Thomas C. Lebo, he dispatched to search other areas of the Llano, locate Indians, and make notes about the country they scouted. Mainly, they were unsuccessful in finding Indians. The one exception was Lieutenant Geddes, who killed one Apache warrior and captured five others (four women and a boy). By the end of the expedition in November, Indians, including Comanche and Kiowa holdouts, had left the Llano Estacado and Shafter's soldiers had returned to Fort Concho.

William R. Shafter and his black troopers had thoroughly explored the Llano Estacado. Together, they had covered twenty-five hundred miles. They had mapped and charted topographical features of the high tableland from the eastern escarpment to the Pecos River and from below

Fort Concho on the south to Tule Canyon on the north. They had visited all the major lakes, including one named Shafter Lake, on the Llano, and connected them by wagon roads to known water sources, such as Punta de Agua, Casas Amarillas, Silver Lake, and in Blanco Canyon, Silver Falls. In some ways, the end of their remarkable expedition marked an end to the magnificent horse-and-buffalo days of the Llano Estacado Indians. Clearly, it marked an end to the soldier-Indian wars in the High Plains region.[22]

Summary

By the time of the Civil War in the 1860s the Comanche population on the Llano Estacado and, indeed, all through a receding Comancheria, had declined. It continued to wane in the reservation period and afterward until well into the twentieth century, when it began to recover. The dwindling numbers and other sociocultural-economic issues encouraged Comanches to accept non-Comanche people, including captives, into their circles. Partly as a result the Llano while still in Comanche possession became a place characterized by a highly multiethnic-multiracial populace. Quanah, for example, the mixed-blood son of a warrior and a white woman, while still in his twenties became an important Comanche leader.

Diseases, of course, but activities associated with raiding and declining bison numbers also factored into the declining population, as did fighting federal soldiers. Troopers, especially those led by "Bad Hand" (as Indians called him) Ranald Mackenzie, kept Comanches and their Kiowa allies on the run and on the move in the days after the Civil War. For the two horse-mounted, bison-hunting nations and their few Plains Apache associates the problems devolved into an abyss of complications that in the long run settled them onto a reservation in southwestern Indian Territory, a dry, sandy area, although in places beautiful, where traditional nineteenth-century farming proved difficult. Although not by choice, they gave up the Llano Estacado and its sweeping, windswept prairies that they loved. The eloquent Yamparika headman Ten Bears said during the Treaty of Medicine Lodge discussions in 1867: "I was born upon the prairie, where the wind blew free and there was nothing to break the light of the sun. I was born . . . where everything drew a free breath. I want to die there."[23]

In the soldier-Indian wars on the Southern Plains after the Civil War, Indians of the Llano Estacado had no chance in a protracted struggle. As early as 1867 most lived on their Indian Territory reservations. Comanches and Kiowas numbered less than five thousand people facing a Texas population of eight hundred thousand. Further, they faced a formidable foe in the US Army with its unlimited resources, an army that raised havoc with Indian populations by destroying their horses, homes, and food sources. In the short run, the Indians defended themselves well, sometimes bringing serious damage to US troops and often frustrating soldiers and their officers. But after 1870, at least from the army's point of view, much of the fighting, including the damaging Red River War, represented little more than mopping-up exercises designed to return Indians to their reservations. But even before the Red River War, the Llano's former inhabitants suffered from actions of bison-hide hunters, who by killing the Comanche and Kiowa mobile bison food supply and general life support, had begun taking a different toll on the Llano's native groups.

6

Hunters, Sheepherders, and Surveyors

In 1875, Comanches and their allies no longer ranged over the Llano Estacado. With nearly all Indians gone, the high, grassy, windswept mesa, often flat and even mysterious but unquestionably inviting in an economic way, became the domain of Anglo bison-hide hunters. Then, in quick succession sheepmen, cattlemen, pioneer farmer-settlers, railroaders, and townspeople followed. In a span of only twenty-five years the Llano, "heaven's harsh tableland," changed from an open, Comanche-dominated hunting preserve to a rural, settled agricultural commonwealth whose Anglo population soon outstripped the largest number of Comanches or other Native Americans to have ever inhabited the region.

The rapid transition began with Anglo bison hunters. At the end of the Red River War in 1875, bison hunters returned to the Texas Panhandle, moving south from Dodge City on the Arkansas River and from the now bison-empty, former killing fields of Kansas. For a brief time, the hunters remained above the Canadian River, hunting Coldwater, Palo Duro, and Wolf Creeks, but they soon set up camps farther south on the edge of the Llano Estacado in the upper Washita drainage system and Sweetwater Creek. Mobeetie in Wheeler County, Texas, became an important gathering spot, especially after the US Army in 1875 established Fort

Elliott nearby. To acquire hides, other hunters killed bison in Central Texas before moving north to the Fort Griffin, Albany, and the Brazos River's Clear Fork country in such Texas counties as Young, Stephens, Shackelford, and Jones. Fort Griffin became the foremost outfitting and marketing center for bison hides during the short period, 1874–79, that bison killing flourished in Texas. From Fort Griffin, freighters hauled the hides to railway connections at Fort Worth.[1]

Bison hunters had first entered the Llano Estacado in 1874 from the second Adobe Walls site. They left subsequent to the fight with Isatai's and Quanah's off-reservation Indians. After federal troops in the Red River War convinced Indians to return to their reservations, the hunters and accompanying skinners and freighters again approached the Canadian and upper Red River tributaries, this time from Fort Elliott and nearby Mobeetie. Bison remained plentiful. Hunters spread out through the breaks and rough ground just east of the Llano as well as the flat prairies above the escarpment. They sold hides to buyers coming from Dodge City, Kansas, or Camp Supply, the army post on the North Canadian River near the Oklahoma Panhandle.

At Camp Supply William McDole (W. M. D.) Lee and Albert E. Reynolds had formed the Lee-Reynolds trading firm. Lee was post sutler at Camp Supply and a successful rancher and businessman. He wanted to control the entire Texas hide trade. Reynolds, a former Indian agent, had been Lee's partner in a number of previous ventures. In 1876, they allied their firm with entrepreneur Charles "Charley" Rath and his partner Robert "Bob" Wright of Dodge City, Adobe Walls, and Mobeetie. Lee and Reynolds provided mountains of trade goods, groceries, flour, equipment, tools, lead, powder, tobacco, and whiskey from their large stores at Camp Supply. Additional supplies came from Dodge City.[2]

Then, at least two developments brought hunters in greater numbers to the Llano Estacado. In one, the Texas government in 1876 created some fifty-four counties out of the old Bexar Land District. The counties covered all the Texas Panhandle and much of the Llano Estacado's South Plains region. As a result, surveyors rushed into the empty land to mark out the territory and oftentimes to find land for real estate agents,

Bison and Their Numbers

Bison have been in North America longer than the humans who hunted them. As members of the Bovidae family of mammals, modern bison are distantly related to such animals as the Asian water buffalo and European aurochs (or wisents).

An ancient species of bison colonized North America perhaps as early as 600,000 years ago. Called Bison latifrons, the early animals were giants, twice the size of modern bison, with huge horns that spread some six feet from tip to tip. The long horns provided a means to fight off predators and afforded a mode of aggressive display toward such large mammals on the plains as mammoths, tapirs, and monster ground sloths. As Ice Age animals, Bison latifrons enjoyed a short, spring calving period so that their young could mature enough to survive their first cold, harsh winter. They spread from Florida to California and as far south as central Mexico.

Bison antiquus descended from the long-horned Bison latifrons. Over a period of fifty thousand or more years, they evolved smaller, and as post–Ice Age animals, they developed a longer breeding season and gave birth to small calves. They were about one-third larger than today's species but with horns shorter than their ancestors' and slightly curved. They adapted well to the short-grass plains, became less selective in eating (they were both

When stampeding, bison could run for many miles. As pictured here, hunters or cowboys may have been guiding them toward a stockade or an area where men could dispatch the big animals for their hides. Courtesy of Southwest Collection/Special Collections Library

grazers and browsers), and saw their winter mortality rates decline. Like their ancestors, Bison antiquus thrived in North America.

Like modern bison, the antiquus species possessed a heavy, distinctive hairy mane, a heritage from their evolution in the far north. The mane became a means of display for aggressive purposes, and as do today's bison, they used it for protection against cold weather by facing into bitter winter storms. The first humans on the Llano Estacado, Clovis and Folsom people (living about 11,400 to 10,200 years ago), hunted a subspecies of Bison antiquus called Bison antiquus occidentalis.

American bison, or buffalo, evolved from Bison occidentalis. Like their ancestors, they adapted well to the post-glacial environment and flourished on the Great Plains. After the big die-off of mammoths and mastodons some 10,000 to 12,000 years ago, they became the largest animal in North America, with a full-grown bull weighing between fourteen hundred and twenty-four hundred pounds and standing five and a half to six feet tall. Cows are smaller in weight and height.

The number of such animals on the Great Plains never reached beyond twenty-five to thirty million. Biologists, zoologists, ecologists, and other scholars, including environmental historian Dan L. Flores, argue impressively that the so-called carrying capacity of the land would not allow for numbers above thirty million. Bison on the Great Plains faced grazing competition from such animals as elk, deer, and pronghorns. Moreover, prairie dogs, whose colonies might be many miles in length, consumed enormous amounts of grass.

Still, the number of bison on the plains was huge. In 1541, Spanish explorer Francisco Vázquez de Coronado wrote, "And I found such a quantity of cows [bison] . . . that it is impossible to number them." In 1871, zoologist Joel Allen examined eyewitness accounts of bison numbers and wrote a scholarly report on the topic. A few contemporary comments in his report included "We could not see their limit either north or west"; "the Plains were black and appeared as if in motion"; and "there is such a quantity of them that I do not know what to compare them with, except the fish in the sea."

Bison numbers declined rapidly in the decades after Allen's report. In fact, their numbers had been in decline long before then. The causes were many, including grazing competition with horses and cattle, European animal diseases (from which bison had no immunity), and the bison-hide trade.

On the Llano Estacado, bison numbers were large in 1875 when Lieutenant Colonel William R. Shafter and his African American troopers (Buffalo Soldiers) saw three separate herds each with approximately one hundred thousand animals. Three years later, bison hunter George Causey was hard-pressed to find any bison on the Llano. Fortunately, the magnificent brown giants have been saved from extinction and now thrive in public parks and on private ranches on the Great Plains, including at Caprock Canyons State Park and Trailway at the edge of the Llano Estacado.

buyers, speculators, and perhaps permanent settlers. Hunters, knowing that pioneer settlers would soon follow, redoubled their efforts to get the bison ahead of them. In a second development, Charles Rath, the German-born entrepreneur and teamster fluent in the Cheyenne language, one of the founders of the bison-hunter Adobe Walls camp, and a major hide merchant at Dodge City, determined to get below the Llano bison herds and establish an outfitting post west of Fort Griffin.

Having formed the partnership with Lee and Reynolds, Rath in the fall of 1876 led a large, striking column of bison hunters, skinners, teamsters, and others out of Mobeetie. The column, perhaps two hundred people plus horses and mule- and oxen-drawn wagons moved straight south—"by the compass"—to the Double Mountain Fork of the Brazos River in southern Stonewall County. Here, after seven weeks en route, they established Rath City (sometimes Camp Reynolds), a little town that soon held Rath's large store, a laundry, two saloons, a barbershop, a blacksmith shop, a dance hall, and a combination restaurant and hotel. A large number of tent "buildings" went up, and men built a sod corral

The bison-hide hunter camp shows meat drying on racks, hides stretched on the ground, and hunters resting in front of their tents of bison hides and canvas. The camps were dirty and smelly. Courtesy of Southwest Collection/Special Collections Library

to hold livestock. Not long afterward hunters brought in the first hides, and within weeks large stacks of them existed in the hide yard, perhaps four acres in size, behind Rath's store.[3]

Established in December 1876, the little but active trade and outfitting magnet saw its busiest season during the winter of 1877–78 when bison hunters sold tens of thousands of hides there. Englishman Frank Collinson, a hunter and trader and later writer, reported seeing one million hides at Rath City that season, an exaggeration no doubt. Regardless, hide buyers there conducted at least $1 million worth of business through the winter. Depending on quality and age of the animal when it was killed, hides brought between $1.50 and $3.00, and agents like Rath sold them for a bit more. In the few years that he operated out of Dodge City, Mobeetie, Rath City, and Fort Griffin, Rath may have bought and sold nearly one million hides and countless wagonloads of dried bison bones at about $6.00 per wagon. Yet, in 1902 he died penniless in Los Angeles.[4]

In 1876 and 1877 there may have been fifteen hundred hunters working West Texas, including the Llano Estacado. Some operated out of

San Angelo and the Concho River country, approaching the Llano from the southeast. Many still used Mobeetie in the north as their base from which they cut southwestward onto the Llano to hunt along the upper Red and Pease River tributaries. Fort Griffin, of course, but also Rath City and a site at Deep Creek (modern Snyder), as well as a number of smaller camps, became bases from which to operate. Hunters did not work alone. Skinners, freighters, camp managers, and others often associated with the hunter—in all perhaps five thousand men—engaged in the dirty business in West Texas.[5]

Some of the men left reminiscences. For the Llano, significant accounts came from Frank Collinson; his literary rival Ohio-born John R. Cook; Alabama-born Joe S. McCombs, who claimed to have killed twelve thousand bison; Willis S. Glenn; John V. and Thomas L. "George" Causey; and J. Wright and John Wesley Mooar, two highly successful hidemen in Texas. Few of them apologized for killing bison. Indeed, in 1928, at a meeting of the West Texas Historical Association in Abilene, J. Wright Mooar said, "Buffalo hunting was a business and not a sport; it required capital, management and work, lots of hard work, more work

Charles Rath, a bison-hide buyer from Kansas, sits on a pile of dried hides at his Dodge City hide yard where the hides awaited shipment to eastern processors. Courtesy of Southwest Collection/Special Collections Library

than anything else." The church-going, seventy-seven-year-old former hunter told his Abilene audience that "the killing of the buffalo [was not] accomplished by vandals." It resembled an industrial enterprise, he suggested, one made possible by better rifles and new hide-tanning technology, and success went to the more daring and efficient of the hunter-businessmen. Many hunters in West Texas came south from the Kansas and Colorado plains; others were Texans—Southerners

Courtesy of Michael Harter

This gigantic pile of bison skulls suggests that the killing of bison reached massive numbers in the mid- to late 1870s. Courtesy of Southwest Collection/ Special Collections Library

recently arrived or native. Most of the hunters, suggested John Cook, were young, Civil War veterans, competent and self-reliant. "Nearly all of them," he wrote, "had read of Daniel Boone wandering alone in the wilds of . . . uninhabited lands east of the Mississippi." And, like latter-day Boones, he noted, "loved the wild, uninhabited region" of the bison plains.[6]

Not all of them represented heroes of romance: "chivalrous, charitable, jovial, kind and considerate." The famous naturalist Ernest Thompson Seton said, "The hunters were the dregs of the border towns." Richard Irving Dodge, a military officer who knew them, described bison hunters as a rough and smelly bunch "unsavory as a skunk." They may have been daring businessmen and fearless adventurers, as J. Wright Mooar remembered, but also they drank heavily and heartily of liquor, cursed incessantly, and one of them, Jim McIntire, bragged, even if greatly exaggerating, that he had "killed Comanche and Kiowa

Indians by the score, and once I killed and skinned [an Indian woman] and made a purse of her breast." Although sometimes brutal and insensitive, they tended to be loyal and trustworthy hunting companions.[7]

They also proved highly efficient at procuring hides—millions of them. In 1875, Lieutenant Colonel William R. Shafter and his black troopers, while scouting the Llano Estacado, saw several bison herds of one hundred thousand or more animals. The huge animals proved gentle enough that Shafter's men rode into one of the herds to lasso an abandoned (or escaped) military horse grazing among them. Three years later, bison could not be found anywhere on the Llano. Historian Ty Cashion writes about such destructiveness: "The killing over the peak seasons was staggering." For all the Great Plains, white hide hunters may have killed 8.5 million bison. The number they killed on the Llano remains unknown, but considering the killing operations that occurred there from bases in Mobeetie, San Angelo, and Rath City, the number may have reached well over a million animals. At one time in the not-so-distant past, some 25 or 30 million of the magnificent and stately looking creatures had inhabited the American Great Plains, but in 1879, with a few exceptions in Palo Duro Canyon, no bison could be found on the Llano Estacado portion of the Great Plains.[8]

The Causey brothers were among the hidemen who operated on the Llano Estacado. As bison herds declined in 1877, the Causeys set up camp at Buffalo Springs in Yellow House Canyon just below present-day Lubbock. It looked like a typical hunting camp: hides lay pegged out on the ground over a wide area, bison tongues hung to sun-dry on racks, tents stood close by, and a wagon or two waited to be loaded with hides for hauling to market at Rath City. Horses and mules grazed nearby. Like most such camps, it stank. R. A. Burgess reported: "The stench and filth around these camps was appalling, and visitors . . . departed nauseated." From their camp in the canyon on most days George rode north a few miles out to a slight rise, later called Causey Hill, to sight bison herds. Upon reaching the top of the knoll, located on the northeast edge of present-day Lubbock, he stood up erect in the saddle on his horse. Then, using large field glasses, he viewed the flat land reaching away toward the horizon as he looked for herds that he planned to hunt for the day.[9]

The Causeys did not stay long at their Buffalo Springs camp. They soon moved up the canyon to Casas Amarillas, the large basin about forty miles west of Lubbock. There, on the west rim overlooking the big bowl, they constructed or added on to a little stone and rock structure that comancheros may have built some years earlier. From this prominent landmark and watering spot with its two lakes and large, deep, natural well later called the "Devil's Ink Well," the Causeys hunted the surrounding area. George Causey, who did most of the hunting, killed a thousand bison during the last big hunting year, 1877–78.

Ciboleros still worked the western Llano Estacado. But, as with other hunters, the results diminished rapidly after 1876. John Cook, for example, saw more wild horses (mustangs) on the Llano than bison in 1876 and 1877. In July 1877, Cook and Sam Carr, another bison hunter, rode up on a herd of horses. The men, probably in northern Martin County west of Sulphur Springs Creek and northwest of modern Big Spring, "had ascended a rise in the plains," remembered Cook, when west and southwest of them they saw "scattered over many thousands of acres of land . . . bands of wild horses." The animals, wrote Cook, "were ranging in unmolested freedom and in perfect quiet." The hunters, awed by the incredible scene, watched the horses for a couple of hours. "As evening came on," Cook concluded, "young colts came running and frisking around in reckless abandon in their wild unfettered freedom."[10]

As bison hunters finished their bloody work, leaders from other businesses entered the Llano Estacado. Sheepherders (pastores) out of New Mexico, surveyors from Dallas, and cattlemen off the prairies south and west of Fort Worth or from Colorado or New Mexico or Kansas followed the last of the hidemen. They came close enough to the hunters that they could hear the big fifty Sharps Rifles (or the .45 Creedmoor Sharps) boom away on the last of the bison.

Pastores may have entered the Llano Estacado as early as 1874, but clearly in 1875 some arrived with Jesús María Trujillo from San Miguel County in New Mexico. Trujillo led his family and five or six other units down the Canadian River in the spring and settled on the south side of the big valley across from Cheyenne Creek. They built a small community—plaza—named Trujillo in Oldham County with stone and adobe homes and a tall, rock corral to hold their livestock, including sheep. Other New Mexicans followed and built their own villages.

Historically, an important group reached the Llano Estacado under the leadership of Casimero Romero. A former comanchero who had lived in Mora County, New Mexico, Romero's pastores arrived in the spring of 1876—about the time the country's Centennial Exposition opened in Philadelphia. The well-to-to Romero, a blue-eyed and fair-skinned Spaniard, led a large party that included a dozen employees (mainly herders), three friends, and their families with at least twelve freight wagons each pulled by four yokes of oxen. They brought supplies to get through the first year plus horses, cattle, and three thousand sheep. They settled near the site of what became the town of Tascosa on the Canadian River.

In the spring of 1877 other sheepherders appeared, most of them friends or acquaintances of Romero. They established plazas at additional sites with water available. Eventually, New Mexican sheep plazas existed up and down the western Canadian River Valley, on the broken plains north of the valley, and on the Llano Estacado south of the river. The plazas ranged in size from one or two families to twenty or more. Some of the plaza dwellers, such as Henry Kimball, a blacksmith, and Theodore Briggs, a soldier in the Red River War, claimed American citizenship. Some Englishmen, such as Jim Campbell and A. B. Ledgard, entered the Canadian to establish a very large sheep operation: perhaps twenty-five thousand head plus some thirty-five hundred cattle. An English-Scot concern, the New Zealand Sheep Company, may have grazed more than sixty thousand animals, but during the severe winter of 1880–81 cold weather and freezing winds on the Llano resulted in the death from exposure of many pastores and a large number of sheep. More than eighty years ago, Edna Kahlbau located several former plazas: at least six in Oldham County, one at Tecovas Springs in Potter County, and one on Tierra Blanca Creek in Deaf Smith County, among many others.[11]

Grazing patterns differed, but all were open-range operations. They grazed their flocks across unfenced and otherwise unoccupied territory, some of which the State of Texas owned and some of which had been set aside for railroads. Many pastores followed circuits out of the Canadian River Valley early in the year to ensure arrival on the Llano Estacado by lambing time. During the summer, they led the flocks across grassy plains from one water hole (a playa or a running creek) to another, circling back weeks later to return to their home range by shearing time. Other herders kept sheep on the Llano and sent shearers and large wagons to meet the flocks for shearing, perhaps fifty miles from the home plaza. In wagons, teamsters hauled the resulting wool to market. In the late fall pastores grazed their flocks back to the home range and placed them within stone and rock corrals during the coldest months of the winter.[12]

Grazing circuits extended from north of the Canadian River to south on the Llano Estacado as far as Tahoka Lake in Lynn County. They included Tule, Quitaque, Blanco, and Yellow House Canyons. They extended from New Mexico down Running Water, Blackwater, and Yellow House Draws. As the Llano's South Plains area filled with sheep operations, grazing circuits became more and more fixed. As a result, some herders in the area, as in the Canadian River Valley, built rough stone corrals on the open range or in the Llano's canyons to shelter themselves and their sheep. Some corrals stood eight feet high.

Some stone and rock corrals existed in far upper Yellow House Draw. Here, in the area between Silver Lake and modern Enochs—in the boundary area between modern-day Cochran, Hockley, and Bailey Counties—Yellow House Draw suddenly cuts a deep, wide swath (a small canyon) for about three miles. In it, several shallow caves pockmark the steep walls and probably provided shelter for herders. A series of rock fences or corrals held sheep in the little canyon. It may have been a place to hold and sort sheep during spring shearing season, but the presence of rock corrals and fences suggests permanent or semipermanent residence. In several West Texas counties as late as the 1920s, cowboys and cattlemen found remains of pastor dugouts and shelters.[13]

Several New Mexico–based herders utilized the area between Running Water and Yellow House Draws. Jose Perea, a highly successful wool grower, using several pastores herded his flocks of thirty thousand sheep to Tahoka Lake and through Yellow House and Blanco Canyons. Because of the great amount of grazing land and water needed for the large number of animals, Perea scattered his woolly *Ovis* widely and took them wherever good grass and water could be found. In the Lubbock area, Zachary T. Williams, a twenty-nine-year-old from Mississippi, grazed his flocks near Buffalo Springs in Yellow House Canyon. He had arrived, he claimed, as early as 1877. Richard Wilkerson, a twenty-six-year-old from Indiana, drove sheep into Blackwater Draw in the vicinity of present-day Lubbock Country Club. John Coleman, a highly successful wool grower, ran a very large spread across what is today Mackenzie Park in Lubbock County. One of his five herders included Andrew Gonzales, a native of Monterrey, Mexico, and one of the first permanent Mexican-American settlers in the county.

Sheepmen of the Llano Estacado, as elsewhere in Texas, bred fine wool sheep varieties to meaty Spanish *churros*, but there is some dispute about the matter. Herders in Texas and New Mexico for two centuries or more had been grazing the lean, small, but long-legged *churros*, as much a mutton variety as a wool producer, but introducing some cross-breeding through the years to upgrade the wool. On the Llano, several herders brought in Spanish Merino and English Cotswold rams to improve *churro* wool. The Merino, the foundation breed of all modern fine-wool sheep, was a broad-backed, smooth-bodied, large-carcassed animal with an ability to walk long distances in compact flocks. It became the range sheep of Texas and the Southwest. Cotswold rams, slightly smaller than Merinos and favored by British herders, were a long-wool mountain breed developed in England that crossed with *churro* ewes with good success.

A large number of "free grazers" also took sheep onto the Llano Estacado. As independent pastores, they pushed their own animals out of Pecos River Valley communities and onto the Llano near Taiban Spring or perhaps near the springs in the upper Cibola Blanca Creek area, both in modern Roosevelt County, New Mexico. Others went up the ramp at Puerto de los Rivajenos in present Quay County. They moved onto the high tableland in the spring, grazed their sheep across the plains from water source to water source, stopped briefly to shear the ewes and rams, and turned back toward home in the fall. Both groups of pastores established residency, but open-range wool growers and later cattle raisers disliked such "drifters," for too often their animals carried communicable diseases, such as scabies, a highly contagious, wasting condition that ruined the fleece as it also devastated the host animal.

About the same time that pastores reached the Llano Estacado, surveyors arrived. Thus, sheepmen, surveyors, and bison hunters all worked through parts of the Texas High Plains in the late 1870s. In addition, cattlemen, as noted, close on the heels of the bison hunters, moved into the Llano Estacado country. Charles Goodnight, for example, a forty-year-old former scout and guide and successful cattle drover and businessman coming from Colorado, after wintering near the Romero Plaza (Tascosa), in 1876 trailed a large herd across parts of the Llano from Tecovas Spring to Palo Duro Canyon. In November, with help from a number of cowboys, Goodnight established a ranch within the present borders of Palo Duro State Park. Numerous bison remained in the canyon, and Goodnight's cowboys kept busy driving them away from the cattle. Earlier, but also in 1876, and farther south, forty-year-old, German-born entrepreneur Henry Clay Smith (Heinrich Schmitt) located a ranch in Blanco Canyon—at about the same moment, incidentally, that Lakota warriors in present-day Montana killed Colonel George A. Custer and some two hundred members of his famed Seventh Cavalry. Smith did not find bison there, but with help he placed about six hundred cattle on the canyon's rich grasses along the White River. Quickly, he hired masons to build a big rock house at the property's headquarters, a place soon called Mount Blanco.

Moreover, in 1876, a few Comanche "fugitives," who apparently had never gone to the reservation, still hunted southern and western sections of the Llano Estacado, including into New Mexico. Additional Comanches, especially young men angry over the rapidly diminishing number of bison in the huge hunting territory they believed had been reserved for them in such treaties as Fort Atkinson (1853) and Medicine Lodge (1867), joined the fugitives. The much-alarmed Comanches saw plenty of disgusting sights. At one place east of the Llano they found, as explained by surveyor O. W. Williams, who held a law license from Illinois but had come to Texas for his health, "a great number of glistening skeletons of buffaloes, apparently slaughtered one or two years earlier." The bones covered two "spots of ten acres each," wrote Williams, with an estimated one hundred "skeletons closely lying as the result of a hunter getting what was called a 'stand.'" Herman Lehmann, a white captive raised as a Comanche remembered, "We would often see great wagon loads of hides being hauled away and would find the carcasses of thousands of slaughtered buffalo." Later, he wrote, "It made us desperate to see this wanton slaughter of our food supply." Such sightings roused Comanche sensibilities, and Kwahadas (mainly) went after bison hunters in their isolated hide camps.[14]

Red Young Man, who had never been to the reservation, and his small band of Kwahadas played a key role in the attacks. At the end of the Red River War in 1875, they had moved south and west deeper onto the Llano Estacado, hid in the Muleshoe Sandhills and Lea-Yoakum Dunes, hunted bison when they could, and camped in such familiar places as Casas Amarillas, Silver Lake, Tahoka Lake, Cedar Lake, and Monument Spring. From time-to-time others, including Batsena, Cotopah, Hishorty, and Esatema, joined them on the Llano. With younger warriors, who sometimes brought their families from the reservation, they hit bison-hunter camps as well as cattle herds, stagecoach lines off the Llano, and on occasion pioneer homesteads.

In early 1877, as Hank Smith's stonemasons worked on the house in Blanco Canyon, Comanches attacked isolated bison hunters. They destroyed Billy Devin's hunting camp near the mouth of Yellow House Canyon and took all the horses. The hunters, wrote John Cook some years later, "barely escaped with their lives." Not many miles away, they wrecked the base camp of Harry Burns and Harold Bradstreet, well-liked hunters from Britain (Scotland?), burning the hides and wagons and taking the ammunition and horses. At the end of February about fifty Comanches found the popular Marshall Sewall alone and out of ammunition after having spent nearly one hundred rounds on shooting bison. They killed him, took his scalp, destroyed his camp, burned his stacked hides, and sliced some choice cuts from the dead bison before riding off without seeing Sewall's skinners and freighters hiding in a draw a short distance from Sewall.[15]

The Comanches hurried away, moving up Yellow House Canyon and into camp in one of its side draws. But, wrote the Comanche-raised Harold Lehmann, "the buffalo hunters took our trail and followed us." When a fight ensued, Comanches divided and one group circled around to the rear of the hunters, captured several of the pursuers' horses, and wounded four men chasing them. The hunters, using their big buffalo guns, held off the Comanche warriors and eventually retreated. The Indians, likewise, pulled out, moving up the canyon and going into camp just below Punta de Agua in modern Lubbock.

As the Comanches hunkered down in something like a winter camp, hunters, ranchers, and settlers complained about what they saw as Indian atrocities. The US Army responded, sending troops onto the Llano Estacado from Fort Richardson in Jack County, Fort Griffin in Shackelford County, and Fort Concho in Tom Green County. And in March 1877, when the weather improved, bison hunters went after Comanches. In particular, they wanted to punish the Indians in Yellow House Canyon. From Rath City on horseback and in three supply wagons accompanied by too much liquor on board, forty-five men well-armed and equipped headed west. They found the Comanches and just after daylight on March 18 attacked in what has become known as the Battle of Yellow House Canyon.

The fight did not go well for the bison hunters. Although they caught the Indians—not expecting a late-winter attack—off guard, the hunters' inexperience in such fighting, lack of discipline, and too much alcohol combined with Comanche skirmishing ability, knowledge of the Yellow House terrain, and determination to protect their women and children all led to a general rout. Hunters charged the camp, but soon Indian warriors had them pinned down. Fighting lasted for several hours, with the hunters mainly trying to hold their positions as Comanches, while getting women and children to safety, took the offensive. An Apache

village stood around a bend in this North Fork of the Double Mountain
Fork of the Brazos River—just up the narrowing canyon, perhaps above
Punta de Agua—but its warriors may not have participated in the fight.

The hunters held their uneasy positions through much of the morning. But with their leader, Hank Campbell, no longer trying to command, their water and ammunition supplies depleting, and several of
their men having been hit in battle and suffering from wounds, the
hunters pulled out and, thoroughly humbled, found their way back to
Rath City. Comanche warriors had shot at least three bison hunters
seriously enough that hidemen placed them on makeshift stretchers.
Others, including their guide, Jose Piedad Tafoya, former comanchero,
also had been injured. One man, Joe Jackson, later died from his wounds.
The Comanches (mainly Kwahadas), according to Herman Lehmann
who participated on the Indian side, suffered only two men wounded
and none killed. When the hunters withdrew, warriors "gathered up
[the women] and children and horses and moved away from there." The
Apaches also left.[16]

A few days later, the Kwahada Comanches camped at Silver Lake on
the Hockley-Cochran County line. A good place to rest, the shimmery
little body of water lay not far west of the large and game-rich Casas
Amarillas basin. The Muleshoe Sandhills toward the north and the
Lea-Yoakum Dunes to the south provided small game and some protection. In present Bailey County, northwest of the lake spread wetlands that
attracted game of all kinds. From their camp at the lake, small groups of
Comanche warriors rode east off the Llano Estacado to sweep through
bison-hunting camps, ranches, and outlying settlements. One raiding
party came within five miles of Rath City, the little, hide-hunter marketing, supplying, and boozing center, and at the spot killed three hunters,
destroyed supplies and equipment, and stole the livestock: horses and
mules.

Then suddenly on May 4, 1877, one of the soldier expeditions on the
Llano looking for these very Indians found their camp at Silver Lake.
The troopers, seventy-two Buffalo Soldiers of Troop G, Tenth Cavalry
and six Tonkawa scouts under muscular and square-shouldered Captain
Phillip L. Lee, attacked. The Comanches had no chance. Nearly all their

warriors, including Herman Lehmann, were absent, hunting bison, searching for bison hunters, and stealing horses and cattle at places as far east as the San Saba and Llano Rivers. The soldiers killed five Indians at the Silver Lake camp and captured six women and sixty-nine horses. The soldiers suffered one death themselves: First Sergeant Charles Baker. Indian families not killed or captured escaped to the southwest, heading toward the Mescalero Sands.[17]

When they returned to Silver Lake on May 5, the Kwahada warriors found a destroyed camp and "horribly mangled" dead bodies. Among the dead, wrote Lehmann, they discovered Batsena, "a very brave warrior," whom the Tonkawa scouts had scalped. Also among the dead, the angry warriors saw the naked body of Batsena's "daughter, Nooki, described as a beautiful Indian maiden, who had been disemboweled and scalped." While they soon located their absent families, the Comanches, discouraged and demoralized, split into smaller groups. Some of them turned back to their reservation in Indian Territory. Other Kwahadas

Silver Lake (also called Laguna Plata or Quemos or Lake Quemada) witnessed much history. Located on the modern Hockley-Cochran County line in Texas, it was a popular stopping and camping place from time immemorial. Indigenous peoples, Spanish explorers, US soldiers, bison hunters, and others used the lake. It was also the site where in 1877 soldiers killed and captured many Comanches. Courtesy of Aaron Lynskey

headed deeper into the Llano Estacado, slipping toward the western escarpment to camp near Portales and Taiban Springs in New Mexico and in the Lea-Yoakum Dunes between Sulphur and Sulphur Springs Draws. A dry, almost waterless stretch of country, it was a semidesert region. There the Kwahadas hoped that bison hunters and federal troopers might remain away from the barren territory.[18]

Younger hotheads among the Kwahadas promised to get revenge—at least on the bison hunters. The small group included Cotopah, Hishorty, and Esatema. With others, they struck again at hidemen, especially those just off the eastern escarpment. Then, shortly after Captain Lee and his Buffalo Soldiers, on their way back to their command post at Fort Griffin, stopped at Rath City and distributed some of the horses and mules taken during the May 4 encounter at Silver Lake, the Comanches made good on their promise. A large Kwahada party struck the important hide town now filled with bison hunters. In a daring, predawn raid perhaps seventy-five warriors rode down Main Street (such as it was), shot up the place, and vanished with all the horses and mules—more than one hundred animals.

For most hidemen, the hunt was over. Many Southerners among them left for Fort Griffin while some Northerners struck out for Dodge City and the Great Plains of Wyoming and Montana. Some hunters, because there remained plenty of bison in the area, stayed around the saloons and dance halls of Rath City and Fort Griffin, waiting for the plains to become safe again. And a small fourth group determined to chase down the Comanche raiding party, punish the thieves, and secure their horses.

The fourth group became part of the "Staked Plains Horror" of 1877. Just days after the Comanches had ridden through a sleeping Rath City and stolen the horses, twenty-four bison hunters led by James Harvey, late of the federal army's Fourth Cavalry, and with guide Jose Piedad Tafoya, who had been wounded in the March 18 fight in Yellow House Canyon, left the hide town for the Llano Estacado. They established a base camp at the mouth of Blanco Canyon, moved up the canyon several miles beyond Silver Falls, and climbed onto the Llano. They found ciboleros hunting the area with little success, turned south, and visited the site of the March 17 fight with Kwahadas at modern Lubbock, and turned west to Casas Amarillas and Silver Lake. For the next two and a half months they scoured the Llano, moving from one water hole to the next and going as far south as Big Spring. As the days turned to weeks and then to months, they watched as the flowers of May and early June, full of color and bloom, shriveled before the hot sun and unrelenting heat of July. In May, John Cook remembered, "we could smell the sweet perfume from [the flowers] and admire their beauty; and for the next six weeks . . . the air was fragrant with their sweet odor." In July, the flowers disappeared, the buffalo and grama grasses browned and curled, the air became hot and dusty, the playas dried up, water holes shrunk, and the Comanches, like the flowers, disappeared. Nonetheless, the bison hunters once again in Casas Amarillas celebrated Independence Day on July 4 and afterward reassessed their unsuccessful efforts at finding Comanches.[19]

Two weeks later, on July 17, the hunters, having moved their base camp to Bull Creek, a headstream of the Colorado River just off the Llano in Borden County, made new plans to find the Comanches. Then, about noon sixty men of Troop A, Tenth Cavalry from Fort Concho with four 6-mule wagons carrying supplies and led by Captain Nicholas M. Nolan, the army veteran from Ireland but now a widower with two children, rode into the bison-hunter camp. They held orders to find the same Kwahadas the hunters had been pursuing. The white hunters and black troopers agreed to join forces and hunt down the Indians. Two days later, with two bison hunters and twenty soldiers remaining to guard the camp, they left the Bull Creek meeting ground.

The combined command, about sixty-two men including guides, headed for Cedar Lake. As they rode west toward the large playa, Nolan and Harvey, who knew one another from the Red River War, talked. Nolan reported that on their way north, he and his men had come across a party of former bison hunters, led by a man named Spotted Jack, herding cattle—Longhorns. The animals, Spotted Jack claimed, belonged to a rancher who wanted to move his cattle beyond the western line of settlement to the edge of the Llano Estacado. Near the head of the North Concho River, Nolan told Harvey, Spotted Jack's cattlemen had lost some horses to Comanche raiders.

Such stories of cattlemen aside, the hunters (mainly Southerners) and soldiers (mainly black men) continued their pursuit. After a dry camp on July 19, the unusual, blended command camped late in the afternoon of July 20 by a large, water-filled playa in Lynn County (probably Guthrie Lake). As they made camp, five Indians from Fort Sill on the Comanche reservation rode into the campsite. Quanah, a Kwahada spokesman who had been a principal figure in the attack on bison hunters at Adobe Walls a couple of years earlier, led them. He carried letters and passes from Colonel Ranald Mackenzie, the new commander at Fort Sill, and James M. Haworth, the Indian agent there, giving Quanah permission to find the off-reservation hostiles and return them to Indian Territory. A few days later, Quanah and his party appeared at Nolan's new camp at Cedar Lake. When Quanah subsequently left, the party of soldiers and hunters followed.

Then, on July 26, while resting at Double Lakes also in Lynn County, scouts, including Jose Piedad Tafoya, sighted the very Comanches the civilian-military command was looking to find. The weather was hot with temperatures over one hundred degrees, water holes and playas empty, including most of Double Lakes, and grasses brown and withered. Some hunters cautioned about going in pursuit. Nolan, however, apparently worried that Colonel Mackenzie wanted the Indian holdouts to surrender to him at Fort Sill and thus receive credit for the significant accomplishment, held different ideas. Nolan wanted to catch the wayward Comanches and thus reestablish his good name after an incident at Cedar Lake in 1875 that had nearly cost him a court-martial.

Thus, at three o'clock on the hot, dry July 26 afternoon, Nolan, Harvey, and their men started out. The next four days produced the "Staked Plains Horror," as newspapers across the country called it. The men soon ran out of water and suffered from sunstroke and other maladies. On the third day, July 28, with the men prostrate for lack of water, the expedition broke up. They had found no Indians. They badly needed water. The bison hunters split from the soldiers. The cavalry detachment, trying to return to its starting point at Double Lakes, broke apart as soldiers strung out for miles and abandoned their equipment and supplies. Some troopers lost their way and wandered off. Four men and many of the horses died. Those men who survived did so in part because they drank their own urine and drank the blood of their dead mounts. Clearly, leadership had failed, but one by one, some of the troopers, beginning on July 30, staggered into Double Lakes, secured water and a bit of rest, and headed back to rescue their debilitated troopmates. Eventually, a relief party arrived at Double Lakes and on August 6 took the soldiers back to the supply camp at Bull Creek.[20]

The bison hunters also suffered from lack of water. But on July 29 most of them made their way to either Silver Lake or Casas Amarillas, where water was available. After reuniting at Casas Amarillas, they moved east and stopped at Punta de Agua, where they found Bill Benson, a hunter who in the intolerable July heat had gone without water four full days before plunging into the wet upper Brazos stream near modern Lubbock. Benson appeared ill, unsteady, and hallucinating; his hair had turned white; and he needed help to stay on a horse. They got him mounted and rode down Yellow House Canyon, planning to return to Rath City.

On August 3, when near the canyon's mouth, the hunters rode into the camp of a surveying party. Coffee, good food, and refreshments followed. The surveyors mentioned that they had seen horses nearby, mainly up the canyon. The next day some of the hunters went after the animals and gathered 125 horses belonging to hidemen. Other hunters headed straight to Rath City, while others headed back to New Mexico to find the Comanches and any horses that might be left there. Still another group followed a Kwahada trail that headed in the direction of the reservation and Fort Sill. By the end of August, all twenty-four hunters had returned to Rath City and the Kwahadas had arrived at Fort Sill on the reservation.

With West Texas and the Llano Estacado clear of Indians, the region seemed safe again for bison hunters. They made preparations for returning to the hunt late in the fall, and as winter approached, hunters clambered onto the plains. Indeed, the winter of 1877–78 produced the largest number of hides for any one year in Texas. By 1879, few bison roamed anywhere in the region except for Charles Goodnight's rangeland in the Palo Duro country.

Surveyors, in the meanwhile, worked their lines through the hot 1877 summer. They stopped work briefly on July 4, the same day that bison hunters were in Casas Amarillas celebrating Independence Day. They measured and charted land between modern Lubbock and Hank Smith's ranch in Blanco Canyon. Indeed, they visited with stonemasons at the ranch. They also went briefly without water but suffered no undue hardships. While at one of their camps about a mile from Smith's unfinished rock house, they met a family from Erath County. For ten days, the family of four and the surveyors traveled and camped together on the Llano Estacado before the family took Ranald Mackenzie's 1872 trail across the Llano and struck out for New Mexico.[21]

Surveyors who met the Erath County family represented one arm of the large Dallas firm of Daugherty, Connellee and Ammerman. The firm, under contract with a speculating company in Dallas and Fort Worth, wanted to locate lands, wrote O. W. Williams, from "the then unlocated public domain." Other surveying teams headed elsewhere, but nearly all of them worked through the fifty-four counties created, as noted, by the state legislature in 1876.[22]

Some speculators eyed the northern Llano Estacado and the Texas Panhandle. In the Amarillo area, for example, Jot Gunter and W. B. Munson, lawyers in Sherman in Grayson County, represented one of the speculating groups. With a contract from the state to survey Panhandle-area counties, later including the huge XIT ranch grant, in exchange for land scrip, the lawyers sent surveyors John Summerfield, W. S. Mabry, and E. C. McLean to the Llano Estacado. The three surveyors and their team first worked the region below the Canadian River near both East and West Amarillo Creeks and west from there. About 1878, as they searched for unlocated lands for Henry B. Sanborn, often called the "Father of Amarillo," they rediscovered heavy-flowing Tecovas Spring. A couple of years later the site became the headquarters for the Frying Pan Ranch that Sanborn and his partner Joseph F. Glidden, the inventor of a superior-designed barbed wire, established on the west edge of the future site of Amarillo.

As surveyors and others measured land in the fifty-four recently created counties, ranchers, farmers, and townspeople moved to the Llano Estacado. On the Llano's South Plains, Hank and Elizabeth Smith and their family represent the first permanent rancher-settlers. Smith, as

Elizabeth Boyle "Aunt Hank" Smith

Elizabeth Boyle Smith (1848–1925) came to America from Scotland with three of her brothers about 1866. Several years later her brothers headed west and settled at Fort Griffin near present-day Albany in Shackelford County, Texas. In December 1873, with her father, who had just arrived from Scotland after his wife's death, Elizabeth joined her brothers. A few weeks later, on December 31, at a New Year's Eve dance, she met Henry Clay "Hank" Smith (Heinrich Schmitt), a cowboy, Civil War veteran, freighter, and entrepreneur. They married on May 19, 1874.

A year or so after their marriage, Elizabeth and Hank began management of the Occidental Hotel in Fort Griffin, a structure Hank had built. With her husband often gone on business, Elizabeth, or "Aunt Hank," as she was beginning to be called, took major responsibility for the hotel. She ran it with a firm hand, graceful furnishings, and fine cooking, and the hotel's popularity grew.

In 1878, the Smiths with their son George and a hired man moved to Blanco Canyon in Crosby County. The canyon cuts a deep gulf into the Llano Estacado. The Smiths moved there to take over a failed cattle-ranching operation and to recoup a bad loan on the land and livestock. During the two previous years Hank had supervised the construction of a large, two-story rock house in the canyon, and after 1878 Aunt Hank turned the "Rock House," as it would be called, into a fine home for their growing family.

Within a couple of years, the Smiths began operating a little store at their ranch headquarters. Hank planted fruit trees and tended to their cattle, sheep, and farm crops while Aunt Hank looked after a garden. In 1879, she became postmistress of the Mount Blanco Station, located in a building a few yards from the Rock House, a position she maintained for thirty-nine years. As her children (there were five who reached adulthood) grew, she taught them and some neighborhood young people in her home, perhaps the first school on the South Plains of the Llano Estacado.

Aunt Hank took great care to ensure the health of her children, and she made a room in her home available for sick travelers and local cowboys. Because she had learned some basic medicine while helping physicians at Fort Griffin, she became something of a nurse and kept a large assortment of medicines at her Mount Blanco home.

In Blanco Canyon, Aunt Hank became a good friend of the wife of H. H. Campbell, who managed the large Matador Ranch about sixty miles away. Other friends included W. C. Dockum and his wife, who lived on a ranch about twenty miles distant; John H. Jacobs and his wife, who helped manage the store at Mount Blanco; and, after 1879, a group of Quaker settlers at the nearby town of Estacado. On occasion, Aunt Hank with her children attended religious services with her Quaker friends. Except for visitors, recreational opportunities were scarce, but there were times when the Smiths with their children and perhaps some neighbors rode south to Silver Falls for swimming and a picnic.

Food was plentiful. Aunt Hank raised garden vegetables and picked wild plums, grapes, and nuts with her children. In addition to beef and mutton, her husband provided deer, pronghorns, and other wild game—even bison the first year they lived in the canyon.

Elizabeth Boyle "Aunt Hank" Smith was a homemaker, nurse, postmistress, schoolteacher, and hostess for a large number of visitors and friends. Her home was a popular and busy place. She was independent and self-reliant, and after her husband's death in 1912, she continued to operate the ranch—"Glorietta Hacienda"—with her sons for several more years. She died in 1925, and her family buried her in Crosby County's Emma Cemetery.

noted, establish a ranch with cattle in Blanco Canyon even as bison hunters operated nearby. In 1877 and 1878, he oversaw the construction of a large home, the "Rock House," in the canyon while surveyors ran their lines just two miles below the house. In 1879, with Elizabeth (or "Aunt Hank," as she was called) he moved his growing family to the popular site, which soon became known as Mount Blanco.[23]

At nearly the same time, neighbors showed up. Paris Cox, who had come to Texas with some bison hunters, after hearing that the state legislature had created the large number of counties from the old Bexar Land District, hurried to Austin. There about 1877 he obtained certificates to the land he had visited with the hunters near the Smith's house and went home to Indiana to recruit settlers to whom he could sell land at twenty-five cents per acre. In 1878, Cox returned to his land. He hired Smith to dig a well, break out thirty acres of land, and plant a variety of crops, all of which Smith and his employee, Charley Hawse, completed with success in 1879 (about the same time that bison had disappeared from the Llano). Shortly afterward, Cox and his wife, Mary, and their two sons with three other families, all Quakers in religious faith, arrived in the fall. They established a little village that later took the name Estacado, soon a thriving farming and ranching community.[24]

In the northern Llano (lower Panhandle) or just off its escarpments, Mobeetie in the east and Tascosa in the west developed as ranching communities. Mobeetie grew from a Charles Rath and Robert Wright supply store established about 1874. It may have held 150 residents a year later, but most people abandoned the place as Comanches, Kiowas, and Cheyennes, having left their reservations, cut through the Texas Panhandle trying to avoid solders during the Red River War. With the establishment in 1875 of Fort Elliott nearby, Mobeetie again became an important trade and supply center. Tascosa grew from the sheep plaza Casimero Romero had established in 1876. Romero's employees and friends built several adobe huts and some corrals, and as other New Mexicans came to the Canadian River and the northern reaches of the Llano, the place became a busy little trade center. Henry Kimball, as noted, set up his blacksmith shop in 1876, and soon a general store and a saloon appeared.

The appearance of such towns as Tascosa, Mobeetie, and Estacado along with concomitant factors, both nationally and locally, brought cattlemen to the Llano Estacado. Nationally, an economic depression caused by the "Panic of 1873" had ended by 1877, and with it beef prices rose again. In addition, railroad companies, which had halted construction during the hard business downturn turn, resumed building and moved onto the Great Plains. Cattle buyers used the railroads to collect Texas cattle that drovers moved to marketing centers along the tracks, especially in Kansas. With financiers in the East and in Europe, especially England and Scotland, looking to invest in western ranching at a time when joint-stock companies made it possible to pool resources, Texas land and cattle companies seemed an attractive proposition.

Locally, the end of Texas and New Mexico bison hunting opened millions of acres of rich grassland for cattlemen, just as it had for wool growers before them. Rainfall amounts on the Llano stayed high, well above the eighteen- to twenty-inch average for several years, especially from 1882 to 1885, creating a superb grassland habitat. With millions of cheap cattle grazing beyond the Western Cross Timbers, the thick post oak belt west of Fort Worth; equipment, accoutrements, and labor costs low and cowboys plentiful; and beef in demand, cattle raising in Texas became popular and practical. Moreover, there seemed some unidentifiable, elusive energy about cattle ranching: men on horseback, power between one's legs, gun on hip, looking down upon the wide-open world around them.[25]

Whatever the case, a cattle-raising boom followed. Cattlemen and cowboys climbed onto the Llano Estacado, bringing with them the big-ranch, open-range (unfenced) cattle industry. In the Llano area, as indicated, Charles Goodnight and Hank Smith in 1876 and 1877 led the way, but others came close behind. In fact, from 1876 to 1885, when brutal weather—long, cold winters and hot, droughty summers—overstocked ranges, and rock-bottom cattle prices took a heavy toll on ranchers and their herds, the Llano Estacado experienced a veritable explosion in the land and cattle business. Although large operators dominated the upper Llano, perhaps 60 percent of cattle-ranching enterprises there, such as those of Jim Mitchell in Oldham County, included small herds of no more than one hundred or two hundred head. Likewise, cattle ranching on the South Plains and its western sections in New Mexico mirrored the northern ranges: that is, although big outfits dominated cattle production, plenty of cattle raisers, like Blanco Canyon's Hank Smith, handled small herds with one or two employees.

Their open-range ranching methods ruled the early years of cattle raising on the Llano Estacado. Big land and cattle companies backed by eastern and foreign investors, cattlemen with large herds off the rich prairies west of Fort Worth, and numerous ranchers with modest droves all pushed their livestock westward ahead of a rapidly advancing Texas population. They all helped create an incomparable cattle boom on the Llano and elsewhere in the American West. This grand and colorful Llano cattle industry is in part the subject of chapter 7.[26]

Summary

On the Llano Estacado, the short decade from 1875 to 1885 included some of the most dramatic events associated with the American West. With the last Comanche holdouts settling on the reservation in Indian Territory and with the larger tribe now relatively small in population numbers, the Comanche nation became less a people of several independent divisions united by kinship, culture, and language and more a single sociopolitical group whose members looked to charismatic leaders for guidance and direction.

Bison hunters, who probably killed fewer animals than popular accounts suggest, experienced a short, harsh, and brutal life on the Llano. To the American consciousness their work was rough and callous (and revolting), but dramatic. That "buffalo hunters" as opposed to, say, "hidemen," attract broad popular attention today can be seen in the large number of books written about them (and witness the space given them in this volume), about bison, and about the near annihilation of the large, beautiful brown beasts that had roamed the Great Plains for tens of thousands of years.

Unlike Southern Plains bison hunting, wool growing during the Llano's open-range era receives little popular interest. Yet the 1880s census, archaeological evidence, and the historical record show that significant numbers of sheep grazed the short grasses of the Llano from below Lynn County north to the Canadian River Valley and from the western escarpment east to Blanco and Yellow House Canyons. Later, ranchers grazed sheep in Martin, Midland, and Ector Counties on the southern edge of the Llano. Early sheepherding, like bison hunting, included isolated and lonely work conducted without relief through bad weather or good. But for about ten years after 1875 herding sheep on the High Plains meant profits and occasional affluence before a stretch of bad weather plus cattle and the men who owned them brushed sheep aside and created opportunities for enormous earnings and sometimes fabulous wealth on the Llano Estacado.

Cattle raising on the Llano Estacado, which also began about 1875, remained a secondary enterprise until a big livestock boom at the end of the decade brought huge eastern- and foreign-owned land and cattle operations to the grassy region in the 1880s.

7

Cattlemen, Cowboys, Farmers, and Settlers

The Llano Estacado became a busy place after 1875. With Comanches, Kiowas, and Cheyennes having returned to their reservations after the Red River War, bison hunters, surveyors, and pastores moved into the High Plains vacuum. Cattlemen, cowboys, and early farmer-stockmen came close on their heels, and other settlers were not far behind. Indeed, as they climbed onto the high tableland, the first permanent non-Indian residents on the Llano—sheepherders, cattlemen, and farmer-stockmen—could hear the booming big guns of hidemen as the hunters cut down the last few remnants of the nearly extinct Llano bison.

Thus, after 1875, the Llano Estacado witnessed several new developments. Cattlemen, for example, drove their herds into the Llano's canyonlands and along the Canadian River Valley. With their cowboys they successfully challenged pastores for water sources and grazing territory before moving their open-range (unfenced) operations onto the Llano's uplands. At the very same time, many pioneer farmers and farmer-stockmen, supported by the state's new landownership legislation, contested cattlemen to the open-range country. Concomitantly, towns and villages appeared, many aided by the extension of railroads, by land speculators, and by local entrepreneurs seeking to carve out a living through merchandising groceries, hardware, clothes and cloth, and sundry other essential goods, plus entertainment and liquor.

Such developments began with an expanding cattle industry. In the West, open-range, free-grass ranching with its horse-mounted cowboys and large herds of drifting Longhorns created, at least for outsiders, a vivid and dramatic mental image: men on horseback, reins held tight, moving feral cattle across a dusty plain. In Texas, the combination of cowboys, cattle, and horses created what Joe B. Frantz called the "Holy Trinity of Texas." This Old West narrative evolved as a result of a nationwide demand for fresh beef after the Civil War. With long-legged, Longhorn cattle roaming loose in South Texas and beyond the Cross Timbers west of Fort Worth, cattle raising from horseback, which had a long tradition in Mexico, seemed an attractive proposition. Partly as a result, many men and some women took a gamble on cattle: round up Longhorns and drive them a thousand miles to market.[1]

The so-called Cattle Kingdom, or "beef bonanza," followed. Europeans, especially from England and Scotland, and American Easterners through joint-stock companies combined their financial resources and joined in the big, colorful, and dramatic enterprise. For a brief time, cattle raising in the West was among the hottest investments in America. The number of cattle-raising operations increased rapidly. Indeed, some ninety years ago, Walter Prescott Webb, the distinguished historian of the Great Plains, suggested that for "rapidity of expansion there is . . . not a parallel to this movement in American history." The booming enterprise, having started in Mexico, moved out of Texas and the Southwest, spread north across the entire Plains where eastern livestock traditions influenced it, filtered west through the Rocky Mountains and Great Basin, and connected with long-established livestock traditions in California. With modifications it reached into Oregon, Washington, and Canada.[2]

On the Llano Estacado, however, the big, open-range cattle-raising boom was short-lived. It extended roughly from 1876 to 1886. Although ranching has continued to the very present, cattle raising on the Llano and in its canyonlands during the brief, colorful open-range period was fraught with difficulties. Complicated by the whims of weather, water

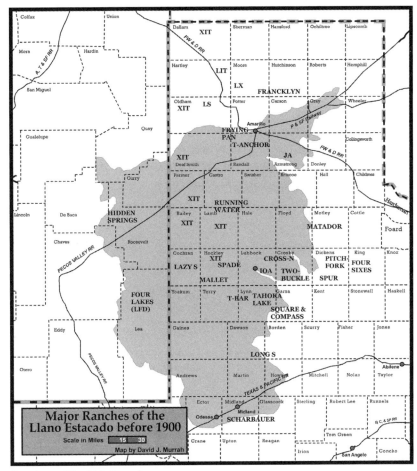

Courtesy of David J. Murrah

shortages, lack of fencing, and fluctuating prices that remained beyond the control of ranch owners and their cowboy employees, ranching was often financially unrewarding.

Yet several cattle raisers on the Llano Estacado made huge profits in the difficult business. They built large, successful ranches, and in the absence of graduated income and inheritance taxes became part of America's upper socioeconomic society. Some constructed impressive homes, sometimes on the ranch, a few times in such large cities as Fort Worth, Dallas, or Austin, but often in a town that because of the local cattle industry was becoming a city. In Amarillo, for instance, South Polk

Charles Goodnight arrived in Palo Duro Canyon about 1876 to establish the JA Ranch just as sheepherders pushed onto the Llano and as bison hunters were destroying the last of the Llano bison. Courtesy of Panhandle-Plains Historical Museum

Street became "Silk Stocking Row" with a fine esplanade and mansions that by contrast with possessions of cowboys and average middle-class Americans seemed like castles of medieval Europe. Whether ranchers were fabulously wealthy, moderately well-off, or marginally productive, one should remember that cattle ranching and cowboying, like farming, were difficult, labor-intensive occupations, but also they were a way of life.

Charles Goodnight in Palo Duro Canyon, Hank Smith in Blanco Canyon, and some of the pastores along the Canadian River who grazed a few cattle were in 1876 and 1877 among the first cattle raisers on the Llano Estacado. Several former bison hunters also turned to cattle raising. In Sterling County, Spotted Jack, a part-Anglo, part-Indian, part-Mexican former guide and hunter, with a few other cowboys in

1877 drove Longhorns near the head of the North Concho River for a rancher moving his animals toward the Llano Estacado. Also in 1877, rancher John Lovelady with his cowboys pushed a small number of cattle toward the northwestern edge of Garza County.

Thomas L. "George" Causey, the former hide hunter, with his brother John moved up Yellow House Draw in 1877 in pursuit of ever-more-scarce bison. They built a sod house at Casas Amarillas, turned to cattle raising, and hunted wolves, deer, and antelope for their hides. A few years later, George Causey sold out to Jim Newman, who moved in with fifteen hundred cattle and acquired "rights" to spread his livestock through the rich basin. The Causeys moved over to New Mexico. George started a ranch with George Jefferson in 1882 near Ranger Lake and Four Lakes in the northern part of Lea County. They raised cattle and rounded up and broke wild mustangs. Later that same year, James

Henry Clay "Hank" Smith supervised construction of his home in Blanco Canyon in 1877 and 1878 before moving into it with his family from Fort Griffin in 1879. It became a popular visiting place during the settlement of the eastern South Plains. Courtesy of Southwest Collection/Special Collections Library

Harvey and Dick Wilkerson built a sod house near Monument Spring south of present-day Hobbs, New Mexico.[3]

On the eastern edge of the Llano, close to Hank Smith in Blanco Canyon, several ranchers took up cattle raising. Cass O. and George Edwards arrived in Crosby County in 1879 and ranched there until 1882. In 1883, Cass Edwards moved to Double Lakes in Lynn County, established the T-Bar Ranch, and built his herd and landholdings. The T-Bar with 130,000 acres became one of the first cattle ranches to be located entirely on the Llano.[4]

Nearby, Jim and Finnis Lindsey briefly held rights to land along the South Fork of the Double Mountain Fork of the Brazos River in Garza and Lynn Counties, but in 1882 two Missouri merchants, Abraham Nave and James McCord, purchased the Lindsey cattle and grazing rights and established the Square and Compass Ranch, half of which spread across the Llano in Lynn County and half below the escarpment in Garza County. Two years later, by leasing and purchasing additional land, the Missourians held some 140,000 acres.[5]

Christopher Columbus "Lum" Slaughter, a Texas-born Dallas banker and businessman, became perhaps the largest land and cattle owner in Texas. As a young teenager, he started into the cattle and cattle-trailing industries with his father and an uncle on the prairies west of Fort Worth. In 1876, the thirty-nine-year-old Slaughter moved two thousand animals to West Texas. Two years later his cowboys drove his herd to the head of the Colorado River and onto the Llano Estacado over parts of Dawson, Martin, and Gaines Counties. Having secured grazing rights to additional land off the eastern escarpment in parts of Borden and Howard Counties (as well as Martin County below the escarpment), Slaughter's Long S Ranch became a huge enterprise extending across nearly one million acres. Then in 1884, he increased his land and cattle holdings by purchasing rights to the one-hundred-thousand-acre Running Water Ranch in Hale and Lamb Counties northwest of present-day Plainview. The town (or water stop) of Slaughter, established in 1882, on the Llano in northeastern Midland County along the Texas and Pacific Railroad got its name from this "Cattle King of Texas."[6]

One of the most luckless operations during the cattle-raising boom period proved to be the large IOA Ranch in Lubbock County. Established near the end of the boom years in 1884 by the Western Land and Livestock Company, based in Iowa and Illinois, the ranch covered through lease and purchase most of the southern half of the county. Stocked with twenty thousand cattle in 1885, its owners enclosed the ranch with barbed-wire fencing, divided it into three pastures, and pumped water with windmills for their livestock from the underground Ogallala reservoir. It never made a profit.[7]

In northern sections of the Llano Estacado (the lower Panhandle), large ranches also dominated the boom years of cattle ranching—most of them known by their brands. The LX Ranch, established in 1877 just north of present-day Amarillo in Potter County, extended between twenty-five and thirty miles to and across the Canadian River. An operation of some four hundred thousand acres, the LX, owned by Colorado investors, included high-bred horses—mares—as well as cattle. One of its first managers, a

Lee Bivins, on the ground at left with hat and tie, and cowboys of the giant LX Ranch at lunch on the range. Courtesy of Panhandle-Plains Historical Museum

fugitive from justice in Wyoming, was William C. Moore. In 1903 the LX became part of the huge holdings of Lee Bivins, a cattleman, general merchandiser, and Amarillo developer.

West of the LX, George W. Littlefield, Mississippi-born cattle trailer, entrepreneur, and philanthropist, in 1877 purchased water rights and founded his LIT Ranch in the Canadian River Valley near Tascosa. It extended for fifteen miles on both sides of the river. Four years later, he sold the ranch and with his half nephew, J. Phelps White, established a big ranch in the Pecos River Valley in New Mexico Territory. In 1883, White and the forty-one-year-old Littlefield moved onto the Llano in Roosevelt County, New Mexico.[8]

Just south of present Amarillo near modern Canyon in Randall County, Texas, spread the large T-Anchor Ranch. Started in 1877 by Leigh Dyer, Charles Goodnight's son-in-law, expanded by former bison hunter Bill Koogle after he became owner, and purchased by others in the 1880s as the GMS Ranch (Gunter, Munson, and Summerfield, the speculators and surveyors of the Panhandle), it succeeded wildly. In 1882, Jot Gunter bought Munson's and Summerfield's share and using the T-Anchor brand made it a huge operation with drift fences west across the plains almost to modern Hereford. One of its first managers was John Hutson, "an eccentric Englishman of noble birth."[9]

The largest of the early ranches on the Llano Estacado was the XIT. Established in 1882 by the Capitol Freehold Land and Investment Company of Chicago, which had been created the year previous to construct a new capitol building in Austin, the ranch was massive. It extended for 220 miles mostly along the New Mexico border from the top of Texas near Buffalo Springs in Dallam County to Yellow House Draw in Hockley County. It covered some 3,050,000 acres. Its owners did not plan to be full-time cattlemen. They wanted to run livestock only until they could sell their land to farmers and settlers and thus recoup their investment in building the State Capitol, which they completed in 1888—although, of course, they did not aim to lose money in ranching.[10]

In operating the ranch, its owners and various managers divided the big spread into several divisions with some ninety-four pastures. At least four of the divisions reached across the Llano Estacado. The

Llano divisions included Alamositas in Oldham County, Escabada in the southwest corner of Deaf Smith County, Spring Lake in northern Lamb County, and Casas Amarillas in Lamb and Hockley Counties. Each division maintained a headquarters operation, and each served a special purpose for raising XIT cattle and the horses needed to herd them. The ranch, according to its principal biographer, employed from "100 to 150 cowboys, with combined remudas of more than 1,000 cow ponies, [who] 'rode herd' upon approximately 150,000 cattle."[11]

On what became the western edge of Amarillo, Joseph F. Glidden and Henry B. Sanborn in 1881 established the Frying Pan Ranch. Glidden, who in DeKalb, Illinois, in 1874 had developed and patented (No. 157,124) a simple but highly effective barbed wire, became wealthy through the wire business. Like other Illinois men of wealth (think IOA and XIT ranches), he wanted to invest in the growing western land and live-stock industry. Sanborn, a smooth-talking salesman for Glidden's Barb Fence Company, joined him. With financial help from Isaac L. Ellwood, Glidden's DeKalb neighbor and partner in the fence company (who later established his Spade Ranch on the Llano Estacado), they acquired through purchase, lease, and possession by right of first occupation, 250,000 or more acres extending from the Canadian River south to the northern edge of the T-Anchor and reaching some fifteen miles east to west. They established headquarters at the much-used and famous Tecovas Spring, and hired Warren W. Wetzel (Wetsel), who had recently married in New York and brought his wife to Texas, as manager.[12]

The LS Ranch, another large operation established during the Llano Estacado's cattle-boom days, spread west of the Frying Pan and, like its neighbor, south from the Canadian. Lucian Scott, a banker and busi-nessman from Leavenworth, Kansas, and W. M. D. Lee, the successful sutler, freighter, and trader from Camp Supply, formed the Lee-Scott (LS) Cattle Company in 1881. Lee, according to one of his biographers, in 1882 drove his buggy up the Canadian River Valley. Far up the river but still in Texas, he stopped at a few sheepherder plazas and with a valise full of money bought out some of the pastores. His method, if, in fact, the story is true, proved effective, and soon several herders removed their flocks and headed back to New Mexico.[13]

Others stayed. Casimero Romero, for example, while keeping some sheep, turned to freighting between his Tascosa village and Dodge City. He had built a large home in Tascosa, a community that had grown from a quiet little friends-and-family plaza into a loud, rough town full of saloons, toughs, rustlers, outlaws, gunslingers, and cowboys off the big ranches on both sides of the Canadian River. Like Romero, other pastores, even when they kept a few sheep or turned to cattle, opened businesses. With other settlers, such as cattleman Jim Mitchell, the pastores helped organized Oldham County in 1881 with Tascosa as the county seat and Jim East as sheriff. East with other officials in the justice system, including Pat Garrett, a former bison hunter who became head of a small company of Texas Rangers and who later killed famous outlaw Billy the Kid, brought order and stability to the upper western Llano, including the wild outlaw haven in Tascosa.

West of there in New Mexico, some of the Llano Estacado ranches reached impressive size. George Littlefield and his partner, Phelps White, in 1883 moved out of the Pecos River Valley, secured large amounts of land for what became their famous LFD brand, and obtained grazing rights to a huge region on the New Mexico side of the big mesa. White, from the time he and Littlefield moved into the Pecos River Valley in 1881, believed that the future of ranching in New Mexico needed to be centered on the Llano, and accordingly he moved through lease and purchase to acquire rights to rich pastures near Mescalero Spring, Four Lakes, and Ranger Lake, all in Lea County near modern Tatum. They secured land at Ranger Lake from George Causey, the former bison hunter whom White had met years earlier in Dodge City.[14]

Farther north in New Mexico many others grazed cattle. One of them was Tom Harris, a former LS wagon boss. Harris had led an unsuccessful cowboy strike at the beginning of the spring roundup in 1883. Most owners refused to accept the cowboy demands for higher wages, and strikers at the conclusion of the roundup lost their jobs. Cattlemen blacklisted them. Without prospects of work, some of the former strikers and other cowboys joined Harris at a tiny community located on a branch of Trujillo Creek in Quay County. The place had been, according to historian Donald F. Schofield, "a past haven for other outcasts such as [comancheros], whiskey peddlers, and the [famous, but young, out-law Billy the Kid and his] gang." From it, Harris and his inner circle of cowboys organized a "syndicate" to raise cattle, corral unbranded cows, mark them with their brands, and later claim them as their own ("mavericking," cattlemen called the practice). The Harris syndicate succeeded for a brief time, but soon Llano Estacado ranchers, led by the LS owner W. M. D. Lee and law officials, including Sheriff Jim East from Oldham County, moved against Harris and his questionable ranching enterprise, ending it.[15]

On the Llano Estacado, big-ranch cattle operations, such as the LS, became easier after livestock owners worked through the difficult issue of water, or lack of it. On hot summer days, each cow needed about fifteen gallons of water. Even in years of high average rainfall, good water remained elusive on the Llano: playas were often gypsum-laden, streams dry or brackish, and lakes—usable ones—few and scattered. The indispensable Ogallala Aquifer, of course, held plenty of sweet water, but getting it to aboveground holding tanks proved challenging until ranchers drilled wells and erected windmills to pump the life-sustaining liquid out of the large underground reservoir.

The first such well-windmill combination on the Llano Estacado, according to archivist, historian, and biographer David B. Gracy II, ap-peared in Roosevelt County, New Mexico. George Causey built it on his Ranger Lake property, probably sometime about 1882. Other ranchers followed, including Willa V. Johnson, who drilled wells on his Kentucky Cattle Company and Two Buckle Ranches in Crosby County. He also located a well in Lubbock County in 1884. C. C. Slaughter had eight wells with windmills operating in Dawson County before 1885. Soon afterward, cattlemen with herds on the northern edge of the Llano in both Texas and New Mexico drilled wells and erected windmills.[16]

From their first operations on the Llano Estacado, cattlemen brought in purebred bulls to breed their Longhorn cows. Although Charles Goodnight brought with him from Colorado in 1876 some Durham bulls, the most popular-breed bulls included Shorthorns, Aberdeen Angus, and especially the white-faced, red-bodied Herefords. Hereford-Longhorn crosses produced small calves that grew quickly, wintered well, and seemed a bit more resistant to the diseases that ravaged other mixed-breed cattle herds. Rancher and first judge of Carson County O. H. "Bull" Nelson, W. M. D. Lee of the LS Ranch, and later Goodnight of the JA all brought in Herefords to improve their herd bloodlines, as did C. C. Slaughter on his Long S Ranch. Neighboring cattlemen followed their lead and encouragement.[17]

To work their big ranches, cattlemen needed herders—cowboys. The majority of such workers identified as Anglo-Americans, but a good number were Hispanic, African American, or Native American. On the Llano Estacado, a few were former pastores, and some of the older cowboys were Civil War veterans—Union and Confederate—still looking for new stakes or refusing to return to quiet, but difficult, farm life. Some identified as "nester kids," sons of pioneer farmers. Indeed, most cowboys were young. Their average age, according to William H. Forbis, who has written about them, was twenty-four, and they remained cowboys an average of only seven years.[18]

In popular stereotype, cowboys have become larger-than-life figures: men on horseback with big hats, perhaps a gun holstered on their hip, a rope in one hand, reins held tight in the other, looking down figuratively and literally on farmers, sheepherders, townspeople, and others around them. Some tried to live up to the overly masculine characterization. Edward Everett Dale, once a ranch hand himself, wrote that many a "cowboy was a wild, reckless type who rode hard, swore hard, and feared neither God nor man." Such a characterization seems too harsh, but to build their own herds, cowboys on occasion stole cattle from their employers. Myths aside, a good cowboy, writes Forbis, remained "a dirty, overworked laborer who fried his brains under a prairie sun or rode endless miles in rain and wind to mend fences or look for lost calves."[19]

Cowboys worked hard for long hours and low pay. They shivered through cold and snow during winter months to turn cattle back to the home range. The line riders among them slept in and lived out of tiny shacks or half-dugouts, alone or with a single companion. They rode out in opposite directions each morning for many miles checking on cattle before turning back to reach their half-dugout or other simple abode near nightfall—all for about a dollar a day plus board.

In the early days of Llano ranching, these employees were rarely called cowboys. They were "waddies," "hands," or "cowhands." The 1880 Panhandle census listed not a single "cowboy" as working on any of the many upper Llano or Panhandle ranches. Rather, the census delineated such workers as "stockman," "sheepherder," "cattle herder," "ranchero," and "raising cows." As indicated, they might be "nester kids." V. W. Whitlock, who spent many years among cowhands, called them "waddies," "wranglers," "hands," and the youngest ones "lints."[20]

Although the use of such terms for cattle hands did not disappear, by the end of the 1880s, the term "cowboy" was in general use. William F. Cody is at least partly responsible for the transition. In 1883, he began his Buffalo Bill's Wild West, a popular outdoor traveling show that included young men herding cattle. He called them cowboys. A year later, he featured one of them as "Buck Taylor: King of the Cowboys." And in 1887, Prentice Ingraham, a hack writer, produced with little originality a dime novel titled *Buck Taylor: King of the Cowboys*. Cody's famous Wild West and Ingraham's pocket-sized and lively-selling novel plus Charlie Russell's "cowboy" paintings must have played a role in ranch hands and others adopting the new term.

Cowboys, by whatever term used, linked up with other ranch employees at branding and castrating time, when most worked on foot with hot fires, hot irons, and sharp knives. With searing irons, they marked live cows with their ranch's identifying marks, and with knives and other "weapons" turned bull calves into steers. They took their meals on the ground and spent little time at rest.

As tough as they were and despite such brutal and violent work as branding and castrating, cowboy life was not all callous and hard. Cowboys lived by Victorian-era social and cultural values. They doffed their hats before women, for example, and removed them when entering the ranch house parlor or eating at the ranch house table. They treated most folks with thoughtful consideration. They dressed in "town clothes" before heading to, well, town. They read plenty of dime novels, trade catalogues, and newspapers, but, as B. Byron Price has indicated, they also read William Shakespeare, Robert Burns, "and other literary classics."[21]

Lysius Gough and Cowboy Poetry

Lysius "Parson" Gough (1862–1940), a Texas cowboy, schoolteacher, and Llano Estacado wheat grower, in 1886 published Western Travels and Other Rhymes, perhaps the first serious collection of cowboy poetry. Called "Parson" because he did not curse, Gough had run away from home, become a cowboy on the T-Anchor Ranch near Canyon, Texas, and finally at age twenty-two attended school at Pilot Point Institute in Denton County. He graduated four years later and eventually became principal of the school. While a student at Pilot Point, he had published his book of poems and later, while principal, married Ida Russell, a former student. They settled on a farm south of Dimmitt in Castro County.

Gough took an interest in a wide variety of issues. He taught school in Dimmitt, planted wheat, experimented with digging wells and irrigating crops, studied law, entered politics, and became in 1891 the first judge of Castro County. In 1898, he moved to Hereford and after 1914 became one of the largest wheat producers on the Llano Estacado. From 1923 to 1928, he served as president of the Texas Wheat Growers Association. He organized the first of what became an annual T-Anchor Ranch cowboy reunion, and he was an important early supporter of the Panhandle-Plains Historical Society. Through it all, he continued to write poetry and published Spurs, Jingles and Saddle Songs in 1935. He and Ida had ten children, six of whom lived into adulthood.

Gough was called by some the "poet laureate" of cowboy poetry, and his verse fit easily into the mainstream of western folk poetry at the turn of the century. That is, in the late 1880s folk poetry, like Gough's work, and rural, agrarian music fell into traditional dance and music forms that were popular in the western farm and ranch country. Poetry at the time, recited around cowboy campfires and in ranch bunkhouses, tended to be simple. It often rhymed, used an iambic meter, and utilized vernacular dialect common in western range country, including the Llano Estacado.

Authors of some of the period's best cowboy poetry remained anonymous. But cowboy poems appeared in self-published books and small pamphlets and in newspapers, magazines, and livestock journals. They were popular. "Lasca," published in a Montana journal in 1882 and written by a visiting London theater critic, was widely recounted by cowboys—and at Chautauqua presentations around the United States. In 1898, Nathan Howard "Jack" Thorpe, while trailing a herd of cattle from New Mexico through the lower Texas Panhandle, wrote "Little Joe the Wrangler," a sad but highly admired verse and often recited on the range and in the ranch house parlor. Another widely narrated cowboy poem, but from the twentieth century, was "Sierry Petes" ("Tying Knots in the Devil's Tail") written by Gail Gardner about 1917, a poem often set to music, often pirated, and often performed on YouTube. Perhaps the most popular of all cowboy poems is Carmen William "Curley" Fletcher's "The Strawberry Roan," first published in his 1917 poetry pamphlet. Poetry events, such as the National Cowboy Poetry Gathering in Elko, Nevada, continue in 2022 to display the popularity of cowboy poetry, a popularity suggested perhaps as early as Lysius Gough's little book of western poems.

While they may have drunk too much liquor, and too often, at local saloons, cowboys enjoyed other kinds of recreation, such as ranch dances. Early in the Llano Estacado's cattle-raising boom era, a custom developed that the ranches, each in turn, ought to hold a big dance party—a "blowout." Held once a year, they became polite but fancy affairs in which ranch owners expected their cowboys to dress neatly and remain sober. The Frying Pan Ranch, as an example, held a blowout at its headquarters at Tecovas Spring in early January 1884. Attendees came from as far as eighty miles away. Late in the afternoon as guests arrived, the Frying Pan hosts provided coffee, sandwiches, and doughnuts. They served supper at nightfall, and after that everyone danced all night with a break for steamed oysters at midnight. About seventy-five people attended, only twenty of whom were women, which means, of course, the ladies remained on the dance floor most of the night. In the morning after breakfast the Frying Pan hosts bid their tired visitors safe travels home.[22]

While hardly recreation, cowboys also joined fellow cowhands at roundup time in the spring and fall. During the open-range era of cattle ranching on the Llano Estacado, multiranch roundups proved common, especially the important spring roundup. During winter months, despite the best efforts of line riders, cattle from adjoining ranches (and from distant spreads) mixed together. In the spring, they needed to be separated and returned to the home range, where all calves received brands and bull calves endured castration. Roundups in the early, open-range era became big semiannual affairs.[23]

Roundups and cattle ranching changed with the widespread adoption of barbed-wire fencing. Such fencing on the Llano Estacado began no later than 1881. A few ranchers, such as owners of the T-Anchor, put in drift fences, some of them extending east-west for miles. At the Frying Pan Ranch, Joseph Glidden and his partner, Henry B. Sanborn, the "Father of Amarillo," enclosed the entire spread with barbed wire and

With few women or older girls available on early western ranches, cowboys sometimes held stag dances in the bunkhouse with men dancing the female part. Courtesy of Southwest Collection/Special Collections Library

The windmill pictured here was built about 1888 in the Casas Amarillas basin. The tallest windmill in the world at the time of its construction, it rose from the basin floor to tower above the Llano Estacado flatlands, where it could catch the region's winds. It toppled over in a sandstorm on Thanksgiving, 1926. Courtesy of David J. Murrah

divided the ranch with an east-west fence that separated the upland prairies from the broken land below the Canadian River escarpment. Altogether, their fence lines extended for 105 miles with four strands of wire (420 miles of it). In 2022, some of the original fence is still in use. Eventually, all Llano and Panhandle cattlemen fenced their ranges with barbed wire—although not always with Glidden's brand. Owners of the huge XIT Ranch enclosed 3,050,000 acres within nearly 1,500 miles of fence (6,000 miles if one counts all four strands).[24]

Fencing had many benefits, of course, but in an important and unsuspecting way it helped block "free grazers" and keep cattle trailers from the Llano Estacado. Beginning in 1881, ranchers, led by O. H. Nelson and Charles Goodnight, opposed drovers moving their South and Central Texas herds through Llano and Panhandle pastures to ranges in Kansas, Colorado, Wyoming, and elsewhere. Because many such Longhorn herds still carried tick fever (Texas fever), ranchers with rifles and shotguns ready (much like Missouri farmers nearly twenty years earlier) established a so-called shotgun quarantine to turn back drovers and their Texas cattle. The ranchers told drovers, including those who tried to follow the handy and direct Potter-Bacon Trail across the Llano to Colorado, to stay off the Llano and away from the Panhandle and to move their livestock along the Rath Trail east of the Llano Estacado or take some other familiar route (the Great Western Trail) to market. Their advice, including threats, proved effective.[25]

To market their cattle, South Plains and northern Llano ranchers in the absence of local rail connections trailed their animals to distant railway shipping points. Most often cattlemen contracted with trailing companies for the job. The earliest ranchers on the Llano sent their cattle to Dodge City along various old freighting trails from Tascosa, Mobeetie, Wild Horse Lake within the present limits of Amarillo, and elsewhere. After 1881, when the Texas and Pacific Railway reached Midland and Odessa, ranchers on the southern Llano, including the southern divisions of the XIT, some in the Yellow House Canyon area, and some in the area southeast of the Mescalero Sands in New Mexico, marketed cattle and bought supplies in Midland, Pecos, or Colorado City. That same year, 1881, the Atchison, Topeka and Santa Fe Railway reached New Mexico, and several ranchers in the upper and western Llano moved their market animals (steers mainly) overland to water stops or communities such as Springer along the rail line and placed them on train cars of the famous railway.

At that time, 1881, Crosby and Lubbock Counties on the Llano's South Plains began receiving non-ranching, pioneer settlers. As noted in chapter 6, it started with Hank Smith in Blanco Canyon in 1877 and Paris Cox and his Quaker community of Estacado in 1879. Several concomitant factors drew people to the area, including the 1876 creation of fifty-four High Plains counties that created a land-speculating frenzy that brought surveyors to the Llano. Moreover, the news of men pushing sheep and cattle through the Llano's eastern canyonlands and up onto the rich, grassy plains encouraged farmers and businesspeople to the region. Such dynamics, coupled with a rapidly growing Texas population, emboldened—pressured even—young, brash adventurers

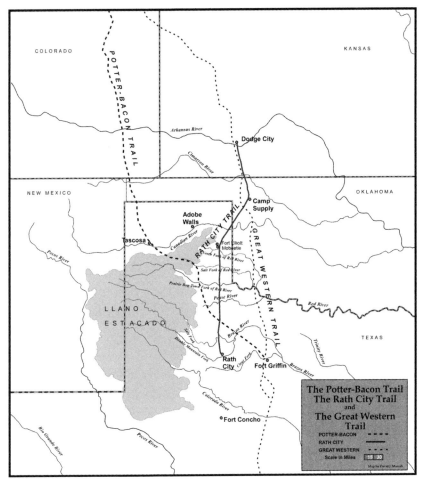

Courtesy of David J. Murrah

and courageous couples to seek opportunities in sparsely settled, cattle-raising-dominated western Texas.

Estacado, under Paris Cox's leadership, attracted some of the first farmers and settlers. Not all of them stayed, but in August 1880, William Hunt from Oklahoma visited Cox and his little farm. Impressed, Hunt wrote in a letter that appeared in *The Texas Almanac for 1883*: "I saw corn, oats, millet, sorghum, melons, Irish potatoes, sweet potatoes, and garden vegetables—all did well." He settled in the town, and others arrived: townspeople, farmers, cattlemen, and cowboys. The farmers with their families bought land from Cox, planted crops, shopped in the budding town, and began building a community. Cattlemen, cowboys, and sheepherders established ranches in nearby Blanco Canyon above and below the Hank Smith ranch and in Yellow House Canyon with some of them reaching far up the canyon and spilling over onto the tableland.[26]

Settlers, including farmers, farmer-stockmen, cowboys, and townspeople, in the area sought to establish a civil society on the South Plains. Most of the Quakers who came to Cox's Estacado community on the Crosby-Lubbock County line, arrived in family units. They built sod and adobe houses, sought supplies from Colorado City on the Texas and Pacific Railway, planted crops on land they purchased from Cox, and set about improving their rugged pioneer lives. Within two years some ten families had arrived, including George W. Singer and his family, who built a sod house and opened a small store. William Hunt, the physician who had written favorably about the Estacado area, farmed and practiced medicine. His daughter, Emma Hunt, started a school. Hunt became postmaster. Townspeople began hauling lumber in freight wagons from the railroad depot at Colorado City about 120 miles distant, and the Quakers built a wood-frame meetinghouse. Additional farmers arrived, planted crops, and traded in town, as did cowboys from area ranches. H. E. Hume and R. L. Stringfellow opened a general merchandise store in the community.[27]

Not all was serene. Cowboys wanted a saloon, but Cox and his Quaker farmers blocked such an establishment. The resulting cowboy-farmer animosity characterized Estacado through its lifetime. And after Hume and Stringfellow opened their general store, George Singer, a German-American Lutheran, and his family moved away. They settled at Punta de Agua, the little horseshoe-shaped water hole that marked the headwaters of the upper Brazos River in Yellow House Draw and located within the present city of Lubbock. An ancient hunting and trading site, the water hole had recently served as a military road crossing point: one trail went from Fort Elliott in the Panhandle south to Fort Stockton in modern Pecos County; the other, an old and well-worn route sometimes called the Mackenzie Trail, connected Fort Griffin in Shackelford County with Fort Sumner in New Mexico.

Singer built a home at the lake about 1882 or 1883 and again opened a general store, this time with a little saloon. He or, at least one time, Rachel freighted merchandise and building supplies from Colorado City on the Texas & Pacific. His store, although only about 360 square feet in size, attracted cowboys, farmers, sheepherders, settlers, drovers, and others, including some Apaches. When Rachel Singer began using the back side of the store as an "eating place," travelers from a wide area stopped by to devour a meal, share a drink, and try her famous biscuits. The federal government in June 1884 appointed Singer postmaster of what it called its "Lubbock" office, a position he held until November 1890.[28]

As such developments occurred in the Blanco–Yellow House Canyons area, the Texas and Pacific Railway in 1881 and afterward created a population "boom" of sorts along the southern Llano Estacado. As owners pushed their railroad from Fort Worth through West Texas in a southwest direction to its junction with the Southern Pacific near Sierra Blanca in Hudspeth County, several towns appeared along its tracks. Colorado City, Midland, and Odessa led the way, but others followed. Colorado City, which had started as a Texas Ranger camp in 1877, became a major cattle-shipping point after 1881. It soon became the county seat for Mitchell County and in 1884–85 held a population of six thousand. Midland, called Midway until 1884 when it got a post office, became a sheep and cattle marketing hub and the Midland County seat in 1885. Odessa, founded in 1881 as a water stop along the railroad, became a livestock distribution center, and the government established a post office there in 1885. In 1891, Odessa, named for Odessa in Ukraine because of the level, grassy prairies in the area, became the seat of Ector County.

Modern Stanton, the seat of Martin County, also began as water stop on the Texas and Pacific. The railroad built a two-story section house, pump, and tank at the site, and in 1881 it became a German Catholic settlement named Grelton, established by John J. Konz and others. It soon became a busy farming community. That same year, Father Christian

D. (Anastasius) Peters, with help from fellow settlers, built West Texas' first Catholic Church in the town and the next year built a two-story monastery for the Mendicant Carmelite religious order. Grelton received a post office in 1883, and soon it held not only the Catholic complex but also a hotel with a wagon yard, school, courthouse, several businesses, and railway operations. It became Marienfeld in 1885 and Stanton in 1890. Then in 1894, a group of nuns of the Sisters of Mercy opened a convent and academy named Our Lady of Mercy. It soon attracted students from much of West Texas.

Wool growers and cattlemen were part of the population growth. Ranchers brought sheep and some goats with them, and many of them also raised cattle and often in the same pastures with sheep. When selling the wool or mohair, they delivered it to Pecos, Midland, or Colorado City and from there on tracks of the Texas and Pacific to Fort Worth. Such ranchers faced the same problems as cattlemen elsewhere on the big mesa: predators and lack of water. They struggled for years to beat back wolves, coyotes, and feral dogs, all of which killed wild turkey, deer, antelope, and small game. But as bison disappeared and ranchers with livestock entered the range, wolves turned on domesticated cattle and sheep, especially young calves and lambs. While livestock owners may have exaggerated damage from predators, the losses were nonetheless real. After government agencies and livestock organizations offered bounties for wolf pelts, farmers and ranchers hunted wolves to near extinction. As noted, former bison hunters, such as Bill Benson and George Causey, turned to wolf hunting to make extra cash, and many early settlers, including ranchers, organized wolf hunts as recreational events. Women sometimes went along.

More difficult than predators for cattlemen was a long stretch of bad weather that began in mid-January 1885. On the sixteenth of the month, after a week of clear and pleasant weather, a huge dark bank of clouds rolled in from the north, bringing with it a cold, snow-filled blizzard and a menacing sheet of dry sleet. The storm became a monster, and its icy blast forced drifting cattle south across Llano and Panhandle rangeland until they reached three- and four-strand barbed-wire fences. Here, the animals pushed into the wire as trailing cattle pressed against them and snow and ice covered and suffocated them. The storm blew through the terrible night and continued off and on for several days. As it continued to whirl and blow, snow created hard-packed drifts around and about the wire-trapped animals. Successive waves of cattle piled in against them.

In time the packed snow and dying cattle created bridges of a sort along fence lines over which additional animals crossed. Cattle from above the Canadian River reached south to the wide river valley, where they received some protection from the storm. Animals on ranges in Potter and Oldham Counties in Texas and in Quay and Curry Counties in New Mexico were not so fortunate. They found only modest breaks along shallow draws on the Llano. Farther south, animals, such as those belonging to C. C. Slaughter in Dawson and Martin Counties, struggled before the cold winds, pushing through or over barbed-wire fences as they moved south and west into rangeland well below the Llano Estacado. On the heels of the storm came a numbing cold that drove temperatures below zero. For several days the cold weather continued and few people ventured out.

The series of storms created havoc. Cattle drifted far to the south beyond their home range, and many froze to death. For example, when he rode out to survey the damage in his Potter County spread, John Grissom, the Frying Pan Ranch range boss—who in 1883 may have been the same J. L. Grissom who signed the original cowboy strike notice—found cattle that bore brands of neighboring ranches mixed with Frying Pan herds and dead animals along all the fences. Ranch cowboys stripped several carcasses of their hides and burned some of the dead animals, but with little heart for the job, they left most of the corpses to wolves, coyotes, and scavengers. Neighboring ranches experienced much the same kind of disaster. Della Tyler Key, a regional historian, wrote that it registered as "one of the worst disasters ever to hit" Potter County and Panhandle-Plains pastures.[29]

In the spring, with cattle having drifted many miles from the home ranch, a major livestock roundup occurred, one perhaps second only in size to the 1883 Panhandle cowboy strike-related event. In the north many ranchers with their cowboys, remudas, and chuck and supply wagons gathered near Tascosa. Farther south other ranchers, led by

C. C. Slaughter of the Long S Ranch, gathered their cowboys, horses, and equipment at Big Spring. Cowboy crews arrived from miles away, each bringing a remuda of several horses that they staked near their ranch chuck wagon. From the staging areas, cowboys rode out each day, gathered livestock, and turned them toward home. They collected thousands of cattle that had drifted before the wind and storms and then separated the animals that had mingled with one another unconcerned about property lines. The Big Spring cowboys found cattle that had drifted as far south as the Devil's River well below the Llano's southern edge. Livestock losses were heavy.[30]

More losses followed. Little rain fell on the Llano Estacado, and the summer of 1885 turned hot, withering grasses and drying out streambeds. In July, President Grover Cleveland ordered Texas cattle out of Indian Territory reservations. Thereupon, cowboys moved tens of thousands of cattle from the Comanche-Kiowa and Cheyenne-Arapaho Reservations to Texas, including the Panhandle and upper Llano, where grass had already thinned from drought and overgrazing and where range fires had burned off thousands of acres. Another cold winter in 1885–86 followed by more droughty weather in the summer caused additional cattle to perish. Moreover, as Panhandle historians have written, the long drought left "annual calf crops short by as much as twenty percent on many ranches." During the same period, cattle prices crashed—badly. The combination of cold winters; hot, dry summers; overstock ranges; and low prices persisted into 1888, collapsing the booming, big-ranch cattle industry.[31]

More than weather and prices caused the boom's collapse. New land laws in the 1880s and afterward strangled many big ranches. The new laws, which at first, as in 1879, benefited cattlemen, soon came to favor farmers and farmer-stockmen who were crowding onto the Llano Estacado. As explained by David J. Murrah, perhaps the preeminent ranching historian of Texas, an increasingly "farmer-oriented Texas legislature sought to end the cattlemen's free use of state land." That is, many ranchers leased from railroads or from the state, alternating sections (640 acres each) of land in checkerboard fashion, making it possible for them to graze without cost the neighboring, unclaimed, and open sections.

When the lease was nearly up, they leased the open sections again. But in 1883, the legislature enacted a law that raised the lease price to four cents per acre, a costly charge for big operators, and in addition the law allowed farmers or other settlers to secure a lease to the open sections for up to ten years. In 1887, a new but similar land law provided that livestock men could buy 160 to 640 acres of unimproved agricultural lands or four sections (2,560 acres) of grazing land for as low as two dollars per acre and take forty years to pay the cost. The laws clearly favored pioneer farmers, and as Murrah indicates, the "introduction of barbed wire complicated the situation." Cattlemen, he writes, "enclosed portions of the public domain," a situation that led farmers to cut fences in order to get to land they had just purchased. But farmers, once having acquired such land, fenced water holes on their property, water sources that ranchers had used for many years, causing cattlemen to respond, further complicating the land issues.[32]

In 1895, the state legislature, as Murrah suggests, "struck a devastating blow at . . . big Texas ranchers." It passed the Four-Section Act, a law allowing prospective settlers to purchase one section of agricultural land at three dollars per acre and three sections of grazing land at one dollar per acre for as little as eighty dollars down and four years to pay. Moreover, the law stated that the buyer/settler must live on the land and "make certain minimum improvements." Such a situation proved impossible for big Texas ranchers. In response to the important law, farmers and farmer-stockmen scrambled for land on the Llano Estacado. Additional laws, or amendments to the Four-Section Act, occurred in 1897 and after the turn of the century.[33]

Cattle raising continued, of course, but several of the huge livestock operations sold out. Others adjusted or went broke. The London-financed Francklyn Land and Cattle Company, which controlled 631,000 acres stretching across the Canadian River and including large parts of Carson and Gray Counties, failed. In the late 1880s, the *Tascosa Pioneer* reported on the company's Diamond F ranges: "The cattle are wasted, scattered, lost, and debts confront a stock-less broken corporation." Byron Price and Fred Rathjen write that the ranch "collapsed almost overnight from the weight of [its] financial burdens" and filed for bankruptcy in 1886.[34]

Other cattlemen quit. The Chicago-based owners of the giant XIT, men who never intended to stay in the cattle business, sold their cattle, horses, and equipment. They marketed the land and often disposed of it in large blocks, dealing away 1.3 million acres between 1901 and 1904 when they moved to shut down their ranching operations.

In 1893, the Iowa- and Illinois-based owners of the troubled IOA Ranch in Lubbock County also quit the volatile business. They marketed their cattle, abandoned leaseholdings, and between 1896 and 1901 sold small tracts of several sections each. Still, the ranch went broke. In 1901, in a foreclosure sale at the Lubbock County courthouse, Herbert L. Kokernot and his uncle John W. Kokernot purchased the remaining one hundred thousand acres.

Owners of the Frying Pan Ranch at Amarillo went in a different direction. By 1893 William H. Bush, son-in-law of Joseph Glidden, had bought out Henry Sanborn and taken over direction of the ranch. Determined to hold on to the land but get out of livestock raising, Bush sold the cattle, horses, and their accoutrements. He planned to plant some crops, including grapes and eucalyptus trees. He soon welcomed, indeed invited, farmers and farmer-stockmen to the Frying Pan, leasing to each on an annual basis four sections under conditions that they protect grass and land, maintain fences, and control noxious weeds and trees. The plan worked, allowing Bush and subsequently his heirs to continue ownership of large portions of the ranch to the present day.

As big ranching operations adjusted to the collapsing cattle boom, the Llano Estacado's two largest cities, Amarillo and Lubbock, got their start. Amarillo came a bit earlier than Lubbock, partly as a result of the Fort Worth and Denver Railroad building through the upper Llano area. Town promoters and speculators helped Amarillo's birth and early growth. Hearing that the big railroad would pass through southern Potter County and turn north through the Panhandle, James T. Berry, a townsite developer working for Colorado City merchants, located a site just below Wild Horse Lake, an important stopping place for drovers trailing cattle herds from the south to Dodge City. Other promoters, one of whom was Henry Sanborn, part owner of the Frying Pan Ranch, challenged Berry and his Colorado City backers with additional townsites.

When the railroad came through in 1887, Berry won out—temporarily. Sanborn, unwilling to quit, backed by his wealthy partner, Joseph Glidden, and aided by a flood in the low-lying area of Berry's town below Wild Horse Lake, got the city's location shifted to his section of land along the rail line and safe from flooding.[35]

Before the flood and shift in location, Berry's Amarillo grew rapidly. Citizens, mostly cowboys, organized Potter County in 1887 and elected W. B. Plemons county judge, James R. Gober sheriff, and other prominent citizens county commissioners. The judge and commissioners held their first meeting in September, and surveyor Henry H. Luckett laid out the town. Less than a year later Amarillo held several stores and saloons, a hotel, a restaurant, law and real estate offices, and about two hundred residents. Soon a newspaper, the *Amarillo Champion*, appeared with H. H. Brooks, a strong-willed Englishman, as publisher.

Yet Sanborn prevailed. He gave away lots; convinced Brooks to publish the paper in his (Sanborn's) addition; built a large, wood-frame, forty-room, yellow-painted hotel; and took timely advantage of the flood, which occurred in the spring of 1889. After the flooded town dried out, citizens put their homes and buildings on skids and moved to higher ground in Sanborn's addition. In 1890, Amarillo's population stood at 482, and Polk Street became the central business district with both general merchandise and specialty stores, saloons, law offices, restaurants, and establishments that catered to the needs of cowboys and cattlemen.[36]

Lubbock's birth, except for the absence of a railroad, mirrored Amarillo's early start. That is, rival promoters sought to build a community on their land, the village shifted its location, and a big hotel played a significant role in founding the town. In brief, Lubbock resulted from a significant amount of human enterprise in the upper Brazos River country, including the growth of the Estacado community and the success of Singer's Yellow House store, both of which attracted pioneer farmers seeking homesteads and businessmen looking for opportunities to open trade. Drovers and cowboys pushing cattle along upper Brazos River draws and an increasing number of travelers in the area represented additional industry. Seeing the activity, Frank E. Wheelock, the young but ambitious manager of the large IOA Ranch, and Rollie Burns, a visionary IOA cowboy, determined to establish a town. With financial help from Dallas speculators, the two IOA employees in 1889 secured land for their community; purchased building materials at Amarillo; and constructed the fancy eighteen-room, two-and-one-half story Nicolett Hotel that on the high, lonesome terrain could be seen from miles away. After construction of the hotel, they invited businessmen and townspeople to take up lots nearby. Soon some fifty people with thirty-eight buildings lived in Lubbock, as Wheelock and Burns called their village, located on the north side of Yellow House Draw in the heart of Lubbock County.[37]

Other promoters and speculators sought their own community that might become the county seat. The most successful of them was Whit E. Rayner, who had previously built a town in Stonewall County. He laid out a settlement in 1890 less than four miles south of Lubbock and below Yellow House Draw. Rayner with several local cattlemen, such as Van Sanders and W. A. Carlisle, and a few speculators, saw their town, South Lubbock, grow. It soon had a population of fifty people, creating a rivalry with Lubbock. Rayner, Wheelock, and their respective backers realized the village—either Lubbock or South Lubbock—that lost the upcoming election in the county seat vote would not survive. To find a solution, they began discussions in June 1890. They met at the big, popular Nicolett Hotel. Near the end of the negotiations in December, Rayner's South Lubbock took the name Monterey, and on December 19, Rayner and several men from Monterey plus Wheelock, Burns, and several others from Lubbock signed an agreement to establish a new town at a separate but nearby location and retain the name of Lubbock for the combined towns. By the end of February 1891, all citizens of the rival communities with their homes and businesses had moved to the new Lubbock, including the large Nicolett Hotel.

Moving the hotel became a spectacular event. Its move attracted many onlookers who watched as workers hauled the building, minus its two-story covered front porch, south across the upper Brazos River just below the junction of the Blackwater and Yellow House streams in present-day Mackenzie Park and then directly to the designated Lubbock County Courthouse Square. For many years, the hotel was a prominent fixture in the city. On March 10, as expected, citizens voted Lubbock the county seat.[38]

Lubbock grew slowly, partly because no railroad ran through Lubbock County and partly because the large IOA Ranch covered the entire southern half of the county. Although ten years after its founding, the community, according to census counts—which cannot always be trusted—held fewer than three hundred people, Lubbock looked as early as 1895 like a busy small town. It contained several stores and mercantile firms, a dentist, six lawyers, a newspaper office, three land agents, a livery stable, the county courthouse and jail, many homes, and two hotels, including the popular and still imposing Nicolett.

Just to the north in Hale County, Plainview challenged Lubbock for leadership on the South Plains. Established in 1887 near a grove of hackberry trees by Z. T. Maxwell, a farmer and sheep raiser from Floyd County, and Edwin Lowden Lowe of Tennessee, Plainview got a post office the same year. It soon became the county seat. Two years later, although without the benefit of a railroad, the community, in the middle of wonderful farming country, counted seventy-five citizens who patronized a hotel, church, and general merchandise store. Part of the town's success related to its proximity to a well-used cattle trail extending from below Yellow House Draw north to Amarillo and the busy cattle-shipping yards at Wild Horse Lake. In 1892, Plainview counted two hotels, a school, newspaper, four churches, and numerous businesses.

In the upper Llano on the Fort Worth and Denver Railroad, a group of speculators led by Robert E. Montgomery in 1887 established Washburn in northwest Armstrong County. The railroad built a section house, depot, and stock pens at the site that had once been part of the AJ Ranch. It also drilled two wells, a double pump station, and a coal chute. The next year, after a short rail line (the Panhandle Railway Company) connected the little town to Panhandle City in Carson County, Washburn boomed, getting a post office in 1888 and becoming a trade center for farmers, ranchers, and neighboring towns.

The town of Panhandle likewise owes its existence to railroads. Established in 1887 as the terminus of the Southern Kansas (Panhandle and Santa Fe) Railway, the town stood among several large ranches.

These horse- and mule-drawn chuck and supply wagons of the JA Ranch were crossing the Red River during an 1898 roundup. Courtesy of Panhandle-Plains Historical Museum

Shortly after its founding as Carson City, it received a post office as Panhandle City and acquired a newspaper (today perhaps the longest active paper in the upper Llano Estacado), and as early as 1888 it held a school, mercantile store, bank, wagon yard, and three saloons. That same year it became the seat of Carson County. Like its sister village, it boomed with the railway extension between Washburn and Panhandle City. A major cattle-shipping point, the town's corrals sometimes held up to sixty-five thousand head of livestock waiting shipment. The unique John Callaghan Hotel hosted distinguished guests as well as gala events. Temple L. Houston, an Oklahoma-based lawyer and son of former Texas governor Sam Houston, visited the town often on legal business. He stayed at the famous hotel while he represented the Santa Fe Railway.

In New Mexico's portion of the Llano Estacado, town building and landholding varied from the Texas side of the 103rd meridian. Ranchers there dominated the High Plains, but the federal government controlled some of the land. As a result, not until after the turn of century, with the exception of some settlers and ranchers at water holes near Portales, Four Lakes, Ranger Lake, and elsewhere, one could not find a remarkable village on the New Mexico side of the Llano. It remained pretty much rangeland, a nearly treeless, mostly flat region under a big, blue sky and stretching off to a far horizon with only occasional shin oaks and cacti to break the ennui. Then, a second wave of farmer-settlers in the late 1890s and after the turn of the century brought new towns, new citizens, and new agricultural enterprises to heaven's harsh tableland in eastern New Mexico and western Texas—the subjects of chapter 8.

Summary

The range-cattle industry's boom years after 1875 represent what western historian Walter Prescott Webb called "perhaps one of the outstanding phenomena in American history."[39] Its cowboys, horses, and cattle created a triad of legendary portions that still thrills the hearts of most rural and many urban Americans. The boom did not last, of course, crippled by such national trends as a downward shift in cattle prices and financial panics in the 1880s and 1890s as well as unpredictable Great Plains weather that produced a rough stretch of cold winters and droughty summers. Overstocked ranges did not help.

About the same time that open-range cattle raising hit its peak, a first wave of farmer-stockmen arrived on the Llano Estacado. Like cattle raisers, they also struggled during the period of financial downturns and the spell of bad weather. When serious droughts in the late 1880s and early 1890s further squeezed profits, farm settlement slowed. Indeed, some early farmer-stockmen in face of drought and other issues abandoned their farms, resulting in a decline in cultivated acres.

After the western cattle industry's shakeout in the early 1890s, a second wave of pioneer farmers began settling the Llano Estacado. More villages appeared, especially along railroads, and citizens began to organize county governments and to seek incorporation of their towns. Although with the arrival of additional farmers and other settlers the population of the Llano increased, the huge mesa, in appearance and character, remained a vast, open land in the 1890s, waiting, one might suggest, additional railroads, land speculators, town promoters, and land-hungry farmers. And when all arrived, they contributed a more settled look to the Llano Estacado, an appearance that continued during the three decades immediately prior to and after World War I.

8

Homesteaders and Townspeople to World War I

From the 1890s, through the nationwide Progressive Era and its reforming spirit before World War I, to the beginning of the Jazz Age in the 1920s, the United States, including the Llano Estacado, witnessed major transformations. Essentially, if oversimplifying, the United States during the 1890s moved from a rural, agrarian nation to an urban, industrial one. New business formations (corporations) and innovative technologies (electric lights, typewriters, elevators, motor cars, use of steel) changed urban life and made new jobs and novel working experiences available and brought many people, including foreign-born citizens, into cities. New York, Boston, Philadelphia, and Chicago led the way, but other cities and smaller urban areas also gained from America's national reordering.

Progressive Era reforms (child labor laws, shortened workdays, more equitable taxation laws among them) influenced Eastern city life and urban employment patterns far more than western Texas and a rural Llano Estacado. During World War I, however, national food and fiber demands placed enormous pressure on Llano farmers and ranchers—indeed, all of American agriculture—to produce ever-more staples to feed and clothe the American nation, its military personnel, and subsequently its allies in Europe and their soldiers. After the war in the 1920s the entire country, including the Llano, after another brief economic downturn to start the decade, witnessed unparalleled affluence and some national "craziness."

For the Llano Estacado, the new era began with sweeping changes. A spate of frightful weather, crashing beef prices, overstocked ranges, and related issues had brought an end to the booming range-cattle industry, transforming it in the early 1890s from high adventure to settled business. As cattle raising shifted further in face of the decade's national financial panic and depression, a growing wave of settlement became an unprecedented rush of farmers and town people to the Llano Estacado. After 1900, population expansion followed in an enormous folk movement, one reminiscent of Americans overrunning Southeast Texas after Stephen F. Austin's initial colonization efforts there in the 1820s.

Pioneer farmers packed into eastern regions of the Llano Estacado. Some moved into land vacated or sold by ranchers. Others purchased land from railroads, land speculators, and town promoters, and the agricultural shift from open-range cattle raising to enclosed ranching and crop farming stepped up. Public land laws that increasingly favored farmers and farmer-stockmen over range-cattle enterprises also played a key role in the agricultural drift on the Llano to farming and ranching within fences.

Moreover, because the State of Texas retained its public lands when it entered the United States, federal land laws did not apply in Texas. Thus,

C. C. Slaughter, in the driver's seat of his converted army ambulance ca. 1900, drove around his ranches in the vehicle until a few years later when he acquired an automobile. Photo from George M. Slaughter Papers, Southwest Collection/ Special Collections Library. Courtesy of David J. Murrah

such national legislative measures as the Homestead Act in 1862, the Timber Culture Act and the Desert Land Act of 1877, and the Timber and Stone Act of 1878, all of which helped make cheap land available to western settlers, were unavailable to Texas pioneers. Rather, in Texas the state gave enormous amounts of land to railroads for construction and maintenance support, and state laws governed land acquisition and use. Some of the first such laws governing Llano land favored cattlemen and big ranching operators. Despite such brilliant studies—we think—as Major John Wesley Powell's 1879 *Report on the Arid Regions of the United States*, legislative favor in Texas changed to farmers. Powell wanted an end to the rigid system of rectangular surveys as suggested in the Homestead Act. Grazing land, he wrote, should be made available to cattlemen and other stockmen in twenty-five-hundred-acre units, and landowners should cooperatively develop the scarce water supplies. Texas farmers, oriented to smaller units in a humid east, opposed in their state any political action to implement Powell's plan. The Texas legislature agreed and, recognizing the political clout of an expanding farmer population, passed the Four-Section Act and its related laws.

Another factor in the agricultural shift to crop farming was the 1902 Texas Supreme Court case *Ketner v. Rogan*. For many years, cattlemen had rented grazing sections from the state for five-year periods and had released the land before the contracts expired. This "lapse-leasing" system blocked settlers, especially farmers, from securing property. As David J. Murrah describes it, J. E. "Ed" Ketner, a settler in Lynn County, "waited for the lease on C. C. Slaughter's Tahoka Lake Ranch to expire" so that he might purchase some land there. "When he learned that Slaughter had renewed the lease prior to its expiration, Ketner [in 1901] filed suit . . . against the Texas land commissioner," Charles Rogan, and Slaughter. A year later, he won the case. After the court's decision, grazing land leased from the state became available for purchase before it could be leased again. Thus, when large blocks of leases expired after 1902, hundreds of thousands of acres became available to land-hungry Texas farmers.[1]

Pioneer farming proved no easy proposition. Some of the first West Texas farmers and farmer-stockmen for various reasons were unable to take full advantage of the new farm technology with its innovative machinery coming out of Chicago, Saint Louis, and elsewhere. But, slowly at first in the 1890s and then with greater rapidity, they adopted large, efficient windmills, horse- or mule-drawn planting and harvesting equipment and plows, and near the turn of the century huge traction engines and then tractors. Before then, breaking the tough prairie sod required great physical strength and special plows with shares strong enough to cut through the thickly matted roots of grass and the some-times "gummy" soils. Finding it difficult and time-consuming work, most farmers tended to break out small areas, get them planted, and then continue to plow up new land as time and weather permitted. In addition, they might raise small numbers of livestock, including cattle, sheep, pigs, and chickens. They were essentially subsistence farmers. Drought, hordes of grasshoppers, economic depression, declining agri-cultural prices, and a shortage of cash all weighed heavily on such early farmer-stockmen. Indeed, in the upper Llano and Panhandle "cultivated property," write B. Byron Price and Frederick J. Rathjen, "declined by about 9,000 acres during the decade, as settlers, broken and defeated by the elements, abandoned their claims wholesale."[2]

For those who stayed, living conditions often remained as bleak as the natural elements. Some pioneer families in the first wave of settlement in the 1880s lived in tents or in wagon boxes (such as three of the first four families at Estacado in Lubbock County) until they had dug a home in the side of a hill or constructed a house built halfway into the ground with a crude frame structure completed above the dugout portion. Other people, especially in the 1890s, built some homes from blocks of sod (four by twelve by eighteen inches usually) cut from the grassy earth. They made roofs with poles upon which they placed additional sod blocks. Although warm in winter and cool in summer, the dugouts and sod houses were small, dirty, and after rainfall, often filled with mud. Some people built a flimsy wooden shack and covered it with tarpaper. As soon as possible, families constructed a frame house.

Pioneer farm families faced an endless round of chores. Men handled the heavy labor of breaking sod and planting, cultivating, and harvest-ing the major crops. Women labored ceaselessly at household duties of

Depicted here is a pioneer farmer's barn of sod with a grass roof plus the oxen he and his son used to break the tough prairie sod in the 1890s. Courtesy of Panhandle-Plains Historical Museum

all kinds, and, among those families who raised milch cows (such as in the German folk colony in Martin County), they often did the milking. Children took responsibility for certain farm chores, such as tending cattle, horses, hogs, chickens, and other livestock that might be found at the farmstead.

Water and fuel were often difficult to obtain. The Llano held few trees except in its draws and canyons from where early settlers could haul wood in wagons. Some settlers, if living near railroads, secured coal for fuel. Water was a different problem. In drought years, as in 1892–94, 1898, 1902, and 1907, creeks and playas dried up, forcing homesteaders to haul water in barrels from distant sources. Eventually, they drilled wells and erected windmills, but too often that proved a haphazard proposition.

In 1890, for example, thirty-two-year-old sheep raiser John Barclay "J. B." McGill, a Lampasas, Texas, newspaperman–turned–wool grower who had recently secured a ranch thirty miles north of Midland, needed to dig a well. He hired well drillers out of Midland, but they bored down to a clay base without finding water. They moved to another location on the ranch and again failed to strike water. McGill himself then tried to hand-dig a well, but he had similar results. Finally, in a fourth effort, this time again with hired well drillers, McGill's workers found water but not in amounts large enough to support the four thousand sheep he planned to move from his ranch near Stanton. Eventually, he and his new bride moved to northern Mexico to raise sheep.[3]

In the early 1890s, when McGill desperately drilled for water north of Midland, most of Texas west of the 98th meridian was in a state of drought. In an attempt to ameliorate the dry conditions, the US government hired R. G. Dyrenforth, a self-proclaimed "general" and rainmaker, to produce rain near Midland. In August 1891, Dyrenforth, who also called himself a "concussionist," and his team unloaded from boxcars of the Texas and Pacific Railway such items as dynamite, gunpowder, cannons, kites, and balloons. Near the edge of town, they set about launching the explosives into the sky, expecting the cannon blasts, booms, and explosions to bring down water in the next day or two. No rain fell, but the exploding dynamite and gunpowder set off several fires in the dry, Midland County grass that subsistence farmers needed for their livestock.[4]

To supplement their subsistence-farming life, many of the earliest pioneers, including those living north and east of Midland, gathered bleached bison bones. The bones, which sometimes sold for six dollars a wagon load, produced a bit of extra profit, especially when drought or other maladies created crop failure. The death of millions of animals during the great bison kill-off of the 1870s left uncounted tons of skeletons on the grassy plains at a time when Eastern manufacturers noted that bones could be made into good fertilizer and used for other products. In places where hunters "got a stand" a few years earlier, bones might be scattered thickly over a ten-acre plot. Pioneer families, adults and children, male and female, collected bones and hauled them to a railroad town (a "bonehead") from where others placed them on train cars for shipment east. A few bone piles awaiting shipment reached huge sizes in length and width and height. "By the late 1890s," according to John T. Becker, "bone pickers received between twenty and twenty-two dollars a ton" for bones. Soon, professional freighters hired out to transport

For extra income, early settlers gathered bison bones from the Llano Estacado prairies and delivered them to railroad sidings known as "Bone Heads." Courtesy of Southwest Collection/Special Collections Library

bones to rail tracks at Amarillo on the Fort Worth and Denver Railroad or at Colorado City on the Texas and Pacific and then carry supplies back home. For some families facing a deep financial crunch, bone gathering kept them on the farm. Some observers, concludes Becker, "have estimated that during the boom years—the 1880s and 1890s—of the bone trade, railroads shipped half a million tons of bison bones out of West Texas, which put $3 million into the pockets of early pioneers."[5]

Despite such financial help, pioneer farming on the Llano Estacado sometimes proved to be overwhelming. In some cases, emotional-psychological issues added to the difficult plight. As explained by Panhandle historian L. F. Sheffy, early Panhandle–South Plains farmer-stockmen came from a settled world characterized by levels of comfort and services that did not exist in their new environment. They may have expected to regain their comfortable standard of living quickly, but many, especially women, were disappointed by the crudity of their new homes and by their failure to re-create the world they had left behind. As a result, some

The road between Post in Garza County and Lubbock featured a difficult climb up the Caprock Escarpment. Courtesy of Southwest Collection/Special Collections Library

people gave up and left their homesteads to settle in town or to return to the region from which they had come. The three families at Estacado living in tents left for home after only a few months on the cold, windy High Plains.[6]

But early settlement was not all bleak. Life in the farm and cattle communities of the Llano Estacado included entertainment, if spartan, of various kinds: dances, horse racing with lots of betting, parties, and holiday celebrations among them. Dances, as noted, might occur at the big ranches, and in the cattle country cowboys at dances always outnumbered females by significant margins, thus keeping women and older girls on the dance floor much of the night. Town folks held similar dances in the courthouse or another large building and sometimes in homes.

In March 1903, the *Lubbock Avalanche* ran an article in which a young woman described her experience at a dance on the Llano Estacado. She had just arrived from the East, the paper indicated, and she was unfamiliar with western-style dancing. Her first dance at the affair was a loud and energetic quadrille (a forerunner of the modern square dance). Her

Overland freighting during the early stages of Llano settlement was an important business that required large teams and big wagons. Courtesy of Panhandle-Plains Historical Museum

partner, she noted, was a young single cowboy whose girlfriend watched from the sideline. As she explained in the newspaper: "It was with many misgivings in spite of my partner's assurance that he would pull me through, that I took my place in the dance.

> Hark y partners.
> Rights the same.

So far, I bowed as did the rest.

> Balance you all.

With the plunge of a maddened steer, my partner came toward me. I smothered a scream as I was seized and swung around like a bag of meal. Before I could get my breath, I was pushed out to answer to:

> First lady to the right;
> Swing the man that stole the sheep,
> Now the one that hauled it home,
> Now the one that ate the meat,
> Now the one that "gnawed the bones."

Not being well acquainted with the private histories of the men in the set, I was at a little disadvantage, but I was seized, swung, and passed on to the next, until I finally arrived breathless at the starting point.

> First gent, swing yer opposite pardner,
> Then yer turtle dove.
> Again yer opposite pardner,
> And now yer own true love.

I blushed in spite of myself at so publicly passing as my partner's "turtle dove" and "own true love," while his sweetheart over in the corner, transfixing me with a jealous glare, saw no humor whatever in the situation. Again came the command:

> First couple to the right,
> Cage the bird, three hands round.

I found myself in the center of a circle formed by my partner and the second couple and then exchanged places with my partner at the call:

> Bird hop out and crane hop in,
> Three hands around and go it again.
> All men left: back to the partner,
> And grand right and left.
> Come to yer partner once and a half
> Yaller hammer right and jaybird left,
> Meet yer partner and all chaw hay,
> You know where and I don't care,
> Seat your partner in the old arm chair.

By this time, feeling quite bruised and battered, I was ready for most any kind of a chair.[7]

If the newspaper and the woman's description were correct, and surely they were, community dances on the Llano Estacado must have been rollicking and lively affairs. They were also popular, common, and widespread. With women outnumbered or even absent on some of the isolated ranches, cowboys sometimes danced with other cowboys, and even at mixed dances, some cowboys tied a ribbon around their right arm to indicate that they would dance the female part.

Other forms of entertainment existed. In cattle country, horse racing became a popular event and, like dancing, attracted people living miles away from the race site, usually a flat section of ground in a pasture where organizers had laid out a temporary track. In town, parties of various kinds were popular, many of them simple events that brought people together to visit and eat or sometimes to play games. Holiday celebrations, especially Christmas and New Year's Eve in winter and the Fourth of July in summer were popular. Independence Day festivities changed over time as towns grew. Eventually, some included parades, speeches, public luncheons, and other events such as horse racing and

Amarillo's lower Polk Street (downtown) in 1895 when Potter County held about five hundred inhabitants. Courtesy of Panhandle-Plains Historical Museum

dances. Picnics also brought people together, as did short excursions to some delightful site: beautiful Silver Falls in Crosby County attracted picnickers from the time that Hank Smith first settled above the falls in Blanco Canyon in the 1870s. As settlement and population increased, bigger towns such as Amarillo found citizens using larger buildings (or constructing "opera houses") for public lectures, traveling minstrel and vaudeville shows, theater presentations (sometimes by local thespians), and end-of-the-school-year presentations by students.

In October 1889, for example, J. B. McGill, the young sheep raiser mentioned earlier, rode into Midland from his "Staked Plains" ranch, as he called it, near Stanton to attend a school and community "spelling match." Once there, he said in a letter to his distant cousin, he "did not accept the invitation to take in the exercises, which was extended" to all audience members while older students were "on the floor." In what McGill called "the juvenile class a five-year-old boy, said to be the 'worst boy in town,' spelled the last word given out" and thereby won the contest over "forty-nine of his classmates." While McGill reflected that "spellers, like poets, 'were born, not made,'" the young spelling bee champion for a month would now wear a medal so designating his honor.[8]

By 1905, South Polk Steet in Amarillo, because of such fine mansions as the Bivins home and its attractive esplanade with a rail trolley to downtown, had become known as "Silk Stocking Row." Courtesy of Panhandle-Plains Historical Museum

Melissa Dora Oliver-Eakle and
Molly D. Abernathy

Two of the most prominent women in pioneer days of the Llano Estacado were Melissa Dora Oliver-Eakle (1860–1931) in Amarillo and Molly Abernathy (1866–1960) in Lubbock. Both married twice, both became large landowners and businesswomen of distinction, and both must be judged "modern women."

Oliver-Eakle was born in Alabama. In 1879, she graduated from Georgia Female Seminary in Macon and five years later married William Oliver, principal stockholder of one of the South's largest textile concerns. In 1890, she visited Amarillo, where her brothers operated Callaway Brothers, a general merchandise store. After her husband's death the next year, she returned to Amarillo to visit and a few years later moved there permanently.

Molly Abernathy was born in Hood County, Texas. She attended AddRan College (forerunner to Texas Christian University) in Thorpe Springs and spent the summers on her parents' ranch in Erath County. In 1886, she married James W. Jarrott, an ambitious but restless schoolteacher who became an attorney, state legislator, merchant, and would-be rancher. They had four children. In 1901, Molly and James with their growing family moved to the Lubbock area to establish a ranch, and a year later, a hired gunman shot and killed the unarmed James Jarrott.

In Potter County, Melissa Dora Oliver-Eakle became one of Amarillo's most influential and colorful entrepreneurs. Upon arriving in Amarillo in 1895, she went to work for her brothers and not long afterward took over management of the large firm, which later became the Amarillo Mercantile Company. Melissa in 1902 married O. M. Eakle, a director of Amarillo National Bank. They had one daughter. Eakle died in 1914, but Melissa had already begun contributing large personal funds (she was independently wealthy) to the city to encourage urban growth. She platted a new subdivision, the Oliver-Eakle Addition, extending the city to the south, which included land that later held Amarillo College and Memorial Park. In the 1920s, she built the ten-story Oliver-Eakle

To hide that she was a woman in a man's world, Melissa Dora Oliver-Eakle went by M. D. Oliver-Eakle in her business dealings after 1900. Courtesy of Panhandle-Plains Historical Museum

Building, one of Amarillo's first skyscrapers. It became the Barfield Building in 1947. "To help disguise the fact that she was a woman in a business world ruled by men," write local historians, she often used the name M. D. Oliver-Eakle. This highly successful woman was a generous philanthropist, providing money for her church, for city parks, for cultural activities, and for local education.

Meanwhile, in Lubbock, Molly D. Abernathy's life and work mirrored that of her Amarillo counterpart. After her husband's death, Molly stayed on land the couple had claimed under the 1895 Four-Section Act, slowly increased her land to sixteen sections, expanded her cattle herd to four hundred registered Herefords, and raised her children. In 1905, she married Monroe G. Abernathy, a pioneer real estate operator, and turned to real estate investing. She moved to Lubbock, took over operation of the old Nicolett Hotel for a time, built a large business office building downtown, and constructed an attractive home overlooking some beautiful topography, Yellow House Canyon, in east Lubbock. As a philanthropist, Molly gave Lubbock land that became Mackenzie Park.

Melissa Dora Oliver-Eakle and Molly D. Abernathy came from rural backgrounds but achieved success as urban businesswomen. They engaged in real estate ventures, built downtown buildings, and gave large sums of money to support charitable causes in their respective cities. They supported women's suffrage, and they were both vocal leaders in the early Progressive Era's temperance crusade and later in the Prohibition movement of the 1920s. Both were community builders and influential shapers of the developing Llano Estacado.

Pioneer life was not all recreation and hard, physical labor. Town and county politics intruded into cultural and economic activities. As ranchers gave way to farmers and other settlers, county governments needed to be established. The state attached politically unorganized counties to a neighboring county already operating. As the local population increased, however, the recent arrivals in one constituency after another chose to organize their own government, disengage the older political connection, select a town for their county seat, elect administrators and officials, and begin with a fresh county entity.

The process worked well for the most part, but sometimes county seat struggles—little political wars—occurred. They could be disastrous, including in some cases the disappearance of towns. It happened at Estacado, the seat of Crosby County. A prosperous new town of nearly two hundred residents in 1890, it contained a little college called Central Plains Academy and, as one visitor noted, "two general stores, a hotel, a lawyer's office, a newspaper, the county courthouse, and a [Quaker] meeting house which doubled for church and school." It lost a vote for county seat in 1891 and soon disappeared. Emma, the new county seat located east of Estacado and closer to the center of Crosby County, served as the political heart of the county for twenty years before losing in 1911 a county seat election to Crosbyton. Emma soon disappeared beneath area cotton fields.[9]

Although railroads had not yet reached Lubbock, the village was beginning
to show considerable activity as settlers moved into the surrounding area.
Courtesy of Southwest Collection/Special Collections Library

Clearly, then, in the early twentieth century the Llano Estacado enjoyed a population boom. Farmers rushed onto the Llano claiming
homesteads whenever good farming land became available, but especially in the eastern counties from Floyd and Hale south through Lynn,
Dawson, and Terry Counties. Farmers wherever they landed on the
Llano raised a variety of crops, of course, but in the eastern counties
especially they soon turned to cotton production. By 1905, growers in
Floyd, Hale, Lubbock, Lynn, Crosby, Dawson, and Hockley Counties
had turned to cotton, and entrepreneurs soon built gins to process the
crop. Before World War I, although grain sorghums, wheat, and alfalfa
remained the more abundant of many farm commodities grown in the
region, cotton became a major cash crop and with gins stimulated local
business and town growth.

Likewise, early in the new century, railroads spread through the
Llano Estacado, also spurring and facilitating population growth. Local
boosters in Amarillo got the Pecos Valley Railroad (eventually part of
the Santa Fe system) to build a line connecting Roswell and Amarillo.
Railroad builders completed it in 1898. The Choctaw, Oklahoma and
Texas (Rock Island) Railroad reached Amarillo from the east in 1903

and continued west. In 1908, after economic difficulties related to a national financial panic of 1907, it reached Wildorado in Oldham County before pushing west from there to Tucumcari, New Mexico, in 1910. The Santa Fe Railway pushed its tracks south from Amarillo to Plainview in 1907 and then to Lubbock in 1909. Wishing to connect its web of West Texas rail lines with its roads farther east, the Santa Fe built a line (the "Coleman Cutoff") from Coleman County through Lubbock in 1911 and northwest from there. In 1913, it reached rapidly growing Clovis, New Mexico, which had begun on the Pecos Valley line in 1906.

Various short lines appeared on the Llano Estacado, and several "paper railroads"—lines planned but not built—encouraged settlement. After the turn of the century in 1900, nearly every town and its boosters understood the importance of railroads, which could make or unmake a community. Railroads could lower transportation costs and shorten travel time for both people and commodities. Leaders in every town wanted one, for railroads, writes Don L. Hofsommer, "had an immediate and dramatic effect on the area [they] served." Matthew C. Vaughn and Samuel D. McCloud, for example, in 1908 platted the town of Virginia

Lonnie Williams, who farmed near Slide in Lubbock County, began freighting supplies from Amarillo through Plainview to Lubbock. Courtesy of Lynette Wilson

City deep in the heart of Bailey County. They laid out streets, including a lakeshore drive, parks, and land for schools, for the "downtown" area, and for a library. They brought in a two-story hotel in which prospective lot buyers might stay until their homes could be built. And they began grading tracks for a railroad they called the Denver and San Antonio Railroad. No railway came, and after four years the town collapsed.[10]

Some of the railroads experienced diverse ownership and went through several name changes. In 1909, the Acme, Red River & Northern Railway became the Quanah, Acme & Pacific and a few years later built tracks southwest from Quanah in Hardeman County to Floydada in Floyd County. The Crosbyton–South Plains Railroad, chartered in 1910 and built from Lubbock to Crosbyton, became, five years later, the South Plains and Santa Fe Railway. The Santa Fe system built a line from Lubbock to Seagraves in 1918, and although it still operated in 2022, it had gone through a number of different ownerships and identities. Likewise, the Santa Fe system built a railway line in 1925 from Lubbock to Bledsoe on the Texas–New Mexico border. Bledsoe for a short time was one of the largest cattle-shipping points in Texas. Later, owners cut the line back to Whiteface. Railroad men built a line south out of Slaton through Wilson and Tahoka in Lynn County to Lamesa. In New Mexico, the Atchison, Topeka and Santa Fe Railroad—hardly a short line, granted—skirted the northwestern edge of the Llano, but with a major depot and shipping point first at Springer in Colfax County and after 1901 at Tucumcari in Quay County, it became important for Llano residents and livestock operators. Farther south, the 110-mile-long Texas–New Mexico Railway, completed in 1930, connected Lovington, New Mexico, and oil fields in the region with the Texas and Pacific Railway at Monahans, Texas.

In Andrews County, the Llano Estacado, Mexico and Gulf Railroad (LEM&G), one of the "paper railroads," encouraged the growth of a community at Shafter Lake, a permanent little playa. Although the line was never built, boosters, led by James T. Cumley, editor of the *Shafter Lake Herald*, promoted the line with gusto, claiming it would run from Dalhart in the Texas Panhandle south through the heart of the Llano Estacado and eventually to the Gulf of Mexico. Cumley's efforts inspired the establishment in 1907 of a town, also called Shafter Lake, at the site.

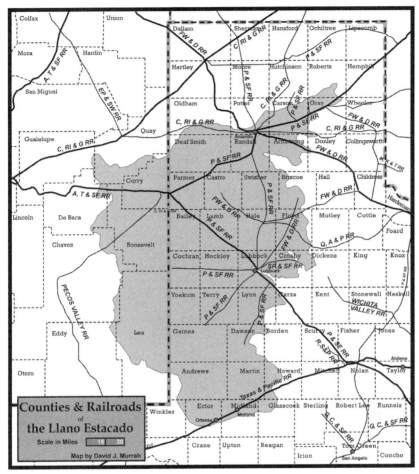

Courtesy of David J. Murrah

In 1910, the town may have included five hundred citizens plus a bank, church, schoolhouse, general store, blacksmith shop, and small hotel. After losing a close election to Andrews in 1910 for location of the county seat, the town of Shafter Lake declined and disappeared. Only a cemetery and what is left of the saline lake remain at the former townsite.[11]

Elsewhere, a number of German settlements (colonies) appeared. About ten miles west of the German Catholic Grelton-Marienfeld-Stanton community, the Texas and Pacific Railway established Germania about 1881. Some forty Lutheran families from Saxony settled there. Later known as Paul, it had disappeared by 1969. Father Joseph Reisdorff became a major figure in establishing German Catholic communities in Texas. In a general sense, he purchased tracts of land, brought in German Catholic settlers from the Midwest, founded a church, saw the community through its initial years, and then moved on to repeat the process in another location. On the Llano Estacado, Reisdorff founded Nazareth in Castro County in 1902, Umbarger in Randall County in 1909, and helped establish Slaton in Lubbock County in 1911. Four years later, German Lutherans joined the Catholic colonists in Slaton. Germans from Fort Wayne, Indiana, founded the community of Rhea in Parmer County about 1910. Their little village on the New Mexico–Texas border developed on a part of the former XIT Ranch. In 1923 German Catholics made up the bulk of the people who founded Pep in Hockley County. The German colonists near Pep settled on forty-two thousand acres of subdivided ranchlands.[12]

Like the German communities, towns and villages appeared from one end of the High Plains to the other, and most of the established towns increased in size and activity. Lubbock's population, for example, rose from less than 300 residents in 1900 to 1,938 in 1910. Amarillo grew from 1,442 people in 1900 to nearly 10,000 inhabitants in 1910 and 15,494 ten years later. Clovis, founded only four years earlier, held a population

Twice a week, during most months between 1905 and 1910, caravans of land buyers from the Midwest got off a train at the Santa Fe depot in Amarillo, boarded automobiles or wagons, and visited prospective land sites on the Llano Estacado on tours led by realtors. Courtesy of Ray Franks and Jay Ketelle

Hugh traction engine breaks out sod in 1906 with prospective land buyers watching with great interest. Courtesy of Panhandle-Plains Historical Museum

3,255 in 1910. Plainview, larger than Lubbock in the first two decades of the new century, began to refer to itself as "The Queen City of the Plains." And Midland and Odessa, key railroad and marketing towns on the lower Llano, also enjoyed population growth, albeit at a slower rate until the discovery of oil there in the 1920s.

Town promoters played key roles in settlement of the Llano Estacado. They secured large tracts of land, advertised—often in the Midwest—the land's value as farm property, brought prospective buyers to the Llano via railroads, and arranged for the sale/purchase of the land and establishment of nearby towns. Railroads also got involved. The Santa Fe, for example, wanted and needed customers living near its tracks; therefore, on two Fridays a month it gathered folks from the Midwest and hauled them to Amarillo, a town of approximately 10,000 inhabitants in 1910. At the Santa Fe depot in the growing city, realtors and land speculators picked up the prospective settlers, placed them in big touring cars—such as the fancy, seven-passenger Pope-Toledo—or in horse-drawn buggies, and took them to available land on the wide prairies.[13]

W. P. Soash proved to be one of the most successful land agents and town promoters. Born in Iowa in 1877, Soash traveled much, worked at a variety of jobs, and gained experience in colonizing lands in the Dakotas. In Texas in 1906, he secured thirty thousand acres of XIT land, built a town on it, and resold the land in smaller tracts to settlers at good profit. In 1908, he bought one hundred thousand acres of Christopher C. Slaughter's Running Water Ranch northwest of Plainview, established the town of Olton, and over time disposed of the property to farmers and townspeople from the Midwest. The very next year, 1909, working again with Slaughter, he secured two hundred thousand acres of the Long S Ranch, laid out and organized the town of Soash about twenty miles north of Big Spring, and moved the headquarters of his business to the new town, which in fact proved an elaborate one for a pioneer community. He built a bank, a hotel, a feed yard, and other installations for the new settlers. While Soash sold plenty of land, this time his town did not prosper and after a short time disappeared.[14]

Amid all the village and town growth, sheep and cattle ranching did not end. Sheep operations remained successful in some southern and western stretches of the Llano Estacado, and sheep feeding operations on the South Plains and around Lubbock kept Lubbock County among those areas in the state with large sheep populations into the 1930s. In Midland and Ector Counties, John Scharbauer, who had come to Texas from New York in 1880, developed a large sheep operation in the 1890s. Indeed, by 1892, although now developing a cattle operation, he had become one of the largest sheep ranchers in the state. After encouraging his brother Christian and his family, including Christian's son Clarence, to come to Midland, John's larger Scharbauer family in 1895 abandoned sheep for cattle. Their Scharbauer Cattle Company, which Clarence later managed with great success, maintained headquarters in Midland but spread through Midland and Ector Counties and into southern New Mexico. Scharbauer City in northeastern Ector County took its name from the family's extensive ranching operations in the area.[15]

Cattle ranching continued and to some extent increased in western and northwestern parts of the Llano in Texas and on the plains of eastern New Mexico. In the Hockley and Cochran Counties, Texas, area between and around the Muleshoe Sandhills and Lea-Yoakum Dunes some huge, late-developing ranching enterprises took hold. Here, in what some ranching historians call "Texas's Last Frontier," David M. DeVitt, Christopher C. Slaughter, and F. G. "Fount" Oxsheer, among others, established cattle ranches on as-yet-unsettled land or property that had once been part of the XIT. They drilled wells; built fences; brought in purebred bulls, especially Herefords, to upgrade their Longhorn stock; struggled in the courts over land issues; engaged in old-fashioned, western fence-cutting wars; and in the 1930s some of them, the DeVitt family and a few of the Slaughter heirs, got more than rich after wildcatters discovered oil in the area (a few good oil wells, according to Texas folklore, will make cattle ranching profitable).

DeVitt, an Eastern newspaperman–turned–Texas rancher, raised sheep with his brother Phillip. They were in the Midland and Howard Counties area soon after the Texas and Pacific Railway came through Big Spring and Midland. By 1890, DeVitt, now married with children, had moved to San Angelo and become one of the town's leading citizens. With a few minority partners, including W. H. Flato Jr. of Kansas City, DeVitt through lease and purchase established his large Mallet Ranch in 1895 in the southwestern part of Hockley County. About fifty thousand acres of the big ranch stretched across both sides of dry and sandy Sulphur Draw, a piece of grazing land that did not attract farmers in the 1890s. Indeed, not until the 1920s, when some of the large ranching operations became farms to produce wheat and cotton, did Hockley and Cochran Counties receive enough people to establish local governments and organize the counties.[16]

Slaughter's Lazy S Ranch, established in 1898, covered nearly all of Cochran County and a good portion of Hockley County. It included some 246,699 acres, and through lease he added more. He brought his oldest son, George, over from the Long S Ranch to manage the Lazy S, or Whiteface, Ranch, a property he developed to ensure (he hoped) the financial future of his wife, children, and grandchildren. George Slaughter trailed some mixed Longhorn stock from the Long S and on the Lazy S bred them with Herefords. For a brief time between 1897 and 1899, the Slaughters used two famous Hereford bulls, Ancient Briton and Sir Bredwell, on the Lazy S and then shipped them to Roswell, New Mexico, where George oversaw the company's Hereford breeding-farm and hay-production operations.[17]

F. G. Oxsheer, from a Central Texas cotton-producing family, turned as a youth to cattle trailing and ranching. With others he invested in land and livestock ventures, one of which before the 1880s cattle-industry crash extended from Gail in Borden County onto the Llano Estacado. After the collapse, he assembled, as others have written, "a patchwork ranch empire stretching from Tahoka Lake in Lynn County to the New Mexico border in Cochran County." Eventually, he held cattle on one and a half million acres. Yet the long drought of the late 1880s and early 1890s caused financial havoc, and Oxsheer turned to his friend and distant relative Christopher C. Slaughter for assistance. Slaughter backed Oxsheer, and the two cattle kings built a huge, successful empire on Cochran and Hockley grazing lands. By 1900, however, Oxsheer had determined to leave the Llano Estacado and go to Mexico. He sold his interests to Slaughter.[18]

Unlike the close Oxsheer-Slaughter relationship, DeVitt and Slaughter found themselves at great odds. As explained by ranching historian David J. Murrah, Slaughter through some questionable procedures had by 1899 "obtained contracts to buy more than 50,000 acres of land that [DeVitt's] Mallet Ranch was leasing" in Hockley County, land the state had set aside for monetary support of schools in other counties (counties would receive proceeds from the sale of such land). DeVitt and Flato objected to the Slaughter acquisition and separately filed suits to prevent Slaughter's purchase. A legal "war" followed. Slaughter won at first, but DeVitt's group countered by buying, or seeking to buy, the school land they were leasing. Slaughter ignored the DeVitt and Flato purchase negotiations and, when the DeVitt lease expired in June 1903, directed his cowboys to move onto the land and build a fence.[19]

DeVitt again turned to the courts, but he also ordered his cowboys to cut the Slaughter fence. Lazy S cowboys rebuilt it and then found it cut again. Five more times through November and December 1903, according to Murrah, Slaughter's cowboys repaired the fence. Cowboys from both ranches began carrying guns, and George Slaughter wrote to his father:

"I think [one of the cowboys] thought he might be called to fight any time." In the meanwhile, the court fight continued through district and federal courts and finally the Court of Appeals in New Orleans in 1905. In the end, DeVitt and Flato got their way, but Slaughter, who pulled out of the contested property, still controlled huge portions of Cochran and Hockley Counties. The ranchers and their heirs continued to raise cattle in the area into the 1930s when wildcatters discovered oil and altered life for nearly all residents of the two late-developing counties.[20]

As DeVitt and Slaughter battled over territory near the New Mexico border, land speculators, farmer-stockmen, town promoters, and others together with the extension of railroads changed other sections of the Llano Estacado. C. W. Post, for example, a wealthy and idealistic American breakfast-drink (Postum) and breakfast-cereal (Grape-Nuts) manufacturer, secured large tracts of land (perhaps 250,000 acres) in western Garza and eastern Lynn Counties to sell in smaller parcels to

Eighteen men and sixty-two horses and mules break out sod on L. E. Cowling's land east of Canyon City, ca. 1906, as townspeople look on. Courtesy of Panhandle-Plains Historical Museum

Wheat and cotton were not the only Llano Estacado crops, as this large field of oats standing shocked illustrates. Courtesy of Panhandle-Plains Historical Museum

farmer-settlers. Fascinated with the elusive American ideal of independent, yeoman farmers, he and his agents divided his holdings into 160-acre farms. Workers, according to his plan, then drilled a well, erected a windmill, and built a home and barn on the property as agents sold the ready-made farm with a small down payment. Post financed the balance through his Double U Company. In the 1910s, Post sold his "improved farms" to hundreds of settlers and at the same time developed the town of Post City in Garza County.[21]

Farther to the northwest, rancher and banker George W. Littlefield became, like Post, a land colonizer. In 1901, he had purchased the southern, or Yellow House, division of the XIT Ranch and a decade later, seeing the large number of farmer-settlers arriving on the Llano Estacado, began to sell Lamb and Hockley County property. By this time, the Santa Fe Railway had cut through his ranchland, and, accordingly, his agents established the town of Littlefield along its tracks, created the Littlefield Lands Company, and over time sold some 310,000 acres of land to twentieth-century pioneers.[22]

Most of the early farm settlers on the Llano Estacado practiced subsistence farming. They raised horses, of course, a few cows perhaps, chickens, and pigs. They planted crops, such as grain sorghum, hay, and Johnson grass, to feed their livestock and raised corn, wheat, and a variety of vegetables to feed themselves. They sold or traded surpluses in town for goods they could not produce themselves.

Nonetheless, very early in the farmer-settlement phase of the Llano Estacado, some agriculturalists turned to cotton. Such a shift seemed natural, for many Llano settlers came from cotton-growing backgrounds in Central and East Texas, and some growers just east of the Llano had with success experimented with cotton. On the Llano before 1903, S. S. Rush in Lubbock County harvested forty acres of cotton. In 1905, cotton growers in Lubbock, Hale, Floyd, Crosby, Hockley, and Lynn Counties planted cotton, and before 1915 cotton became an important part of the South Plains economy. Cotton gins followed, and between 1900 and 1909 all the cotton-producing counties of the South Plains counted a gin or two in their leading cities.

As cotton agriculture spread through the farm and ranch country of the Llano Estacado, town builders sought a college for their communities. The little college Central Plains Academy at Estacado in Crosby County had lasted only two years. The school at Stanton, Our Lady of Mercy, which opened in 1894, attracted secondary students far more than college undergraduates. Lockney Christian College, located at tiny Lockney in Floyd County and founded in 1894 by such Church of Christ members as the John Baker family, struggled for membership. In 1897, the surveyor Willis D. Twichell with the intellectual bon vivant James D. Hamlin established Amarillo College near downtown in the Potter County seat, but always on the edge of bankruptcy, it closed in 1910.

In the meanwhile, at Plainview the Nazarene Church in 1907 founded Central Plains Holiness College. It was impressive with separate dormitories for men and women and a large, four-story building with twenty-seven rooms and an enrollment of more than two hundred students. It did not succeed financially, and the church sold the buildings to the

Methodist Church, South in 1909. The Methodists renamed the school Seth Ward College, a two-year institution. Fires that destroyed its buildings in 1914 and 1916 forced the little school to close.[23]

Also in Plainview, at the time the dominant community on the Llano Estacado south of Amarillo, Baptist theological officials in 1908 established Wayland Baptist College. It came about as a result of a gift of ten thousand dollars and twenty-five acres of land from James Henry Wayland and his wife. Two years later, the school, although its administrative-classroom building was still under construction, offered its first classes. Wayland Baptist University, its promotional literature suggested, was in 2022 the oldest college in continuous operation on the Llano.

Technically, the Wayland Baptist argument may be correct, but in 1909 the Texas legislature established West Texas Normal College (WT) in Canyon City (Canyon), a town of about fourteen hundred residents and the seat of Randall County. The teacher-training school opened in 1910 east of the downtown area on forty acres of pastureland dominated by prairie dogs and cattle. Some 227 students attended classes the first semester. In terms of enrollment, the college grew slowly in its early years, at least for its fall and spring terms. Each summer, however, a large number of teachers who wanted to complete their degrees enrolled at WT, as students had come to call their little school. A fire destroyed its first building, but after restoration, the main administrative-classroom building held eighty-five rooms. In 1916 it was the largest academic building in Texas.[24]

The establishment of the teacher-education college in Canyon encouraged other West Texans, including those in Lubbock and Amarillo, to secure an agricultural college—perhaps a branch of Texas A&M—in the region. Both the legislature and scheming Governor James "Pa" Ferguson agreed, and in February 1917 a bill providing for a West Texas A&M College became law. Ferguson created a locating committee with himself as a member, and after it completed a search for a community to host the new college, the committee, Ferguson announced, had selected Abilene. But shortly afterward, other committee members realized that Ferguson was wrong. The committee in fact had not voted for Abilene. Committee members, angry over the governor's scheming, joined with other leaders who favored Ferguson's removal from office for such actions and for his veto of the University of Texas budget. They believed he needed to be impeached. In September, the state legislature took appropriate action, and shortly afterward Ferguson left office. The new governor, William P. Hobby, in face of urgent demands related to World War I postponed the West Texas A&M college movement.[25]

By this time, World War I had been under way in Europe for three years, and in June 1917 the United States had become involved. The war's impact on the Llano Estacado, although several thousand miles and across an ocean away from the fighting, grew after 1914 and after 1917 became significant. The war not only ruined the agricultural college movement but also adversely impacted the enrollment of others. At West Texas Normal in Canyon, for example, 375 male students joined the American military and 7 of them lost their lives. Young men from Llano towns, farms, and ranches, like the college men, enlisted in one of the branches of the US Armed Forces. Moreover, the federal government with a catchy program of slogans, such as "raise-more-sheep," encouraged ranchers to expand their livestock numbers and farmers to produce more cotton.[26]

To replace their sons or younger hired help who had gone off to fight in the "Great War," many farmers across the United States out of necessity bought tractors and large machinery. During the war, demands for meat, especially lamb and beef; wheat; wool; and cotton reached important new highs. Beef prices skyrocketed. And a worldwide demand for wheat created a situation urging farmers to break up large numbers of acres of grazing land for wheat production.

With young men at war, women entered the workforce in greater numbers. They took positions as clerks, secretaries, and saleswomen. In Amarillo, for instance, White and Kirk, a large department store that claimed it was the city's oldest retail business, hired additional women, including some in administrative positions. Local hotels and restaurants also hired more female employees. Women joined the staff of the *Amarillo Daily News*, and others took control of their family businesses. Likewise, many farm women expanded their roles beyond gathering eggs, milking cows, and feeding chickens.

Phebe Warner

Phebe Kerrick Warner (1866–1935) was a writer, promoter, public speaker, and major influencer of projects and causes for the Texas Panhandle and Llano Estacado. A pioneer of the region, Warner, according to her biographer June Steele, through her speeches, newspaper columns, and general promotions carved out an impressive career as a Progressive Era reform activist. She organized women's clubs, advocated enhancement in all aspects of rural life, promoted issues relevant to Panhandle citizens, and "spearheaded the drive to create a state park in Palo Duro Canyon."

Born at Belle Plain, Illinois, Phebe Kerrick grew up on the family farm. In 1893, she graduated from Illinois Wesleyan University. She taught at Illinois Women's University before traveling to Claude in Armstrong County, Texas, in 1898, where, writes Steele, as one of the county's first residents, "she married Dr. William Arthur Warner" and "began a lifelong career of community-building." Except for in Amarillo, William Warner at the time was the only physician within a hundred miles of Claude, the county seat with a courthouse and a few businesses that served area farmers and ranchers.

For rural farm and ranch women, the upper Llano Estacado was a lonely place. Soon realizing that the distance between homesteads and the number of miles between communities added to the loneliness and isolation, Phebe Warner "began to organize settlers to bridge the gaps of distance between their homes." She encouraged some women to gather for quilting and sewing sessions where they might visit and share ideas and to join such men's activities as house or barn raisings. She pushed other women, especially those living in town, to meet for literary studies. "The meetings," notes Steele, "soon grew in popularity and took on greater purpose." In time, the women organized the Wednesday Afternoon Club, and it attracted attention beyond Claude and Armstrong County.

At the same time Warner was making speeches, commonplace but inspirational little talks. Directed at farm women of Armstrong

County, the popular presentations gained regional attention and led to an increasing number of invitations to speak at church meetings, high school graduations, and community events. Many of her addresses touched on what she conceived as the "plight of rural women." By 1916, she had become a highly sought public speaker with invitations coming from across the state.

After one such lecture in El Paso, Peter Molyneaux, an editor for the Fort Worth Star-Telegram, invited Warner to write articles and other pieces for his newspaper. She agreed, writes Steele, and thus launched "a twenty-year career in journalism, one that would extend to dozens of Texas publications." She became famous in the Texas Panhandle and across the state. Between 1916 and her death in 1935, Warner was a crusading spirit, using her columns and speeches to tackle a host of issues she deemed worthy, relevant, in need of attention, and solvable. Such matters included, but were not limited to, school reform, efficient local government, improving rural life, women's status in society, the Progressive Era "Good Roads" movement, and a state park system for Texas. As to the latter topic, as much as anybody and more than most people, Phebe Warner promoted the establishment of Palo Duro Canyon State Park, one of the Llano Estacado's truly significant natural phenomena.

On the Llano Estacado, several agricultural developments occurred. Before the war, most farmers raised a variety of crops, including cotton, with grain sorghum, alfalfa, wheat, and Sudan grass among the dominant plantings. During World War I, the demand for cotton rose and prices increased. The same thing, of course, occurred with wool and mohair, beef and lamb, and wheat, but on the South Plains, write some historians, to "take advantage of the favorable trend [in cotton], . . . farmers planted more." In Lubbock County, for example, farmers produced 947 bales in 1915, 3,496 bales in 1918, and 13,865 bales a year later. The shift to cotton, making it something of a monocrop, continued in the 1920s.[27]

On the northern edge of the Llano Estacado, wheat became the major farm crop. The shift started just before World War I when wheat began selling for $1.00 per bushel. In response, local ranchers sold and leased land to pioneer farmers who broke the sod for wheat. The large Frying Pan Ranch, for example, urged its farmers and leaseholders to plant wheat, and after James Bush arrived to manage the ranch, thousands of acres of Frying Pan grazing lands became wheat fields. Other big ranches followed the Frying Pan lead, and in 1912 the Santa Fe Railway shipped from the Texas Panhandle, writes Garry L. Nall, "a total of 2,850 cars containing 2,850,000 bushels" of wheat. During World War I, as the price of wheat reached $2.71 cents per bushel, even greater expansion occurred. At the end of the war in 1918, growers on the Llano Estacado and north across the Canadian River raised wheat on nearly six hundred thousand acres.[28]

Unfortunately, World War I produced anti-German sentiments across the United States and on the Llano Estacado. Amid such cries as "Halt the Hun," schools discontinued German-language classes, for example, and discriminated against traditional German foods. Yet on the Llano, many people of German descent enlisted in American armed forces. Others bought war bonds and participated in the national Food Administration's effort to conserve food through its slogans "Meatless Tuesdays," "Wheatless Wednesdays," and "Porkless Saturdays." They planted "Victory Gardens," home vegetable patches, and some German Americans tried to downplay or even hide their ethnic background.

By the time World War I ended in November 1918, a global pandemic had brought tragedy. The disease—unfairly named "Spanish influenza"—killed twenty-two million or more persons worldwide and nearly seven hundred thousand people in the United States. It lasted about nine months, erupting suddenly in the spring of 1918 and ending only after the onset of cold weather in the winter of 1919. On the Llano Estacado, individuals, as they did in 2020–21 with the COVID-19 pandemic, took to wearing masks (some soaked with camphor-phrenic), avoided contact with others, and paid close attention to their own personal hygiene.

In Lubbock, Mayor Charles E. Parks in October 1918 encouraged the city commissioners to close schools, theaters, and other public gathering places. In December, the commission forbade all public meetings. In Amarillo, N. S. Griggs, a local mortician, indicated that at one time he was conducting every day between one and six funerals for flu victims. At West Texas Normal College in Canyon the school closed several times during the pandemic. Students and faculty members contracted the disease, and a few student deaths occurred. In fact, across the Llano Estacado, graveyard headstones in many cemeteries provided mute evidence of people who died during the epidemic.[29]

One of the faculty members at WT who contracted flu, but perhaps not the global variety, was Georgia O'Keeffe, soon to become perhaps America's most controversial artist. O'Keeffe, who had taught art in the Amarillo public schools from 1912 to 1914, joined the WT faculty in 1916. Two years later, illness and other considerations took her away from Canyon and the Llano Estacado, but she never forgot what she remembered as the wonderful High Plains and the rugged Palo Duro Canyon. Indeed, she enjoyed her years teaching on the Llano and often recalled with fondness her experiences on the "empty plains." Likewise, her students remembered her with kindness, many of them stating she was the best teacher they ever had. While she lived in Amarillo, many citizens saw her as a bit strange with her dress, her manly appearance, and her leisure time spent card playing with men in the back room of the hotel-boardinghouse on Polk Street where she lived.[30]

During the years O'Keeffe spent time on the Llano Estacado, road construction became an important activity. Most major highways before World War I enjoyed names: Bankhead Highway, Lincoln Highway, and others. On the Llano Estacado, one of the most unusual systems of roadways included the Ozark Trails, started in 1913 by William Hope "Coin" Harvey, an entrepreneur and presidential campaign organizer as well as a health resort operator. He wanted to improve roads in the near Southwest and thus get vacationers to his hotel and spa in the Ozark Mountains. Harvey did not build the roads, but he advertised and promoted them, latching on to the nationwide "Good Roads" movement of the Progressive Era. By 1916, thousands of people had joined Harvey's Ozark Trails Association (OTA), and in 1917, reportedly, nearly twenty thousand people attended an OTA meeting in Amarillo, temporarily doubling the city's population.

With as yet no national or Texas system of numbered highways, named highways used various symbols or signs to mark their roads. The Ozark Trails highways used diamond-shaped signs with a white background and a green "OT," sometimes between two green stripes. After 1918, James E. Swepston of Tulia began encouraging towns to build pyramids or obelisks to designate the Ozark Trail highway through their community. The plan called for twenty-five-foot-tall concrete obelisks, painted white with green lettering, and perhaps a bit of travel information and maybe lights for illumination. Leaders in several towns in northwest Texas built the pyramids. On the Llano Estacado, the obelisks appeared in Farwell, Tulia, Dimmit, Nazareth, Tampico Station (in Hall County) in Texas and in other towns in New Mexico. By 1925, the system had been replaced by numbered highways. Some of the famous Route 66 across the Llano had once been part of the Ozark Trails system.[31]

Clearly, by the end of World War I better roads for a growing number of automobiles and trucks in America and on the Llano Estacado had become a necessity. In the 1920s, the war's influence, as noted in the next chapter, reached into additional areas of American life.

Summary

The Llano Estacado saw major changes in its landscape and demography in the thirty years before 1920. The arrival of new settlers, the appearance of railroads, the development of towns and cities, the transformation of grassland into cotton and wheat fields, and the impact of World War I all played a role in the Llano shift from a seemingly wide-open cattle country to a rural commonwealth dominated by such booming urban areas as Amarillo, Plainview, Clovis, and Lubbock.

In the 1890s, drought and a national economic depression, the worst of the century, shaped the region's activities. Well drilling, fence building, and crop farming characterized much of the period, but people living on the Llano and moving to the area also built schools and churches to supplement their little towns. Nearly always the schools and churches, plus the local courthouse in county seat communities, became the center of social pursuits and essentially unsophisticated cultural endeavors. Pioneer life meant long hours spent at difficult, time-consuming tasks, but even the very first settlers sought social outlets in horse racing, house parties, town and country dances, and holiday celebrations.

After the turn of the century in 1900, a veritable flood of farmer-settlers arrived on the eastern Llano Estacado. Aided by railroads, land speculators, and town builders, they overran the place as they carved out their farms and towns and grew their cities. Nonetheless, even as some ranchers sold their land to the new arrivals, others, such as C. C. Slaughter and David DeVitt, created new, large ranching operations on the Llano in such places as Cochran and Hockley Counties.

World War I also affected the Llano Estacado, as it did all of the United States. On the Llano's young farms, it encouraged a shift from horse- and mule-drawn wagons and equipment to tractor-pulled plows and harvester machines. The war encouraged the shift from subsistence farming to one-crop operations with cotton or wheat the principal commodity. It led to other changes as well and at its end helped bring the global flu epidemic to the Llano Estacado. The war's end set in motion many developments that occurred in the 1920s.

Georgia O'Keeffe

Georgia O'Keeffe (1887–1986), one of America's truly significant artists, lived, worked, and painted on the Llano Estacado for nearly four years. She taught art in the public schools of Amarillo from 1912 to 1914 and served as art instructor at West Texas State Normal College (West Texas A&M University) from 1916 to early 1918, before illness and other considerations took her to the little town of Waring in Kendall County northwest of San Antonio and eventually back to New York. As noted by John T. "Jack" Becker and others, O'Keeffe loved the Llano Estacado with its spectacular sunrises and sunsets and the enormous wildness of Palo Duro Canyon. From the rugged canyon and the Llano's unbelievable flatness she drew inspiration, ideas, themes, and colors that influenced her work for much of the rest of her life. To her, the cold of winter, the heat of summer, and the dusty winds of spring in Amarillo and Canyon held an enchantment and a fascination she could not explain in her letters but sought to describe in her drawings and paintings. O'Keeffe enjoyed teaching, and many of her students remembered her as an unusual but effective instructor.

In Amarillo, O'Keeffe lived in a hotel-boardinghouse, the Magnolia Hotel, on South Polk Street on the edge of downtown. Farther south on Polk, the wide dirt and gravel street with a trolley (streetcar) and steel rails to carry residents to and from the downtown shopping district was becoming known as "Silk Stocking Row." Several huge and stately mansions lined South Polk Street as did some splendid trees, and a grassy esplanade began where the trolley line ended. Each school day, O'Keeffe walked or took the trolley south to Amarillo High School. On weekends, she walked or caught a ride onto the empty plains, sometimes going as far as Palo Duro Canyon.

Amarillo was a busy little city of just under twelve thousand people in 1912 and 1913, a town that enjoyed a growing sophistication, but it still carried some "Old West" baggage. On September 14, 1912, for example, John Beal Sneed, a prominent citizen of Amarillo, in cold blood shot and killed from behind (probably)

Albert G. Boyce Jr., also a leading resident of the city, as Boyce walked up Polk Street, passed Polk Street Methodist Church, and went toward downtown. The Boyce-Sneed feud involved an unfortunate love triangle occurring while O'Keeffe lived in Amarillo. Indeed, her hotel was only a couple of blocks away from where Sneed ambushed his wife's lover.

O'Keeffe perhaps added to the edge-of-settlement image. Twenty-four years old, she wore her hair pulled back in a tight, short-looking style, dressed in plain black outfits, spent little time with other teachers, ate in the hotel's dining room, and, when she was not out walking, played poker and dominoes in a back room with the hotel's male guests.

Later in Canyon, town residents, and perhaps her colleagues as well, saw O'Keeffe as a bit odd. There were her dark clothing, of course, her men's-style shoes, and her hair fashions, but there were also her late-night or early-morning walks, her scandalous automobile rides with a male student, and her general eccentricities, such as going to a men's barbershop to have her shoes polished and having no curtains on her bedroom windows.

Georgia O'Keeffe loved the High Plains and its canyons. As noted, the land inspired her and soon influenced her painting forms, patterns, and methods. Indeed, she had been producing a lot of black-and-white charcoal images until her Llano experience. Once on the Llano Estacado, she returned to watercolor and a wider range of colors in painting. Moreover, college students and colleagues remembered her as a superb teacher who encouraged fresh ideas and the same creativity that she herself had found on the Llano Estacado.

9

Pre–Jazz Age to Post–World War II Era

From the end of World War I to the end of World War II people of the Llano Estacado, like people everywhere in United States, experienced events at times disrupting of their way of life and at times reassuring and bolstering it. In the 1920s, for example, the entire country, after a brief economic downturn, saw an era of unprecedented affluence and with it a continued shift in America from a rural society to an urban one. This prosperous "Roaring Twenties" decade—the Jazz Age—came to an abrupt and premature end in 1929 with the unexpected stock market crash and the subsequent Great Depression of the 1930s. Business failure brought economic hardship to a wide spectrum of America, including the Llano, and it did not end until World War II in the early 1940s unleashed in the United States a gigantic war machine. Full employment followed and with it an end to some of America's worst hard times.

This thirty-year era of a surging, shrinking, and resurging economy began in the early 1920s. For the Llano Estacado, it centered on agriculture and the long, lingering influence of World War I. During the war, as we have seen, global demands for wheat, meat, wool, mohair, and cotton were enormous. As America and its allies defeated Germany and its wartime partners in 1918, the demands subsided—but only partially. In at least fourteen Llano Estacado counties, for example, sheep raising or feeding continued at a favorable pace, and in 1930, each of the counties produced between five thousand and thirty thousand sheep and lambs, but sheep-raising methods had changed. With fewer herders available, sheepmen grazed their animals within mesh-wire fences or fed them within small enclosures. Wool and lamb production, while slowing, continued into World War II, when it boomed again.[1]

For Llano wheat growers, production in the 1920s became complicated. During the war, farmers on the Llano Estacado and all through the Great Plains increased production. Above-average precipitation on the Llano, high market prices, and the earning value of wheat per acre versus grazing livestock per acre contributed to the expanding cultivation of the popular cereal grain, particularly winter wheat. Wheat producers prospered. After the war in the early 1920s, as Europe rebuilt its farms and increased its wheat output, global prices collapsed. To make up for the declining market returns and offset income losses, wheat farmers on the Llano and across the larger Great Plains plowed up more native grassland (and planted more wheat), a circumstance that historians, environmentalists, and economists have come to call the "big plow up." Huge amounts of grazing land in the upper Llano Estacado became

In the late 1920s near Post an automobile is climbing the Caprock Escarpment along a dirt road leading onto the Llano Estacado where US Highway 84 is located today. Courtesy of Paul Carlson

extensive wheat fields. In some counties, such as Potter, wheat acreage nearly doubled between 1925 and 1931. When market values continued low or even declined, wheat producers faced troubling uncertainty and sometimes farm foreclosures.

Many of the same conditions applied to cotton production. As prices declined, cotton growers broke out more land to expand acreage. At the same time, many farmers shifted away from grain sorghum, Sudan grass, and alfalfa in favor of cotton, which on the South Plains, like wheat in upper parts of the Llano, produced greater income per acre than other crops. As did wheat farther north, cotton growing in South Plains counties transformed regional agriculture. Cotton, like wheat, became a major cash crop.

Cotton agriculture more than other crops inspired irrigation on the Llano Estacado's South Plains. In drought years, or even during those summers when precipitation remained slightly below normal, water was in short supply. To offset the lower-rainfall years, cotton growers, as well as other farmers, turned to crop watering. Use of drilled wells and windmills to pump water for livestock from the large underground Ogallala

This postcard, dated 1920, indicates that Lubbock, because of its railroad and highway connections, was known as "The Hub of the Plains." Courtesy of Sally Abbe and Cindy Martin

Lonnie Williams with his daughter DeLois Williams Alexander planting cotton on his farm in south Lubbock County near Slide in 1931. Courtesy of Lynette Wilson

Aquifer had been around since the first cattlemen urged their herds onto the Llano. Between 1910 and 1912, several Llano farmers had drilled or dug wells for irrigation. Such farmers included D. L. McDonald near Hereford, the Chicago-based Coldron Land Company near Muleshoe, J. J. Slaton west of Plainview, and George Boles east of Lubbock. But windmills could not pump water in amounts needed for large-scale crop irrigation. A solution was found when George W. Littlefield and Arthur P. Duggan near Littlefield drilled wells and used gasoline-powered engines to pump water for their crops. Nonetheless, as Donald Abbe and others have written, "The high cost of drilling, equipping, and maintaining a well . . . [and the need] to devise practical methods for applying the water to their land" slowed large-scale irrigation for a decade or more.[2]

With or without irrigation, the big plow up for cotton and wheat altered the Llano Estacado's landscape, especially on the South Plains.

As cotton agriculture expanded there, what had been a semiarid farm and grazing land became for nearly seven months a year a semidesert of brownish-red fields and windblown dirt and dust. Even as late as 2022, cotton fields on average remained green for only four months a year with about a month of brilliant white while cotton awaited harvesting. The ecological shift proved to be a lasting influence of the big plow up.

During the 1920s a shift away from horse and mule power to tractors, trucks, and automobiles occurred. An "industrial revolution" Donald Worster called it, one in which mechanization supplanted "men and animals with fossil-fuel power." Between 1910 and 1930, Worster notes, "the labor needed to plant and harvest the nation's wheat fell by one-third, while the acreage jumped by almost the same amount." And, of course, the flatlands of the Llano Estacado "were especially suitable for mechanized farming."[3]

Big, heavy, steam-powered traction engines had been around for several decades, but smaller, gasoline-powered tractors came late to the Llano Estacado. Yet, in 1917, more than one hundred companies, including at least temporarily Henry Ford's big automobile corporation, made the smaller tractors. In the Panhandle–South Plains area, according to Worster, the most popular tractors proved to be versions of the red-colored Farmall, the gray and orange Case, the bright green John Deere, and the McCormick-Deering 15-30.[4]

Manufacturers, led by the John Deere and William McCormick companies, also turned out bigger and better plows. Many farmers adopted disk plows that did not dig as deep as the older moldboard plows, and they could be pulled along the ground faster. The disk plows held other advantages as well, for, according to Worster, they chopped up the ground to allow for water absorption, "killed weeds efficiently, and, when used often enough, left a finely pulverized surface layer."[5]

Mechanization in other areas also expanded. Harvesters for wheat improved. Threshing machines evolved to be bigger, and eventually farm-manufacturing companies, led by the McCormick company, turned out large machines that combined harvesting and threshing—combines they came to be called. Cotton farmers rapidly adopted mechanization, for tractors seemed especially suited for row crops such as cotton. Quickly, too, tractor-pulled or mounted equipment suited to cotton cultivation developed, and when they could afford it, farmers on the Llano Estacado purchased such equipment as soon as it became available. Nonetheless, most cotton growers in the South Plains region continued to use horse and mule power well into the 1930s and some afterward. They hired seasonal and migrant workers to pull cotton bolls from the plants ("pick" cotton) as they dragged a large sack in which to place the cotton. Some people could pull one thousand pounds of cotton per day. Despite the reluctance or financial inability of some farmers to embrace changes in cotton production, mechanization in the 1920s increased.

During the 1920s, the national prohibition of alcoholic beverages turned out to be a strange and unfortunate experience. Many counties and towns on the Llano Estacado were "dry"—that is, had outlawed the manufacture, sale, and transportation (and sometimes consumption) of beer, wine, and other spirits—even before World War I. Nonetheless, the idea of conserving wheat combined with a general willingness of Americans to adopt a spartan lifestyle to aid the war effort led to a national prohibition through the Eighteenth Amendment to the Constitution. The amendment passed Congress in 1917, and in January 1919—well after the war's end made such conservation unnecessary—the required number of states (thirty-six) had at last ratified it. The amendment, however, did not define "intoxicating liquors." Shortly afterward, therefore, the Volstead Act defined an alcoholic beverage as one having 0.5 percent (1/2 of 1 percent) alcohol by volume, and in 1920 "Prohibition" was law.

In hindsight, Prohibition was a mistake. It could not be enforced. It inspired illegal and too often dangerous home brewing ("bathtub gin"), bootlegging, racketeering, and related crime as never seen before in the United States. Prohibition remains an example of Americans' unwillingness to submit to unpopular legislation and regulations. In many "dry" counties on the Llano Estacado, bootlegging from New Mexico had been common before World War I. Now, in the 1920s, "rum runners," especially those operating from such larger towns as Amarillo, Plainview, and Lubbock, shifted their procurement sources to El Paso and its neighbor Juárez across the Rio Grande. Some men in Amarillo before their arrests in 1924 made several trips to El Paso. Each time they stole a big automobile from a local dealer, drove it to the border, loaded it with liquor, and returned to Amarillo, where they ditched the stolen vehicle and sold the contraband, making up to $15,000 on each trip, or about $160,000 in 2022 currency.[6]

Home brewing became common. In rural areas and small towns, setting up a modest still was not difficult. In larger towns, some enterprising distillers ran fairly large, but illegal, operations. Other "dealers" found ways to acquire liquor for redistribution. In Amarillo, for instance, Prohibition enforcers led by Sheriff Burton Roach in 1922 arrested two couples for "having intoxicating liquors in their possession for sale." Roach and his men collected in a house about "two hundred and twelve quarts of whisky, some pints, a few packages of champagne and forty gallons of alcohol, with a total value of approximately $8,000." They also found a large stock of alcohol in a hole behind the house. It contained bottles, according to the labels, of liquor from England, Canada, and Mexico.[7]

"Speakeasies"—clandestine drinking and socializing clubs—appeared. In Lubbock, some restaurants or other establishments located downtown just off Broadway made liquor available in their "private" back rooms, which became the speakeasies or "nightclubs," even if they did not operate at night. In Amarillo, at the end of the 1920s the new fourteen-story, six-hundred room Herring Hotel, built by Cornelius T. Herring, opened. In its basement, one might attend the posh Old Tascosa nightclub. Some of the more fashionable establishments required memberships and attracted women. Indeed, women who had never entered or even consider visiting a pre-Prohibition bar or swinging-door corner saloon could in 1920s Lubbock and Amarillo be found in illegal nightclubs and taprooms. Some of the females were "flappers," mainly young women who adopted short hair and short skirts and painted their cheeks and lips red. They might listen to jazz music, dance to the lively strains of the iconic Charleston, drink a trendy highball, and smoke a cigarette—Lucky Strikes and Pall Malls were popular.

In the 1920s, an unsettled fear of communism spread across America, including the Llano Estacado. Causes for the "Big Red Scare," as it was called, were many: the 1919 Boston police strike, Seattle general strike, and other labor walkouts; the bombing in Washington, DC, at the home of America's chief police official, Attorney General A. Mitchell Palmer; the 1920 arrest and subsequent trial of Nicola Sacco and Bartolomeo Vanzetti, philosophical anarchists, for the murder of a Massachusetts paymaster and his guard; and police raids on suspected socialists, including some in conservative Montana, and other "left-wingers." Part of the legacy of the Red Scare became a national crusade for "100 percent Americanism" and restrictions on immigration.

On the Llano Estacado, the antiforeign, antiradical mood appeared in various forms, the most virulent being the disgusting Ku Klux Klan. Although the name remained the same as the anti-black, anti-carpetbagger post–Civil War Klan, the modern organization, which started about 1915, was different. It continued to harass African Americans, but on the Llano, it also claimed to be a crusade to stop bootleggers, destroy "unclean" literature, promote Protestantism, support Anglo-Saxon ideals, and defend women and Christian morals. It challenged Roman Catholics, organized labor, foreigners, and other groups it deemed un-American. The Klan attracted doctors, lawyers, engineers, druggists, bankers, businessmen, store owners, clergymen, and accountants, but most of its members came from the ranks of less educated, less financially secure citizens. It enjoyed some political success in Texas, including on the Llano.

The 1920s Klan proved to be short-lived. It was something of a scam, for half of its costly initiation fee went to the national organization. Klan members also bought their expensive robes, hoods, and other paraphernalia as well as propaganda literature from the national Klan headquarters. The Klavern (as the local group was called) received some of the membership fee plus annual dues. Once people revealed the secret organization as a self-promoting con based on the initiation fee, annual dues, and paraphernalia charges, the Klan fell apart, especially after 1926, even if it did not disappear.[8]

On the Llano Estacado, the Ku Klux Klan became active in Amarillo, Lubbock, and elsewhere. It proved popular in many small towns. In the little community of Slaton with a population of about nine hundred people in Lubbock County, the Klavern held a parade in which three thousand members, including some women, marched before allegedly ten thousand observers. The Slaton Klan beat a farmer who had abused his wife, enforced Prohibition, and supported Protestant churches by providing money to them.[9]

The Slaton Klavern may also have been responsible for the 1922 tarring and feathering of Father Josef M. Keller. A German immigrant and the Catholic priest of a rapidly growing parish, Father Keller, who had arrived in Slaton in 1917 to replace the church founder Father Joseph Reisdorff (who retired but stayed in Slaton), may have been a bit eccentric. He strongly supported his home country, going to the point of chastising the Slaton newspaper editor for anti-German comments in the paper, the *Slatonite*. In any case, on the night of March 4, 1922, masked and armed men entered the Keller home, bound and gagged him, and hauled him several miles out of town into the middle of a cotton patch. There men stripped, whipped, and beat him, after which they poured hot tar on the priest, covered the sticky tar with feathers, and left the man to his own devices. Keller walked back to town, found help to remove some of the tar and feathers, and the next day left Slaton. He spent a year in recovery in Saint Louis and afterward settled in Wisconsin at a small-town parish. He died in 1939.[10]

The Amarillo Klavern counted nearly four hundred members in early 1923. It engaged in the usual Klan activities. Its members donned their robes and hoods, held parades, and conducted secret meetings with, of course, secret passwords and secret handholds. They moved about at night, burned fiery crosses, and threatened and flogged people for any manner of "wrongdoing." The floggings became bad enough that in 1923 Lieutenant Governor T. W. Davidson sent Texas Rangers to investigate. The Rangers arrested T. W. Stanford, a Klansman, for his role in endangering a Potter County citizen. In court, Stanford received a prison sentence, but a criminal appeals court overturned the conviction. The Klan died in Amarillo nearly as quickly as it arose, in part perhaps because J. L. Nunn, publisher and general manager of the *Amarillo Daily News*, and David M. Warren, the newspaper's managing editor, showed no sympathy for Klan activity.[11]

The Lubbock group, Texas Klan Number 199, engaged in the usual activities. Under the leadership of C. C. Livingston, the local Exalted Cyclops, the Klavern enforced Prohibition, sought to stop bootlegging, used lighted crosses to make threats, held secret meetings, and intimidated victims who had raised its ire and resentment. In the summer of 1923, writes Winfred G. Steglich, "twelve hooded and robed Klansmen entered the open-air tabernacle" (tent) at "the Cumberland Presbyterian Church on 16th Street" in the city's nascent African American community (the Flats) "and presented the pastor a sealed envelope." The note inside contained a racially charged message to the black congregation, but little else occurred. The Lubbock Klavern reached a peak that summer and declined afterward.[12]

In New Mexico, the Ku Klux Klan attracted few followers. On the Llano Estacado, little evidence for its presence exists. The New Mexico population included a large number of Roman Catholics, Hispanics, and Native Americans, none of whom, obviously, found membership in the secret fraternal organization appealing. A Klavern operated briefly at Forrest in Quay County. In Roswell, located in the Pecos River Valley and off the Llano, Pioneer Klan Number 15 boasted of keeping Roman Catholic teachers out of Roswell's schools but admitted "wherever it raised its head, people complained."[13]

On the other hand, people on the Llano Estacado supported America's "Good Roads" program. As noted in chapter 8, the OTA with its tall obelisks crossed the Llano Estacado, most notably through its northern reaches. More important, the idea of improved—meaning graded, graveled, well-drained, and sometimes paved—roadways encouraged the growth of the Texas State Highway Department, established in 1916, the creation of county highway departments, and the development of automobile travel. By the 1920s a numbering classification for both federal and state highways had begun, and as a result the need and use for named highways declined. The Ozark Trails system, which reached its peak in the mid-1920s, faded away. Most of the colorful obelisks disappeared, and much of OTA's northern route through the Llano became the iconic Route 66. Its southern trails became numbered highways.

Improved highways encouraged automobile travel—lots of it—and tourism, but now it included middle-income families. In response, businessmen and -women on the Llano Estacado opened rest stops, gasoline stations, roadside restaurants, and motor courts. Also, the Highway Department in 1917 had begun publishing an annual official highway map. In the 1920s, the maps showed more and more of the Llano roadways. Moreover, in Amarillo, the largest "city" in the region and located along the recently commissioned Route 66, city officials and entrepreneurs laid out a camping site for long-distance travelers. And big bus companies expanded operations on the improved Llano roads and highways.

Both Lubbock and Amarillo grew in the 1920s. Although cattle and wheat industries continued to influence Amarillo's economy, the discovery and opening of the large Panhandle Oil and Gas Field greatly spurred the city's growth, which in 1927 reached a population of more than fifty-two thousand. In addition to oil and gas production, helium extraction from natural gas became important for the city. The US Bureau of Mines secured drilling rights to a gas field northwest of Amarillo

The US government helium plant located west of Amarillo as pictured in 1931.
Courtesy of Panhandle-Plains Historical Museum

and in 1927 opened an extraction plant about seven miles west of the city at Soncy on the Rock Island Railroad. Within two years Amarillo had become known as the "Helium Capital of the World."[14]

Lubbock's growth in the 1920s (its population increased from four thousand to ten thousand) related to different factors. The emergence of the city as a transportation hub with its railroads and highways represented one factor. Its further development as the center of a highly productive agricultural area was another. Then, the establishment of Texas Technological College hastened its passage to urban prominence. Texas Tech began on February 10, 1923, when Governor Pat Neff signed the bill creating the college into law. Shortly afterward a five-man board traveled across West Texas to choose from among thirty-six communities the institution's location. On the Llano Estacado, leaders in Amarillo, Plainview, tiny Wilson in Lynn County, and of course Lubbock all submitted a brief and a proposal seeking the institution. On August 8, the board chose Lubbock. The school, with Paul Whitfield Horn as president and Fort Worth's newspaper mogul Amon Carter as chairman of the board, opened in the fall of 1925, enrolling more than nine hundred students its first semester.

Amarillo also got a college—at last. Having failed at getting West Texas Normal, Texas Technological College, and in 1927–28 a Methodist Church–related University of Amarillo (by transferring and renaming the church's Clarendon College), city leaders, led by Lee Bivins and such area legislators as George Ordway and James Guleke, got a state-authorized two-year institution, Amarillo Junior College. It opened in September 1929 with eighty-seven students. In 2022, Amarillo College (AC), as it is often called, included six campuses and enrolled over ten thousand students, reflecting the city's large population growth.

Population growth and economic expansion also occurred in Midland and Odessa as well as in Hobbs in New Mexico. Petroleum keyed the growth in these Permian Basin communities. In scattered parts of West Texas in the 1920s, wildcatters had made several new discoveries of oil with prolific fields found in the Panhandle and the Permian Basin. Statewide during the decade, oil-based industries, such as refining of oil and pipeline construction, increased significantly, and Permian Basin cities, including Hobbs, benefited from the expansion. The towns grew as entrepreneurs opened service, transportation, supply, pipeline, and related petroleum companies, creating a huge demand for workers, housing, and businesses to support them. Together, Odessa and Midland became the hub of the Permian's giant oil industry.[15]

The decade brought more than oil and economic growth to the Llano Estacado. In the Littlefield area, thousands of acres of grazing land became farming country, after the Littlefield Land Company—beginning as early as 1912—offered its property to buyers. To facilitate its sales, the company sent buses to Oklahoma and East and South Texas to bring farmers to Littlefield to look over the land. "I was astonished," remembered Ed Aryain, a recently arrived Syrian store owner in the 1920s, "to hear that the raw prairie land around Littlefield was selling for forty dollars an acre. I thought this was an awfully high price for unbroken raw land. How wrong I was." Small farms spread across Lamb and northeastern Bailey Counties.[16]

As such twentieth-century "pioneers" arrived, Protestant churches expanded in both number and practitioners. Baptist, Methodist, Church of Christ, and Christian (Disciples of Christ) churches dominated, but plenty of others appeared. Roman Catholic churches, which had existed on the Llano from a very early date, gained in number in the 1920s, in part because the number of Hispanics of Catholic orientation increased. Jewish communities appeared in larger cities, particularly Lubbock and Amarillo, and expanded over the next several decades.

Another important phenomenon in the 1920s was the growth of service clubs: Rotary, Elks, Kiwanis, and Lions Clubs, for example. They seemed a part of the Jazz Age's fascination with "joining" and with fraternal organizations. The clubs grew rapidly during the decade. Businessmen organized them in most small towns of the Llano Estacado. Each week, middle-class citizenry gathered for a luncheon, good fellowship, and perhaps a bit of singing. More than that, however, the clubs engaged in community service and charitable activities. Amarillo led the way with its popular Rotary Club, and Lubbock in early 1921 was not far behind. Sometimes, as in Lubbock, the Rotary group and the Elks

Club joined together in providing gifts and food for needy families in the city, particularly at Christmas.

Also, in one of nature's wonders, mockingbirds, the state bird of Texas, began nesting on the Llano Estacado in the late 1920s and early 1930s. According to famous Texas naturalist Roy Bedichek, mockingbirds, although "quite common about the clearings and in towns and villages," are rare in dense woods, such as the forests of eastern Texas, and they "stayed off the plains of western Texas until that section settled up and" the new residents "planted trees about their" homes and farmsteads. Mockingbirds became "one of the first of the tree-nesting species" to "come up into the open country" of the Llano. The growing presence of trees had changed the Llano's landscape, and as a result, mockingbirds and such similar tree-nesting birds as wrens, robins, and threshers, arrived in flocks. William G. McMillan Sr., a "birder" of no little experience from Lubbock, wrote to Bedichek saying that in the early 1930s the "mockingbird came to Lubbock in noticeable numbers."[17]

By that time, the early 1930s, the United States and the Llano Estacado stood deep in the Great Depression, a national financial, manufacturing, and economic disaster of epic proportions. It was, and remains, the worst monetary loss and business downturn in the nation's history. Its many causes range from agricultural and industrial overproduction that lowered prices, high tariffs that reduced foreign purchases, and weaknesses in the economy that at the end of the 1920s slowed business activity. Perhaps the new but little understood phenomenon of easy credit and installment buying also played a role. Installment buying in the 1920s encouraged a consumer culture in America that worked well until a waning of purchasing power bit into manufacturing sales and residential and commercial construction—which had been major drivers of the decade's business prosperity.

Epitomized by the stock market crash in 1929 and dramatized by Wall Street's "Black Tuesday" collapse on October 29, the Depression brought economic difficulties of all kinds. Unemployment attained disastrous levels, which, some accounts suggest, reached as high as 33 percent of the American workforce. Consumer spending and confidence dropped, reductions in capital investments occurred, and manufacturing slowed. Ultimately, construction activity slackened, agriculture suffered, many businesses failed, banks closed, and human misery became common.

In Texas and on the Llano Estacado, as elsewhere in the United States, many people lost jobs and went on relief. Merchants and shopkeepers cut workers, which added to the unemployed numbers. Some farmers and ranchers lost their land to bankruptcy, and schools and local governments became impoverished as tax receipts dropped. Commodity prices crashed. Oil, for example, in 1931 decreased to five cents a barrel and cotton dropped to five cents a pound in 1932. Food prices declined. In Texas and on the Llano, bread cost on average as little as four cents a loaf, beef eighteen cents per pound, and milk four or five cents a quart. A hamburger might cost a nickel. Nonetheless, because they were without work or on relief, many people remained unable to pay the low prices.

In part, such hard times created a brief but disgusting phenomenon: the appearance of public enemies. They were petty thieves, bank robbers, and in general small-time crooks who sometimes committed spectacular crimes and who became stone-cold killers, especially of police officers. Because their bank robberies often proved popular among Americans who had lost a lifetime of savings when their bank folded, they also became folk heroes to some people. Their leaders included John Dillinger, Charles "Pretty Boy" Floyd, Katherine "Ma" Barker, and Alvin "Creepy" Karpis. They operated mainly in the Midwest and on the Great Plains. In Texas, after Governor Miriam A. "Ma" Ferguson in a bit of political spite fired all the Texas Rangers, the Texas-based thieves and thugs raced around the state robbing gas stations and small businesses and killing "cops," as they called peace officers. Among them were the just plain mean, indeed vicious, Clyde and Marvin "Buck" Barrow and their paramours, Bonnie Parker and Blanche Caldwell. In August 1932, broke and on the run, Bonnie and Clyde with sometime partner Ray Hamilton landed on the Llano Estacado in southeastern New Mexico, where Bonnie spent hours and boxes of shells improving her shotgun shooting. Down off the western escarpment, the three stopped at the home of Dorsie M. Stamps, Bonnie's aunt, who lived on the outskirts of Carlsbad. They stayed there a few days, but when someone recognized

Bonnie Parker was a blonde-haired, cigar-smoking, and poetry-writing killer who with Clyde Barrow shot police officers, store owners, and bystanders as they made their way in stolen automobiles around the Southwest in the early 1930s. Courtesy of Southeastern New Mexico Historical Society

their stolen Ford V-8 Coupé, they kidnapped the deputy sheriff, Joe Johns, and headed again to Texas along some of the Llano's back roads. When they approached San Antonio some six hundred miles later, they released Johns. The outlaws then headed north through Texas to Oklahoma and Missouri. Two years later, in May 1934, Bonnie and Clyde died in an ambush along a lonely forest road near Iowa, Louisiana.[18]

More characteristic of the Llano Estacado was the blowing dirt in the 1930s and the development of the idea of a Southern Plains "Dust Bowl." Much of the dust and dirt can be attributed to the big plow up. As noted earlier, farmers had cultivated additional ground to plant more wheat or cotton in response to high demand and soaring prices during World War I. When prices for both commodities dropped after the war, growers in the 1920s compensated by plowing up additional acres and planting more wheat and cotton. When they blew, strong winds of the Great Plains and the Llano Estacado picked up the dust and dirt that after cotton harvest lay bare in the fields and carried it, like blowing snow, into drifts against buildings, fence lines, and railroad tracks, and too often far beyond the Great Plains, occasionally to places along the Atlantic Coast. Sometimes huge, black clouds of dust rolled across the Panhandle–South Plains area, turning days to nights and bringing cases of dust pneumonia to the plains. On the Llano's dirt-bare South Plains, the blowing dirt and dust was an ecological disaster, one that replays itself every spring.[19]

Economically, farmers and ranchers on the Llano Estacado had been struggling since the cotton and wheat price collapse after World War I. During the 1930s Depression, they continued to wrestle with low prices, crippling farm and equipment mortgages, and generally high costs for feed and seed. Now adding to their woes came a severe stretch of drought and high temperatures. For many summer days in the 1930s, thermometers eclipsed the one-hundred-degree mark, sometimes by several degrees, and drought complicated farming. In 1933 and 1934, for example, rainfall amounts averaged only 9.96 inches. Agricultural historian Garry L. Nall writes that for the twelve years between 1929 and 1940, "rainfall failed to reach the normal 19.67 inches at Amarillo" nine times.[20]

Horrific dust- and sandstorms, caused by years of drought and empty fields, swept across the South Plains—the central Llano Estacado—and the Southern Great Plains during the 1930s. Courtesy of Southwest Collection/Special Collections Library

Blowing dirt also contributed to agricultural distress. The Soil Conservation Service tracked dust storms on the Great Plains. In listing such storms in which visibility dropped to less than a mile, it cited fourteen in 1932, thirty-eight in 1933, twenty-two in 1934, forty in 1935, sixty-eight in 1936, and seventy-two in 1937. Extensive heat, high winds, and little rainfall all contributed to the so-called dirty thirties. When large amounts of static electricity accompanied strong winds, the storms became extraordinary events. On Sunday afternoon, April 14, 1935, for example, an enormous dust storm blew down from the north and across the Llano Estacado at seventy or more miles per hour. Rolling, swirling, and "boiling" black clouds, "a solid bank of dust" recalled Raleigh Middleton, billowed sixty or more feet high, turning a bright spring day to dark. Automobiles stalled, lights came on, chickens went to roost, and breathing became difficult, especially for cattle and horses, which were soon covered with a thick coat of dust. The tall, spectacular front rose high and dark, and dust, said the pilot of an airplane forced to land north of Lubbock, extended "[four] miles in the air."[21]

Although dramatic, the April 14 "Black Sunday" storm was not the worst dust- and sandstorm. H. T. Coleman from the Amarillo area, while admitting the Black Sunday "duster," as he called it, was more noteworthy, said the storm a month earlier on March 3 measured worse, and William G. DeLoach of Sudan in Lamb County noted in his diary that "of my 37 years on the plains . . . the sand storm of [March 3] was the worst I ever saw," and in the margin he wrote, "Bad oh bad." The March storm, one of many that month, has been called a "smothering, grit-filled 'freak of nature.'"[22]

Blowing dirt and widespread drought may have characterized the Great Depression on the Llano Estacado, but economic difficulties of all kinds existed. In short, at the time that Franklin D. Roosevelt won election as President of the United States in November 1932, the Depression neared disastrous proportions, and when he took office four months later in March 1933, the American economy was edging toward chaos. Perhaps the most urgent issue as Roosevelt took office was a nationwide banking crisis. Banks were failing. The problem was bad enough in Michigan that the governor, calling for a euphemistic "bank holiday," close banks in the state to prevent so-called runs on deposits that in some places found people withdrawing their money and closing their accounts in such numbers that banks went broke. Governor Ma Ferguson, who had taken office a second time in January 1933, on March 2 closed the state banks in Texas. Roosevelt, as one of his first duties as president, declared a national bank holiday, shutting down the nation's banking industry.

Two weeks later, after federal inspection, banks began to reopen. In the meantime, serious inconveniences occurred. People could not cash checks, including paychecks. A shortage of currency developed, and many folks hoarded money. Business slowed even more as trade became dull and activities that depended on currency—cash—declined. Because of the currency shortage, merchants could not give change. Yet people adjusted, and bartering quickly caught on, with some people in Lubbock trading groceries, for example, for seats at baseball games—particularly those of the local Lubbock Hubbers baseball club.

With the banking crisis under control, President Roosevelt and the federal government turned to the larger economy. During the first one hundred days of his presidency, Roosevelt introduced a dozen or more programs scholars have come to call the "New Deal" to get people back to work, to shore up the nation's financial structure and institutions, to reorder the economy, to aid the country's agricultural and manufacturing industries, to protect the environment, and in general to get the nation's anemic markets moving again. The federal government would do it through relief for the unemployed, recovery of the economy, and reform in financial, business, and monetary institutions.

New Deal programs impacted favorably on the Llano Estacado, especially in agriculture, the environment, and employment. The Agricultural Adjustment Act (AAA) provided price supports and crop and livestock quotas for farmers and ranchers. The Civil Works Administration (CWA), Public Works Administration (PWA), and gigantic Works Progress Administration (WPA) programs made key contributions in providing jobs through work projects, sometimes only minor chores but more often significant and lasting endeavors. In Amarillo and Lubbock, federally employed workers repaired and built water and sewer lines, parks, roads, and public facilities. The WPA took on a wide range of activities to get people to work, not only in the major cities but also in small towns and rural areas. It provided work in nonconstruction activities for unemployed teachers, students, actors, historians, artists, writers, and other intellectuals. There were detractors, of course, especially toward the short-lived CWA and the WPA, for what critics called "make-work" projects or "boondoggle" activities, such as raking leaves and cleaning ditches. And in fact, the US Supreme Court declared parts of the AAA and PWA laws unconstitutional.

The more popular Civilian Conservation Corps (CCC) establish work camps across the region. At the camps it provided minimum wages to young men with government-sponsored jobs in conservation projects. Such workers constructed dams, built roads and buildings, created and improved parks, and prepared recreation areas or access to them. The Buffalo Lake National Wildlife Refuge in western Randall County was one such facility that federally employed workers improved. In 1938, they built a dam across Tierra Blanca Creek. Behind the dam, Buffalo Lake

A typical CCC camp in the late 1930s at Palo Duro Canyon from where workers constructed roads, cabins, rest areas, and hiking trails. Courtesy of Panhandle-Plains Historical Museum

attracted fishermen, swimmers, boaters, campers, significant numbers of waterfowl and other migratory birds (eight hundred thousand ducks and geese in the 1960s) on the Central Flyway, and it offered great facilities until the mid-1970s, when the creek and springs that fed it dried up and a 1978 flood impaired the dam, causing officials to reconsider the empty lake's purpose. In 1992, officials built a new flood-control structure, but the place is dry except after heavy rains. Federally employed personnel and CCC workers also built Muleshoe National Wildlife Refuge in Bailey County. The refuge with its three lakes attracts thousands of migratory birds as well as local wildlife. Likewise, the CCC played a key role in Palo Duro Canyon State Park, where from their camps CCC workers built roads, cabins, and hiking trails.

On the Llano's South Plains, the federal government's Ropesville Resettlement Project drew national attention. The project, one of seventy-eight similar programs, grew out of Roosevelt's Federal Emergency Relief Administration, created in 1933. Located near Ropesville, in extreme southeastern Hockley County, the program aimed to get suffering farmers, workers, sharecroppers, or former landowners on a small family farm. Project leaders purchased some forty-one hundred acres from the Spade Ranch, carved the property into smaller units with a 768-square-foot house, outhouse, shed, chicken house, and a well and windmill. By 1937 leaders had the project ready for its first families and had been approved for an additional forty-eight farms. The project with a total of seventy-seven farms ended in 1943 when the farms came under individual ownership.[23]

In both the Permian Basin and the Texas Panhandle, the petroleum industry in the 1930s with its drilling, transporting, piping, servicing, and refining sectors became more and more a major part of the Texas economy. But it was not without problems. As the gigantic East Texas oil field came on line during the decade, gross overproduction occurred and oil prices dropped to below the cost of production. There followed a period of confusion, illegal drilling, general chicanery, and lawsuits. To stabilize the industry, the state stepped in, brought order, and set drilling quotas and production limits designed to normalize prices so that production output and market demand might remain in line.[24]

Great Plains Shelterbelt Project

In 1934, the US government, led by President Franklin D. Roosevelt, established the Shelterbelt Program (after 1936 it became known as the Prairie States Forestry Project) to help alleviate problems of dirt and dust blowing away from the Great Plains and destroying its rich topsoil. Created within and operated by the Forest Service in its first years, it eventually became part of the Soil Conservation Service. Designed in part to relieve unemployment problems in the Great Plains states, the project hired thousands of workers who before 1942 planted two hundred million trees from western and northern Texas, including the northeastern Llano Estacado, to Canada.

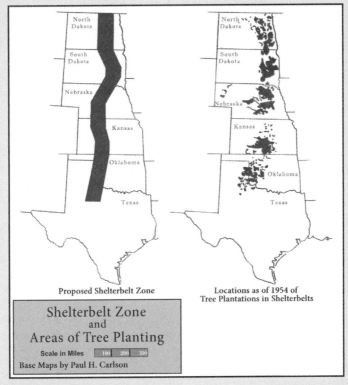

The maps, based on a 1934 New York Times article and a 1954 government report, show the controversial "Shelterbelt Zone" and the actual planting sites as of 1954. Courtesy of Paul Carlson

Workers planted trees as shelterbelts and windbreaks. They placed the tree belts and breaks on private farm or ranch property along roadways and section lines and around homesteads. Designed to slow the wind and thus halt wind-erosion problems, shelterbelts often included several rows of different sizes and species of trees. Farmers who cared for the young trees found that as the trees grew over time, the shelterbelts worked—at least to a limited extent. The belts also attracted wildlife, including deer, gamebirds, rabbits, fox, and squirrels, and coyotes who hunted them.

With the Texas headquarters in Wichita Falls, project personnel hired workers; sought nurseries to produce young tree plantings; and contacted farmers, ranchers, and county officials to locate sites for shelterbelts. Eventually, the Works Progress Administration and the Civilian Conservation Corps took over most of the tree-planting work. Farmers and ranchers in several northeastern Llano Estacado counties, including Roberts, Gray, Donley, Armstrong, and Carson, plus others in the northern Panhandle received shelterbelts and windbreaks. Some of them are still working.

In its early years, there was plenty of criticism for the Shelterbelt Program. Farmers did not want to give up much land for windbreaks that might be seventeen to twenty-one rows of trees wide or about ten acres for a quarter section (160 acres) of land. A reduction of rows per shelterbelt followed. Ten-row shelterbelts became common with fewer rows for windbreaks around homesteads.

Many people, including some forest experts, argued that forest plantations, such as shelterbelts, would not work on the semiarid plains. But farmers and ranchers who took even minimal care—fencing from livestock, some water in the first year, careful soil preparation for planting—of the trees on their property saw that within a few years the shelterbelts provided important benefits.

A major criticism involved funding. Several authorities believed that relief funds should not be used on projects whose success could not be judged adequately for years. As a result, an original appropriation of fifteen million dollars for the shelterbelts was cut to one million dollars. The Works Progress Administration stepped in with money to save the project.

An early press release and announcement of the shelterbelt project included a map to indicate where the trees would be planted. Through misinterpretation, the map suggested that a solid belt of trees one hundred miles wide and running from Texas to Canada would be planted with trees. While such a solid forest of trees was never considered, the map created a public relations nightmare. Heavy ridicule followed.

The Prairie States Forestry Program came to an end in 1942. A detailed planting report issued twelve years later evaluated the program as a mild success: it put people to work, ameliorated some wind erosion and saved soil, attracted wildlife, and in general improved the attractiveness of farm and ranch homesteads of those who participated.

Whether in the oil patch, on the farm or ranch, or in town during the Great Depression, life and living activities on the Llano Estacado continued. With people unemployed and money short, the activities of necessity became simple, less costly affairs. Movie theaters with their low fares and cheap popcorn did fine, for many citizens found in local theaters an avenue of escape. Indeed, some of the most popular movies in the 1930s featured well-dressed and wealthy Americans in large, extravagant homes. Miniature golf proved popular. Gasoline refueling stations likewise performed well in the Depression years as automobiles, like theaters, provided an inexpensive means of escape through Sunday-afternoon drives or short excursions to a rural campground or picnic area. Silver Falls in Crosby County, as in the nineteenth century, was a popular destination, especially for Texas Tech students.

To enhance childhood education, the state, by merging small, rural school districts, reorganized its public school's structure. Massive consolidation followed. In the process, three or four, and sometimes five,

Joe Fortenberry and Changing Basketball Rules

Joe Fortenberry (1911–93) was one of the Llano Estacado's most notable athletes. A basketball player of outstanding skill, he was also a player of exceptional height for the 1920s and early 1930s. This 1929 Happy High School graduate, notes sportswriter Clay Coppedge, "basically revolutionized the game of basketball by giving fans—and reporters—their first glimpse of what we know today as the slam dunk." He also played on the college team at West Texas State Teachers College (West Texas A&M University) that was advertised in 1933 as "The Tallest Team in America."

Fortenberry was born in tiny Leo in Cooke County. His family moved to the Happy area when he was a youth, and he learned basketball at Happy High School. He helped lead the Happy Cowboys to county and regional championships before enrolling at West Texas State, where he became an All-American in 1932–33. His teams at West Texas repeatedly won the Texas Intercollegiate Athletic Association championship, and they won a total of six times before the conference dissolved in 1933, the year Fortenberry graduated from West Texas.

According to the university's chief historian Marty Kuhlman, Fortenberry was six feet, nine inches tall. Thus, he towered above the opposing players, and as he possessed a good leaping ability, he proved nearly impossible to guard. There were other very tall players—at a time when most players were under six feet—on the team, which led to the "tallest team" moniker. After graduation in 1933, Fortenberry went to work for Globe Refinery in what Coppedge calls "basketball-mad McPherson, Kansas, where he was the star" on the Globe Refinery–sponsored Amateur Athletic Union (AAU) team, the McPherson Globe Oilers. The team won the 1936 AAU national championship.

Shortly afterward, Fortenberry was in New York to try out for the US Olympic basketball team. Michael McKnight, writing for Sports Illustrated in 2015, indicated that "when Joe Fortenberry, a farm boy from Happy, Texas threw one down at the West Side YMCA in New York City on March 9, 1936, he may not have been the first man to dunk a basketball, but he was the first to do it in an aesthetically stirring way, and in front of the right people." Arthur J. Daley of the New York Times was there. He wrote of Fortenberry's dunks: "This new version of the lay-up shot left observers simply flabbergasted." Fortenberry made the Olympic team, and in Berlin, site of the 1936 games, his US team went undefeated and won the gold medal while playing outside, once in a rainstorm.

Some basketball rules soon changed, and Clay Coppedge claims Fortenberry was responsible. A rules committee abolished the practice of starting every possession with a jump ball. Joe was too tall and too good. The committee also outlawed goaltending, in part because Joe had a talent for swatting balls away from the basket.

During World War II, Fortenberry played with the Army Air Corps team. Afterward he married and with his wife and three children settled in Amarillo. He accepted a position with Phillips Petroleum Company and played for the Phillips 66ers AAU team. In 1959, he became the first athlete inducted into the Panhandle Sports Hall of Fame. Joe Fortenberry died in Amarillo in 1993, an eighty-two-year-old former farm boy from Happy who changed the game of basketball.

rural school districts on the Llano Estacado, each located at a crossroad hamlet or tiny village, became one district centered at a larger community. The Cooper Rural High School district in Lubbock County, for example, in 1936 combined schools at Slide, Barton, New Hope, and Union with a larger one at Woodrow. In 2022, it is the very large Lubbock-Cooper Independent School District. Because local schools provided community identity, were a consumer of local business products and services, and offered housing for teachers and administrators, a town or village that lost its school through consolidation declined or died. Partly as a result, Slide, Barton, New Hope, and Union are in 2022 only dots on highway maps. Clearly, however, consolidation improved the state's educational delivery system.[25]

Higher education continued apace. Texas Technological College suffered a brief period of declining enrollment at the beginning of the Depression but weathered the economic storm and saw the number of its students increase later in the decade. The college, led by Mary Woodward Doak and William Curry Holden, opened a historical museum on campus. Short of funds during the Depression, leaders delayed its construction but by 1936 had received enough money to build a basement or ground-floor facility. In 1927, officials in New Mexico established Eastern New Mexico Junior College in Portales in Roosevelt County, but the Depression delayed its construction. It opened in 1934, became a four-year institution with the name Eastern New Mexico College in 1940, and in 1949 with the establishment of some graduate programs became Eastern New Mexico University. Amarillo College, which had opened in the late 1920s, attracted in the 1930s many students in part because they could remain close to home during the Depression.

At the same time, Llano Estacado–based musicians, artists, writers, scholars, and others made significant contributions to intellectual and cultural life. In the 1920s and 1930s, Hattie M. Anderson and L. F. Sheffy, historians at West Texas State College in Canyon, were driving forces behind the Panhandle-Plains Historical Society located on campus. J. Evetts Haley, a superbly gifted storyteller and feisty conservative politician and historian, became editor of the society's journal, the *Panhandle-Plains Historical Review*. His work with the society led to the publication of such major studies as *Charles Goodnight: Cowman and Plainsman* and *The XIT Ranch of Texas and the Early Days of the Llano Estacado*. Sheffy led efforts that resulted in the creation in 1933 of the Panhandle-Plains Historical Museum.[26]

At Texas Tech University, William Curry Holden not only became curator of the West Texas Museum on campus but also, like his good friend Haley, was among the first to write about West Texas. Holden's *Alkali Trails*, a social and economic study of West Texas, first pub-

Polk Street in downtown Amarillo lit up the night in 1938. Courtesy of Panhandle-Plains Historical Museum

lished in 1930, remained in print for many years, and in 1998 Texas Tech University Press reprinted the major work. Holden became an internationally famous anthropologist and archaeologist for his work in the discovery and development in the 1930s of the Lubbock Lake Landmark, his expeditions to and studies of the Yaquis in northern Mexico, and his scholarly papers on the ancient Antelope Creek ruins near the Canadian River. Holden and Haley worked together to make the museum's initial collections a formal department as the Southwest Collection in the college in the 1950s. By 2022, their little department had morphed into the Southwest Collection/Special Collections Library, one of the superior academic archives in the United States.

Llano Estacado musicians were also busy. The famed Texas musician Bob Wills from Turkey in Hall County formed his Texas Playboys band in 1934 and played at venues in Lubbock and Amarillo. His popular western swing melodies—sometimes called "hillbilly" harmony—paved the way for modern country-and-western music. For several weeks in the 1930s,

In the 1940s, Lubbock was a thriving, rapidly growing, and modern city with a busy downtown as shown in this view along Broadway. Courtesy of Southwest Collection/Special Collections Library

Roy Rogers (Leonard Slye) and his musical group, the Sons of the Pioneers, honed their skills at Amarillo and Lubbock radio stations. In 1939, Woody Guthrie, the twenty-nine-year-old singer-songwriter from Pampa, high up on the northeastern edge of the Llano, penned "So Long, It's Been Good to Know You" about the Llano's 1935 Black Sunday dust storm. Guthrie was a significant figure in American folk music, and his *Dust Bowl Ballads* album is considered a major contribution to American music.

Near the end of the 1930s the cycle of drought about which Guthrie wrote ended as rainfall increased again. On the Llano Estacado, economic circumstances, however, although improved since the worst hard times, still kept many people out of work, farm conditions for staple-crop agriculture fragile, and oil production searching for stability. Then, suddenly, World War II brought an end to the Depression and changed life and activities across America and on the High Plains.

World War II had started in mid-1939 when England and France challenged Germany over the latter's aggressive advance through western Europe. It expanded as Italy, the Soviet Union (Russia), and, in the Far East, Japan became involved. The United States entered the spreading conflict after Japan attacked the American military installations at Pearl Harbor in Hawaii on December 7, 1941. Fighting on land and sea around the world made it a truly global war with dozens of countries involved.

After the Pearl Harbor attack, people on the Llano Estacado volunteered in significant numbers to fight the Japanese and German aggressors. Before the deadly strike, Llano citizens, like those elsewhere in the United States, were divided on the course to follow vis-à-vis the conflict in Europe: stay neutral or provide non-fighting support. After Pearl Harbor, opposition to American involvement in the war—from those who wanted the country to remain neutral—disappeared. The *Amarillo Daily News*, in a statement that reflected Llano sentiment, stated: "At last we have unity. We are aroused. We have the Will to win." The day after the attack people jammed local military recruiting stations in Amarillo, Clovis, Lubbock, Plainview, and elsewhere. They wanted to serve and wanted to get into the fighting as quickly as possible. Many got their wish, including women, who joined auxiliary military groups with some of the women eventually flying large transport planes.[27]

Some men got into the war very soon. As early as November 1940, Texas National Guard troops from the Panhandle (142nd Infantry and 131st Field Artillery) mobilized in Amarillo. One group, the Second Battalion of the 131st Field Artillery, headed for Brownwood, Texas, for further training. Shortly afterward, men of this battalion volunteered for overseas duty and headed for the South Pacific, where they landed on the island of Java. Then, on March 2, 1942, less than three weeks after the Pearl Harbor attack, Japanese troops overran the island and captured the Americans. As B. Byron Price and Frederick J. Rathjen write, all "contact with the Second Battalion was lost . . . and at a terrible price [it] became immortalized as the Lost Battalion of Java."[28]

New Mexico soldiers, many from the Llano Estacado, also suffered. Some eighteen hundred men from Eddy and surrounding counties served in the 200th Coast Artillery Regiment in the Philippines. They were there in December 1941 when Japan attacked and forced thousands of American and Philippine soldiers onto the Bataan Peninsula. Four months later, on April 9, 1942, the fighting ended when over seventy-five thousand exhausted and hungry men, overwhelmed by the better-armed and supplied Japanese forces, surrendered. The Japanese army, not prepared for the large number of prisoners, marched the captives, without food or water, north some sixty-five miles to holding camps. During the march, the prisoners received unmerciful and inhumane treatment, including clubbing, shooting, bayoneting, and beheading. Between three thousand and ten thousand people died in the "Bataan Death March," including half of the members of the 200th Coast Artillery Regiment.[29]

On the Llano Estacado soon after the Pearl Harbor attack, the US Army Air Forces established several training bases: Amarillo Army Air Field, Clovis Army Air Field, Hobbs Army Air Field, Lubbock Army Air Field, and Pampa Army Air Field among them. Moreover, in 1942, the Army Air Forces located glider-plane training bases at Plainview Field in Hale County and at Lamesa Field in Dawson County but in April 1943 transferred the Plainview operations to Lamesa. In addition, in Lubbock, the South Plains Army Airfield, located at the town's Municipal Airport, also trained glider pilots. Established in 1942, the sixteen-hundred-acre "airfield," writes Don Abbe, "became a small city. Several thousand people lived and worked around the clock at" the site north of Lubbock. "Over [80] percent of the approximately six thousand World War II glider pilots," Abbe concludes, "trained at the facility."[30]

In addition to the air bases, the Army Air Forces contracted with civilian flying schools to provide basic flight training and prepare pilots for the war. In Lubbock, Clent Breedlove, who operated two small private airports on the city's south side and ran a teaching program called Civilian Pilot Training, became head of the Army Air Forces' local College Training Detachment (CDT). The detachment soon "became known as the Texas Tech Pre-flights program," writes John W. McCullough, an aviation historian, and by "June 1944, an estimated 3,750 student pilots of the 309th CDT had trained with Breedlove and his instructors" at either Breedlove Field or his nearby Dagley Field.[31]

The new training bases and expanded airfields on the Llano Estacado created important changes for the cities and towns. Housing demands skyrocketed and construction booms followed. Work opportunities became plentiful. Indeed, sometimes jobs went unfilled, even as women in very large numbers returned to the workforce. Not only did wartime demands end the Great Depression in Llano cities, but also, as Abbe and others have written, "the intense demand for agricultural products created an agricultural boom" and high "commodity prices led to full-scale utilization of the land to produce cash crops."[32]

In southeastern New Mexico, the US military established twenty-six precision bombing practice targets. Located on the ground in isolated areas, the Army Air Forces used the targets to train pilots and bombardiers. Associated with some of the region's air training centers, such as those in Clovis and Hobbs, plus others just off the Llano Estacado (including Carlsbad Army Air Field), the sites reached significant size. One south of Melrose in Curry County called the Melrose Bombing Range was huge. Some targets at the sites included wooden pyramids to serve as bull's-eyes, and some were illuminated at night. At least two of the targets stood some seventy miles east of Roswell. More elaborate targets, called geoglyphs, included "large dirt berms in concentric circles," write Donna Blake Birchell and John LeMay, that "formed bulls-eyes surrounded by the whitewashed outlines of factories, plants and ships, complete with smokestacks." A few geoglyphs existed on the western edge of the Llano Estacado, including one near Hobbs that was used from 1942 to 1945. Some of the geoglyphs were berms up to eighteen hundred feet in diameter, six feet high, and fifteen feet across. In 2022, several of them can still be seen, especially from the air.[33]

The Llano Estacado also became home to several prisoner-of-war (POW) camps. One of six major POW camps in southeastern New Mexico existed near Hobbs. In Texas by the end of the war, twenty-one POW camps and twenty temporary facilities housed fifty thousand Axis soldiers, most of them Germans. One of Texas' largest POW camps existed at Hereford in Deaf Smith County. It held more Italian soldiers than German. Just off the Llano, a holding camp existed at McClean in Gray County. Very few prisoners attempted to escape, and eventually

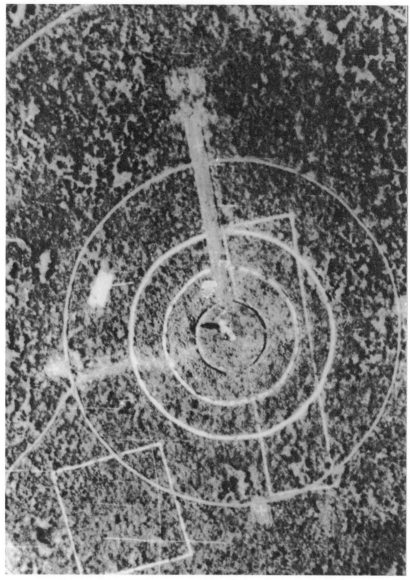

In southeastern New Mexico military geoglyphs, or bombing targets, can be found in Carlsbad, east of Roswell, and south of Melrose. Some, as the one shown here, are large and sophisticated with buildings and extensive berms. Courtesy of Donna Blake Birchell and the Southeastern New Mexico Historical Society

many of them went to work on area farms or accepted other off-camp employment.

Japanese Americans on the Llano Estacado were not treated as well. The Santa Fe Railway had located several of their Japanese American workers in Clovis after 1909 when the town was founded, and over the subsequent years a small but vibrant Japanese ethnic community developed. Japanese children attended both public and private schools in Clovis, and the railroad promoted their fathers to highly skilled positions, especially machinists. "In 1941," write Dolores Mosser and Sammie Simpson, "thirty-two Japanese—fifteen adults and seventeen children—lived in Clovis." After the shocking Pearl Harbor attack placed all Japanese American citizens and Japanese nationals in the United States in danger, Santa Fe Railroad and government officials removed (relocated) the Clovis Japanese, for their protection, to an abandoned CCC camp near Fort Stanton, New Mexico. They had lost their jobs, their homes, their personal possessions, and their livelihood—even though they worked in militarily significant positions.[34]

The Pantex Army Ordnance Plant northeast of Amarillo also proved vital to the war effort. Created in 1942, "Pantex," as locals called it, manufactured bombs and artillery shells. The huge complex put a large number of Amarillo and area residents back to work and bolstered the Amarillo economy, but it brought the dangers of foreign wars close to home. On November 30, 1944, one of the "white" trains—referring to the white canvas used as covers on the train cars—from Pantex carrying 165 five-hundred-pound bombs jumped the tracks at Tolar, New Mexico, caught fire, burned, and detonated the bombs. The explosion destroyed Tolar, leveling or damaging every building in town. Because most residents, including children, were away at work or school, the death toll was small, but the blast was enormous and could be felt some sixty-five miles away.[35]

At the time of the Tolar blast, World War II, although its end was nearly a year away, had turned in favor of the Allies. The massive D-Day assault of German positions in Europe on June 6, 1944, was less than five months away. North Africa had been retaken and Allied forces were in Italy. In the Far East, Allied forces were island-hopping their way toward

Japan, taking one Japanese-held position after another, including the Philippines and the island of Java, where thousands of Llano Estacado soldiers had died.

Clearly, the war spurred economic growth on the Llano Estacado. Ranchers aided by huge market demands both at home and abroad delivered extraordinary numbers of livestock, especially sheep and cattle. Likewise, farmers supported by favorable rainfall amounts produced astonishing crop yields, not only for cotton and wheat but also grain sorghum and alfalfa. In the upper Llano beef and wheat production between 1940 and 1945 had "increased astronomically." On the South Plains, cotton cultivation swelled to the point where the Llano subregion became "one of the leading cotton producing areas in the nation" and the world.[36]

In the Llano's larger cities, population growth proved spectacular. Defense work at airfields, new opportunities in housing construction and related industries, and with businesses creating jobs for both men and women, large numbers of people moved to Amarillo, Lubbock, Clovis, Midland, and Odessa. Amarillo's population, for example, increased from, 51,686 people in 1940 to 74,246 in 1950. Lubbock's population more than doubled, from 31,853 persons in 1940 to 71,747 in 1950. The Permian Basin's expanding oil industry during the war also led to significant growth in Midland and Odessa.[37]

The war impacted the Llano Estacado in another important way. It forced Llano citizens to view a world far from their High Plains homeland and transformed much of the region's social and intellectual landscape. "Prior to World War II," notes Bishop Leroy T. Matthiesen, the region "was redneck country insulated from the remainder of the world." Then the war drew thousands of young men from the east to places like Amarillo, Clovis, Hobbs, Lubbock, Midland, and Odessa. It also sent Llano "volunteers and draftees by the thousands to the world outside." Moreover, the Llano's African American and Hispanic populations increased during the war, helping make all citizens "more tolerant of people who differed from them."[38]

During and after the war, life in rural areas of the Llano Estacado changed. The Rural Electrification Administration, created in 1934 as part of Roosevelt's New Deal, through dozens of government-sponsored rural cooperatives slowly brought electric power to rural areas. Electric lighting, heating, and handy household appliances followed, easing life for rural families, especially women. On the other hand, rural populations declined and tiny crossroad communities faded away, in part, as noted, through school consolidation and in part as a result of the trend toward larger and larger farms. In addition, the state's 1949 Colson-Briscoe Act created the Texas Farm to Market Roads, a system that extended paved roads through the state and the Llano Estacado to improve the means of getting crops and livestock to market. But in an unforeseen result, the better roadways made it possible for farmers and ranchers to move off their rural property and use the good roads to travel back and forth from new homes in town. That same year, the state's Gilmour-Aikin laws renewed and expanded school consolidation on the Llano Estacado. The subsequent closing of schools added to the increasing number of Llano ghost towns. Indeed, consolidation after 1949 reduced the number of school districts in Texas from 6,409 to 1,539.

On the Llano Estacado after 1949, consolidation of schools, improved rural roads and highways, a growing city population, an agricultural trend to fewer but larger farms, and the increasing influence of petroleum in the economy set the stage for the Llano's impressive urbanization and large-scale agribusiness activity in the second half of the twentieth century—the subjects of chapter 10.

Summary

During the thirty years between 1920 and 1950, the Llano Estacado continued to transform itself. It was as always in its past a place in flux. Influenced in large measure by two global wars, shifting weather patterns and ecological developments, and an increasing fascination with national social and cultural trends, the Llano and its citizens, like Americans everywhere, faced prosperity with confidence and troubled times with determination. The Jazz Age involved such unsettling developments as the Red Scare and such upsetting institutions as the Ku Klux Klan, but also it included some attractive collective craziness, some economic prosperity, some social and intellectual growth, and with new, modern conveniences some easier living patterns.

Then, suddenly, the Great Depression, with its high unemployment and its agricultural hardship together with an oil industry in chaos, revealed altogether too much of the stress and harshness associated with living on the Llano Estacado. Fortunately, federal government programs and the Llano citizens' own determination to adjust and persevere through the hard times sustained life for those impacted most severely by the deep economic slump. Those people less harshly squeezed during the 1930s aided others and supported traditional social and cultural programs of the past.

Although much had changed during the 1930s, much had remained the same. Then came World War II. The war returned prosperity to the Llano Estacado and got the region's people working again. The US War Department (soon to be the Department of Defense) through its Army Air Corps brought several airfields with soldiers and airmen from across the country to the Llano. Population gains in cities followed, but such gains, at least in part, contributed to the rural population decline that continued into the 1950s and afterward.

10

Urbanization and Agribusiness

With World War II over, people living on the Llano Estacado turned to domestic issues, several of which impacted the region in positive ways. Many homebound soldiers, unwilling to return to farm life and the cotton field, found major housing shortages in their hometowns. But, fortunately, builders and construction companies for the first time in years could acquire materials to create such housing units as apartment complexes and single-family homes. The building boom that followed the war and the pent-up demand (dating to the stock market crash in 1929) for modern home appliances, plus bursting savings accounts and big spending, all combined to unleash a decade of prosperity that launched America and the Llano Estacado into a period of unparalleled growth.

In Amarillo, many citizens at first found the new prosperity elusive. In August 1945, the huge Pantex Plant closed as did the nearby Cactus Ordnance Plant. A year later, the Amarillo Army Airfield shut down. The War Manpower Commission indicated that forty-seven hundred military positions in the city had been lost, which, of course, threw a lot of families into unemployment lines. Yet other jobs became available in construction and in trucking and transportation. Moreover, Amarillo, already the administrative key to Panhandle oil operations, became the center of an expanding upper Llano Estacado agribusiness industry, and city leaders sought to fill job opportunities associated with a huge swell in irrigated farming.

Thus, after some initial setbacks, Amarillo, like such other Llano Estacado cities as Plainview, Lubbock, and the Permian Basin oil towns of Midland and Odessa, enjoyed economic growth. The development included a house-building surge. With an increasing population but little construction activity during the 1930s Depression and with wartime lumber restrictions, the postwar housing expansion was a nationwide phenomenon, one that continued through much of the 1950s. In fact, a major feature of the post–World War II Llano Estacado was the region's construction-based prosperity.

In Amarillo, such growth continued despite a destructive tornado in 1949. That stormy blast, occurring on May 15, ripped through the city, killing five people, injuring nearly three hundred others, and bringing major wreckage to houses and businesses in several parts of the city. It flattened a twenty-block area in south Amarillo, damaged forty-five aircraft at the little Tradewinds Airport, leveled buildings at the Tri-State Fairgrounds, and blew a Santa Fe train of thirty-five cars off the tracks, killing and injuring dozens of horses. Accompanying rain, which was heavy, flooded large parts of the city.[1]

Except for the tornado, events in Lubbock and on the South Plains mirrored those in Amarillo and the Texas Panhandle. The Lubbock Army Airfield closed in 1945, for example, but four years later the US Department of Defense reactivated it as Reese Air Force Base. Lubbock's population surged, more than doubling from 31,853 inhabitants in 1940 to 71,747 in 1950. Major expansion in cotton cultivation across the South Plains in the 1950s and the continued growth of Texas Technological College helped push the Lubbock population to 128,691 in 1960. Also during the 1950s, the city became a center for agribusiness activity, much of it associated with irrigation on farms. New manufacturing plants and distribution facilities opened, providing irrigation pumps, piping and other tubular supplies, as well as sprinkler systems and related service operations. Older cotton mills and processing plants expanded and new ones opened. Like Amarillo on the northern edge of the Llano Estacado, Lubbock, in the heart of the South Plains, became a center for marketing fertilizers and pesticides, and in both cities, new businesses to sell and distribute farm equipment appeared.

The Graham-Hoeme plow with its chisel-like plowshares sold across the United States and around the world. It highly influenced and aided Llano Estacado agriculture. Courtesy of Panhandle-Plains Historical Museum

One of the most effective new pieces of agricultural equipment was the Graham-Hoeme chisel plow. Created in rough form by Fred Hoeme, an Oklahoma wheat grower, in the late 1930s and perfected by William T. Graham, an inventive and experimental farmer near Silverton in Briscoe County, Texas, in the early 1940s, the plow with chisel-like plowshares reached under the topsoil and broke open the ground. The action, as historians B. Byron Price and Frederick J. Rathjen note, "helped the soil catch and retain rainfall while leaving the topsoil intact and covered with a stubble mulch, which, in turn, served to hold moisture and to prevent soil from blowing." It proved to be, they note, a major "technological innovation in the cause of soil and water conservation."[2]

After Hoeme sold his share in the invention, Graham opened a manufacturing shop in Amarillo. By the end of the 1940s, he employed over one hundred workers to build the plow, and in the 1950s the company, now the Graham Plow Company, Inc., "attracted," according to Amarillo historians, "world-wide attention" and sold the machine on a growing international market. Like Joseph Glidden's original barbed wire, however, the plow was easily copied, and despite dozens of patents on it, big agricultural-machine manufacturing corporations built their own versions of Graham's effective and popular plow. As a result, in the 1960s the Graham Plow Company went out of business.[3]

The new plow came just in time to help alleviate a long, difficult drought in the 1950s. Begun in parts of the Llano Estacado in 1949, the drought turned vicious in 1951 and afterward. In the upper Llano rainfall amounts declined well below levels to sustain agriculture. Amarillo, for example, recorded only 12.15 inches of rain in 1952, an amount some six inches short of average, and in 1956, the worst year in terms of the 1950s drought, only 9.94 inches of rain fell on the city. In Lubbock, just over 10 inches of rain fell in 1956, and during the thirteen years from 1947 through 1959 rainfall totals reached above the 18.23-inch average in only two years (1949 and 1957). The overall average in Lubbock during the drought was 13.38, but 11.36 if the two above-average years are eliminated.[4]

Without irrigation, the low rainfall amounts were not enough to sustain crop agriculture. In other parts of the Llano, such as in Lamb and Cochran Counties, rainfall amounts also dropped. Indeed, most of the South Plains experienced rainfall totals of three to five inches below normal. In Lamb County, farmer William DeLoach in 1956 complained of a "cat" of a sandstorm in May and an inability to plant his cotton for lack of moisture. He later got seed in the ground, but in September he wrote in his diary, "The crop on my place is in bad shape as well as all other dry land crops. Too dry." Called the "great drought" by some observers, the 1950s dry spell proved devastating to many farmers, especially dryland operators, that is, those farmers without irrigation systems.[5]

Several developments grew from the drought. In one, there was a dramatic increase in field irrigation made possible by the availability of powerful, fuel-driven pumps and cheap natural gas to run them. The number of wells on the High Plains increased from 14,000 irrigating 1.86 million acres in 1950 to 27,500 irrigating 3.5 million acres four years later. The number of irrigated acres continued to increase through the end of the 1950s and into the 1960s and afterward. Indeed, the number did not level off until after 1997.[6]

In another development, Amarillo and Lubbock, as noted, became hubs for equipment manufacturing, sales and service, and well-drilling operations. Their banks provided financing to establish expensive well and irrigation systems. By the early 2000s, however, as the number of irrigated acres on the Llano Estacado had begun a slow decline, irrigation-equipment manufacturing like center-pivot systems began to concentrate elsewhere on the Great Plains, such as in Kansas and Nebraska.

In a third change, irrigation, which worked well with row crops, boosted further the production of cotton and grain sorghum. In turn, the popularity of tractors and tractor-drawn equipment in the 1950s and afterward increased, and concomitantly more farm implement and tractor dealerships opened in places like Littlefield, Plainview, Hereford, Lamesa, Morton, and Brownfield. On the South Plains, many farmers made cotton their only crop and thus abandoned any pretense to diversified farming.

Moreover, just as agricultural scientists improved cotton varieties and enhanced seed qualities, engineers upgraded irrigation technology. From

In the early 1950s, natural gas–powered irrigation pumps proved a boon for agriculture on the semiarid Llano Estacado. Courtesy of Panhandle-Plains Historical Museum

on-ground irrigation in the beginning to the use of aluminum piping in the 1960s, polyvinyl chloride (PVC) thermoplastic in the 1970s, and flexible throwaway plastic piping in the 2000s, changes were constant. At the same time, belowground drip irrigation gained some attention, and, of course, in 2022, huge center-pivot systems dominated all crop—cotton, wheat, grain sorghum, sunflower, and others—irrigation on Llano Estacado farming operations.[7]

Additional innovations and scientific and technological advances in irrigation strategies—in fact, in all agriculture—have changed farming and ranching. In cotton growing, for example, as explained by John T. "Jack" Becker and others, "with the use of computers and satellite technology" in 2022, "a South Plains farmer" using wireless phone connections essentially "can irrigate his cotton from his home or from his truck." Modern computer "software can show [a] farmer pictures of his cotton taken by satellites hundreds of miles in space." Such technology allows cotton growers "to look at [their] fields, check weather conditions, and then communicate with [their] center pivot" system receiver units "to apply the correct amount of moisture on [the] cotton." In some cases, such technology might also suggest to growers when their "cotton is being stressed by insect pests or a chemical deficiency." Both problems might be handled, Becker and others suggest, "by putting the correct agricultural chemicals" in proper amounts in water being sent through the complex system.[8]

Finally, irrigation with its costs, equipment, and maintenance needs together with a concomitant growing sophistication in mechanization helped reorder society and demography on the Llano Estacado. A broad range of striking developments followed. In cotton cultivation, for example, as explained by Don Abbe and others, mechanical harvesters in the 1950s and afterward eliminated the need for seasonal workers, such as migrant cotton harvesters, and together with the spreading use of irrigation, mechanization led to agricultural consolidation. "Farms," they write, "got larger and larger, but there were fewer of them." Rural populations declined, schools merged, and tiny towns disappeared. Through much of the Texas portion of the Llano Estacado, most counties in the 1960s lost population. Some lost as much as 50 percent of their residents.[9]

In Roosevelt County, New Mexico, several towns disappeared or declined. Bethel, located several miles west of Portales, vanished. A group of Church of Christ homesteaders from Lockney, Texas, founded Bethel in 1901. A year later the settlers built a school and "boasted that it was one of the few two-teacher schools in the county." In 1903, the school enrolled 243 students. Local historians argue that this "farming and ranching community became well known for its rich soil" and for the cotton its farmers produced. The Bethel Gin, one of the first cotton gins in the county, opened in the 1950s. But, not long afterward, cotton growing slowed in the area and the gin closed in the late 1960s. The town is no more. Caprock in northwestern Lea County was a thriving community in the 1930s with a school, store, gasoline station, and homes, but in the 2020s it contained empty buildings and a couple dozen folks living in the ranch area.[10]

In some ways, Kenna, along the Atchison, Topeka and Santa Fe Railway some thirty-five miles southwest of Portales, mirrors Caprock.

Kenna in Roosevelt County, New Mexico, is a ghost town along US Highway 70. It is pictured here about 1947 as Rural Electrification administration (REA) workers extended power lines in the area. Courtesy of Gayle Walke

Established as a campsite in the 1890s for workers as they built the railroad, Kenna became a permanent village after 1899. Within ten years, the growing town boasted a post office, a bank, two hotels, and several stores and saloons. By 1909, Kenna had become one of the largest cattle-shipping points in the state. In 2022, it was empty but with a tiny community church and a few people living in the surrounding area.

Similar stories exist for other Roosevelt County communities. In 2022, they seemed to have little chance for a future good life. Arch is a ghost town. Floyd has a small store and a few people in the surrounding area. Elida, which held 534 people in 1960, counted 176 folks in 2020. Causey totaled 52 inhabitants in 2020. Lingo is a ghost town. Milnesand with its unusual name and 35 people in 2020 was home to an annual prairie chicken festival from 2002 to 2012. Through much of the twentieth century in Roosevelt County, people sold farms and businesses and left their rural communities. Portales, the largest city in the county with a population of 12,123 in 2020, benefited from the rural decline, but it too endured population pressure from Clovis, a larger city with Cannon Air Force Base only eleven miles distant.

REA workers endure a dust storm near the beginning of the long 1950s drought at the village of Milnesand along State Highway 206 in far-southern Roosevelt County, New Mexico. Courtesy of Gayle Walker

In Quay County, Forrest, founded after the turn of the century, held a post office between 1908 and 1969 and a school that won the state high school basketball championship in 1933. The school closed in 1957. The last store in Forrest shuttered in 1975. There is little left as people moved away. Noting the region's demographic shifts, Abbe and others write that as people in "rural areas of the [Llano Estacado] left the land" in the late twentieth century, cities "grew much faster, reflecting a transition to an urban economy."[11]

The urbanization of the Llano Estacado, in what was and remains largely open farm and ranch country, grew from more than rural immigration. The continued expansion in petroleum mining and oil's auxiliary businesses attracted people far from the Llano Estacado and spurred growth in Amarillo, Hobbs, Lubbock, and especially Midland and Odessa. Lubbock and Amarillo became transportation hubs with their airports, major railroads, and trucking companies. Interstate Highway 40 in the Amarillo area and Interstate Highway 20 through Midland and Odessa also facilitated urban growth. Military spending associated with airfields in Clovis, Amarillo, and Lubbock further encouraged the growth—especially in Amarillo, where, write Price and Rathjen, in "1967 about 16,000 personnel were station at Amarillo Air Force Base." The government, however, deactivated the air base in 1968, for a time crippling the Amarillo economy. In fact, the Amarillo population declined by some ten thousand residents between 1966 and 1970. The city recovered, of course, aided by a heavy-construction industry that built highways, suburban-like shopping malls, and large housing subdivisions.[12]

College and university growth on the Llano Estacado also helped the trend toward urbanization. For example, Lubbock Christian University, started as part of a secondary school in 1954, branched off as a junior college in 1957 and a senior college in 1972. In 2015, now with university status, it enrolled nearly two thousand students. The University of Texas Permian Basin, authorized by the legislature in 1969 and founded in 1973 in Odessa, enrolled over six thousand students in 2017. That same year Eastern New Mexico University in Portales, the largest regional college in the state, also enrolled over six thousand students. In Hobbs, the University of the Southwest, a private Christian school founded in 1962, registered about one thousand students in 2020. New Mexico Junior College, established in Hobbs in 1966, enrolled nearly four thousand students in 2017. The establishment and spectacular growth (almost exponential) of Texas Tech University's gigantic medical school complex in Lubbock plus its medical branches in Amarillo and Midland and the Texas Tech School of Veterinary Medicine in Amarillo, which opened with sixty-four students in 2021, also encouraged the trend toward the Llano's peculiar style of urbanization.

Urban growth aside, agribusiness remained a driving force in the region's economy. Cattle feeding, for instance, which had been around for a long time, expanded in the upper Llano and Panhandle in the 1960s and afterward. Two men were particularly responsible: Paul Engler, a Nebraska cattle buyer, and W. L. Stangel, retired Texas Tech agricultural professor. Engler saw exceptional promise in the Amarillo area for cattle feeding: a "mild climate," as Becker and others have written, "open spaces, abundant cattle, and the proximity to large amounts of corn and grain sorghum." Engler opened Hereford Feedyard in Amarillo. Stangel, while traveling through Arizona and California, writes Becker in *West Texas*, "noted the large number of West Texas cattle being fed West Texas grain" and thus encouraged entrepreneurs, like Engler, to establish cattle-feeding operations in West Texas close to sources for both cattle and feed. Stangel's promotion and Engler's success soon got others involved, and "the number of cattle on feed . . . [increased] from 220,000 in 1966 to 1.3 million in 1980." Becker notes that at "one time nine giant feedyards fattened cattle near Amarillo. Some yards held up to 100,000 head. Cactus Feeders, founded in 1975 by Engler and Thomas H. Dittmer, became in 1985 the largest custom feeder in the world." According to Orville Howard, it funneled "more than $1 billion into the Texas Panhandle economy" and annually "finished out more than 800,000 head of cattle."[13]

After 2000, dairy farming expanded on the Llano Estacado. From early in its pioneering period, some farmers—maybe a lot of them—kept a milch cow or two on their property. After the turn of the century, William Henry Bush of the Frying Pan Ranch encouraged farmers and stockmen of the Amarillo area to try dairy farming. In Illinois, Bush saw how milch cows provided ample income to dairymen. Although a few men and some women tried it, dairying did not catch on in the 1920s and 1930s as farmers turned more toward cotton and wheat production and then wrestled with the Depression. After World War II, dairying gained some ground, and then in the late 1990s and after 2000, dairy operations on the Llano Estacado exploded. Curry and Roosevelt counties in New Mexico were the first to attract major dairy operators, several of them Pacific Coast dairymen who found eco-friendly conditions on the southern High Plains less restrictive than the increasingly prohibitive environmental laws in California. Dairy farming, characterized by very large operations, soon expanded into Texas. Hockley, Cochran, Lamb, Hale, Randall, Potter, and Bailey Counties all became home to big dairies. Dairy operations on the Texas portion of the Llano averaged two thousand milking cows. In New Mexico, one dairy farm in Quay County apparently handled in scattered locations nearly forty thousand animals, milking the cows twice daily—a lot of milk indeed.[14]

While major dairy production was rather new to the Llano Estacado, petroleum mining and oil production remained a staple of the region's economy. They continued to provide jobs and income for Llano citizens and contribute to county and school district revenue pools. The Permian Basin fields in the Hobbs, Midland, and Odessa areas, of course, remained the largest producing regions. After discovery in Hockley County of the Slaughter Field in the late 1930s, oil production there grew in the 1940s, 1950s, and afterward. Development of fields near Post in Garza County and through Plains in Yoakum County and near Denver City along the Yoakum-Gaines county line in the 1930s and 1940s further promoted oil production. Two decades later, oil boycotts by the Organization of Petroleum Exporting Countries (OPEC) dramatically increased oil and gas prices, and a growing demand for petroleum, write Abbe and others, "led to exploration throughout the South Plains." Oil men developed small pools "in Lubbock, Lynn, and other formerly oil-less counties." Oil prices shot up, bringing jobs, immigrants, and prosperity to much of the Llano Estacado, helping produce a significant oil boom through much of the state.[15]

The boom did not last. In the mid-1980s, oil prices plummeted. The

Permian Basin economy entered a severe recession and all but the strongest oil-related companies went bankrupt. Employment crashed. The Panhandle oil fields and Amarillo, their administrative center, also suffered hard times. Indeed, through much of the state, the oil-based slump caused bank failures, unemployment, and general economic stagnation. In the 1990s, the Llano Estacado, the Permian Basin, Amarillo, and the rest of the state recovered from the sharp downturn. The unfortunate boom-and-bust cycle in the oil patch continued into the 2000s with the financial ups and downs occurring in part because the Texas and Llano petroleum industries cannot control global oil prices.

Llano Estacado citizens, however, do indeed control the region's music forms and fashions. From cowboy dances and blowouts in the 1880s through a big-band era and western swing in the 1930s and 1940s to rock and roll in the 1950s and afterward, the Llano has a rich musical tradition. As part of that tradition, Lubbock's Buddy Holly became a national figure in the nation's popular rock-and-roll music scene, and he inspired plenty of others, including Mac Davis of Lubbock and apparently the Beatles, the unsurpassed music group from Liverpool, England.

Other musicians from the Llano Estacado gained national fame and respect. They include Jimmy Dean of Plainview; Don Williams of Abernathy; Virgil Johnson of Lubbock; Tanya Tucker of Seminole; Roy Orbison of Wink; Waylon Jennings of Littlefield; Ralna English, who attended Texas Technological College; Roger Williams, who was an Amarillo disk jockey; Guy Penrod of Hobbs; Odis Echols of Clovis; and others such as Sonny Curtis, Joe B. Mauldin, Bob Montgomery, Nicky Sullivan, and Jerry Allison, who sang with Holly's group the Crickets. More recently, the Flatlanders band of Butch Hancock, Joe Ely, and Jimmy Dale Gilmore has dominated Texas and Llano music. Jay Boy Adams, the Maines Brothers, and the Hispanic group the Home Boys, all from Lubbock, have gained fame. Natalie Maines of the Dixie Chicks has received international notoriety. Andy Wilkinson, a former musician-in-residence at Texas Tech's Southwest Collection/Special Collections Library, has encouraged and led a large group of young country-western singers, songwriters, and performers. In opera, Lubbock's David Gaschen appeared for several years on Broadway as the phantom in *Phantom of the Opera*, and in late 2021 he began performing as Jean Valjean in *Les Misérables*. The Llano's Mary Jane Johnson also gained fame as an opera singer.

Development, growth, and support for such musicians came from several colleges and universities. Texas Tech University, South Plains College, and West Texas A&M University all have strong music and theater traditions. Nonacademic organizations likewise have supported singers and songwriters. One of the more significant such institutions on the Llano was the Norman Petty Recording Studio in Clovis. Petty, a successful musician and songwriter, recorded Holly, of course, but also Buddy Knox, Jimmy Gilmer and the Fireballs, and others. Jennings, Orbison, Red Stegall, and Bobby Fuller cut their earliest recordings at the famous studio. In Lubbock, the Cotton Club, established in 1939 and later owned by local and Texas musician Tommy Hancock, hosted Bob Wills, Elvis Presley, Little Richard, Buddy Holly, and others. Also, many young musicians got their start playing at Christopher R. Stubblefield's tiny Stubb's Bar-B-Q joint on East Broadway. More recently Don Caldwell and the Cactus Theater have promoted young musicians, and the Lubbock Lights festival has gained popularity. Petty's studio, the Cotton Club, and Stubb's Bar-B-Q are gone, but in New Mexico the Lea County Fair and Rodeo concerts each August in Lovington and the Clovis Musical Festival each September continue to attract a wide variety of amateur and professional entertainers. Large audiences, especially on Hispanic Heritage Celebration night at the Clovis festival, attend to listen and watch.[16]

The outdoor musical drama *Texas* ("TEXAS Outdoor Musical") also provided plenty of training for young singers and dancers. The Texas Panhandle Heritage Foundation guides the big production, but under some financial pressure due to the COVID-19 pandemic, it joined with the Panhandle-Plains Historical Society/Museum in 2021 to produce the popular musical. The Cultural Foundation of the Texas Panhandle, whose mission is to preserve the cultural underpinnings of the region, serves as an umbrella-like advisory body for the two sponsoring groups.

Reasons for the robust Llano Estacado music traditions are many, of course. In a big, broad interpretation, historian David Hackett Fischer looked to England of the deep past. That is, he traces the Llano's music norms and customs back east through Texas and the Old South to Virginia and ultimately to southern and western England of the seventeenth century. In his big book *Albion's Seed*, he suggests that many folkways, habits, forms, and traditions relating to the South and to Texas came from southwestern England. In America, as people made their way west, their folkways changed and evolved, but germs and seeds of the original spread, moving through the South and continuing west as families moved. The "germs," as Fischer calls them, included music traditions. Perhaps. And perhaps on the Llano Estacado, as novelist John Green might say, music isn't optional.[17]

Writers, some associated with Llano Estacado universities, also made significant contributions to the region's cultural milieu. The number seems countless. In Amarillo and the Panhandle area Loula Grace Erdman, who wrote the prize-winning novel *Years of the Locust* and other books, led the way. Kimberly Willis Holt received national awards for her books, including the prestigious National Book Award for *When Zachary Beaver Comes to Town*. Al Dewlen, a newspaper-man-turned-novelist, enjoyed enormous success for his literary accomplishments. His *Twilight of Honor* was an international best seller and became the basis for a popular Hollywood film, but among Llano residents, *The Bone Pickers*, set in Amarillo, is perhaps his most-admired book. John R. Erickson, a Panhandle rancher, has published seventy-five books and hundreds of serious ranch articles but is best known for his highly popular Hank the Cowdog series, which has sold ten million copies worldwide. Carol Sobieski, a screenwriter, penned movies for television, including *Christmas Sunshine*. Exceptional cowboy poets include Buck Ramsey and Red Stegall. Ramsey, who was born on a farm near New Home in Lubbock County but grew up in the Amarillo area, is best known for *Grass*, his long epic poem of cowboy life. The brilliant, Amarillo-based Stegall, a songwriter, recording artist, and television and movie personality, has been called the "Cowboy Poet of Texas."[18]

In the Lubbock and South Plains area writers have produced a number of fine works. Jane Gilmour Rushing, who received a PhD from Texas Tech and later taught at the university, wrote a number of books, many of them set in West Texas. Her groundbreaking *Mary Dove*, about interracial marriage on the frontier, is a mastery of character and place. Singer, songwriter, poet, and playwright Andy Wilkinson has received several honors for his compositions, including five Western Heritage "Wrangler" Awards for his dramas and other publications. Walt McDonald, a Lubbock native, retired air force colonel, and former college professor, published many fine collections of poetry, including such Western Heritage "Wrangler" Award winners as *The Digs in Escondido Canyon, All That Matters: The Texas Plains in Photographs and Poems*, and *Whatever the Wind Delivers*. In 2001, state officials named him the poet laureate of Texas. The Caprock Writers and Illustrators Alliance with over 150 members brings writers together and assists with the sponsorship of the Lubbock Book Festival, usually held each September. In Hobbs, Jim Harris, a short-story writer, folklorist, historian, and poet, continues to publish well-honed selections, including reviews and short pieces for New Mexico magazines. Alex Ross of Lubbock became a writer and artist of comic books.

The Llano Estacado has produced many fine artists and entertainers, some of whom became national celebrities. Glenna Goodacre designed the beautiful Sacagawea dollar for the United States Mint and the Vietnam Women's Memorial in Washington, D.C. Ben Sargent, a cartoonist, won the Pulitzer Prize for editorial cartoons in the *Austin-American Statesmen*. Among other wonderful projects, Paul Milosovich painted covers for country-and-western albums, and his *Texas Golf Legends* contains one hundred portraits of famous golfers. Eddie Dixon, Wyman Meinzer (the Texas state photographer), Terry Allen, Garland Weeks, and James C. Watkins all gained national reputations, as did Tulia's Kenneth Wyatt, known for his wonderful western and faith-based paintings. The Llano's Bess Hubbard is known throughout the nation for her paintings and sculptures.

Likewise, the Llano Estacado can boast of its natives or residents who gained some measure of fame as entertainers. Besides many of them mentioned earlier, there is Tula Finklea, who made the "big time" as Cyd Charisse, a dancer who starred in several movies, including *Ziegfeld Follies*; Vivien Fay, who danced in a Marx Brothers film and with Lucille Ball; and Carolyn (Baker) Jones, who played Morticia in the television series *The Addams Family*. Lubbock Monterey High School graduate Barry Corbin starred in the original but offbeat television series *Northern Exposure*, and G. W. Bailey, who, among other roles, was Rizzo in the long-running television hit series *M*A*S*H* and Lt. Louie Provenza in *Major Crimes*. There are plenty of others, including such fine actors as Lee Horsley of Muleshoe and Woody Harrelson of Midland.

Llano Estacado–based historians associated with local universities made important contributions to the region's intellectual life. William Curry Holden and Ernest Wallace, Texas Tech historians, published several influential books and professional journal articles treating the Llano Estacado. Perhaps no one has published as many scholarly historical studies on as eclectic a range of subjects as David J. Murrah, former archivist and historian at Texas Tech. Although called "the preeminent ranching scholar of his time," Murrah has written also on religion and churches, environment and geography, cities and counties, and historians and artists, and he has edited additional volumes. Frederick J. Rathjen of West Texas State (WT, now West Texas A&M) University wrote, among other works, *The Panhandle Frontier*, which remains the most thorough study of the region's early years. Other historians associated with the Llano include Hattie M. Anderson, Garry L. Nall, Dan L. Flores, L. F. Sheffy, and John Miller Morris, whose *El Llano Estacado* is a masterpiece of historical and environmental writing.

Museums and archives continue to contribute to the Llano's social and cultural life. The major archives are the Southwest Collection/Special Collections Library at Texas Tech, the Neta Stewart Haley Memorial Library and J. Evetts Haley History Center in Midland, and the Panhandle-Plains Historical Museum and Archives at West Texas A&M. History museums exist seemingly everywhere on the Llano Estacado. Most are small, such as the Last Frontier Museum in Morton, but good, and they effectively preserve and communicate local history. The Lea County Museum in Hobbs, the Permian Basin Petroleum Museum in Midland, the Carson County Square House Museum in Panhandle, the National Quarter Horse Hall of Fame and Museum in Amarillo, the Museum of Texas Tech University (although now more an art concern than a history museum), and the National Ranching Heritage Center in Lubbock are among the better ones. The finest history museum on the Llano, and perhaps the largest one in Texas, is the Panhandle-Plain Historical Museum in Canyon. It is superb. For dramatic museum effects the astonishing American Wind Power Center and the agricultural museum FiberMax Center for Discovery in Lubbock are marvelous, as is the Blackwater Draw Archaeological Site near Portales.

Museums represent an important aspect of the Llano's tourism-vacation industry, a business that continues to impact the big mesa's economy, society, and culture. In Hobbs, Zia Park Casino Hotel & Racetrack not only brings money to the city but also creates jobs, and it has contributed to the city's population growth over the past decade. One of the Llano's strangest tourist points is Cadillac Ranch, located along Interstate Highway 40 (old Route 66) a few miles west of Amarillo. It is a free, open-space attraction with ten Cadillacs half-buried, nose-down, in the dirt in one of the late Stanley Marsh 3's wheat fields. Financed by Marsh, a group of art hippies who called themselves the Ant Farm placed the Cadillacs, ranging from a 1949 Club Sedan to a 1963 Sedan de Ville, in a line facing west with their big fins sticking out of the ground. Tourists in growing numbers stop on the access road, walk out to the automobiles, and paint or mark or scribble a message on the Cadillacs. On the twentieth anniversary of the site in 1999, Marsh held a large celebration—a "cocktail party in a wheat field," he called it—and invited all to come attired formally in suits and cocktail dresses. Many did, and they enjoyed mounds of hors d'oeuvres and beverages available on two large tables each under a big tent. Several years later Marsh moved the Cadillacs a few miles farther west. "The girls," he said, "were bothered by Amarillo's smog."

Of larger significance, dedication of Sanford Dam on the Canadian River in 1966 opened up a major tourist attraction and water recreation area. Plans to control the shallow, sandy river date back to at least the Dust Bowl days of the mid-1930s, and at that time different supporters of a dam saw various uses for it: recreation, flood control, irrigation, and a future water source for the city of Amarillo. Time passed, agencies formed and reorganized, and officials in Austin supported funding measures. But no dam followed. In the late 1940s conditions and events

Stanley Marsh 3

Stanley Marsh 3 (1938–2014), was, like Georgia O'Keeffe, a Panhandle artist and eccentric, but, unlike O'Keeffe, Marsh was, until controversy rocked his world, one of the most lovable characters of Amarillo and the upper Llano Estacado. He was also a successful businessman, large-ranch owner, media mogul, philanthropist, jovial raconteur, and prankster. He was a character, someone said of him, and he worked hard at being one. Perhaps best remembered for his Cadillac Ranch, the unusual but whimsical public art exhibit of ten half-buried Cadillacs along Interstate Highway 40, Marsh, wrote Alex Shoumatoff, was "The Wizard of Amarillo."

The scion of a Panhandle oil and gas family, Marsh was born in Amarillo. He attended the University of Pennsylvania and there received a bachelor's degree in economic history and a master's degree in American studies with a concentration in history. He loved art, painted some, and encouraged nearly all artistic pursuits. In 1967, Stanley married attorney Gwendolyn "Wendy" Bush O'Brien, a member of a Panhandle ranching family, and the couple had five adopted children. He and Wendy gave large sums of money to such charitable organizations as schools, universities, and teaching hospitals.

Although a financially successful businessman, Marsh preferred to have fun, play games, and patronize the arts. He also poked fun at himself and at pretentiousness. He once said, "Art is a legalized form of insanity, and I do very well at it." He funded an uncommon amount of unusual public art. Besides Cadillac Ranch, he paid for Floating Mesa, a huge natural mesa around which he had artists wrap a narrow band of white-painted plywood so that from a distance the mesa seems to be afloat. He hired men with road graders and Caterpillar tractors to clear off land and build a giant replica of a pool tabletop, painted the monster green, and located huge soft pool balls (thirty-eight inches in diameter) and long pool sticks on it.

Marsh's Dynamite Museum involved a group of young men whose special project was to place mock traffic signs around the city. They traveled about Amarillo with a trailer (containing signs and sign-emplacement supplies) pulled by a big, gaudy pink Cadillac topped by a large pink pig statue. The signs bore such messages as "Road Ahead," "Steal This Sign," and, one supposes, the maxim for the project: "ROAD DOES NOT END."

Marsh encouraged and sponsored the writing of local and regional history—another of his favorite subjects. In 2011, he suffered a series of strokes and a year later found himself the defendant in several child abuse–related lawsuits. The allegations—nothing but "lies, lies, lies," said his wife, Wendy—broke his heart. Stanley Marsh 3 died under hospice care in 2014, but he should be remembered as one of the Llano Estacado's most colorful characters.

At the twentieth anniversary celebration of the Cadillac Ranch outdoor museum Stanley Marsh 3, standing in the center in a top hat, discusses his project with visitors. Courtesy of Ellen Carlson

moved toward building the long-sought structure. Then the Korean War intervened. Finally, in May 1953 Texas governor Allen Shivers signed legislation creating the Canadian River Municipal Water Authority (CRMWA). The new agency, to which eleven Llano Estacado cities belong, began the slow process of securing land, settling mineral rights, obtaining funds, designing the dam and pipelines, and solving related problems. Nine years later construction began, and four years after that on a cold and windy (November 1, 1966) day 1,250 people attended official ceremonies marking the opening of the dam, out of which flowed at the time the longest aqueduct in the world.

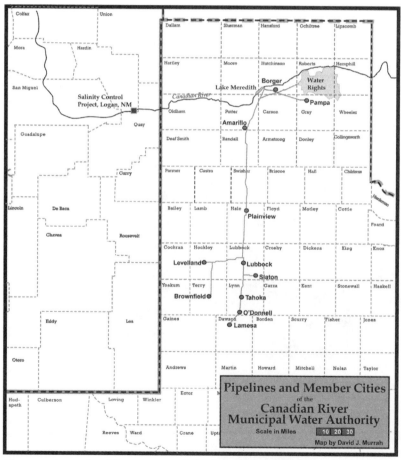

The map shows the cities, towns, and pipelines that are part of the Canadian River Municipal Water Authority. Courtesy of David J. Murrah

Although dry in 2022, Buffalo Lake once provided fishing, swimming, boating, and other recreation for people in the Canyon-Amarillo area. Courtesy of Panhandle-Plains Historical Museum

Behind it, the dam created huge Lake Meredith. Named for A. A. Meredith, one of the key figures in the long struggle to have the dam constructed, the lake provided a multi-recreational area that in its early history attracted a million visitors per year. Also significant, the lake provided municipal water for eleven members of the CRMWA, which operated the dam, some 322 miles of pipelines in its aqueduct system, pumping stations, and water treatment plants. For over three decades the CRMWA provided good water for its member cities, but after 2000 all of them, led by Amarillo and Lubbock, began to seek additional sources for the precious resource, including from wells that reached into the Ogallala Aquifer in Roberts County.[19]

At the same time that Amarillo leaders in the late 1930s sought a dam across the Canadian River, others succeeded in getting a dam across Tierra Blanca Creek in western Randall County. Government-employed workers with the CCC and the WPA built the barrier, a big, 835-foot-long earthen dam across Tierra Blanca Creek south of Umbarger. Behind the structure, water sipped and drifted into the creek bottom, creating

Buffalo Lake, a seven-mile-long body of water that proved to be a key recreation spot for Amarillo, Canyon, and neighboring areas until the early 1970s. By then, natural springs that fed the lake had dried up as a result of a dropping water table in the Ogallala Aquifer, and the US Interior Department allowed the lake to empty due to silting and to a major fish-kill as a result of organic material buildup (pollution) from upstream feed yards. Although it held thirteen-hundred-acre feet of water in 1973, authorities closed the lake to fishing, swimming, and boating. Then it went dry.

And then a heavy rainstorm occurred on May 26, 1978. The lake filled with three-thousand-acre-feet of water before spilling over the dam. Major flooding followed—along Tierra Blanca and nearby Palo Duro Creeks, streams that merge near Canyon. The gigantic flood caused a huge amount of property damage in Canyon and downstream through several housing developments and bedroom communities and still farther downstream in Palo Duro Canyon State Park. People lost homes, automobiles and trucks, pets, and uncountable personal possessions. The resulting damage created a sight that local residents spent much of their lives trying to forget. Also, Interior Department personnel determined the dam at Buffalo Lake was unsafe and needed to come down. When local groups objected, government officials replaced the earthen dam with a concrete structure but not until 1992. In 2022, the former lake is dry. Nonetheless, the large Buffalo Lake National Wildlife Refuge attracts sizable numbers of birds plus prairie dogs, owls, mule and white-tailed deer, wild turkeys and on occasion bobcats, porcupines, and eagles, including bald eagles in winter.[20]

As suggested by the 1978 Randall County flood, Llano Estacado weather, like climate conditions all across the Great Plains, can be dangerous, destructive, unexpected, and unforgiving. It remains a big and constant factor in Llano life and living, especially for farmers and ranchers, who each morning monitor local weather reports on radio or television before stepping outside to survey the skies, inspect range grass or farm crops, and when appropriate check their rain gauges. Even with irrigation systems, farmers and ranchers are often at the mercy of "Mother Nature."

Llano Estacado meteorological conditions might be good and favorable, of course—as they often are. Early each morning nearly any time of year, as well as most all day during autumn's agricultural harvest months, the Llano's weather can be beautiful. In devastating instances, however, the weather and a sometimes fickle Mother Nature, as at Canyon in 1978, bring destruction and desolation. The 1941 flood on the Canadian River represents another terrible example. Following several days of heavy rains in northwestern Llano and Panhandle country, the river on September 22, 1941, spilled—roared really—out of its banks. It flooded the river valley from New Mexico through Texas to Oklahoma. The rushing, snarling, roiling floodwaters broke gas lines, downed bridges, isolated communities, closed US Highway 87, and prevented trains from crossing the wide valley. North of Amarillo, the river rose twenty-four feet, with water surging to within inches of the Highway 87 bridge. Flood damage altered the thinking of those groups who wanted a dam across the Canadian and brought a measure of urgency to the project, but the Japanese bombing of Pearl Harbor in December ended the dam idea—temporarily.

In 1956, an area-wide, massive snowstorm closed Route 66 and effectively shut down the upper Llano Estacado. The "Plains Lies Paralyzed" read a headline in *Amarillo Daily News*. Occurring on February 1 and 2, the winter storm dropped twenty-nine inches of snow on Plainview; twenty-four inches on Hereford, Happy, and Dimmit; eighteen inches on Canyon; fourteen inches on Portales and Amarillo; twelve on Clovis; eleven on Lubbock and Hobbes; and similar amounts on cities and towns in between. Freezing temperatures dropped into the single digits and in some places below zero, and as the wind picked up, deep drifts of snow formed.

The storm closed major parts of the region. Traffic halted along city streets in Plainview and Amarillo and through rural roads and highways, including, as noted, Route 66. US Highway 87 from south of Plainview to north of Amarillo closed. In rural stretches of the two busy highways even loaded passenger busses got stuck as snow drifted across the highways and piled up along roadside edges, thus stranding bus occupants. Downed power lines cut communication in many cities and between some of them. Schools and businesses closed, of course, and in extensive parts of the region the upper Llano Estacado became immobilized. Several folks, especially men, died of heart attacks while shoveling snow or trying to free automobiles from snowdrifts, and in rural Hale County a "woman died in childbirth," writes Mike Cox, "because she could not get medical treatment in time." The storm contributed to at least twenty human deaths and caused the loss of thousands of cattle and other livestock. Snow-removal activity continued for up to a week in places, and government agencies, such as the Strategic Air Command in Amarillo, dropped hay from planes for several days to save livestock at isolated ranches.[21]

The heavy winter snowfall came during one of the worst droughts in the twentieth century. Thus, it provided some moisture to a land starved for water (no measurable rainfall had occurred since October 1955). Children took advantage of closed schools and for nearly a week enjoyed the deep snow by digging caves into snowdrifts that sometimes reached to rooftops, building giant snowmen, and constructing other large creatures, such as in Plainview where they built a long, large snow dragon.[22]

In Lubbock, a tornado on May 11, 1970, like the 1956 snowstorm, proved to be a major event and for Lubbock a turning point on many levels. The tornado, or tornadoes as there may have been two or three of them, caught Lubbock and its citizens by surprise. It was an F5-category storm that struck late in the evening, bringing with it powerful, swirling winds, hail, and heavy rainfall. The massive storm cut a wide swath through downtown, the neighboring Guadalupe residential area, and along busy Fourth Street by Texas Tech University before turning north along Highway 87 and cutting through Lubbock International Airport, West Texas Air Terminal, and the exclusive Country Club residential area.

The tornado resulted in the death of twenty-six people with an additional eighteen hundred suffering injuries. Property loss was also huge. The storm damaged some ten thousand homes, completely destroying eleven hundred of them. Across the tornado's circling path, perhaps eighteen hundred people became homeless. It damaged ten thousand automobiles, and about five hundred businesses sustained wreckage of some kind. It cut utilities, including water supplies, and it created havoc with traffic flow and communication systems: in those days before cell phones, twenty-five thousand telephones lost service. It toppled power lines and spread debris across streets, including main thoroughfares. Some underpasses filled with water, blocking access to portions of the city. At an estimated property damage of $840 million, it was one of the costliest tornadoes in America to that time.

In the aftermath, Lubbock and its citizens, led by youthful mayor Jim Granberry, sought and received federal and state relief funds. Residents also passed a $13.6 million recovery bond package that repurposed and rebuilt the near-downtown area, where major damage had occurred. In the end, the influx of federal and state money, the revitalization of the area just north and east of downtown, and the dispersal of minority citizens through the city represent important and permanent transformations and perhaps a major economic turning point for Lubbock.[23]

Clearly, Llano Estacado weather is unusual and sometimes difficult to fathom. March 20, 2021, for example, opened with a cool, beautiful morning on the eastern South Plains. A thunderstorm developed before noon, and hail the size of peas fell, pulling some emerging leaves off Siberian elm trees and cottonwoods. The storm passed and the sun came out, warming up the day. In the early afternoon another storm moved through the region, and a large measure of hail fell—it covered the ground like snow. Late in the afternoon wind picked up, and heavy dust in darkening amounts rolled through the area. That evening a beautiful sunset closed the remarkable day. As celebrated comedian Yakov Smirnoff might say of Llano weather: "What a country!"

The Amarillo-area Pantex Ordnance Plant reflected another of the Llano's almost absurd yin and yang conundrums. The plant spurred economic growth on the northern Llano Estacado. It employed about twenty-three hundred people, and independent contractors who handled construction and repair activities engaged many more. Yet in 1981, the plant created a national nightmare for Amarillo citizens. The story began earlier when the US Defense Department in late 1980 wanted to place its embryonic MX missile system in the Clovis, New Mexico, or

Dalhart, Texas, areas. Texans objected. The story and the issue shifted a few months later to the Pantex Plant, where area residents assembled nuclear bombs. The matter exploded in August 1981 when Catholic bishop Leroy T. Matthiesen called for "individuals involved in the production and stockpiling of nuclear bombs to . . . resign from such activities, and to seek employment in peaceful pursuits." He wanted to abolish nuclear weapons.[24]

Amarillo-area reaction was swift and hostile. Citizens condemned Matthiesen in letters, notes, cards, and telephone calls. But in Canyon, faculty members at West Texas State University, who supported the bishop, invited him to speak. He did, further roiling the issue. Pantex and the work there received international attention, most of it negative. National radio and television networks interviewed Matthiesen, and he spoke again in New York City against nuclear weapons, the morality of assembling nuclear warheads, and the Pantex Plant in general. He debated with Amarillo pastors and continued to push his point. For nearly two years, Pantex remained in the news, but eventually local and national attention shifted away from Pantex and the MX missile system.

Although it was mainly an economic, intellectual, and moral issue, the Pantex difficulty was also a political issue. Political conservatives tended to defend the plant and the people who worked there, and in the 1980s they were often members of the Republican Party. In fact, most Llano citizens, the voting records suggest, have been supporting Republican candidates and positions since the late 1950s, when they began to shift their support away from the conservative wing of the Democratic Party to Republican candidates and positions. The voter swing was gradual, however, and as late as 1968 conservative Democrat Preston Smith of Lubbock won election as governor of Texas. He served in the position from 1969 to 1973 and, among other accomplishments, played a key role in the establishment of the Texas Tech University Health Sciences Center in the 1970s.[25]

In the years after Smith's term ended, Llano Estacado residents, especially those living in Texas, continued and even increased their political shift to conservative Republican positions and candidates. They supported Republican presidential and gubernatorial candidates in each election and likewise backed local Republican candidates for nearly every state Senate and House of Representatives seat. Even conservative Democrats had little chance. Popular Kent Hance of Dimmit switched to the Republican Party, and in 2001, George W. Bush, a Republican from Midland, began the first of two terms as president of the United States.

Local, state, and national elections of November 3, 2020, reflected current political trends, at least on the Texas portion of the Llano. That is, although Democrat Joe Biden won the 2020 election to become the forty-sixth president of the United States, President Donald Trump, Biden's Republican opponent, and other Republican candidates received a greater share of votes from Llano Estacado citizens than their Democratic opponents. In rural counties of the region, the percentage of support for Trump and the Republicans went well beyond 50 percent. Indeed, in the New Mexico counties on the Llano Estacado, 70 percent of the voters cast Republican ballots.

In urban counties, such as Lubbock County, President Trump and the Republicans also did well, but vote patterns are instructive. Only 66.14 percent of 183,627 registered voters turned out in Lubbock County, but it was the highest turnout since 1984. Trump carried precincts with a majority of Anglo voters, sometimes taking 81 percent of the vote. Biden won 85 percent or more of the vote in precincts with a heavy black population. Trump won in a couple of precincts with a large concentration of Latino voters, but in most of them Biden garnered up to 67.8 percent of the vote. In districts with a high concentration of college students, Biden carried the two Texas Tech precincts; Trump won in the Lubbock Christian University sector.[26]

Likewise, US Senator John Cornyn easily won reelection in Lubbock County. He received 79,549 votes (65.4 percent) of the 121,459 votes cast in that race. Cornyn did better in most Lubbock County precincts than President Donald Trump. His opponent, Mary Jo "MJ" Hagar, a motorcycle-riding military veteran, received only 36,319 votes, a count less than Democratic presidential nominee Joe Biden. Voting in rural counties of the Llano Estacado, including those in New Mexico, shows even stronger support for Republican candidates all along the ballot. Indeed, in August 2021, signs appeared on buildings in towns and on barns or other structures in many rural areas calling for support for Donald Trump in the 2024 presidential election.

The 2020 election aside, women and other minorities on the Llano Estacado clearly have made gains in politics, education, and business leadership. As early as 1940, African American residents on the Llano had organized a chapter of the National Association for the Advancement of Colored People (NAACP), and the League of United Latin American Citizens (LULAC) started a chapter in Lubbock in 1951. The two groups became effective agents of a growing minority population on the Llano. By the 1970s Hispanic Froy Salinas had been elected to the Texas House, where he represented District 75-B. He served well into the 1980s. Also in the 1980s, Maggie Trejo became a member of the Lubbock City Council, and Thomas "T. J." Patterson, an African American and former newspaper editor, began his long and distinguished political career. In Amarillo, Debra McCartt, an Anglo and former schoolteacher, in 2005 became the first woman to serve as mayor of the city.[27]

In education, there were additional gains for women. Janis Rivas was the first woman to head the Amarillo Independent School District (AISD) board of trustees. Her leadership in the early 2000s was both dynamic and beneficial for AISD. In 2004, the Texas Plains Girl Scout Council named her one of its Women of Distinction. In Lubbock, Kathy Rollo in 2018 became superintendent of the large Lubbock Independent School District. Shortly afterward, Lori Rice-Spearman assumed the presidency of the huge Texas Tech University Health Sciences Center, a teaching hospital with system branches in Amarillo and the Permian Basin.

In business, women and other minorities have made spectacular gains. They head ranches (Mary Emeny and Nina Ritchie), trucking firms (Jane Gripp and Hazel Kelley Wilson), manufacturing companies (Barbara Miller), and hundreds of other firms, including retail outlets, law practices, private schools, and real estate concerns. Women have served as state and federal district judges, including 72nd District of Texas judge Pat S. Moore and US District judge for the Northern District of Texas Mary Lou Robinson. The record is amazing, but upon thoughtful consideration, one that should be found as unsurprising as it is noteworthy.

Finally, two important developments need further emphasis. First, in the twenty-first century population trends on the Llano Estacado show large cities increasing in numbers of residents, small towns declining in inhabitants, and villages disappearing. To use the term "ghost town" seems harsh, especially to people who might live there, but abandoned villages are scattered through the Llano: Tokio, Shafter Lake, Tredway, Bronco, Kenna, Quarter Way, Arch, County Line, Soash, Virginia City, Estacado, Emma, and Becton are among hundreds of them. Failed farms, bankrupt ranches, school consolidations, and young people seeking opportunities in cities each contributed (and contributes) to the ghost town phenomenon, from one point of view a cheerless counternarrative to a hallowed American dream.

The second development is a change in ethno-demographics. As noted, many villages have disappeared from the Llano Estacado. But in the first years of the twenty-first century even midsize towns are losing populations. Brownfield in 1980 counted 10,387 residents, but in 2020 the number had dropped to 9,808. Lamesa totaled 11,790 inhabitants in 1980, but only 9,505 in 2020. Littlefield dropped from 7,409 in 1980 to 5,992 forty years later. The Muleshoe population has fared better, increasing from 4,842 in 1980 to 5,158 in 2010, but then dropping to 5,134 in 2020. Moreover, Hispanics, particularly Mexican Americans, have not only increased their population numbers in many towns and cities, but in many smaller ones they have come to dominate political positions, such as mayor and city council positions as well as members of local school boards.[28]

Agribusiness remains an important aspect of the Llano Estacado. The United States is the world's largest producer of grain sorghum, with much of it grown in West Texas and on the Llano Estacado. The Llano's South Plains contains "the largest contiguous cotton patch in the world." Cattle feeding on the northern edge of the Llano and wheat growing across the Panhandle and upper Llano Estacado profoundly affect the regional economy. Because it has been the largest customer for America's grain sorghum and a major producer of cotton, China, by raising sorghum tariffs—as it did in 2018—or dumping its cotton reserves—as it did in 2014—can impact the global market in agricultural products produced on the Llano Estacado.[29]

Population of Counties on the Llano Estacado in Texas and New Mexico

Texas Counties	1880	1890	1900	1910	1920	1930	1940
Andrews	0	24	87	975	350	736	1,277
Armstrong	31	944	1,205	2,682	2,816	3,329	2,495
Bailey	0	0	4	312	517	5,186	6,318
Borden	35	222	776	1,386	965	1,505	1,396
Briscoe	12	0	1,253	2,162	4,560	5,590	4,056
Carson	0	356	469	2,127	3,078	7,745	6,624
Castro	0	9	400	1,850	1,948	4,720	4,631
Cochran	0	0	25	65	67	1,963	3,735
Crosby	0	82	788	1,765	6,084	11,023	10,046
Dawson	24	29	37	2,320	4,309	13,573	15,367
Deaf Smith	38	179	843	3,942	3,747	5,979	6,056
Dickens	28	295	1,151	3,092	5,876	8,601	7,847
Donley	160	1,056	2,756	5,284	8,035	10,262	7,487
Ector	0	224	381	1,178	760	3,958	15,051
Floyd	3	529	2,020	4,638	9,758	12,409	10,659
Gaines	8	68	55	1,255	1,018	2,800	8,136
Garza	36	14	185	1,995	4,253	5,586	5,678
Glasscock	0	208	286	1,143	555	1,263	1,193
Gray	56	203	480	3,405	4,663	22,090	23,911
Hale	0	721	1,680	7,566	10,104	20,169	18,813
Hockley	0	0	44	137	137	9,298	12,693
Howard	50	1,210	2,528	8,881	6,962	22,888	20,990
Lamb	0	4	31	540	1,175	17,452	17,606
Lubbock	25	33	293	3,624	11,096	39,104	51,872
Lynn	9	24	17	1,713	4,751	12,372	11,931
Martin	12	264	332	1,549	1,146	5,785	5,556
Midland	0	1,033	1,741	3,464	2,449	8,005	11,721
Motley	24	139	1,257	2,396	4,107	6,812	4,994
Oldham	387	270	349	812	709	1,404	1,385
Parmer	0	7	34	1,555	1,699	5,869	5,890
Potter	28	849	1,820	12,424	16,710	46,080	54,265
Randall	3	187	963	3,312	3,675	7,071	7,185
Roberts	32	326	620	950	1,469	1,457	1,289
Swisher	4	100	1,227	4,012	4,388	7,343	6,528
Winkler		18	60	442	81	6,784	6,141
Terry	0	21	48	1,474	2,236	8,883	11,160
Yoakum	0	4	26	602	504	1,263	5,354
Texas Total	**1,005**	**9,652**	**26,271**	**97,029**	**136,757**	**356,357**	**397,336**

NM Counties	1880	1890	1900	1910	1920	1930	1940
Chaves	0	0	4,773	16,850	12,075	19,549	23,980
Curry	0	0	0	11,443	11,236	15,809	18,159
De Baca					3,196	2,893	3,460
Eddy			3,229	12,400	9,116	15,842	24,311
Lea					3,545	6,144	21,154
Quay				14,912	10,444	10,828	12,111
Roosevelt				12,064	6,548	11,109	14,549
NM Total	**0**	**0**	**8,002**	**67,669**	**56,160**	**82,174**	**117,724**
Grand Total	**1,005**	**9,652**	**34,273**	**164,698**	**192,917**	**438,531**	**515,060**

This population chart indicates by decades the number of people in thirty-seven Texas counties and seven New Mexico counties. Large portions of several counties, such as Howard and Garza in Texas and Reaves and Eddy in New Mexico, are not on the Llano Estacado; thus, their total numbers inflate the Llano's actual population.

1950	1960	1970	1980	1990	2000	2010	2020
5,002	10,372	13,450	13,323	14,338	13,004	14,786	18,610
2,215	1,966	1,895	1,994	2,021	2,148	1,901	1,848
7,592	9,090	8,487	8,168	7,064	6,594	7,165	6,904
1,106	1,076	888	859	799	729	641	631
3,528	3,577	2,794	2,529	1,971	1,790	1,637	1,758
6,852	7,781	6,378	6,682	6,576	6,516	6,182	5,807
5,417	8,923	10,394	10,556	9,070	8,285	8,062	7,371
5,928	6,417	5,326	4,825	4,377	3,730	3,127	2,547
9,582	10,347	9,085	8,859	7,304	7,072	6,059	5,133
19,113	19,185	16,604	16,184	14,349	14,965	13,833	12,456
9,111	13,187	18,999	21,665	19,153	18,561	19,372	18,583
7,177	4,963	3,737	3,539	2,571	2,762	2,444	1,770
6,216	4,449	3,641	4,075	3,696	3,828	3,677	3,258
42,102	90,995	91,805	115,374	118,934	121,123	137,130	165,171
10,535	12,369	11,044	9,834	8,497	7,771	6,446	5,402
8,909	12,267	11,593	13,150	14,123	14,467	17,526	21,598
6,281	6,611	5,289	5,336	5,143	4,872	6,461	5,816
1,089	1,118	1,155	1,304	1,447	1,406	1,226	1,116
24,728	31,535	26,949	26,386	23,967	22,744	22,535	21,227
28,211	36,,798	34,137	37,592	34,671	36,602	36,273	32,522
20,487	22340	20,396	23,230	24,199	22,716	22,935	21,537
26,722	40,139	37,796	33,142	32,343	33,627	35,012	34,860
20,015	21,986	17,770	18,669	15,072	14,709	15,799	17,878
101,048	156,271	179,295	211,651	222,636	242,628	278,831	310,639
11,030	10,914	9,107	8,605	6,758	6,550	5,915	5,596
5,,541	5,068	4,774	4,684	4,956	4,746	4,799	5,237
25785	67,717	65,433	82,636	106,611	116,009	136,872	169,983
3,963	2,870	2,178	1,950	1,532	1,426	4,799	1,063
1,672	1,928	2,258	2,283	2,278	2,185	2,052	1,758
5,787	9,583	10,509	11,038	9,863	10,016	10,269	9,869
73,366	115,580	90,511	98,637	97,874	113,506	121,073	118,525
13,774	33,913	53,885	75,062	89,673	104,312	120,725	140,753
1,031	1,075	967	1,187	1,025	887	929	827
8,249	10,607	10,373	9,723	8,133	8,378	7,854	6,971
10,064	13,652	9,640	9,944	8,626	7,173	5,410	7,791
13,107	16,286	14,118	14,581	13,218	12,761	12,651	11,831
4,339	8,032	7,344	8,299	8,786	7,322	7,879	7,694
556,674	830,987	820,004	927,555	953,654	1,007,920	1,110,287	1,212,340
39,884	57,649	43,335	51,103	57,849	61,382	65,645	65,157
23,174	32,691	39,517	42,019	42,207	4,5044	48,376	48,430
3,725	2,991	2,547	2,454	2,252	2,240	2,022	1,698
40,421	50,783	41,119	47,855	48,605	51,658	53,829	62,314
30,577	53,429	49,554	55,993	55,765	5,5511	64,727	74,455
13,912	12,279	10,903	10,577	10,823	1,0155	9,041	8,746
16,391	16,198	16,479	15,695	16,702	1,8078	19,846	19,191
168,084	226,020	203,454	225,696	234,203	244,068	263,486	279,991
724,758	1,057,007	1,023,458	1,153,251	1,187,857	1,251,988	1,373,773	1,492,331

Source: Compiled by David Murrah, 2021.

A large Lubbock County cotton patch stands ready for harvest in late October.
Courtesy of Ellen Carlson

For nearly seven months after harvest, cotton fields stand empty, and in the early
spring high winds pick up the dry, rich dirt and send it miles away. Courtesy of
Ellen Carlson

China's actions notwithstanding, after 2000, diversified farming strategies and dryland farming again attracted farmers, especially younger ones. A few farmers have turned to raising hemp (cannabis). In 2022, thirty-three growers held licenses to plant hemp in the Lubbock region, and two held a similar license in the Panhandle area. The crop, drilled in like wheat, grows tall, and farmers harvest the tops for seed production and then use the stalk for a number of industrial purposes: CBD oil, textiles, bioplastics, and others. Although an easy crop to grow, it is a tricky business. Farmers need to monitor government laws and regulations about acre use, overproduction, and other issues. Yet in the Lubbock area in 2021, hemp growers made per-acre better returns than cotton producers, and Slaton opened a big warehouse to store the fall harvest.[30]

The table grape and wine industry has also made gains. In 2022, the Llano Estacado was home to a large number of small wineries, and the number of them was growing. One of the oldest was Llano Estacado Winery near Lubbock, but newer vineyards, sometimes with accompanying wineries, can be found in New Mexico and from Yoakum, Terry, and Lynn Counties north to Parmer, Castro, and Swisher Counties on the Texas side of the Llano. Most wineries are doing well and already winning awards for the taste quality of their wines.

Wineries and grape growing are not without problems. Vineyards are labor intensive and need hands-on, as opposed to machine-driven, attention. More difficult has been what growers call herbicide damage. In 2021, owners of Reddy Vineyards in Brownfield claimed losses of 90 percent of their Tempranillo grapes due to windblown drift of dicamba herbicide from nearby cotton fields. With them, other grape growers brought suit against Bayer-Monsanto and BASF, who made the herbicide. Results of the lawsuits are as yet unknown but will be significant in the South Plains area in part because, according to reporter Matt Dotray, "more than 85% of all the wine grapes grown in Texas are grown within one hour of Lubbock, and the grapes are produced, sold or used by the state's $13.1 billion wine industry."[31]

Wine, vineyards, and urbanization notwithstanding, the Llano Estacado in the early twentieth century retained its western flavor, rural character, and provincial appearance. Its big open spaces; baby-blue, often cloudless sky; friendly people; strong economic opportunities; and broad cultural scope are balanced by its nearly ceaseless winds, blowing dust, dry atmosphere, boom-and-bust economy, and great distances. In short, the Llano can be a hard place in which to live, and, thus, it remains heaven's harsh tableland.

Summary

The Llano Estacado has seen important, and sometimes major, shifts in its demography, political alignment, and ways its citizens made a living, their religious preferences, and their social and cultural endeavors and understandings. Cotton growing, processing, and marketing in the central Llano, oil production in the extreme southern and southwestern edges, and cattle raising and feeding in the northern area controlled the Llano's economy during the long period after World War II. Yet, during it, the Llano, mostly rural in disposition, came to be dominated by an urban-centered population. The idea of change, perhaps, remains the clarifying catchword for the Llano's modern era.

Clearly, agribusiness activity remains strong and innovative on the Llano Estacado. Yet in 2022, the large region, although still mainly rural in temperament and outlook, is dominated politically, socially, and intellectually by its big cities and growing urbanization. Predicting the Llano's future is hazardous, but such a mission distinguishes the epilogue.

Epilogue

Change is constant. During the past thirty-five or so years—within the lifetime of many of us—enormous technological transformations have occurred across the globe. They include such things as the magic of powerful smartphones, tiny computers with huge processing systems, the incredible internet, and instant satellite communications, all of which have reshaped human society. Electric automobiles and battery-powered cigarettes, email and zoom conferences, e-books, and Google Earth represent more of the innovations influencing our world today. Moreover, many miraculous breakthroughs in medicine and medical practice, including amazing advances in surgical procedures, seemed inconceivable a generation ago.

Sometimes the change is rapid and unrelated to intellectual and technological innovations—such as occurred on the eastern edge of Llano Estacado on May 24–25, 2021. A heavy rainfall on May 24 produced a roaring uncontrollable runoff of water that in just a few hours carved a deep, wide gorge through what once had been a dry, shallow draw within the city boundaries of far southeast Lubbock. The water eroded its left bank, cutting a deep channel into it and undercutting the bank. Then the churning, driving force twisted and drove into the opposite bank. As the water moved, it tore large blocks of rich, reddish-brown earth from an empty cotton field and moved soil downstream, dumping it into the upper North Fork of the Double Mountain Fork of the Brazos River. It moved into Buffalo Springs Lake and possibly from there to Lake Ransom Canyon and on down the river. Not only did the field suffer a sudden loss of acreage, but also the new gulf threatened a major roadway over the once-quiet little draw.

More often change happens slowly. On the Llano Estacado, the two-thousand-year-long drought during the Archaic years aided the slow buildup and creation of Llano sand dunes. The appearance and later disappearance of the sensitive little prairie vole occurred over hundreds of years. During the past one million years, glaciers at one-hundred-thousand-year intervals have spread over North America, perhaps eight times. Each time they expanded and subsequently thawed, the glaciers altered plant and animal life in the Northern Hemisphere. Often, they advanced and retreated in response to global activities related to carbon dioxide (CO_2) and oxygen levels. Global warming in 2022, which is melting glaciers at alarming rates, is closely linked to a rise of CO_2 in the atmosphere. As both masters and caretakers of our planet, we know global warming is occurring, but we seem unable to take steps to stop it.[1]

Global warming is not just a problem for the Llano Estacado. In 2021 and 2022, the Colorado River's Lake Mead on the Arizona-Nevada border and Lake Powell near Page, Arizona, have severe water shortages. Lake Mead has shrunk 152 vertical feet, its lowest level since the reservoir was filled in the 1930s. The lake provides water for cities from Denver to Phoenix and for 4.5 million acres of farmland. The situation is critical. Felicia Marcus, a water authority from Stanford University, said the critical water depletion "should represent an earthquake in people's sense of urgency" and it "should ring 'alarm bells' across the West."

Nearby, Lake Powell behind Glen Canyon Dam rests at only 27 percent capacity, meaning, said Bureau of Reclamation Commissioner Camille Touton, that the Colorado River dam is in danger of reaching the minimum level of water required to generate power for millions of people across the Southwest. While the Lake Mead and Lake Powell problems may not immediately impact the New Mexico–Texas High Plains, both the short- and long-range futures of the Llano Estacado are tied to global warming.[2]

For the Llano Estacado, global warming means among other things a spreading desert environment. And, indeed, the Chihuahuan Desert relentlessly pushes northward across the Rio Grande and onto the Llano's southwestern corner. An expanding desert environment with less rainfall, more heat, and shifting plant and animal life is an inevitable result, some of it even in our lifetime. Moreover, future weather patterns appear set to impact farming and ranching on the Llano, both of which must exist in a more arid ecological framework.

As part of that framework, soil-conservation efforts must be addressed. Tons of rich and irreplaceable topsoil on the South Plains blow away each year, none of which is replaced. In some places, such as near Plains in Yoakum County, a few farmers in the late 1950s abandoned crop farming as usable soils disappeared into the wind. Also, heat-tolerable and drought-resistant crops must be the focus of future (and probably chaotic) farming activities on the Llano Estacado. Large livestock, such as beef cattle and milch cows, will be hard-pressed in the coming heat.

Water, or lack of it, is also a messy issue, not only for agriculture but also for the survival of Llano cities. For various reasons, both human and natural, the Lake Meredith reservoir has proved insufficient in supplying the needs for Llano Estacado cities that are part of its Canadian River Municipal Water Authority. In 2003, the authority reduced its allocations to member cities and in 2011 temporarily ceased water withdrawals.

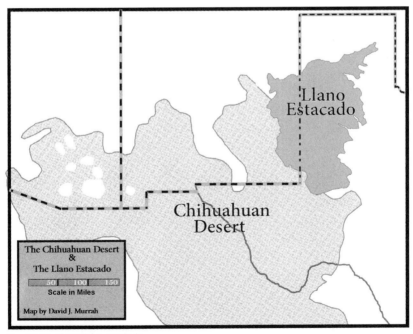

Courtesy of David J. Murrah

Moreover, the Ogallala Aquifer water table continues to drop, and the aquifer has been the only source of the life-giving fluid for some Llano communities for many years, including, until recently, the rapidly growing Lubbock suburb of Wolfforth. As we have seen, the lake at Buffalo Lake National Wildlife Refuge west of Canyon went dry in the 1970s as aquifer water levels dropped and springs stopped flowing. Many High Plains residents trust that in the near future modern well-drilling technologies will bring fresh, usable water at a reasonable cost from ancient aquifers far beneath the Ogallala Formation. One hopes it is more than a pipedream.

While water supplies remain a major concern, renewable energy sources, such as wind power, will clearly be part of the Llano Estacado's future. Indeed, they already are. Minnesota-based Xcel Energy, which supplies electrical power to much of the Llano, has been adding wind energy into its regional generating mix for more than twenty years. Xcel has boosted its wind power output at the large Sagamore Wind Project near Portales, New Mexico, and the Hale Wind Project near Plainview, Texas. In 2022, the power company derived nearly 40 percent of the region's electric supply from wind energy. The amount should increase in the future.[3]

Oil- and petroleum-based energy sources should be adequate for the near future. Of course, concerns exist, and long-range supplies are problematic. Moreover, refineries on the Llano are short in number and aging. Gas and gasoline deliveries from the few refineries that exist on the Llano, because of distribution contracts, often go to places off the Llano Estacado. In many areas, helium supplies, not unlike oil and gas, have been depleted. The helium plant at Soncy, located on Amarillo's western edge, is gone. It closed for various reasons, including lack of helium reserves. Moreover, the use of fossil fuels remains a major contributing factor to greenhouse gases (carbon dioxide, methane, nitrous oxide) and subsequently global warming.

Much of modern wildlife, which once flourished on the Llano Estacado, is gone. Pronghorns are gone—or nearly so. In what Andrew H. Knoll calls movements "in the long symphonic dance of Earth and life," changes in the Llano's plant and animal species have occurred.

Oil pump jacks and wind turbines are ubiquitous on the Llano Estacado. They represent major sources of energy for the region and state. Courtesy of Tim McLaurin

Many Ice Age animals are gone, and pronghorns, an animal that may have originated in the American West a million years ago, once grazed everywhere on the Llano. In 2022, they are found on the Llano mainly in New Mexico rangeland, at Texas state parks, and on private ranches.[4]

Prairie dogs have been more successful—although at least one of the five major species, the Utah Prairie Dog, is nearing extinction. In 1901, many millions of the furry, little black-tailed prairie dog, the most common species, could be found on the Llano Estacado, covering thousands of square miles. They are in a state of decline. In 2022, however, one can see them in open grasslands and trying to maintain colonies within the limits of Llano towns and cities. Can prairie dogs be saved? Probably. Yet most people do not seem willing to do it, as many folks, seeing them as pests, poison them, shoot them, drown them, or plow up their rural colonies and destroy their urban settings.[5]

We saved wild bison—sort of. In the Llano Estacado area, Charles Goodnight, the Palo Duro rancher, in 1876 found a small bison herd when he settled in the big canyon. He kept his ranch hands busy keeping his cows away from the last wild bison in the area. Over time, the Good-night bison herd grew in number, but plenty of problems remained. As he took steps to manage the herd, he quite unintentionally bred "wildness" out of the animals. Inbreeding became a problem. Deleterious alleles (a recessive genetic "load" that might result in low juvenile survival, in-uterine mortality, sperm abnormalities, and related problems) devel-oped, causing birth defects and low birth rates in his small herd. In 1997, Texas Parks and Wildlife officials moved some of the Goodnight bison to Caprock Canyons State Park and Trailway, established in 1982. There, bison biologists are now working to preserve and develop the animals as a wild herd of one thousand or more bison.[6]

As are bison, elk may be returning to the Llano Estacado—at least ten-tatively. Pat Ginn in early June 2021 saw a herd of approximately twenty elk close to his family farm north of Petersburg in extreme southeastern Hale County. It was not the first time in recent years that people had seen elk on the Llano. This time the small herd may have been moving from Blanco Canyon northwest through Conservation Reserve Program (CRP) grasslands, where plenty of food existed, toward the Muleshoe Wildlife Refuge, and on to New Mexico uplands.

Like elk, mule deer are also something of a puzzle. On the Llano Es-tacado in the last few years, their numbers have increased. Reminiscent

Elk in summer of 2021 near Petersburg in southeastern Hale County, Texas.
Courtesy of Pat Ginn

New agricultural enterprises, such as hemp (cannabis) growing, dairy farming, and viticulture, shown here, are diversifying agribusiness on the Llano Estacado. Courtesy of Ellen Carlson

of pronghorns, they survived on the New Mexico plains and canyonlands for thousands of years, but in much of the Texas portion of the Staked Plains most mule deer in 2022 can be found only at parks and within private, fenced areas.[7]

Mule deer and elk may be survivors or returners to the Llano Estacado, but some unwanted, invasive species have appeared in recent years. Feral hogs and fire ants are among them. The prolific hogs damage farm crops, and they root into wet lowland cattle pastures, ravaging the grassland and adding to rangeland disorder. These now-wild creatures seem to be an irrepressible invader. Fire ants represent another strange creature from afar. They arrived on the Llano through many sources, including in the root balls of trees being hauled in trucks by nurseries from East Texas. Because they prefer a moist habitat, fire ants often settle in irrigated plots of grassy ground and near homes in towns and cities. In addition, there are feral house cats. Although technically not an invasive species, feral cats in growing numbers are raising havoc on small-bird populations. The impact of these natural-born killers on lizard and such small rodent populations as rural mice and by extension snakes has not yet been fully determined. Feral dogs remain as destructive of small wildlife and livestock as they did one hundred years ago. Africanized bees are likewise causing havoc, this time among essential honeybee colonies.[8]

Invasive species are not new to the Llano Estacado. In the 1870s and 1880s, Russian thistles (tumbleweeds) and Siberian elms entered the region. Both species probably came with some of the first German-Russian immigrants to the Canadian plains. Other evidence suggests that Ukrainian farmers inadvertently brought with them thistle seeds mixed with flax seeds. The thistles, native to the Ural Mountains in Russia, thrive in salty and alkaline soils. Farmers in South Dakota in 1877 first noticed the noxious plants. As farmers tilled the land, making it easy for plants to proliferate, tumbleweeds in the 1870s and 1880s spread briskly through the Great Plains. In the spring of each year across the Llano, dead tumbleweeds can sometimes be found piled deep against fence lines.

Siberian elms on the Llano Estacado have a similar history. A native of Siberia, the tree arrived on the North American plains in the 1860s. Wind dispersed its abundant seeds across the land, and as a result of its drought-resistant qualities, the elm prospered on the plains and spread through the semiarid land. Because the tall plant grows rapidly, people on the Llano Estacado used it for windbreaks, lumber, and shade. They still do.

More destructive on the Llano Estacado has been the water-robbing saltcedar, or tamarisk. Brought to America in the early 1800s, the plant, originally from the Middle East, was envisioned as an ornamental bush that would attract bees and hummingbirds and control erosion along rivers and streams. But its roots drive deep into the ground, and through them each plant takes up some two hundred gallons of water a day. Tamarisk widened its range with ease as wind and birds dispersed its seeds onto the Llano, where it became established wherever a bit of water might be found. Nearly impossible to kill, the plant has become an environmental monster. In many places, it has nearly choked all other life—with such exceptions as birds, butterflies, rodents, and creatures who hunted them—out of the Pecos River.[9]

While saltcedar, like feral hogs, is thriving, destructive, and hard to eliminate, small towns on the Llano Estacado are struggling to stay alive. The number of towns and villages increased in the early twentieth century as the last regions of western Texas—and, indeed, some of the last areas of the United States—became settled with farmers and townspeople looking to support them. However, school consolidation in the 1930s, improved roads after the 1949 Colson-Briscoe Act, modern trucks and automobiles, and additional school consolidation in the 1950s rendered crossroad communities and tiny villages increasingly needless. In southeastern Roosevelt County, New Mexico, such former active communities as Floyd, Bethel, and Arch exist only on maps and in photos and memories. Even several county-seat towns have lost population with the closing of cafés, hotels, and other small businesses made unnecessary by the quick transportation available through better roads, trucks, and automobiles. In 2022, while the largest cities on the Llano Estacado increased in population, the decline of rural towns was relentless.[10]

Grain sorghum, as shown in this Bailey County, Texas, field with Jon Lemon, does well on the Llano Estacado and has been a popular crop on the High Plains for many years. Courtesy of David J. Murrah

Clearly, over the last 175 years on the Llano Estacado, "heaven's harsh tableland," invasive species plus habitat disruption, agricultural overexploitation, and human population growth have changed the landscape. The region remains flat, of course, but particularly on the South Plains section, environmental and physical change makes the Llano unrecognizable from just over a century ago. Early highway maps dating to the 1920s and 1930s, for example, show several of the main arteries between Llano towns and cities as "unimproved roads." In 2022, those former unimproved roads were paved, sometimes four-lane, highways with driving speed allowed up to seventy-five miles per hour.

Such changes reflect what many anthropologists, scientists, and other scholars call the Anthropocene epoch—an age in which humans have profoundly reshaped the globe and its biodiversity. Such scholars argue that the Anthropocene evolved from the Holocene no later than the beginning of the Industrial Revolution in the early-mid nineteenth century, creating over time a human-centered planet. And in just over a century and a half, humans have transformed the Llano Estacado. We have pushed out many of its wild animals, brought in timid sheep and docile cattle, built huge brick and concrete cities, used up much of its water supplies, developed many of its mineral resources nearly to the point of exhaustion, and increased its human population some five hundred times.

Of course, humans have also done many things well. Colleges and universities on the Llano Estacado graduate thousands of students each year, and graduate schools at several universities offer specialized training and education. The medical school at Texas Tech University and a new Texas Tech veterinary school in Amarillo contribute mightily to science, to health, and to the intellectual and cultural life of the Llano. High-impact wind and weather research at Texas Tech's National Wind Institute, part of the Department of Geoscience, has received international recognition for its work in atmospheric science. In fact, the National Oceanic and Atmospheric Administration in 2021 selected Texas Tech through its Wind Institute to be part of a broad, cooperative group of universities to provide high-impact research on such severe weather hazards as tornadoes and hurricanes. Other Llano-based universities, such as Lubbock Christian, Wayland Baptist, West Texas A&M, and Eastern New Mexico, have developed their own research specialties that have received national and even international distinction and added to the Llano's vigorous cultural and intellectual soul.

Success reaches beyond intellectual life. Cannon Air Force Base in Clovis, for example, brings people from a wide variety of places to the Llano, and likewise activity in the oil fields attracts companies and their employees to the wider Midland-Odessa area. The new arrivals add to the ethnic and demographic mix, social fiber, and cultural life of the Llano Estacado. The South Plains region provides a very large percentage of America's cotton output, and cattle-feeding operations around Amarillo lead the nation in innovation.

Moreover, during the past thirty or more years, tourism has become an important part of the Llano Estacado's economic success. Once something of a "flyover country," the Llano, through the innovation, inventiveness, and imagination of its citizens, has become a place of destination. Museums abound on the Llano, and they include small-town- or county-based history museums and big-university-associated art museums. The Permian Basin Petroleum Museum in Midland, the Panhandle-Plains Historical Museum in Canyon, the Blackwater Draw archaeological site near Portales, the Quarter Horse Museum and the Don Harrington Discovery Center in Amarillo, the Square House Museum in Panhandle, the Western Heritage Museum in Hobbs, and the Library of the Presidents in Odessa represent superb institutions, providing a superior museum experience.

In Lubbock alone, at least eight major museums and research institutions attract visitors, a large number of whom come from afar, such as from Europe, Asia, and South America. Major Lubbock attractions include the Lubbock Lake Landmark archaeological site, the Museum of Texas Tech University, the Science Spectrum, the FiberMax Discovery Center, the American Wind Power Museum, the Buddy Holly Center, the Southwest Collection/Special Collections Library at Texas Tech University, and the National Ranching Heritage Center. All focus on Llano Estacado and West Texas themes, issues, and personalities. Similarly, the Texas Tech University International Center for the Study of Arid and Semi-arid Lands brings scholars to the Llano Estacado, particularly from countries of northern Africa and the Near East.

In addition, such events as the annual Clovis Musical Festival, the Fourth on Broadway celebration (July 4, Independence Day) in Lubbock (which some years has brought as many as one hundred thousand people to the downtown area), and other Llano community commemorations have proved popular. Moreover, Zia Park Casino Hotel & Racetrack in Hobbs and the summer musical drama *Texas* in Palo Duro State Park also bring large numbers of visitors to the Llano Estacado.

B. Bryon Price and Frederick J. Rathjen write about numerous recreational opportunities in the upper Llano Estacado. They point to the *Texas* musical, of course, but they also make note of water opportunities at Lake Meredith, once "a virtual inland sea," where fishing, swimming, boating, and camping are available. "Adjacent to it," they write, are the "Alibates Flint Quarries and Texas Panhandle Pueblo Culture National Monument." Also, "Caprock Canyons and Palo Duro Canyon state parks qualify as among the most scenic and geologic gems of the Southwest, and provide camping, hiking, and related recreation."[11]

Such examples illustrate that far from being an empty land in the middle of nowhere (a land that people should avoid or hurry across), the Llano Estacado has plenty about which to boast. Its recreational activities, its cultural resources, its intellectual and inventive achievements, and its friendly and industrious citizens represent only a few of them. Its cool summer evenings, its often-spectacular sunsets, its big, blue, cloudless skies; rich farm- and ranchland; vital oil reserves; enormous open space; and stunning vistas counter many severe aspects of the big, broad region and its geographic monotony. Despite its many flaws, the Llano Estacado of eastern New Mexico and western Texas in 2022 remains a compelling place that contributes vital petroleum products and provides essential food and fiber commodities to the entire nation. Moreover, it continues to attract a growing and diversified population whose citizens love the region perhaps because, as heaven's harsh tableland, the Llano is not an easy place in which to live. As Smirnoff said, "What a Country!"

Notes

Chapter 1

1. From the chorus of an old, familiar gospel hymn, "On Higher Ground" (lyrics by Johnson Oatman Jr., music by Chas. H. Gabriel). The quoted line suggested the title for this book: a wonderful, but often harsh, land. In place of "Heaven's" in the chorus, some versions use the word "Canaan's." David J. Murrah called my attention to the old hymn.

2. Davis, *The Flatlanders*, 201. Clearly, the size and extent of the Llano Estacado depends on how its landmass is defined, and on that score, there is little agreement among scholars. See, for example, Morris, *El Llano Estacado*, 1–2; Carlson and Murrah, *Historic Tales of the Llano Estacado*, 11, 13–14; Holliday, *Paleoindian Geoarchaeology*, 9; Flores, *Horizontal Yellow*, 170. For a different view, see "Llano Estacado," in Tyler, Barnett, and Barkley, *New Handbook of Texas*, 4:251; and Bogener and Tydeman, *Llano Estacado*, 131.

3. See Erickson, *Bad Smoke, Good Smoke*, 5–21, 27, 31–124.

4. For the long drought, see *Lubbock Avalanche-Journal*, February 15, 2022.

5. S. Williams, "The South Plains and 'Southern-ness,'" 145–65.

6. See Meinig, *Imperial Texas*, 104–7.

7. Davis, *The Flatlanders*, 5; Chaplo, *Amarillo Flights*, 1; Carlson and Murrah, *Historic Tales of the Llano Estacado*, 14.

8. Morris, *El Llano Estacado*, 261; "Llano Estacado," 4:251. For several early descriptions of the Llano Estacado, see Weniger, *The Explorers' Texas*, 16–22; Archambeau, "Lieutenant A. W. Whipple's Railroad Reconnaissance," 12–13.

9. Connellee, "Some Experiences of a Pioneer Surveyor," 90; Carlson and Murrah, *Historic Tales of the Llano Estacado*, 13.

10. See Connor, "The Mendoza-Lopez Expedition," 3–29; John, *Storms Brewed in Other Men's Worlds*, 739–49.

11. Wedel, *Prehistoric Man on the Great Plains*, 25–26; Johnson, "The High Plains and Their Utilization," 607–741.

12. See Holliday, *Paleoindian Geoarchaeology*, 8–12. For a succinct but superb discussion of ancient West Texas, see Monte L. Monroe, "The West Texas Environment," in Carlson and Glasrud, *West Texas*, 11–28. See also Rathjen, *The Texas Panhandle Frontier*, 1–3; Carlson, *Deep Time and the Texas High Plains*, 5–7, 21–23. For earlier discussions, see W. C. Holden, "The Land," in L. Graves, *A History of*

Lubbock, 1–7; H. Charles Hood and James R. Underwood Jr., "Geology of Palo Duro Canyon," in Guy, *Story of Palo Duro Canyon*, 12–14; Kimmel, *Exploring the Brazos River*, 21.

13. See High Plains Associates, "Six-State High Plains–Ogallala Aquifer Regional Resources Study," 2–2 to 2–6. See also Rathjen, *The Texas Panhandle Frontier*, 13–14; Hood and Underwood, "Geology of Palo Duro Canyon," 12–13.

14. Morris, *El Llano Estacado*, 128.

15. Chaplo, *Amarillo Flights*, 19, 20, 22; Morris, *El Llano Estacado*, 27; Flint, *No Settlement, No Conquest*, 358.

16. Chaplo, *Amarillo Flights*, 19; see also photos on pages 21 to 24.

17. Morris, *El Llano Estacado*, 126, 127.

18. Holliday, *Paleoindian Geoarchaeology*, 130.

19. Morris, *El Llano Estacado*, 121. See also Meredith McClain, "Another Look at the Llano Estacado's Name," in Carlson and Murrah, *Historic Tales of the Llano Estacado*, 37–39.

20. Morris, *El Llano Estacado*, 78, 121–25. See also Foster, *Historic Native Peoples of Texas*, 186; and Chapman and Bolen, *Natural History of Texas*, 143, 155–56.

21. Holliday, *Paleoindian Geoarchaeology*, 10, 114, 130; Morris, *El Llano Estacado*, 123–24. See also Gene Lynskey, "Hidden in the Sand," in Becker and Murrah, *Caprock Chronicles*, 37–40.

22. Gerald E. Schultz, "The Paleontology of Palo Duro Canyon," in Guy, *The Story of Palo Duro Canyon*, 61–64.

23. Czerkas and Czerkas, *Dinosaurs*, 13, 219–23, 227; Welty, *The Life of Birds*, 2, 593, 600–601; Alvarez, *T. rex and the Crater of Doom*, x, 5–11.

24. See Vaughn M. Bryant Jr. and James Schoenwetter, "Pollen Records from Lubbock," in Johnson, *Lubbock Lake*, 36–40. For counter ideas, see Courtwright, *Prairie Fire*, 18; Axelrod, "Rise of the Grassland Biome," 163–201. See also Fagan, *Ancient North America*, 65; Waldo R. Wedel and George C. Frison, "Environment and Subsistence," in Raymond J. DeMallie, ed., *Plains*, vol. 13, pt. 1, of Sturtevant, *Handbook of North American Indians*, 46.

25. Fagan, *Floods, Famines and Emperors*, 56–57; Hawkes, *Atlas of Early Man*, 16, 17, 22–23; Josephy, *500 Nations*, 12–17; Fagan, *Ancient North America*, 73–74; Harari, *Sapiens*, 20–21. See also Knoll, *Brief History of Earth*, 205, 208–11.

26. Anyonge and Roman, "New Body Mass Estimates for *Canis dirus*," 209–12; Benton, *When Life Nearly Died*, 218–19; Robert Wright, "The Paleontology of Palo Duro Canyon," in Guy, *Story of Palo Duro Canyon*, 75–77; Wedel and Frison, "Environment and Subsistence," vol. 13, pt. 1, 52–54.

27. Eileen Johnson and Vance T. Holliday, "Archeology and Late Quaternary Environments of the Southern High Plains," in Perttula, *The Prehistory of Texas*, 285–89; Carlson, *Deep Time and the Texas High Plains*, 40–44; Jack T. Hughes, "Archeology of Palo Duro Canyon," in Guy, *Story of Palo Duro Canyon*, 37–38, 47–48.

28. Dates used here are from Johnson and Holliday, "Archeology and Late Quaternary Environments," 284. For arguments that the Clovis tradition is almost two thousand years older, see Fagan, *Ancient North America*, 13, 81, 88–89. Recently,

ancient footprints discovered in White Sands National Monument and the missile range area nearby, although far from the Llano Estacado, may be judged as left by people of a social group much older than the Clovis culture. We await analysis.

29. Carlson, *Deep Time and the Texas High Plains*, 36–37; Holliday, *Paleoindian Geoarchaeology*, 23–24.

30. Taylor and Sturtevant, *The Native Americans*, 7–9; Fagan, *Ancient North America*, 79–85; Black, *Secrets in the Dirt*, 20–23.

31. Holliday, *Paleoindian Geoarchaeology*, 177–79, 183–84, 195–97; Fagan, *Ancient North America*, 93; Fagan, *Floods, Famines and Emperors*, 56, 73–79.

32. Carlson, *Deep Time and the Texas High Plains*, 43; Ernest G. Walker, "An Overview of Prehistoric Communal Bison Hunting on the Great Plains," in Cunfer and Waiser, *Bison and People*, 122; Holliday, *Paleoindian Geoarchaeology*, 166–67.

33. Johnson and Holliday, "Archeology and Late Quaternary Environments," 285–86; Holliday, *Paleoindian Geoarchaeology*, 50–51.

34. Dolores Mosser, "Arch Lake Woman," in Carlson and Murrah, *Hidden History of the Llano Estacado*, 20–23. See also Mosser and Simpson, "*La Pista de Agua Vida*," 45–58.

35. *Lubbock Avalanche-Journal*, August 2, 2020, sec. B-1; Carlson, *Deep Time and the Texas High Plains*, 48–49; Holliday, *Paleoindian Geoarchaeology*, 31–32.

Chapter 2

1. Over the last thirty or so years, many scholars have been suggesting that with the beginning of the Industrial Revolution in the 1840s a new epoch, the Anthropocene epoch, began. It is a human-centered era, one in which compelling evidence shows that humans have modified the global climate and perhaps the otherwise natural and cyclical order of atmosphere and ocean interaction. But far more than climate is involved in the idea of an Anthropocene, including the destruction of the ozone, nuclear weapons and power, plastics, and disappearance of wild animals and natural resources.

2. The dates used here are from Johnson and Holliday, "Archeology and Late Quaternary Environments," 284–93.

3. See, for example, the several chapters related to the Southern High Plains (Llano Estacado) and its prehistory in Perttula, *The Prehistory of Texas*, where encapsulating dates, terms and emphases, and approaches are different.

4. Consider, for example, such climate phenomena as the altithermal (hypsithermal or mid-Holocene warm period, ca. 6,500–4,500 years ago), the Medieval Warm Period (Medieval Climate Optimum or Medieval Climate Anomaly, ca. 900–1250), the Little Ice Age (ca. 1300–1850), and the western North America drought of the 1950s.

5. Fagan, *Ancient North America*, 47; see also Perttula, *The Prehistory of Texas*, 284–93.

6. Holliday, *Paleoindian Geoarchaeology*, 155; Spencer et al., *The Native Americans*, 22–24.

7. Holliday, *Paleoindian Geoarchaeology*, 184–85; Fagan, *Ancient North America*, 117–18.

8. Susan C. Vehik, "Hunting and Gathering Tradition: Southern Plains," in DeMallie, *Plains*, vol. 13, pt. 1, of Sturtevant, *Handbook of North American Indians*, 146; Holden, "The Land," 7.

9. See Fagan, *Ancient North America*, 118, 120; Bailey, *American Plains Bison*, 13–18; Kurten and Anderson, *Pleistocene Mammals of North America*, 334–38; Ernest G. Walker, "An Overview of Prehistoric Communal Bison Hunting on the Great Plains," in Cunfer and Waiser, *Bison and People*, 131–33, 146–47.

10. Mowrey and Carlson, "Native Grasslands of the High Plains," 29.

11. Johnson and Holliday, "Archeology and Late Quaternary Environments," 290–92.

12. Ibid., 290–91; Vance T. Holliday, "Cultural Chronology," in Johnson, *Lubbock Lake*, 23.

13. Vehik, "Hunting and Gathering Tradition," 149; Johnson and Holliday, "Archeology and Late Quaternary Environments," 290–91; Holliday, *Paleoindian Geoarchaeology*, 129–33, 184–85.

14. Johnson and Holliday, "Archeology and Late Quaternary Environments," 290; Holliday, *Paleoindian Geoarchaeology*, 184–85.

15. Holden, "The Land," 3–5, quote on 4–5.

16. Johnson and Holliday, "Archeology and Late Quaternary Environments," 292.

17. Ibid.

18. Timothy G. Baugh, "Holocene Adaptations in the Southern High Plains," in Schlesier, *Plains Indians*, 270–73; Hughes, "Archeology of Palo Duro Canyon," 42, 43, 44; Vehik, "Hunting and Gathering Tradition," 153.

19. See Fagan, *The Little Ice Age*, 15–21, 47.

20. Baugh, "Holocene Adaptations in the Southern High Plains," 271; Vehik, "Hunting and Gathering Tradition," 154; Hughes, "Archeology of Palo Duro Canyon," 42, 43, 44. A good discussion of causes for the Little Ice Age is in Fagan, *The Little Ice Age*, 55–58.

21. Hughes, "Archeology of Palo Duro Canyon," 43. See also Baugh, "Holocene Adaptations in the Southern High Plains," 274 (map), 277–79; Robert E. Bell and Robert L. Brooks, "Plains Village Tradition: Southern," in DeMallie, *Plains*, vol. 13, pt. 1, of Sturtevant, *Handbook of North American Indians*, 213–19; Fagan, *Ancient North America*, 146.

22. Foster, *Historic Native Peoples of Texas*, 6–8, 107–8, 186–87.

23. Fagan, *Floods, Famines and Emperors*, 90; Foster, *Historic Native Peoples of Texas*, 7. See also Diamond, *Collapse*, 12–13, 219.

24. Snow, *The Archaeology of North America*, 90; Hyde, *Indians of the High Plains*, 4–7; Fagan, *Ancient North America*, 146.

25. Johnson and Holliday, "Archeology and Late Quaternary Environments," 284.

26. Britten, *The Lipan Apaches*, 50–54; Morris, *El Llano Estacado*, 19–20; John, *Storms Brewed in Other Men's Worlds*, 20.

27. Britten, *The Lipan Apaches*, 51, 56; Morris, *El Llano Estacado*, 62–63; Susan C. Vehik, "Cultural Continuity and Discontinuity in the Southern Prairies and Cross Timbers," in Schlesier, *Plains Indians*, 251.

28. Hughes, "Archeology of Palo Duro Canyon," 40, 45; Holden, "Texas Tech Archaeological Expedition," 43–52; John, *Storms Brewed in Other Men's Worlds*, 58; Vehik, "Cultural Continuity and Discontinuity," 283–85.

29. Eileen Johnson, "Cultural Activities and Interactions," in Johnson, *Lubbock Lake*, 133, 136–37; Baugh, "Holocene Adaptations in the Southern High Plains," 285–86; Vehik, "Cultural Continuity and Discontinuity," 157; Morris, *El Llano Estacado*, 62, 76; Britten, *The Lipan Apaches*, 51, 56; Hickerson, *The Jumanos*, 24–25.

30. See Donald J. Lehmer, "Plains Village Tradition: Postcontact," in DeMallie, *Plains*, vol. 13, pt. 1, of Sturtevant, *Handbook of North American Indians*, 245, 252, 254–55.

31. Britten, *The Lipan Apaches*, 59.

32. Ibid., 7.

33. Sanchez, "A Trip to Texas in 1828," 251; Bollaert, "Observations of the Indian Tribes in Texas," 277.

34. Britten, *The Lipan Apaches*, 6.

35. Morris E. Opler, "Lipan Apache," in DeMallie, *Plains*, vol. 13, pt. 2, of Sturtevant, *Handbook of North American Indians*, 945.

36. Henry F. Dobyns, "Lipan Apache," in Hoxie, *Encyclopedia of North American Indians*, 337; Britten, *The Lipan Apaches*, 56–57, 61–64.

37. Baugh, "Holocene Adaptations in the Southern High Plains," 267.

38. Hamalainen, *The Comanche Empire*, 11, 71, 79 (map); Kavanagh, *Comanche Political History*, 63–83; John, *Storms Brewed in Other Men's Worlds*, 306–12.

39. Lowie, *Indians of the Plains*, 10–11; John, *Storms Brewed in Other Men's Worlds*, 505, 772n; Hamalainen, *The Comanche Empire*, 101.

40. Spencer et al., *The Native Americans*, 22–24.

Chapter 3

1. George Parker Winship, "The Coronado Expedition, 1540–1542," in Morris, *El Llano Estacado*, 18, 41 (map).

2. Bolton, *Coronado*, 244–81.

3. See Morris, *El Llano Estacado*, 41 (map), 43, 70; Holden, "Coronado's Route across the Staked Plains," 3–20; J. Williams, "Coronado," 190–220; Winship, *The Coronado Expedition, 1540–1542*, 279, 302.

4. Morris, *El Llano Estacado*, 99–103; Flint and Flint, *Coronado Expedition to Tierra Nueva*, 302–19, 370–83. See also Inglis, "The Men of Cibola," 1–24.

5. Morris, *El Llano Estacado*, 136. See also John, *Storms Brewed in Other Men's Worlds*, 33, 44–55.

6. Morris, *El Llano Estacado*, 139. See also John, *Storms Brewed in Other Men's Worlds*, 46–47; Simmons, *The Last Conquistador*, 97–98, 109–11, 160–61.

7. Morris, *El Llano Estacado*, 138–43; John, *Storms Brewed in Other Men's Worlds*, 44–54; Simmons, *The Last Conquistador*, 124–26, 160–61.

8. Hickerson, *The Jumanos*, 88–102; Fedewa, *Dark Eyes, Lady Blue*, 21, 24–26; Fedewa, *Maria of Agreda*, 44–46, 53–59, 64–67.

9. Sammie Simpson and Paul H. Carlson, "The Llano Estacado's *La Pista de Agua Viva*," in Carlson and Murrah, *Hidden History of the Llano Estacado*, 26–29; W. C. Holden, "Indians, Spaniards and Anglos," in L. Graves, *A History of Lubbock*, 25–26; Felix D. Almaráz Jr., "An Uninviting Land: El Llano Estacado, 1534–1821," in Vigil, Kaye, and Wunder, *Spain and the Plains*, 78–79; Rathjen, *The Texas Panhandle Frontier*, 53–54.

10. Rathjen, *The Texas Panhandle Frontier*, 53–54; Morris, *El Llano Estacado*, 143–44; Nickerson, *The Jumanos*, 91–94; Fedewa, *Maria of Agreda*, 44–46, 53–39, 64–67.

11. Morris, *El Llano Estacado*, 145.

12. See Hamalainen, *The Comanche Empire*, 70–73.

13. Noyes, *Los Comanches*, 80. See also Hamalainen, *The Comanche Empire*, 120–23; Kavanagh, *Comanche Political History*, 110–12; John, *Storms Brewed in Other Men's Worlds*, 668–75; Russell M. Magnaghi, "The Genizaro Experience in Spanish New Mexico," in Vigil, Kaye, and Wunder, *Spain and the Plains*, 122; Kessell, *Kiva, Cross, and Crown*, 401–5.

14. Morris, *El Llano Estacado*, 173; Bolton, *Texas in the Middle of the Eighteenth Century*, 127–33.

15. Morris, *El Llano Estacado*, 173–74; Flores, *Caprock Canyonlands*, 101, 112; Bolton, *Texas in the Middle of the Eighteenth Century*, 127–33.

16. Morris, *El Llano Estacado*, 174–75; Kavanaugh, *Comanche Political History*, 136–39; Hamalainen, *The Comanche Empire*, 130; John, *Storms Brewed in Other Men's Worlds*, 142–44; Bolton, *Texas in the Middle of the Eighteenth Century*, 127–33.

17. John, *Storms Brewed in Other Men's Worlds*, 738; Kavanaugh, *Comanche Political History*, 140.

18. Kenner, *The Comanchero Frontier*, 78–97; Paul H. Carlson and Randy Vance, "Comancheros," in Carlson and Murrah, *Hidden History of the Llano Estacado*, 33–35.

19. Kenner, *The Comanchero Frontier*, 98–114; US Supreme Court, Deposition of S. E. Stilwell, O. T. #4, 732.

20. Carlson and Vance, "Comancheros," 35.

21. Kenner, *The Comanchero Frontier*, 78.

22. Morris, *El Llano Estacado*, 179; Kavanagh, *Comanche Political History*, 154. For Alferez Francisco Amangual's significant and dedicated work in the San Antonio area before taking on the responsibility of finding a shorter road to Santa Fe, see John, *Storms Brewed in Other Men's Worlds*, 621, 641–43, 649–50.

23. Morris, *El Llano Estacado*, 179, 181.

Chapter 4

1. Hamalainen, *The Comanche Empire*, 102, 111. Granted, the number of Indians in New Mexico, 10,369, and in Texas, even not including Comanches, was enough to make the total population, including Indians, of Texas and New Mexico count well above 40,000.

2. John, *Storms Brewed in Other Men's Worlds*, 468. See also Thomas W. Kavanagh, "Comanche," in DeMallie, *Plains*, vol. 13, pt. 2, of Sturtevant, *Handbook of North American Indians*, 904–5.

3. John, *Storms Brewed in Other Men's Worlds*, 505, 766; Kavanagh, "Comanche," 900–901.

4. For the marriage and Kiowa-Comanche truce, see Kavanagh, *Comanche Political History*, 144–46; Betty, *Comanche Society before the Reservation*, 7.

5. "Map of Texas, 1835."

6. See Rathjen, *The Texas Panhandle Frontier*, 83–88.

7. Pike, *Prose Sketches and Poems*, 40, 44. See also Paul H. Carlson, "Down Blackwater Draw in 1832," in Carlson and Murrah, *Historic Tales of the Llano Estacado*, 77–79; Favour, *Old Bill Williams*, 90–94.

8. Pike, *Prose Sketches and Poems*, 49.

9. Ibid., 52.

10. Ibid., 54; Carlson, "Down Blackwater Draw in 1832," 78; J. E. Haley, *Albert Pike's Journeys in the Prairie*, 43–75.

11. Kavanagh, *Comanche Political History*, 279, 281; Betty, *Comanche Society before the Reservation*, 88, 92–93; Hamalainen, *The Comanche Empire*, 240–41, 245–46.

12. Paul H. Carlson, "The Comanche War Trail," in Carlson and Murrah, *Historic Tales of the Llano Estacado*, 60.

13. Ibid. See also Richardson, *Comanche Barrier to South Plains Settlement*, 97–102; C. Williams, *Texas' Last Frontier*, 82, 86, 220; Hamalainen, *The Comanche Empire*, 219–32; Kenner, *The Comanchero Frontier*, 71, 133–34; Wallace and Hoebel, *The Comanches*, 45, 261.

14. Carlson, "The Comanche War Trail," 60. See also Adams, "Embattled Borderland," 205–20.

15. Rathjen, *The Texas Panhandle Frontier*, 72; Gregg, *Commerce of the Prairies*, 305–18.

16. Rathjen, *The Texas Panhandle Frontier*, 73. See also Gregg, *Commerce of the Prairies*, 308–11.

17. Spellman, *Forgotten Texas Leader*, 79–92, 197n55; Rathjen, *The Texas Panhandle Frontier*, 67–69; Kendall, *Narrative of the Texan Santa Fe Expedition*, 1:189–205; Carroll, *The Texan Santa Fe Trail*, 137–42.

18. Dary, *Entrepreneurs of the Old West*, 76–87; Rathjen, *The Texas Panhandle Frontier*, 74–75; Lavender, *Bent's Fort*, 246–47, 308–10: Marc Simmons, "A Teenager's Adventures on the Frontier," in Simmons, *The Old Trail to Santa Fe*, 161–63.

19. Rathjen, *The Texas Panhandle Frontier*, 93–94. See also Carroll, "Journal of Lieutenant J. W. Abert," 9–113.

20. Rathjen, *The Texas Panhandle Frontier*, 101–2.

21. Ibid., 102.

22. Ibid., 103.

23. Ibid., 106.

24. Luke Lea, *Annual Report of the Commissioner of Indian Affairs*, November 27, 1850, in Prucha, *Documents of United States Indian Policy*, 81–83.

Chapter 5

1. Kavanagh, *Comanche Political History*, 399–404.

2. See Kappler, *Indian Affairs*, 2:600–602; Wallace and Hoebel, *The Comanches*, 300.

3. Kavanagh, *Comanche Political History*, 415.

4. Ibid., 410–18; D. Jones, *The Treaty of Medicine Lodge*, 110–16, 129, 130–34; A. A. Taylor, "Medicine Lodge Peace Council," 98–118.

5. Wallace and Hoebel, *The Comanches*, 313. Population figures in Jerrold E. Levy, "Kiowa," in DeMallie, *Plains*, vol. 13, pt. 2, of Sturtevant, *Handbook of North American Indians*, 920–21; Kavanagh, "Comanche," 900–901.

6. Carlson and Vance, "Comancheros," 34.

7. Ranald S. Mackenzie, Fourth Cavalry, to Assistant Adjutant General; Smith and Carlson, "Locating the Battle of Blanco Canyon," 99–118; Wallace, *Ranald S. Mackenzie's Official Correspondence*, 41–44; Carter, *On the Border with Mackenzie*, 210–11; Wallace, *Ranald S. Mackenzie on the Texas Frontier*, 44–56.

8. Wallace, *Ranald S. Mackenzie on the Texas Frontier*, 64–67.

9. Ibid., 70, see also 68–74; Rathjen, *The Texas Panhandle Frontier*, 159–61; Wallace, *Ranald S. Mackenzie's Official Correspondence*, 71–119.

10. Wallace, *Ranald S. Mackenzie on the Texas Frontier*, 68. See also Rathjen, *The Texas Panhandle Frontier*, 159–61.

11. Wallace, *Ranald S. Mackenzie on the Texas Frontier*, 78–84; Kavanagh, *Comanche Political History*, 432–35; Rathjen, *The Texas Panhandle Frontier*, 159–63; Hamalainen, *The Comanche Empire*, 334–35. See also Mackenzie's reports in Wallace, *Ranald S. Mackenzie's Official Correspondence*, 133–58.

12. Kavanagh, *Comanche Political History*, 432–38; Richardson, *Comanche Barrier to South Plains Settlement*, 185–87; Hamalainen, *The Comanche Empire*, 337–38.

13. J. L. Haley, *The Buffalo War*, 67–78; Rathjen, *The Texas Panhandle Frontier*, 128–31; Baker and Harrison, *Adobe Walls*, 21, 51–52, 69.

14. If J. Wright Moore, one of the most successful of all bison hunters, is correct, the Indians were playing a dangerous and deadly game. That is, their attacks were designed to get the government to offer more in the way of rations of flour, cloth, and other goods. In effect, they were gaming the system.

15. J. L. Haley, *The Buffalo War*, 125–27, 161–67, 179–83, 187, 190–91, 194; Rathjen, *The Texas Panhandle Frontier*, 164–74; Wallace, *Ranald S. Mackenzie*

on the Texas Frontier, 137–46; Nye, *Carbine and Lance*, 213–28; Hamalainen, *The Comanche Empire*, 336–41; Chambers and Carlson, *Comanche Jack Stilwell*, 80–89; Cruse, *Battles of the Red River War*, 32–113. For reports from commanders in the field, see Wallace, *Ranald S. Mackenzie's Official Correspondence*, 76–176.

16. Hamalainen, *The Comanche Empire*, 351.

17. Utley, "'Pecos Bill' on the Texas Frontier," 4–13; Leckie and Leckie, *The Buffalo Soldiers*, 144–49.

18. Sturm, "Notes of Travel"; Nye, *Carbine and Lance*, 235; J. L. Haley, *The Buffalo War*, 208–9; Kavanagh, *Comanche Political History*, 450–51; Chambers, "Fort Sill's Emissaries," 58–68; Chambers and Carlson, *Comanche Jack Stilwell*, 89–91.

19. Heitman, *Historical Register and Dictionary of the United States Army*, 1:750. See also Miles, "Fort Concho in 1877," 29, 33, 34.

20. William R. Shafter to J. H. Taylor, Assistant Adjutant General, Department of Texas, September 29, 1875, William R. Shafter Papers (Shafter Papers); Shafter to Taylor, January 4, 1876, in United States, William R. Shafter, Letters Received, Appointments, Commission, and Personal Branch; Carlson, "Itinerary of a Scout," 130–40.

21. See Austin, *Jal, New Mexico*, 8.

22. Shafter to Taylor, September 29, 1875, Shafter Papers; Shafter to Taylor, January 4, 1876, ACP File, AGO, RG 94, NA; Carlson, "Itinerary of a Scout," 11–18; Crimmins, "Shafter's Explorations in West Texas," 82–96. See also Leckie and Leckie, *The Buffalo Soldiers*, 144–52; US Department of War, "Map of the Country Scouted."

23. Kavanagh, *Comanche Political History*, 415.

Chapter 6

1. See Cashion, *A Texas Frontier*, 170–76; Pace and Frazier, *Frontier Texas*, 176–80; *Fort Worth Daily Democrat*, January 25, 1877; Strickland, "The Recollections of W. S. Glenn," 40–41.

2. Schofield, *Indians, Cattle, Ships, and Oil*, 39–40; Rath, *The Rath Trail*, 143–44; Mooar, *Buffalo Days*, 64.

3. Rath, *The Rath Trail*, 143–45; Cheryl Lewis and Paul H. Carlson, "Rath City," in Carlson and Murrah, *Hidden History of the Llano Estacado*, 48–50; Pace, *Buffalo Days*, 74–76; Holden, *Alkali Trails*, 61.

4. Lewis and Carlson, "Rath City," 48; Cashion, *A Texas Frontier*, 176–81.

5. Cashion, *A Texas Frontier*, 177. See also Geoff Cunfer, "Overview: The Decline and Fall of the Bison Empire," in Cunfer and Waiser, *Bison and People*, 1, 15–22; Flores, "Bison Ecology and Bison Diplomacy," 465–85; Flores, *American Serengeti*, 113, 120–22, 128–32.

6. Mooar, "Frontier Experiences of J. Wright Mooar," 91–92; Mooar, *Buffalo Days*, 63; Cook, *The Border and the Buffalo*, 348.

7. Cook, *The Border and the Buffalo*, 317; Branch, *The Hunting of the Buffalo*, 196–97; McIntire, *Early Days in Texas*, 224, but also see 103. See also Lehmann, *Nine Years with the Indians*, 170–71; Baker and Harrison, *Adobe Walls*, 5–8.

8. Cashion, *A Texas Frontier*, 177. See also Cunfer and Waiser, *Bison and People*, 10, 15, 37; Flores, *American Serengeti*, 11–35.

9. *Crosbyton Review*, March 20, 1936. See also Jenkins, "A History of Estacado," 24.

10. Cook, *The Border and the Buffalo*, 252.

11. Arnot, "My Recollections of Tascosa," 61; Kahlbau, "Ghostly Plazas," sec. C, 4.

12. Taylor, "Pastores in the Texas Panhandle," 1–46; Romero, "Spanish Sheepmen on the Canadian," 46–48; Wentworth, *America's Sheep Trails*, 118–20.

13. See Murrah, *C. C. Slaughter*, 34, 44.

14. O. Williams, "From Dallas to the Site of Lubbock," 8; Lehmann, *Nine Years with the Indians*, 171.

15. Cook, *The Border and the Buffalo*, 188. See also Lehmann, *Nine Years with the Indians*, 171–72; Sandoz, *The Buffalo Hunters*, 269–70.

16. Lehmann, *Nine Years with the Indians*, 173–74. See also Sandoz, *The Buffalo Hunters*, 272–80; Griggs, "Battle of Yellowhouse Canyon," 37–50; Lewis, "Bluster's Last Stand," pt. 1, 14–18, pt. 2, 20–25. For the hunter's point of view, see Cook, *The Border and the Buffalo*, 204–32; Collinson, *Life in the Saddle*, 101–6; Strickland, "Recollections of W. S. Glenn," 42–63.

17. US Department of War, Regimental Returns, Tenth Cavalry; Cook, *The Border and the Buffalo*, 232–40; Smith, *The Old Army in Texas*, 161; Leckie and Leckie, *Buffalo Soldiers*, 158.

18. Lehmann, *Nine Years with the Indians*, 185–86. See also Smith, *The Old Army in Texas*, 161; Leckie and Leckie, *The Buffalo Soldiers*, 158; Carlson, *Buffalo Soldier Tragedy of 1877*, 48.

19. Carlson, *Buffalo Soldier Tragedy of 1877*, 37. See also Cook, *The Border and the Buffalo*, 246–49.

20. Carroll, "Nolan's 'Lost Nigger' Expedition of 1877," 55–75; Crimmins, "Captain Nolan's Lost Troop," 16–31; Charles L. Cooper, letter to his father, August 30, 1877, in *Lynn County News*, Tahoka, Texas, October 19, 1933. Copies of the letter also appeared in the New York *Daily Tribune*, September 8, 1877, and in Nunn, "Eighty-Six Hours without Water," 360–64. See also US Department of War, Proceedings of a General Court Martial; King, *Brief Account of the Sufferings*, 2–10.

21. O. Williams, "From Dallas to the Site of Lubbock in 1877," 3–21.

22. Ibid.

23. Sosebee, *Henry C. "Hank" Smith and the Cross B Ranch*, 1, 6, 87–111.

24. Curry, *Sun Rising on the West*, 164–65; Hutto, "Mrs. Elizabeth (Aunt Hank) Smith," 45; Ericson, *Aunt Hank's Rock House Kitchen*, 7–11.

25. Webb, *The Great Plains*, 224–27; Jordan, *North American Cattle-Ranching Frontiers*, 7–8, 217–18.

26. Murrah, *C. C. Slaughter*, 39, 45; Webb, *The Great Plains*, 225, 228–30; Hagan, *Charles Goodnight*, 45.

Chapter 7

1. Frantz, *Texas*, 135.

2. Webb, *The Great Plains*, 207, 225. See also Jordan, *North American Cattle-Ranching Frontiers*, 208–9, 215–36.

3. Austin, *Jal, New Mexico*, 13.

4. Seymour V. Connor, "The First Settlers," in L. Graves, *A History of Lubbock*, 45–53; Abbe, Carlson, and Murrah, *Lubbock and the South Plains*, 25, 27–30; Abbe and Carlson, *Historic Lubbock County*, 16–19.

5. Abbe, Carlson, and Murrah, *Lubbock and the South Plains*, 29–31.

6. Ibid., 25, 27–28; Murrah, *C. C. Slaughter*, 41–45, 47–48.

7. Holden, "Indians, Spaniards and Anglos," 40–42; Don Abbe, "The IOA Ranch, Lubbock County, Texas," in Carlson and Murrah, *Hidden History of the Llano Estacado*, 60–62; Abbe, Carlson, and Murrah, *Lubbock and the South Plains*, 30.

8. Hamlin, *The Flamboyant Judge*, 30; Gracy, *A Man Absolutely Sure of Himself*, 107–8, 118–19, 141, 157–58. For first Panhandle ranches, see J. E. Haley, *The XIT Ranch of Texas*, 40–48. Littlefield, whose children had both died in infancy, turned to his nephews to manage his ranch holdings, and in 1883 he settled with his wife in Austin.

9. Hamlin, *The Flamboyant Judge*, 30. See also Rathjen, *The Texas Panhandle Frontier*, 185–86; Nolan, *Tascosa*, 21–26.

10. See Pool, *Historical Atlas of Texas*, 120–22, especially map, 122.

11. J. E. Haley, *The XIT Ranch of Texas*, 3. See also David J. Murrah, "The XIT Ranch Windmill," in Carlson and Murrah, *Hidden History of the Llano Estacado*, 51; McCallum and McCallum, *The Wire That Fenced the West*, 121–27; Abbe, Carlson, and Murrah, *Lubbock and the South Plains*, 30; Murrah, *Rise and Fall of the Lazy S Ranch*, 13–15; Nordyke, *Cattle Empire*, 103–11.

12. Hamlin, *The Flamboyant Judge*, 112–15; Carlson, *Empire Builder in the Texas Panhandle*, 22–27; Nolan, *Tascosa*, 112, 117–18; McFadden, "From Invention to Monopoly," 25–43; McCallum and McCallum, *The Wire That Fenced the West*, 31–36, 41. Glidden's friend and DeKalb, Illinois, neighbor Isaac L. Ellwood purchased half interest in Glidden's design, and together they formed the Barb Fence Company. Later Glidden sold his half interest to the big Washburn and Moen Manufacturing Company, while Ellwood retained his share. Both men became wealthy from barbed wire, and both invested in the booming Texas cattle industry. Because the Glidden patent is easy to copy, plenty of people challenged his patent rights, and for years Glidden kept busy in the courts with copyright infringement proceedings. See McClure, "History of the Manufacture of Barbed Wire," 16–23.

13. Kahlbau, "Ghostly Plazas," sec. C, 4; Schofield, *Indians, Cattle, Ships, and Oil*, 53, 59–60;

14. Gracy, *A Man Absolutely Sure of Himself*, 141, 158–59. Littlefield and White sold their LIT brand and grazing rights in the western Panhandle.

15. Schofield, *Indians, Cattle, Ships, and Oil*, 65. See also Zeigler, "The Cowboy Strike of 1883," 32–46. For a series of interviews with the strike participants and others associated with Tom Harris, see J. Evetts Haley Papers, Interview Files.

16. Gracy, *A Man Absolutely Sure of Himself*, 142; Murrah, *C. C. Slaughter*, 57; Holden, *Alkali Trails*, 50; *Taylor County News*, April 24, 1885. See also Baker, "Windmills of the Panhandle Plains," 71–110.

17. Murrah, *C. C. Slaughter*, 56–57; Schofield, *Indians, Cattle, Ships, and Oil*, 53–54, 60.

18. Forbis, *The Cowboys*, 17. See also Dobie, *Cow People*, 161–64; Rollins, *The Cowboy*, 39–42.

19. Forbis, *The Cowboys*, 17. See David J. Murrah, "Cowboys, Treasures, and Chance Meetings: West Texas Ranch Oral Histories," in possession of David J. Murrah, Rockport, Texas. See also Dale, *Cow Country*, 223; Clay, *My Life on the Range*, 56; Dobie, *The Longhorns*, 27–28; Rollins, *The Cowboy*, 70–73; Alexander Mackay, "Cowboy Life on a Western Ranch," 1890, edited by James A. Brink and Charles L. Wood, photocopy and typescript in Alexander Mackay, Reference File.

20. See Rathjen, *The Texas Panhandle Frontier*, 186–88; Rollins, *The Cowboy*, 39–41; James R. Wagner, "*Cowboy*: Origin and Early Use of the Term," in Carlson, *The Cowboy Way*, 11–20; Moore, *Cow Boys and Cattle Men*, 5–6. For a slightly different view, see Jordan, *North American Cattle-Ranching Frontiers*, 50, 180, 213, 232; Whitlock, *Cowboy Life on the Llano Estacado*, 155.

21. B. Byron Price, "Ghosts and Cowboys: Buck Ramsey and the Cowboy Poetry Tradition," in Braucher and Ramsey, *Buck Ramsey's Grass*, xi.

22. Whitlock, *Cowboy Life on the Llano Estacado*, 247–48; Carlson, *Empire Builder*, 29; Holden, *Alkali Trails*, 165–68.

23. See Whitlock, *Cowboy Life on the Llano Estacado*, 139–40, 153–58.

24. Carlson, *Empire Builder*, 22–23; Price and Rathjen, *The Golden Spread*, 57, 701; J. E. Haley, *The XIT Ranch in Texas*, 3.

25. Hagan, *Charles Goodnight*, 76–77, 80–81; Price and Rathjen, *The Golden Spread*, 53–57.

26. William Hunt, "Northwest Texas," in *The Texas Almanac for1883*, 117.

27. H. C. (Hank) Smith, "Along down the Reminiscent Line," *Crosbyton Review*, February 29, 1912. See also Paul H. Carlson, "Estacado, Texas," in Carlson and Murrah, *Historic Tales of the Llano Estacado*, 149–52.

28. For Singer's store, see Henry B. Crawford, "George Singer and His Yellow House Store," in Carlson and Murrah, *Hidden History of the Llano Estacado*, 71–73; Seymour V. Connor, "The First Settlers," in L. Graves, *A History of Lubbock*, 55–56, 65–66n43; Holden, *Rollie Burns*, 75; J. E. Haley, *The XIT Ranch of Texas*, 47–48.

29. Key, *In the Cattle Country*, 28; Carlson, *Empire Builder*, 32–34.

30. See Price and Rathjen, *The Golden Spread*, 55; and Murrah, *C. C. Slaughter*, 57–58.

31. Price and Rathjen, *The Golden Spread*, 60. See also Murrah, *C. C. Slaughter*,

57–60; Holden, *Alkali Trails*, 45–47; Abbe, Carlson, and Murrah, *Lubbock and the South Plains*, 27; White, *The Forgotten Cattle King*, 43–47; Texas Sheep and Goat Raisers Association, newspaper clippings, Morgue Files; *Tascosa Pioneer*, August 27, 1887.

32. Murrah, *C. C. Slaughter*, 55. See also Price and Rathjen, *The Golden Spread*, 57–61, 63; White, *The Forgotten Cattle King*, 65n2, 66–67; Abbe, Carlson, and Murrah, *Lubbock and the South Plains*, 34–35.

33. Murrah, *C. C. Slaughter*, 84, but see also 104.

34. Price and Rathjen, *The Golden Spread*, 60.

35. Carlson, *Empire Builder*, 44–47; Price and Rathjen, *The Golden Spread*, 68–71; Crudington, "Old Time Amarillo," 79–113.

36. Carlson, *Amarillo*, 31–36; Carlson, *Empire Builder*, 44–47; Price and Rathjen, *The Golden Spread*, 68–71; Key, *In the Cattle Country*, 45–38; Crudington, "Old Town Amarillo," 87.

37. Seymour V. Conner, "The Founding of Lubbock," in L. Graves, *A History of Lubbock*, 72–80; Abbe, Carlson, and Murrah, *Lubbock and the South Plains*, 45–46.

38. Conner, "The Founding of Lubbock," 72–80; Carlson, "The Nicolett Hotel," 8–19; Lubbock Heritage Society et al., *Lubbock*, 9; Hunt, *Early Days upon the Plains*, 5–10.

39. Webb, *The Great Plains*, 225.

Chapter 8

1. Murrah, *C. C. Slaughter*, 105, and see 154n2; Texas v. Rogan, 68 *Southwestern Reporter* (Texas), 775–76 (1902); Abbe, "The History of Lynn County," 25–26; Hill and Jacobs, *Grass Roots Upside Down*, 54–57; Carlson, *Empire Builder*, 105.

2. Price and Rathjen, *The Golden Spread*, 62–63. See also Sheffy, "Experimental Stage of Settlement," 87.

3. John Barclay McGill to Mollie McCormick, February 11 and February 23, 1890, in Reeve, *My Dear Mollie*, 161–63. See also Carlson, *Empire Builder in the Texas Panhandle*, 103–4.

4. See Barnett, *Rain*, 156–57; "The Curious Case of R. G. Dyrenforth," in Coppedge, *Texas Singularities*, 26–28.

5. John T. "Jack" Becker, "Picking Bison Bones for Profit," in Carlson and Murrah, *Historic Tales of the Llano Estacado*, 90–92. See also Gard, *The Great Buffalo Hunt*, 300–304.

6. Sheffy, "The Experimental Stage of Settlement," 78–103; Carlson, *Empire Builder*, 103–4; Curry, *Sun Rising on the West*, 164, 166.

7. *Lubbock Avalanche*, March 6, 1903. See also Holden, *Alkali Trails*, 166–67.

8. McGill to McCormick, October 7, 1889, in Reeve, *My Dear Mollie*, 113. See also Spikes, *As a Farm Woman Thinks*, 23, 31.

9. Carlson and Murrah, *Historic Tales of the Llano Estacado*, 150. See also Jenkins et al., *Estacado*, 150–52.

10. Hofsommer, *The Quanah Route*, 17; Dolores Mosser, "Virginia City in Bailey

County, Texas," in Carlson and Murrah, *Hidden History of the Llano Estacado*, 161–63.

11. *Shafter Lake Herald*, October 7, 1907; Starck and Carlson, "Shafter Lake," 31–33, 38; Starck and Carlson, "The Llano Estacado, Mexico and Gulf," 18–21.

12. Matthew Tippens to Paul Carlson, March 14, 2021, letter in possession of author. See also Jordan, "German Settlement of Texas after 1865," 193–212.

13. *Amarillo Evening News*, June 4, 1901; *Amarillo Weekly News*, June 28, 1901; Clark, *Three Stars for the Colonel*, 20–21; Carlson, *Amarillo*, 63–64; Franks and Ketelle, *Amarillo, Texas II*, no. 94.

14. See William M. Pearce, "William P. Soash," in Connor, *Builders of the Southwest*, 218–21; Blodgett, *Land of Bright Promise*, 48, 52, 54, 58–59, 73–85, 91–92; Franks and Ketelle, *Amarillo, Texas II*, no. 94; Jennifer Spurrier, "W. P. Soash and Excursion Trains to the South Plains," in Carlson and Murrah, *Hidden History of the Llano Estacado*, 129–31; Pope, "A Failed Plains Empire," 109–20; Gracy, "Selling the Future," 1–75.

15. See Carlson, *Texas Woollybacks*, 193, 201; Seymour V. Connor, "Clarence Scharbauer, Sr.," in Connor, *Builders of the Southwest*, 206–9.

16. See Murrah, *Oil, Taxes, and Cats*, x, 9–11, 15–16; *Texas Almanac, 2020–2021*, 221, 272.

17. Murrah, *C. C. Slaughter*, 83–102; David J. Murrah to Paul H. Carlson, March 30, 2022, letter in possession of author; David J. Murrah, "Texas's Last Frontier" and "Closing Texas's Last Frontier," both in Carlson and Murrah, *Historic Tales of the Llano Estacado*, 98–100, 101–5.

18. White, *The Forgotten Cattle King*, 11–12, 62–63, 67; Fleming and Murrah, *Texas' Last Frontier*, 10–11. See also White, "F. G. Oxsheer," 106–15.

19. David J. Murrah, "The Last Great Fence Cutting War," in Carlson and Murrah, *Historic Tales of the Llano Estacado*, 105.

20. Murrah, "The Last Great Fence Cutting War," 107; Murrah, *C. C. Slaughter*, 88–89; Murrah, *Oil, Taxes, and Cats*, 24–27; Murrah, *Rise and Fall of the Lazy S Ranch*, 51–53. There are several depositions concerning the court fight in Mallet Land and Cattle Company v. C. C. Slaughter, Court of Civil Appeals Records, 1905.

21. Eaves and Hutchinson, *Post City, Texas*, 7–9, 36–40, 112–16, 161–62; Abbe, Carlson, and Murrah, *Lubbock and the South Plains*, 36; C. W. Post, Reference File.

22. Gracy, *Littlefield Lands*, 9–13; Gracy, *A Man Absolutely Sure of Himself*, 225–26, 274–78; Abbe, Carlson, and Murrah, *Lubbock and the South Plains*, 36.

23. See Murrah, *"And Are We Yet Alive?,"* 84–85, 87; Carlson, *Amarillo*, 56–57.

24. Kuhlman, *Always WT*, 2–6, 13–16, 26.

25. Abbe, Carlson, and Murrah, *Lubbock and the South Plains*, 51–52; Carlson, *Centennial History of Lubbock*, 58–59.

26. Texas Crop and Livestock Reporting Service, *Texas Historic Livestock Statistics, 1867–1976*, 27; Kuhlman, *Always WT*, 65; Carlson, *Texas Woollybacks*, 193–96; Hamilton, "Trends in the Sheep Industry in Texas," 7; "World War I's Impact on Wool and Lamb," 47.

27. Abbe, Carlson, and Murrah, *Lubbock and the South Plains*, 38–39.

28. See Nall, "Panhandle Farming," 68–93; Nall, "Specialization and Expansion," 46–67.

29. *Randall County News*, October 21, 1918; Joyce Mills Brayle to Ruth Lowes, August 21, 1981, V. R. Lowes Papers; Crosby, *America's Forgotten Pandemic*, 209; Kuhlman, *Always WT*, 65; Carlson, *Centennial History of Lubbock*, 61; Carlson, *Amarillo*, 86–87.

30. Matthews, "Influence of the Texas Panhandle on Georgia O'Keeffe," 107–36; Carlson and Becker, *Georgia O'Keeffe in Texas*, xi, 1, 7–24, 29–30.

31. *The Oklahoma County News* (Jones), May 18, 1917; Paul H. Carlson, "Ozark Trails Roadways in West Texas," in Carlson and Murrah, *Hidden History of the Llano Estacado*, 66–68. See also Elvis E. Fleming, "The Ozark Trails in the Pecos Valley," in Fleming and Williams, *Treasures of History III*, 228–37.

Chapter 9

1. Hamilton, "Trends in the Sheep Industry in Texas," 6–11, 42–45; Carlson, *Texas Woollybacks*, 199–201.

2. Abbe, Carlson, and Murrah, *Lubbock and the South Plains*, 39. See also D. Green, *Land of Underground Rain*, 6, 38–48, 72–73, 76.

3. Worster, *Dust Bowl*, 89–90. See also Abbe, Carlson, and Murrah, *Lubbock and the South Plains*, 38.

4. Worster, *Dust Bowl*, 90–91.

5. Ibid., 90.

6. *Amarillo Daily News*, April 6 and 17, 1924.

7. Ibid., April 13, 1922. See also Carlson, *Amarillo*, 106–8.

8. Chalmers, *Hooded Americanism*, 28–35, 39–40, 45; Carlson, *Amarillo*, 103–5.

9. Childers and Martin, *Slaton's Story*, 5.

10. Several sources treat the Father Keller tarring and feathering. See, for example, Villanueva, *Remembering Slaton, Texas*, 45–51; Robert Sledge, "Slaton and the Ku Klux Klan, 1921–1926," in Carlson and Murrah, *Hidden History of the Llano Estacado*, 134–37; Childers and Martin, *Slaton's Story*, 18; *The Slatonite* (Slaton, Texas), March 29, 1922; *Lubbock Avalanche*, March 7, 1922; *Sheboygan Press*, December 18, 1939. See also Hardesty, *Pioneer Preacher of the Plains*, 143; Sweeney, "Ugly Mask of Vigilante Justice," 24–34.

11. Ku Klux Klan (Amarillo) Records, 1921–25, membership roster, A158.4E; Stanford v. State (No. 8457), Court of Criminal Appeals of Texas, 161–62; *Dallas Morning News*, April 15, 1923; Morton Harrison, "Gentlemen from Indiana," in Mowry, *The Twenties*, 145–54; Carlson, *Amarillo*, 104–5; *Amarillo Daily News*, April 12, 1922, and April 1, 4, 26, and 29, 1924; Alexander, *Ku Klux Klan in the Southwest*, 81.

12. Carlson, *Centennial History of Lubbock*, 66–67.

13. Chalmers, *Hooded Americanism*, 223–24; Moncus, *Quay County, New Mexico*, 85.

14. US Bureau of Mines, "Helium Capital of the World—Amarillo," in Hammond, *Amarillo*, 157–59; *Amarillo Daily News*, August 28, 1928; C. W. Seibel, "The Development of Helium Production as Now Carried on at Amarillo, Texas, by U. S. Bureau of Mines, Department of Interior," in Weaver, *Panhandle Petroleum*, 117–23; Seibel, "Government's New Helium Plant," 550–52.

15. Weaver, *Oil Field Trash*, 107–16, 121–22; Olien and Olien, *Oil in Texas*, 147–62.

16. Aryain, *From Syria to Seminole*, 112–13. See also Gracy, *Littlefield Lands*, 95–99, 101–8.

17. Bedichek, *Adventures with a Texas Naturalist*, 203n2. For birdlife on the Llano Estacado in the 1930s, see Hawkins, "Bird Life in the Texas Panhandle," 110–50.

18. Literature on public enemies of the early 1930s is voluminous. See, for example, Burrough, *Public Enemies*. For Bonnie and Clyde on the Llano Estacado and at Carlsbad, see Birchell and LeMay, *Hidden History of Southeast New Mexico*, 32–38; Hynd, *We Are the Public Enemies*, 50–51; Baker, *Gangster Tour of Texas*, 9–10.

19. See Worster, *Dust Bowl*, 10–12, 15; Bonnifield, *The Dust Bowl*, 61–85; Hurt, *Dust Bowl*, 33–47; Nall, "Dust Bowl Days," 43; Neugebauer, *Plains Farmer*, 161, 163; Carlson, "Black Sunday," 5–17.

20. Nall, "Dust Bowl Days," 43.

21. Raleigh Middleton, interview with Paul H. Carlson, November 2, 1990, in Carlson, "Black Sunday," 12, 17; *Lubbock Evening Journal*, April 17, 1935 See also G. C. Applewhite, interview with Richard Mason; Gerald McCathern, interview with Monte L. Monroe. Most newspapers on the Llano Estacado during the first week after "Black Sunday" covered the event. They can be accessed in the Southwest Collection/Special Collections Library at Texas Tech University, the Panhandle-Plains Historical Museum Archives at West Texas A&M University, and in newspapers online. Secondary sources on Black Sunday are numerous: a recent piece is Heather Green Wooten, "'So Long, It's Been Good to Know You': Black Sunday, April 14, 1935," in Scheer, *Eavesdropping on Texas History*, 154–73.

22. *Amarillo Globe*, April 15, 1935; Neugebauer, *Plains Farmer*, 161, 163; Wooten, "'So Long, It's Been Good to Know You,'" 159. See also Lewis T. Nordyke to Marvin Jones, November 8, 1941, in Marvin Jones Papers, Box 2, Folder 1.

23. See Johnson, "Rural Rehabilitation in the New Deal," 279–95; Kennedy, "Harvesting History," 1–2.

24. See Olien and Olien, *Oil in Texas*, 167–79; Weaver, *Oil Field Trash*, 92–97, 107–16; Weaver, *Panhandle Petroleum*, 28–33. See also Olien, "Rag Town Life," 15–29.

25. See *Lubbock Avalanche-Journal*, June 16, 2017.

26. See Bowman, "After Suffrage," 59–70, 74–77; Kuhlman, *Always WT*, 42–43, 74, 164–65; Hill, *Panhandle-Plains Historical Society and Its Museum*, 11, 17.

27. *Amarillo Daily News*, December 9, 1941. See also Flynn, "Living History," 145–46.

28. Price and Rathjen, *The Golden Spread*, 105. See also "Old Troop 'B' Called into Action," *Amarillo Daily News*, April 5, 1942; Stokesbury, *A Short History of World War II*, 204–7.

29. Birchell and LeMay, *Hidden History of Southeast New Mexico*, 117–19; Stokesbury, *A Short History of World War II*, 208–11; Buchanan, *The United States and World War II*, 1:101–2.

30. Don Abbe, "Lubbock's Major Military Bases of World War II," in Carlson and Murrah, *Hidden History of the Llano Estacado*, 177, 178. See also Price and Rathjen, *The Golden Spread*, 106; Buchanan, *The United States and World War II*, 1:120–25; Abbe, Carlson, and Murrah, *Lubbock and the South Plains*, 60–61; Paxton, "Silent Wings and Subtle Legacy," 10–23. Clovis air base is now Cannon Air Force Base; the US military repurposed the Amarillo, Hobbs, Lubbock, and Pampa facilities after the war and then eventually decommissioned them.

31. John W. McCullough, "Clent Breedlove's Lubbock Airfield," in Carlson and Murrah, *Hidden History of the Llano Estacado*, 173–75; McCullough, "Pre-flights on Tech Campus," 19–34. See also Buchanan, *The United States and World War II*, 1:122.

32. Abbe, Carlson, and Murrah, *Lubbock and the South Plains*, 61.

33. Birchell and LeMay, *Hidden History of Southeast New Mexico*, 125–27.

34. Dolores Mosser and Sammie Simpson, "The Santa Fe Railroad and Japanese Americans of Clovis," in Carlson and Murrah, *Historic Tales of the Llano Estacado*, 160. See also McAlavy and Kilmer, *High Plains History of East-Central New Mexico*, 92–93.

35. See Chaplo, *Amarillo Flights*, 111.

36. Price and Rathjen, *The Golden Spread*, 107; Abbe, Carlson, and Murrah, *Lubbock and the South Plains*, 61.

37. For population figures, see Bean, *Texas and Texans in World War II*, 323; Murrah, "County Population Chart," 1.

38. Matthiesen, *Wise and Otherwise*, 192–93, 199–200. See also Carlson, *Amarillo*, 141.

Chapter 10

1. *Amarillo Daily News*, May 16, 17, and 18, 1949; Price and Rathjen, *The Golden Spread*, 108–9. See also Franks and Ketelle, *Amarillo Texas II*, nos. 4–9 and accompanying text.

2. Price and Rathjen, *The Golden Spread*, 109. See also Franks and Ketelle, *Amarillo Texas II*, nos. 14 and 15; Carlson, *Amarillo*, 162–63.

3. Franks and Ketelle, *Amarillo Texas II*, nos. 14 and 15; Price and Rathjen, *The Golden Spread*, 109. See also Neugebauer, *Plains Farmer*, 279–80.

4. Price and Rathjen, *The Golden Spread*, 109; Estaville and Earl, *Texas Water Atlas*, 12; Neugebauer, *Plains Farmer*, 167–68, 305, 317.

5. Fleming and Murrah, *Texas' Last Frontier*, 93; Neugebauer, *Plains Farmer*, 306, 307.

6. Cunfer, *On the Great Plains*, 199.

7. See Becker, Awasom, and Henry, *Cotton on the South Plains*, 7–8.

8. Ibid., 9.

9. See Abbe, Carlson, and Murrah, *Lubbock and the South Plains*, 62–63, quote on 63.

10. See Fleming, "Caprock Once Thriving," 4–5. The literature on ghost towns is abundant. See Baker, *Ghost Towns of Texas*, 40–42, 107–9, 137–39, 149–51; Way, "Bartonsite," 83–95.

11. Abbe, Carlson, and Murrah, *Lubbock and the South Plains*, 63; Burroughs, *Roosevelt County*, 73–77; Moncus, *Quay County, New Mexico*, 84–85; Mulhouse, *Abandoned New Mexico*, 10–14, 21, 34–38, 41–44.

12. Price and Rathjen, *The Golden Spread*, 111; see also Carlson, *Amarillo*, 166–67.

13. John T. "Jack" Becker, "The Texas Panhandle," in Carlson and Glasrud, *West Texas*, 38–39. See also Richard Mason, "The Cotton Kingdom and the City of Lubbock," in L. Graves, *Lubbock*, 15; Garry L. Nall, "The Cattle Feeding Industry on the Texas High Plains," in Dethloff and May, *Southwestern Agriculture*, 105–15; Price and Rathjen, *The Golden Spread*, 124; Carlson, *Amarillo*, 186, 217.

14. Wayne Hardin, New Mexico rancher and commercial operator, interview with author.

15. Quotes in Abbe, Carlson, and Murrah, *Lubbock and the South Plains*, 69.

16. Weiner, "History of the Lubbock and West Texas Musical Heritage," 175–92.

17. Fischer, *Albion's Seed*, 4–10. See also Paul H. Carlson, "Buddy Holly, Beethoven, and Lubbock in the 1950s," in Untiedt, *First Timers and Old Timers*, 92; Weiner, "West Texas and Lubbock Music during the Fifties," 7–17, 118–26; Joe E. Specht, "Put a Nickel in the Jukebox: The Texas Tradition in Country Music, 1922–50," in Clayton and Specht, *The Roots of Texas Music*, 66–94.

18. B. Byron Price, "Ghosts and Cowboys: Buck Ramsey and the Cowboy Poetry Tradition," in Braucher and Ramsey, *Buck Ramsey's Grass*, xii–xv. See also *Lubbock Avalanche-Journal*, July 31, 2021.

19. See *Amarillo Daily News*, May 11, 1949, November 1, 1966, and November 2, 1966; George W. Finger, "Sanford Dam and Reservoir," in Hammond, *Amarillo*, 99–107; Flynn, "Living History," 180; Price and Rathjen, *The Golden Spread*, 121. The eleven cities include Borger, Pampa, Amarillo, Plainview, Lubbock, Levelland, Slaton, Tahoka, Brownfield, O'Donnell, and Lamesa.

20. *Amarillo Times*, December 16, 1939; *Canyon News*, May 17, 1951; *Amarillo Sunday Globe-News*, May 29, 1978, December 21, 1986, and April 17, 1988; *Amarillo Globe-News*, May 2 and 24, 1979; *Amarillo Daily News*, August 29, 1991; *Lubbock Avalanche-Journal*, June 30, 2021; Willson, *May 26, 1978*, 18.

21. M. Cox, *Texas Disasters*, 162; *Amarillo Daily News*, February 1, 2, 4, and 5, 1956; *Plainview Daily Herald*, February 6, 1956; *Amarillo Globe-News*, February 2, 1956.

22. M. Cox, *Texas Disasters*, 155–65; *Amarillo Daily News*, February 4, 1956; *Plainview Daily Herald*, February 6, 1956.

23. See L. Graves, *Lubbock*, 83–85, 120–21, 147–49, 172; *Lubbock Avalanche-Journal*, May 12–15, 1970; Carlson, *Centennial History of Lubbock*, 125–29.

24. Matthiesen, "Statement on the Production and Stockpiling of the Neutron Bomb," 2. The literature is abundant. See Matthiesen, *Wise and Otherwise*, 139–41, 153–55; Mojtabai, *Blessed Assurance*, 46–47, 52; *Amarillo Globe-News*, February 6, 1981.

25. See Hunt, "Host and Hostage," 338–63.

26. Pearson, "Trump Wins in Lubbock County and Texas," 1–2.

27. See Sosebee, "Dashed Hopes and Gained Opportunities," 67–86; Stuntz, "Early African American Community in Amarillo," 63–71.

28. *Texas Almanac, 2006–2007*, 371–81; *Texas Almanac, 2020–2021*, 383, 393, 395, 397. See also *Lubbock Avalanche-Journal*, August 13, 2021.

29. *Lubbock Avalanche-Journal*, May 2, 2021.

30. *Lubbock Avalanche-Journal*, December 16, 2020. In 2022, hemp agriculture was in a period of transition. In regard to the demand for CBD "everything was down and regulations from federal and state policy makers complicated matters." A result has been that large amounts of hemp languish in barns and at storage facilities, and as the industry matures, much smaller crops may be characteristic of hemp's future.

31. *Lubbock Avalanche-Journal*, June 8, 2021. See also *Lubbock Avalanche-Journal*, June 13 and 19, 2021.

Epilogue

1. Since the beginning of the Industrial Revolution in the early nineteenth century, the global temperature has risen about 1.1 degrees Celsius. The world and we humans must avoid the 1.5-degree Celsius rise, the point at which many climatologists think that the planet will start to experience irreversible climate change and its subsequent far-reaching catastrophe.

2. *Lubbock-Avalanche-Journal*, June 12, 2021.

3. Ibid., June 22, 2021.

4. Knoll, *A Brief History of Earth*, 208.

5. R. Graves, *The Prairie Dog*, 12, 19.

6. See Bailey, *American Plains Bison*, 77, 192; Isenberg, *Destruction of the Bison*, 175–76, 178, 180.

7. In the past fifteen years, mountain lions have been seen hunting in or nosing around both Blanco and Ransom Canyons.

8. The number of introduced plants and animals to Texas, including the Llano Estacado, is high, and in several cases the invasive species have created ecological disasters. See reference to Cliff Shackelford in Courtney, "The Texanist," 142–43.

9. D. Williams, "East Invades West," 79–87. Water-robbing mesquite has been around for a very long time, but fires, which once came to the Llano Estacado every three to five years, kept the noxious plant at bay. The first explorers, bison hunters, and soldiers on the Llano found mesquite roots in most all the draws

running through the High Plains. See Weniger, *The Explorers' Texas*, 20, 23; Lt. Col. William R. Shafter to J. H. Taylor, Asst. Adj. Gen., Department of Texas, Jan. 4, 1876, in Crimmins, "Shafter's Explorations in Western Texas," 82–96.

10. David J. Murrah, "County Population Chart," compiled by and in possession of David J. Murrah, Rockport, Texas; Fleming and Murrah, *Texas' Last Frontier*, 56–72; *Texas Almanac 2006–2007*, 371–81; Mulhouse, *Abandoned New Mexico*, 57–73.

11. Price and Rathjen, *The Golden Spread*, 125.

Bibliography

Manuscript Collections, Theses, Dissertations, Interviews

Abbe, Donald. "A History of Lynn County." Master's thesis, Texas Tech University, 1974.

Applewhite, G. C. Interview with Richard Mason, October 15, 1980. Transcript in Southwest Collection/Special Collections Library, Texas Tech University.

Buffalo Lake National Wildlife Area. Reference File. Panhandle-Plains Historical Museum, Canyon.

Bush, William H. Collection. Amarillo Public Library, Amarillo.

Emeny, Mary. Interview with author, July 24, 2021. Notes in possession of author.

Flynn, Sean J. "Living History: John L. McCarty and the Texas Panhandle." PhD diss., Texas Tech University, 1999.

Glenn, Willis Shelton. Papers. Southwest Collection/Special Collections Library, Texas Tech University.

Haley, J. Evetts. Papers: Interview Files. Panhandle-Plains Historical Museum, Canyon.

Hardin, Wayne. Interview with author, July 26, 2021. Notes in possession of author.

Ingalls, Timothy. Interview with author, July 24, 2021. Notes in possession of author.

Jenkins, John Cooper. "A History of Estacado: A Quaker Community and Its Environs." Master's thesis, Hardin-Simmons University, 1952.

Jones, Marvin. Papers. Southwest Collection/Special Collections Library, Texas Tech University.

Ku Klux Klan (Amarillo). Records, 1921–25. Southwest Collection/Special Collections Library, Texas Tech University.

Lost Troop Expedition. Reference File. Southwest Collection/Special Collections Library, Texas Tech University.

Lowes, V. R. Papers. Panhandle-Plains Historical Museum, Canyon.

Mackay, Alexander. Reference File. Southwest Collection/Special Collections Library, Texas Tech University.

Mackenzie, Ranald S., Fourth Cavalry. Letter to Assistant Adjutant General, Department of Texas (DT), November 15, 1871 (filed as Fort Richardson, 521 DT 1871). Letters Sent, US Army Commands, Record Group (RG) 98, National Archives (NA), Washington, DC.

———. Reference File. Southwest Collection/Special Collections Library, Texas Tech University.

Mallet Land and Cattle Company v. C. C. Slaughter. Court of Civil Appeals Records, 1905. National Archives, Fort Worth.

"Map of Texas, 1835." Southwest Collection/Special Collections Library, Texas Tech University.

Martin, Tom. Papers. Southwest Collection/Special Collections Library, Texas Tech University.

McCathern, Gerald. Interview with Monte L. Monroe, September 23, 2015. Transcript in Southwest Collection/Special Collections Library, Texas Tech University.

McFadden, Joseph M. "From Invention to Monopoly: The History of the Consolidation of the Barbed Wire Industry, 1873–1899." PhD diss., Northern Illinois University, DeKalb, 1968.

Mooar, John Wesley. Papers. Southwest Collection/Special Collections Library, Texas Tech University.

Murrah, David J. "County Population Chart." Compiled by and in possession of David J. Murrah, Rockport, Texas.

———. "Cowboys, Treasures, and Chance Meetings: West Texas Ranch Oral Histories." Unpublished manuscript, 1992. Manuscript in possession of David J. Murrah, Rockport, Texas.

———. Letter to Paul H. Carlson, March 30, 2021. Letter in possession of author.

Parker, Quanah. Reference File. Southwest Collection/Special Collections Library, Texas Tech University.

Patrick, Marvin A. "A Survey of Colonization Companies in Texas." Master's thesis, University of Texas at Austin, 1925.

Pearson, Neale J. "Trump Wins in Lubbock County and Texas." Manuscript, November 19, 2020. Photocopy in possession of author.

Phillips, Francis. "The Development of Agriculture in the Panhandle-Plains Region of Texas to 1920." Master's thesis, West Texas State Teachers College, Canyon, 1946.

Post, C. W. Papers. Southwest Collection/Special Collections Library, Texas Tech University.

———. Reference File. Southwest Collection/Special Collections Library, Texas Tech University.

Shafter, William R. Letters Received, Appointments, Commissions, and Personal Branch. Adjutant General's Office, RG 94, NA.

———. Papers. Stanford University Library, Stanford, California. Photocopy, 1861–1898, Southwest Collection/Special Collections Library, Texas Tech University.

Silver Falls. Reference File. Southwest Collection/Special Collections Library, Texas Tech University.

Steele, June M. "Phebe Warner: Community Building in the Texas Panhandle, 1898–1935." Master's thesis, Texas Tech University, 2000.

Terrell, Peggy Joyce. "Colonel R. S. Mackenzie's Campaign against the Southern Plains Indians, 1865–1875." Master's thesis, Texas Tech University, 1953.

Texas Sheep and Goat Raisers Association. Records. Southwest Collection/Special Collections Library, Texas Tech University.

Tippens, Matthew. Letter to Paul Carlson, March 14, 2021. Letter in possession of author.

US Department of War. "Map of the Country Scouted by Colonels Mackenzie and Shafter, Capt. R. P. Wilson and Others in the Years 1874 and 1875." Drawn by Alex L. Lucas. Adjutant General's Office (2832 AGO 1876), RG 94, NA.

———. Proceedings of a General Court Martial, Fort McKavett, Texas; Special Orders No. 169, Headquarters Department of Texas, San Antonio, September 26, 1877; trial of Sergeant William L. Umbles, convened on October 15, 1877. Photocopy in Museum Research Library and Archives, Fort Concho National Historic Landmark, San Angelo, Texas.

———. Regimental Returns. Tenth Cavalry, May–June, 1877. Adjutant General's Office, RG 94, NA.

Government Documents

Cummins, William R. *Report on the Geography, Topography, and Geology of the Llano Estacado or Staked Plains.* 3rd Annual Report of the Geological Survey of Texas. Austin: State Printing Office, 1891.

Fujita, Tetsuya T. *Lubbock Tornado of May 11, 1970.* Report, June 1970. Photocopy in Tom Martin Papers, Southwest Collection/Special Collections Library, Texas Tech University.

Heitman, Francis B. *Historical Register and Dictionary of the United States Army.* 2 vols. Washington, DC: Government Printing Office, 1903.

High Plains Associates. *Six-State High Plains Ogallala Aquifer Regional Resources Study.* Report to the US Department of Commerce and the High Plains Study Council, 2nd printing. Austin: High Plains Associates, 1982.

Johnson, W. D. "The High Plains and Their Utilization." US Geologic Survey, *Twenty-First Annual Report,* pt. 4 (1900): 601–741.

Kappler, Charles J., ed and comp. *Indian Affairs: Laws and Treaties.* 5 vols. Washington, DC: Government Printing Office, 1904–41.

Marcy, Randolph B. *Exploration of the Red River of Louisiana in the Year 1852.* H. R. Executive Document, 33rd Cong., 1st Sess. Washington, DC: A. O. P. Nicholson, 1854.

———. *Route from Fort Smith to Santa Fe, Letter from the Secretary of War . . . February 21, 1850.* H. R. Executive Document, No. 45, 31st Cong., 1st Sess., 1852. Rare Books section, Southwest Collection/Special Collections Library, Texas Tech University.

Mooney, James. "Calendar History of the Kiowa Indians." In *Seventeenth Annual Report of the Bureau of Ethnology,* 1895–96, pt. 1. Washington, DC: Government Printing Office, 1898.

Read, Ralph A. *The Great Plains Shelterbelt in 1954.* Bulletin No. 441. Lincoln, NE: Rocky Mountain Forest and Range Experimental Station, 1958.

Sanborn v. Bush. 91 *Southwestern Reporter,* 883 (Texas, 1906).

Stanford v. State (No. 8457). Court of Criminal Appeals of Texas, January 21, 1925. 268 *Southwestern Reporter,* 161–62.

Sturm, Jacob J. "Notes of Travel in Search of the Qujahj-di-ru Band of Comanches." Letters Received, Military Department of Missouri, 1875 S248/2. RG 98, NA.

Texas Crop and Livestock Reporting Service. *Texas Historic Livestock Statistics, 1867–1976.* Bulletin 131. Austin: Texas Department of Agriculture, 1976.

Texas v. Rogan. 68 *Southwestern Reporter,* 775–76 (Texas, 1902).

Urban, Lloyd V., and H. Wayne Wyatt, eds. *Proceedings of the Playa Basin Symposium, 1994.* Lubbock: Texas Tech University, 1994.

US Department of Commerce, Environmental Sciences Services Administration. *The Lubbock, Texas, Tornado, May 11, 1970: A Report to the Administration.* Natural Disaster Survey Report 70–1, Rockville, Maryland, July 1970.

US Supreme Court. *United States v. State of Texas,* 1894. Deposition of S. E. Stilwell, March 31, 1894, Supreme Court. RG 267, NA.

Newspapers

Abilene Reporter-News, 1959

Amarillo Daily News, 1922, 1924, 1928, 1941, 1949, 1966, 1991

Amarillo Evening News, 1901

Amarillo Globe, 1935

Amarillo Globe-News, 1956, 1979, 1981

Amarillo Globe-Times, 1956

Amarillo Sunday Globe-News, 1938, 1978, 1986, 1988

Amarillo Times, 1939

Amarillo Weekly News, 1901

Atlanta Daily Constitution, 1877

Canyon News, 1939

Crosbyton Review, 1912, 1936

Fort Worth Daily Democrat, 1877

Galveston Daily News, 1873, 1875–77

Jacksboro Frontier Echo, 1877

Lubbock Avalanche, 1903, 1922

Lubbock Avalanche-Journal, 1970, 1978, 1990, 2002, 2016–22

Lubbock Evening Journal, 1935

Lynn County News (Tahoka, Texas), 1933

New York Daily Tribune, 1877

New York Times, 1867, 1877, 1934

Oklahoma County News (Jones), 1917

Plainview Daily Herald, 1956

Post (Texas) *Dispatch,* Golden Jubilee ed., 1957

Randall County News (Canyon), 1918

Record (Forth Worth), 1907

Roswell Daily Record, 1998
Roswell Record, 1892
Saint Louis Globe-Democrat, 1877
San Antonio Daily Express, 1877, 1908
Shafter Lake Herald, 1907
Sheboygan Press, 1939
Slatonite (Slaton, Texas), 1922
Tascosa Pioneer, 1887
Taylor County News (Abilene), 1885.
Wichita Daily Beacon, 1897

Books

Abbe, Donald R., and Paul H. Carlson. *Historic Lubbock County: An Illustrated History.* San Antonio: Historical Publishing Network, 2008.

Abbe, Donald, Paul H. Carlson, and David J. Murrah. *Lubbock and the South Plains: An Illustrated History.* 2nd ed. Tarzana, CA: Preferred Marketing, 1995.

Alexander, Charles C. *The Ku Klux Klan in the Southwest.* Lexington: University of Kentucky Press, 1965.

Alvarez, Walter. *T. rex and the Crater of Doom.* Princeton, NJ: Princeton University Press, 1997.

Armitage, Shelley. *Walking the Llano: A Texas Memoir of Place.* Norman: University of Oklahoma Press, 2016.

Aryain, Ed. *From Syria to Seminole: Memoir of a High Plains Merchant.* Edited by J'Nell Pate. Foreword by John R. Wunder. Afterword by Edward Aryain and Jameil Aryain. Lubbock: Texas Tech University Press, 2006.

Austin, Orval H. *Jal, New Mexico: Tough as an Old Boot.* Waco: Davis Brothers, 1976.

Bailey, James A. *American Plains Bison: Rewilding an Icon.* Helena, MT: Sweetgrass Books, 2013.

Baker, T. Lindsay. *Gangster Tour of Texas.* College Station: Texas A&M University Press, 2011.

———. *Ghost Towns of Texas.* Norman: University of Oklahoma Press, 1986.

Baker, T. Lindsay, and Billy R. Harrison. *Adobe Walls: The History and Archeology of the 1874 Trading Post.* Foreword by B. Byron Price. College Station: Texas A&M University Press, 1986.

Barnett, Cynthia. *Rain: A Natural and Cultural History.* New York: Crown Publishers, 2015.

Bean, Christopher B., ed. *Texas and Texans in World War II, 1941–1945.* Foreword by Randolph "Mike" Campbell. College Station: Texas A&M University Press, 2022.

Becker, John T. "Jack," Innocent Awasom, and Cynthia Henry. *Cotton on the South Plains.* Charleston, SC: Arcadia Publishing, 2012.

Becker, John T. "Jack," and David J. Murrah, eds. *Caprock Chronicles: More Tales of the Llano Estacado.* Introduction by Paul Carlson. Charleston, SC: History Press, 2021.

Bedichek, Roy. *Adventures with a Texas Naturalist.* Foreword by H. Mewhinney. Text Illustrations by Ward Lockwood. Austin: University of Texas Press, 1961.

Benton, Michael J. *When Life Nearly Died: The Greatest Mass Extinction of All Time.* London: Thames and Hudson, 2003.

Betty, Gerald. *Comanche Society before the Reservation.* College Station: Texas A&M University Press, 2002.

Birchell, Donna Blake, and John LeMay. *Hidden History of Southeast New Mexico.* Charleston, SC: History Press, 2017.

Black, Mary S. *Secrets in the Dirt: Uncovering the Ancient People of Gault.* College Station: Texas A&M University Press, 2019.

Blackshear, James Bailey. *Fort Bascom: Soldiers, Comancheros, and Indians in the Canadian River Valley.* Norman: University of Oklahoma Press, 2017.

Blodgett, Jan. *Land of Bright Promise: Advertising the Texas Panhandle and South Plains, 1870–1917.* Austin: University of Texas Press, 1988.

Bogener, Stephen, and William Tydeman, eds. *Llano Estacado: An Island in the Sky.* Introduction by Barry Lopez. Lubbock: Texas Tech University Press, 2011.

Bolton, Herbert Eugene. *Coronado: Knight of Pueblos and Plains.* Albuquerque: University of New Mexico Press, 1964.

———. *Texas in the Middle Eighteenth Century: Studies in Spanish Colonial History and Administration.* Austin: University of Texas Press, 1970.

Bonnifield, Paul. *The Dust Bowl: Men, Dirt, and Depression.* Albuquerque: University of New Mexico Press, 1979.

Branch, E. Douglas. *The Hunting of the Buffalo.* Introduction by J. Frank Dobie. Lincoln: University of Nebraska Press, 1962.

Braucher, Scott, and Betty Ramsey, eds. *Buck Ramsey's Grass: With Essays on His Life and Work.* Foreword by B. Byron Price. Lubbock: Texas Tech University Press, 2005.

Britten, Thomas A. *The Lipan Apaches: People of Wind and Lightning.* Albuquerque: University of New Mexico Press, 2009.

Brown, Norman Wayne, and Sarah Bellian. *Early Settlers of the Panhandle Plains.* Foreword by Chuck Parsons. Charleston, SC: Arcadia Publishing, 2013.

Brune, Gunner. *Springs of Texas.* Introduction by Helen C. Besse. 2nd ed. 2 vols. College Station: Texas A&M University Press, 2002.

Brusatte, Steve. *The Rise and Reign of Mammals: A New History, from the Shadow of the Dinosaurs to Us.* New York: Mariner Books, 2022.

Buchanan, A. Russell. *The United States and World War II.* 2 vols. New York: Harper and Row, 1964.

Burley, Jeffrey, ed. *Encyclopedia of Forest Science.* Cambridge, MA: Academic Press, 2004.

Burns, Ruth White, and Rose Powers White. *A Man Was a Real Man in Them Days.* Clovis, NM: CreateSpace, 2012.

Burrough, Bryan. *Public Enemies: America's Greatest Crime Wave and the Birth of the FBI, 1922–34*. New York: Penguin Group, 2004.

Burroughs, Jean M., ed. *Roosevelt County: History and Heritage*. Portales, NM: Bishop Printing, 1975.

Carlson, Paul H. *Amarillo: The Story of a Country Town*. Lubbock: Texas Tech University Press, 2006.

———. *The Buffalo Soldier Tragedy of 1877*. College Station: Texas A&M University Press, 2003.

———. *The Centennial History of Lubbock: Hub City of the Plains*. Virginia Beach, VA: Donning Company Publishers, 2008.

———, ed. *The Cowboy Way: An Exploration of History and Culture*. Lubbock: Texas Tech University Press, 2000.

———. *Deep Time and the Texas High Plains: History and Geology*. Lubbock: Texas Tech University Press, 2005.

———. *Empire Builder in the Texas Panhandle: William Henry Bush*. College Station: Texas A&M University Press, 1996.

———. *Texas Woollybacks: The Range Sheep and Goat Industry*. College Station: Texas A&M University Press, 1982.

Carlson, Paul H., and John T. Becker. *Georgia O'Keeffe in Texas: A Guide*. Buffalo Gap, TX: State House Press, 2012.

Carlson, Paul H., and Bruce A. Glasrud, eds. *West Texas: A History of the Giant Side of the State*. Norman: University of Oklahoma Press, 2014.

Carlson, Paul H., and David J. Murrah, eds. *Hidden History of the Llano Estacado*. Charleston, SC: History Press, 2017.

———. *Historic Tales of the Llano Estacado*. Charleston, SC: History Press, 2020.

Carroll, H. Bailey, ed. *Guadal P'a: The Journal of Lieutenant J. W. Abert, from Bent's Fort to St. Louis in 1845*. Canyon, TX: Panhandle-Plains Historical Society, 1941.

———. *The Texan Santa Fe Trail*. Canyon, TX: Panhandle-Plains Historical Society, 1951.

Carter, Robert G. *On the Border with Mackenzie; or, Winning the West from the Comanches*. New York: Antiquarian Press, 1961.

Cashion, Ty. *A Texas Frontier: The Clear Fork Country and Fort Griffin, 1849–1887*. Norman: University of Oklahoma Press, 1996.

Chalmers, David M. *Hooded Americanism: The History of the Ku Klux Klan*. 2nd ed. New York: New Viewpoints, 1981.

Chambers, Clint E., and Paul H. Carlson. *Comanche Jack Stilwell: Army Scout and Plainsman*. Norman: University of Oklahoma Press, 2019.

Chaplo, Paul V. *Amarillo Flights: Aerial Views of Llano Estacado Country*. Introduction by Walt Davis. College Station: Texas A&M University Press, 2020.

Chapman, Brian R., and Eric G. Bolen. *The Natural History of Texas*. Foreword by Andrew Sansom. College Station: Texas A&M University Press, 2018.

Childers, Almarine, and Elizabeth Martin. *Slaton's Story: The History of Slaton, Texas, 1900– 1979*. Slaton, TX: Slaton Historical Society, 1979.

Clark, James A. *Three Stars for the Colonel: The Biography of Ernest O. Thompson, Father of Petroleum Conservation*. New York: Random House, 1954.

Clay, John. *My Life on the Range*. Chicago: privately printed, 1924.

Clayton, Lawrence, and Joe W. Specht, eds. *The Roots of Texas Music*. College Station: Texas A&M University Press, 2003.

Collinson, Frank. *Life in the Saddle*. Edited by Mary Whatley Clark. Norman: University of Oklahoma Press, 1963.

Connor, Seymour V., ed. *Builders of the Southwest*. Lubbock: Texas Technological College, 1959.

Cook, John R. *The Border and the Buffalo*. Foreword by David Dary. Austin: State House Press, 1989.

Copeland, Fayette. *Kendall of the Picayune*. Foreword by Robert W. Johannsen. Norman: University of Oklahoma Press, 1997.

Coppedge, Clay. *Texas Singularities: Prairie Dog Lawyers, Peg Leg State Robberies and Mysterious Malakoff Men*. Illustrations by Sarah Hayes. Charleston, SC: History Press, 2019.

Courtwright, Julie. *Prairie Fire: A Great Plains History*. Lawrence: University Press of Kansas, 2011.

Cox, James. *Historical and Biographical Record of the Cattle Industry and the Cattlemen of Texas and Adjacent Territory*. St. Louis, MO: Woodward and Tiernan Printing, 1895.

Cox, Mike. *Texas Disasters: True Stories of Tragedy and Survival*. Guilford, CT: Glove Pequot Press, 2006.

Crosby, W. Alfred. *America's Forgotten Pandemic: The Influenza Epidemic of 1918*. New York: Cambridge University Press, 1989.

Cruse, J. Brett. *Battles of the Red River War: Archeological Perspectives on the Indian Campaign of 1874*. Foreword by Robert M. Utley. College Station: Texas A&M University Press, 2008.

Cunfer, Geoff. *On the Great Plains: Agriculture and Environment*. Foreword by Dan L. Flores. College Station: Texas A&M University Press, 2005.

Cunfer, Geoff, and Bill Waiser, eds. *Bison and People on the Great Plains: A Deep Environmental History*. Foreword by Sterling Evans. College Station: Texas A&M University Press, 2016.

Curry, W. Hubert. *Sun Rising on the West: The Saga of Henry Clay and Elizabeth Smith*. Crosbyton, TX: Crosby County Pioneer Memorial, 1979.

Czerkas, Sylvia J., and Stephen A. Czerkas. *Dinosaurs: A Global View*. Rev. ed. New York: Barnes and Noble Books, 1995.

Dale, Edward Everett. *Cow Country*. Norman: University of Oklahoma Press, 1965.

Dary, David. *Entrepreneurs of the Old West*. New York: Alfred A. Knopf, 1986.

Davis, John T. *The Flatlanders: Now It's Now Again*. Austin: University of Texas Press, 2014.

Dethloff, Henry C., and Irvin M. May Jr., eds. *Southwestern Agriculture: Pre-Columbian to Modern*. College Station: Texas A&M University Press, 1982.

Diamond, Jared. *Collapse: How Societies Choose to Fail or Succeed*. New York: Penguin Books, 2005.

Dobie, J. Frank. *Cow People*. Austin: University of Texas Press, 1964.

——. *The Longhorns*. New York: Bramhall House, 1942.

Eaves, Charles Dudley, and C. A. Hutchinson. *Post City, Texas: C. W. Post's Colonizing Activities in West Texas*. Introduction by David J. Murrah. Post, TX: Garza County Historical Museum, 1998.

Elam, Earl H. *Kitikiti'h: The Wichita Indians and Associated Tribes, 1757–1859*. Hillsboro, TX: Hill College Press, 2008.

Erickson, John R. *Bad Smoke, Good Smoke: A Texas Rancher's View of Wildfire*. Lubbock: Texas Tech University Press, 2021.

Ericson, Georgia Mae Smith, comp. *Aunt Hank's Rock House Kitchen: A Cookbook with a Story*. Crosbyton, TX: Crosby County Pioneer Memorial Museum, 1977.

Estaville, Lawrence E., and Richard A. Earl. *Texas Water Atlas*. Preface by Andrew Sansom. College Station: Texas A&M University Press, 2008.

Fagan, Brian. *Ancient North America: The Archaeology of a Continent*. 3rd ed. London: Thames and Hudson, 2001.

——. *Floods, Famines and Emperors: El Niño and the Fate of Civilizations*. New York: Basic Books, 1999.

——. *The Little Ice Age: How Climate Made History, 1300–1850*. New York: Basic Books, 2000.

Favour, Alpheus H. *Old Bill Williams: Mountain Man*. Introduction by William Brandon. Norman: University of Oklahoma Press, 1962.

Fedewa, Marilyn H. *Dark Eyes, Lady Blue: Maria of Agreda*. Lubbock: Texas Tech University Press, 2020.

——. *Maria of Agreda: Mystical Lady in Blue*. Albuquerque: University of New Mexico Press, 2009.

Fischer, David Hackett. *Albion's Seed: Four British Folkways in America*. New York: Oxford University Press, 1989.

Fleming, Elvis E., and David J. Murrah. *Texas' Last Frontier: A New History of Cochran County*. Morton, TX: Cochran County Historical Commission, 2001.

Fleming, Elvis E., and Ernestine Chesser Williams. *Treasures of History III: Southeast New Mexico People, Places, and Events*. Roswell: Historical Society of Southeast New Mexico, 1995.

Flint, Richard. *No Settlement, No Conquest: A History of the Coronado Entrada*. Albuquerque: University of New Mexico Press, 2008.

Flint, Richard, and Shirley Cushing Flint, eds. *The Coronado Expedition to Tierra Nueva: The 1540–1542 Route across the Southwest*. Boulder: University Press of Colorado, 1997.

Flores, Dan. *American Serengeti: The Last Big Animals of the Great Plains*. Lawrence: University Press of Kansas, 2016.

———. *Caprock Canyonlands: Journeys into the Heart of the Southern Plains*. Austin: University of Texas Press, 1990.

———. *Horizontal Yellow: Nature and History in the Near Southwest*. Albuquerque: University of New Mexico Press, 1999.

Forbis, William H. *The Cowboys*. New York: Time-Life Books, 1973.

Foster, William C. *Historic Native Peoples of Texas*. Austin: University of Texas Press, 2008.

Franks, Ray, and Jay Ketelle. *Amarillo, Texas: A Picture Post Card History*. Amarillo: Ray Franks Publishing Ranch, 1986.

———. *Amarillo, Texas II: A Picture Postcard History*. Amarillo: Ray Franks Publishing Ranch, 1987.

Frantz, Joe B. *Texas: A History*. New York: W. W. Norton, 1976.

Gard, Wayne. *The Great Buffalo Hunt*. With drawings by Nick Eggenhoffer. Lincoln: University of Nebraska Press, 1968.

Gracy, David B, II. *Littlefield Lands: Colonization on the Texas Plains, 1912–1920*. Austin: University of Texas, 1968.

———. *A Man Absolutely Sure of Himself: Texan George Washington Littlefield*. Foreword by J. Phelps White III. Norman: University of Oklahoma Press, 2019.

Graves, Lawrence L., ed. *A History of Lubbock, Part I: Story of a Country Town*. Lubbock: West Texas Museum Association, 1959.

———, ed. *Lubbock: From Town to City*. Lubbock: West Texas Museum Association, 1986.

Graves, Russell A. *The Prairie Dog: Sentinel of the Plains*. Lubbock: Texas Tech University Press, 2001.

Green, Donald E. *Land of Underground Rain: Irrigation in the Texas High Plains, 1910–1970*. Austin: University of Texas Press, 1973.

Green, John. *The Anthropocene Reviewed: Essays on a Human-Centered Planet*. New York: Dutton, 2021.

Gregg, Josiah. *Commerce of the Prairies*. Edited by Max Moorland. Norman: University of Oklahoma Press, 1954.

Guthrie, R. Dale. *Frozen Fauna of the Mammoth Steppe*. Chicago: University of Chicago Press, 1990.

Guy, Duane, ed. *The Story of Palo Duro Canyon*. New Introduction by Frederick W. Rathjen. Lubbock: Texas Tech University Press, 2001.

Hagan, William T. *Charles Goodnight: Father of the Texas Panhandle*. Norman: University of Oklahoma Press, 2007.

Haley, J. Evetts, ed. *Albert Pike's Journeys in the Prairie, 1831–1832*. Canyon, TX: Panhandle-Plains Historical Society, 1969.

———. *The XIT Ranch of Texas and the Early Days of the Llano Estacado*. Norman: University of Oklahoma Press, 1953.

Haley, James L. *The Buffalo War: The History of the Red River Uprising of 1874*. Abilene, TX: State House Press, 2007.

Hamalainen, Pekka. *The Comanche Empire.* New Haven, CT: Yale University Press, 2008.

Hamlin, James D. *The Flamboyant Judge: The Story of Amarillo and the Development of the Great Ranches of the Texas Panhandle.* Edited by J. Evetts Haley and William Curry Holden. Canyon, TX: Palo Duro Press, 1972.

Hammond, Clara T., comp. *Amarillo.* Amarillo, TX: George Autry, 1971.

Hamner, Laura V. *Short Grass and Longhorns.* Norman: University of Oklahoma Press, 1965.

Harari, Yuval Noah. *Sapiens: A Brief History of Humankind.* New York: Harper-Collins Publishers, 2015.

Hardesty, John Pettigrew. *Pioneer Preachers of the Plains: Memories and Meditations of Seventy-One Years in Texas.* Plainview, TX: Hardesty, 1951.

Hawkes, Jacquetta. *The Atlas of Early Man.* Assisted by David Trump. New York: St. Martin's Press, 1976.

Hayhoe, Katherine. *Saving Us: A Climate Scientist's Case for Hope and Healing in a Divided World.* New York: One Signal Publisher, 2021.

Hickerson, Nancy Parrott. *The Jumanos: Hunters and Traders of the South Plains.* Austin: University of Texas Press, 1994.

Hill, Frank P., and Pat Hill Jacobs. *Grassroots Upside Down: A History of Lynn County.* Foreword by David J. Murrah. Austin: Nortex Press, 1986.

Hill, Joseph A. *The Panhandle-Plains Historical Society and Its Museum.* Canyon: West Texas State College, 1955.

Hofsommer, Don L. *The Quanah Route: A History of the Quanah, Acme & Pacific Railway.* College Station: Texas A&M University Press, 1991.

Holden, William Curry. *Alkali Trails or Social and Economic Movements of the Texas Frontier 1846–1900.* Foreword by Lawrence L. Graves. Lubbock: Texas Tech University Press, 1998.

———. *Rollie Burns: or An Account of the Ranching Industry on the South Plains.* Foreword by David J. Murrah. College Station: Texas A&M University Press, 2000.

Holliday, Vance T. *Paleoindian Geoarchaeology of the Southern High Plains.* Foreword by Thomas R. Hester. Austin: University of Texas Press, 1997.

Hopping, R. C. *The Ellwoods: Barbed Wire and Ranches.* Lubbock: West Texas Museum Association, Texas Tech University, 1962.

Hoxie, Frederick E., ed. *Encyclopedia of North American Indians.* Boston: Houghton Mifflin, 1996.

Hunt, George M. *Early Days upon the Plains.* Lubbock: Lubbock Avalanche, 1919.

Hurt, R. Douglas. *The Dust Bowl: An Agricultural and Social History.* Chicago: Nelson-Hall, 1981.

Hyde, George E. *Indians of the High Plains: From the Prehistoric Period to the Coming of Europeans.* Norman: University of Oklahoma Press, 1968.

Hynd, Alan. *We Are the Public Enemies: Our Era of Evil and the People Who Made It.* New York: Fawcett, 1949.

Isenberg, Andrew C. *The Destruction of the Bison*. New York: Cambridge University Press, 2000.

Jenkins, John Cooper, et al. *Estacado: Cradle of Culture and Civilization on the Staked Plains of Texas*. Crosbyton, TX: Crosby County Pioneer Memorial Museum, 1986.

John, Elizabeth A. H. *Storms Brewed in Other Men's Worlds: The Confrontation of Indians, Spanish, and French in the Southwest, 1540–1795*. 2nd ed. Norman: University of Oklahoma Press, 1996.

Johnson, Eileen, ed. *Lubbock Lake: Late Quaternary Studies on the Southern High Plains*. College Station: Texas A&M University Press, 1987.

Jones, Douglas C. *The Treaty of Medicine Lodge: The Story of the Great Council as Told by Eyewitnesses*. Norman: University of Oklahoma Press, 1966.

Jordan, Terry G. *North American Cattle-Ranching Frontiers: Origins, Diffusion, and Differentiation*. Albuquerque: University of New Mexico Press, 1993.

Josephy, Alvin M., Jr. *500 Nations: An Illustrated History of North American Indians*. New York: Alfred A. Knopf, 1994.

——. *The Indian Heritage of America*. New York: Alfred A. Knopf, 1970.

Kavanagh, Thomas W. *Comanche Political History: An Ethnohistorical Perspective 1706–1875*. Lincoln: University of Nebraska Press, 1996.

Kehoe, Alice B. *North American Indians: A Comprehensive Account*. 2nd ed. Englewood Cliffs, NJ: Prentice Hall, 1992.

Kelton, Steve. *Renderbrook: A Century under the Spade Brand*. Fort Worth: Texas Christian University Press, 1989.

Kendall, George Wilkins. *Narrative of the Texan-Santa Fe Expedition*. 2 vols. London: Wiley and Putnam, 1884; facsimile, Austin: Steck, 1935.

Kenner, Charles L. *The Comanchero Frontier: A History of New Mexican–Plains Indian Relations*. Norman: University of Oklahoma Press, 1994.

Kessell, John L. *Kiva, Cross, and Crown: The Pecos Indians and New Mexico 1540–1840*. Albuquerque: University of New Mexico Press, 1987.

Key, Della Tyler. *In the Cattle Country: History of Potter County*. Wichita Falls, TX: Nortex, 1966.

Kimmel, Jim. *Exploring the Brazos River: From Beginning to End*. Foreword by Andrew Sansom. College Station: Texas A&M University Press, 2011.

King, Joseph Henry Thomas. *A Brief Account of the Sufferings of a Detachment of United States Cavalry from Deprivation of Water during a Period of Eighty-Six Hours While Scouting the Staked Plains of Texas*. Fort Davis, TX: Charles Krull, post printer, 1877.

Knoll, Andrew H. *A Brief History of Earth: Four Billion Years in Eight Chapters*. New York: Custom House, 2021.

Kuhlman, Marty. *Always WT: West Texas A&M University Centennial History*. Stillwater, OK: New Forums Press, 2010.

Kurten, Bjorn, and Elaine Anderson. *Pleistocene Mammals of North America*. New York: Columbia University Press, 1980.

Lavender, David. *Bent's Fort*. Lincoln: University of Nebraska Press, 1972.

Leckie, William H., with Shirley A. Leckie. *The Buffalo Soldiers: A Narrative of the Black Cavalry in the West*. Rev. ed. Norman: University of Oklahoma Press, 2003.

Lehman, Herman. *Nine Years with the Indians, 1870–1879: The Story of the Captivity and Life of a Texan among the Indians*. Edited by J. Marvin Hunter. Austin: Von Boeckman-Jones, 1927.

Lowie, Robert H. *Indians of the Plains*. Preface by Raymond J. DeMallie. Lincoln: University
of Nebraska Press, 1982.

Lubbock Heritage Society, Pamela Brink, Cindy Martin, and Daniel Sánchez. *Lubbock*. Charleston, SC: Arcadia Publishing, 2013.

Matthiesen, Leroy T. *Wise and Otherwise: The Life and Times of a Cottonpicking Texas Bishop*. Amarillo: n.p., n.d.

McAlavy, Don, and Harold Kilmer, eds. *Curry County, New Mexico*. Dallas: Taylor Publishing, 1978.

———. *High Plains History of East-Central New Mexico*. Clovis, NM: High Plains Historical Press, 1980.

McCallum, Henry D., and Frances T. McCallum. *The Wire That Fenced the West*. Norman: University of Oklahoma Press, 1965.

McCartor, Robert L., and George S. Tyner. *Eye of the Storm*. Lubbock: Texas Tech University Press, 1986.

McIntire, Jim. *Early Days in Texas: A Trip to Hell and Heaven*. Kansas City, MO: McIntire Publishing, 1902.

Meinig, D. W. *Imperial Texas: An Interpretive Essay in Cultural Geography*. Introduction by Lorrin Kennamer. Austin: University of Texas Press, 1969.

Mojtabai, A. G. *Blessed Assurance: At Home with the Bomb in Amarillo, Texas*. Boston: Houghton Mifflin, 1986.

Moncus, Mary Lynn. *Quay County, New Mexico, 1903–2003: A Pictorial History*. Virginia Beach, VA: Donning Company Publishers, 2003.

Mooar, J. Wright. *Buffalo Days: Stories from J. Wright Mooar as Told to James Winford Hunt*. Edited by Robert F. Pace. Abilene, TX: State House Press, 2005.

Moore, Jacqueline M. *Cow Boys and Cattle Men: Class and Masculinities on the Texas Frontier, 1865–1900*. New York: New York University Press, 2010.

Morris, John Miller. *El Llano Estacado: Exploration and Imagination on the High Plains of Texas and New Mexico, 1536–1860*. Austin: Texas State Historical Association, 1997.

Mowry, George E., ed. *The Twenties: Ford, Flappers, and Fanatics*. Englewood, NJ: Prentice-Hall, 1963.

Mulhouse, John M. *Abandoned New Mexico: Ghost Towns, Endangered Architecture, and Hidden History*. Virginia Beach, VA: Arcadia Publishing, 2020.

Murrah, David J. *"And Are We Yet Alive?": A History of Northwest Texas Conference of the United Methodist Church*. Foreword by Bishop D. Max Whitfield. Buffalo Gap, TX: State House Press, 2009.

———. *C. C. Slaughter: Rancher, Banker, Baptist.* Foreword by Cynthia Slaughter Pattison. 2nd ed. Norman: University of Oklahoma Press, 2012.

———. *Oil, Taxes, and Cats: A History of the DeVitt Family and the Mallet Ranch.* Lubbock: Texas Tech University Press, 1994.

———. *The Rise and Fall of the Lazy S Ranch.* Foreword by Paul H. Carlson and M. Scott Sosebee. College Station: Texas A&M University Press, 2021.

Nabokov, Peter, ed. *Native American Testimony: A Chronicle of Indian-White Relations from Prophecy to the Present, 1492–1992.* Foreword by Vine Deloria Jr. New York: Viking Penguin, 1991.

Neugebauer, Janet M., ed. *Plains Farmer: The Diary of William G. DeLoach, 1914–1964.* Illustrated by Charles Shaw. College Station: Texas A&M University Press, 1991.

Nolan, Frederick. *Tascosa: Its Life and Gaudy Times.* Lubbock: Texas Tech University Press, 2007.

Nordyke, Lewis. *Cattle Empire: The Fabulous Story of the 3,000,000 Acre XIT.* New York: William Morrow, 1949.

Noyes, Stanley. *Los Comanches: The Horse People, 1751–1845.* Albuquerque: University of New Mexico Press, 1993.

Nye, Colonel W. S. *Carbine and Lance: The Story of Old Fort Sill.* Rev. and enl. ed. Norman: University of Oklahoma Press, 1974.

O'Brien, Dan. *Great Plains Bison.* Lincoln: University of Nebraska Press, 2017.

Olien, Diana Davids, and Roger M. Olien. *Oil in Texas: The Gusher Age, 1895–1945.* Austin: University of Texas Press, 2002.

Owsley, Douglas W., Margaret A. Jodry, Thomas W. Stafford Jr., C. Vance Haynes Jr., and Dennis J. Stanford. *Arch Lake Woman: Physical Anthropology and Geoarchaeology.* College Station: Texas A&M University Press, 2020.

Pace, Robert F., and Donald S. Frazier. *Frontier Texas: History of a Borderland to 1880.* Abilene, TX: State House Press, 2004.

Parker, William B. *Notes Taken during the Expedition Commanded by Capt. R. B. Marcy, U. S. A., through Unexplored Texas, 1874.* Edited by George B. Ward. Austin: Texas State Historical Association, 1990.

Perrin, Tim, Warren McNeill, et al., eds. *Pioneering Spirit, Extraordinary Faith: Stories and Essays about LCU's First 60 Years.* Lubbock: Lubbock Christian University, 2017.

Perttula, Timothy K., ed. *The Prehistory of Texas.* College Station: Texas A&M University Press, 2004.

Pike, Albert. *Prose Sketches and Poems Written in the Western Country.* Edited by David J. Weber. College Station: Texas A&M University Press, 1987.

Pool, William C. *A Historical Atlas of Texas.* Maps by Edward Triggs and Lance Wren. Austin: Encino Press, 1975.

Price, B. Bryon, and Frederick W. Rathjen. *The Golden Spread: An Illustrated History of Amarillo and the Texas Panhandle.* Northridge, CA: Windsor Publications, 1986.

Prucha, Francis Paul, ed. *Documents of United States Indian Policy.* 2nd ed., exp. Lincoln: University of Nebraska Press, 1990.

Rath, Ida Ellen. *The Rath Trail.* Wichita, KS: McCormick-Armstrong, 1961.

Rathjen, Frederick W. *The Texas Panhandle Frontier.* Introduction by Elmer Kelton. Rev. ed. Lubbock: Texas Tech University Press, 1998.

Reeve, Agnesa, comp. *My Dear Mollie: Love Letters of a Texas Sheep Rancher.* Dallas: Hendrick-Long Publishing, 1990.

Richardson, Rupert Norval. *Comanche Barrier to South Plains Settlement.* Edited by Kenneth R. Jacobs. New Introduction by A. C. Greene. Austin: Eakin Press, 1996.

Robinson, Charles M., III. *The Indian Trial: The Complete Story of the Warren Wagon Train Massacre and the Fall of the Kiowa Nation.* Spokane, WA: Arthur H. Clark, 1997.

Rollins, Philip Ashton. *The Cowboy: An Unconventional History of Civilization on the Old-Time Cattle Range.* Foreword by Richard W. Slatta. Rev. and enl. ed. Norman: University of Oklahoma Press, 1997.

Sandoz, Mari. *The Buffalo Hunters: The Story of the Hide Men.* Lincoln: University of Nebraska Press, 1978.

Scheer, Mary L., ed. *Eavesdropping on Texas History.* Denton: University of North Texas Press, 2017.

Schlesier, Karl H., ed. *Plains Indians, A.D. 500–1500: The Archaeological Past of Historic Groups.* Norman: University of Oklahoma Press, 1994.

Schofield, Donald F. *Indians, Cattle, Ships, and Oil: The Story of W. M. D. Lee.* Austin: University of Texas Press, 1985.

Simmons, Marc. *The Last Conquistador: Juan De Oñate and the Settling of the Far Southwest.* Norman: University of Oklahoma Press, 1991.

———. *The Old Trail to Santa Fe: Collected Essays.* Albuquerque: University of New Mexico Press, 1996.

Smith, Thomas T. *The Old Army in Texas: A Research Guide to the US Army in Nineteenth-Century Texas.* Austin: Texas State Historical Association, 2000.

Snow, Dean R. *The Archaeology of North America.* Norman: University of Oklahoma Press, 1991.

Sosebee, M. Scott. *Henry C. "Hank" Smith and the Cross B Ranch: The First Stock Operation of the South Plains.* College Station: Texas A&M University Press, 2021.

Spellman, Paul N. *Forgotten Texan: Huge McLeod and the Texan-Santa Fe Expedition.* Foreword by Stanley E. Siegel. College Station: Texas A&M University Press, 1999.

Spencer, Robert F., Jesse D. Jennings, Elden Johnson, Arden R. King, Theodore Stern, Kenneth M. Stewart, and William J. Wallace. *The Native Americans: Ethnology and Backgrounds of the North American Indians.* 2nd ed. New York: Harper and Row, 1977.

Spikes, Nellie Witt. *As a Farm Woman Thinks: Life and Land on the Texas High Plains, 1890–1960*. Edited by Geoff Cunfer. Foreword by Sandra Scofield. Lubbock: Texas Tech University Press, 2010.

Stephens, A. Ray, and William M. Holmes. *Historical Atlas of Texas*. Phyllis M. McCaffree, Consultant. Norman: University of Oklahoma Press, 1989.

Stokesbury, James L. *A Short History of World War II*. New York: William Morrow, 1980.

Sturtevant, William C., ed. *Handbook of North American Indians*. 20 vols. Washington, DC: Smithsonian Institution, 2001.

Taylor, Colin F., and William C. Sturtevant, eds. *The Native Americans: The Indigenous People of North America*. London: Salamander Books, 1991.

Texas Almanac, 2006–2007: Sesquicentennial Edition, 1857–2007. Dallas: Dallas Morning News, 2006.

Texas Almanac, 2020–2021. 70th ed. Austin: Texas State Historical Association, 2020.

The Texas Almanac for 1883. Galveston, TX: Richardson, Belo, 1883.

Tyler, Ron, Douglas E. Barnett, and Roy R. Barkley, eds. *The New Handbook of Texas*. 6 vols. Austin: Texas State Historical Association, 1996.

Untiedt, Kenneth L., ed. *First Timers and Old Timers: The Texas Folklore Society Fire Burns On*. Denton: University of North Texas Press, 2012.

Vigil, Ralph H., Frances W. Kaye, and John R. Wunder, eds. *Spain and the Plains: Myths and Realities of Spanish Exploration and Settlement on the Great Plains*. Niwot: University Press of Colorado, 1994.

Villanueva, James. *Remembering Slaton, Texas: Centennial Stories, 1911–2011*. Charleston, SC: History Press, 2011.

Wallace, Ernest. *Ranald S. Mackenzie on the Texas Frontier*. Foreword by David J. Murrah. College Station: Texas A&M University Press, 1993.

———, ed. *Ranald S. Mackenzie's Official Correspondence Relating to Texas, 1871–1873*. Lubbock: West Texas Museum Association, 1967.

———, ed. *Ranald S. Mackenzie's Official Correspondence Relating to Texas, 1873–1879*. Lubbock: West Texas Museum Association, 1968.

Wallace, Ernest, and E. Adamson Hoebel. *The Comanches: Lords of the South Plains*. Norman: University of Oklahoma Press, 1952.

Weaver, Bobby D. *Oilfield Trash: Life and Labor in the Oil Patch*. College Station: Texas A&M University Press, 2010.

———, ed. *Panhandle Petroleum*. Canyon, TX: Panhandle-Plains Historical Society, 1982.

Webb, Walter Prescott. *The Great Plains*. New York: Grosset and Dunlap, 1931.

Wedel, Waldo R. *Prehistoric Man on the Great Plains*. Norman: University of Oklahoma Press, 1978.

Welty, Joel Carl. *The Life of Birds*. 3rd ed. Philadelphia: Saunders College Publishing, 1982.

Weniger, Del. *The Explorers' Texas: The Lands and Waters*. Austin: Eakin Publications, 1984.

Wentworth, Edward N. *America's Sheep Trails: History, Personalities*. Ames: Iowa State College Press, 1948.

White, Benton R. *The Forgotten Cattle King*. College Station: Texas A&M University Press, 1986.

Whitlock, V. H. (Ol' Waddy). *Cowboy Life on the Llano Estacado*. Norman: University of Oklahoma Press, 1970.

Whitten, Cathy. *Slaton*. Charleston, SC: History Press, 2015.

Williams, Clayton W. *Texas' Last Frontier: Fort Stockton and the Trans-Pecos, 1861–1895*. Edited by Ernest Wallace. College Station: Texas A&M University Press, 1982.

Willson, Carol. *May 26, 1978: The Story of the Randall County Flood*. Canyon, TX: Staked Plains Press, 1979.

Winship, George Parker. *The Coronado Expedition, 1540–1542*. Chicago: Rio Grande Press, 1964.

Worster, Donald. *Dust Bowl: The Southern Plains in the 1930s*. New York: Oxford University Press, 1979.

Periodicals

Adams, David B. "Embattled Borderland: Northern Nuevo Leon and the Indios Barbaros, 1686–1870." *Southwestern Historical Quarterly* 95 (October 1991): 205–20.

Anderson, H. Allen. "The West Texas Museum and Its Hidden Treasure: The Story of the Peter Hurd Mural." *West Texas Historical Review* 94 (2018): 52–67.

Antevs, Ernst. "Climatic Changes and Pre-White Man." In "The Great Basin with Emphasis on Glacial and Postglacial Times." *University of Utah Bulletin* 38, Biological Series 10 (1948): 168–91.

Anyonge, William, and Chris Roman. "New Body Mass Estimates for *Canis dirus*, the Extinct Pleistocene Dire Wolf." *Journal of Vertebrate Paleontology* 26, no. 1 (2006): 209–12.

Archambeau, Ernest R. "The First Federal Census in the Panhandle, 1880." *Panhandle-Plains Historical Review* 23 (1950): 2–102.

———. "Lieutenant A. W. Whipple's Railroad Reconnaissance across the Panhandle of Texas in 1853." *Panhandle-Plains Historical Review* 44 (1971): 1–128.

Arnot, John. "My Recollections of Tascosa before and after the Coming of the Law." *Panhandle-Plains Historical Review* 6 (1933): 61–64.

Axelrod, Daniel I. "Rise of the Grassland Biome, Central North America." *Botanical Review* 51 (April–June 1985): 163–201.

Baker, T. Lindsay. "Windmills of the Panhandle Plains." *Panhandle-Plains Historical Review* 53 (1980): 77–110.

Blodgett, Jan. "Land Promotion and Advertisement in West Texas." *West Texas Historical Association Year Book* 60 (1984): 35–46.

Bollaert, William. "Observations of the Indian Tribes in Texas." *Journal of the Ethnological Society of London* 2 (1850): 262–83.

Bowman, Tim. "After Suffrage: Hattie Anderson, Angie Debo, and Gender Politics in West Texas History." *West Texas Historical Review* 96 (2020): 59–81.

Carlson, Paul H. "Black Sunday—the South Plains Dust Blizzard of April 14, 1935." *West Texas Historical Association Year Book* 67 (1991): 5–17.

———, ed. "Itinerary of a Scout across the Llano Estacado in 1875." *West Texas Historical Review* 91 (2015): 8–20.

———. "The Nicolett Hotel and the Founding of Lubbock." *West Texas Historical Review* 90 (2014): 8–19.

———. "Sheepherders and Cowboys: A Comparison of Life-Styles in West Texas." *West Texas Historical Association Year Book* 58 (1982): 3–18.

Carroll, H. Bailey, ed. "The Journal of Lieutenant J. W. Abert from Bent's Fort to St. Louis in 1845." *Panhandle-Plains Historical Review* 14 (1941): 9–113.

———. "Nolan's 'Lost Nigger' Expedition of 1877." *Southwestern Historical Quarterly* 44 (July 1940): 55–75.

Chambers, Clint E. "Fort Sill's Emissaries to the Quahada Comanches on the Staked Plains." *West Texas Historical Association Year Book* 72 (1996): 58–68.

Collins, Marilyn. "'Coin' Harvey's Ozark Trails Association: Early Road Markers Preserved in Texas." *West Texas Historical Association Year Book* 85 (2009): 168–74.

Connellee, C. U. "Some Experiences of a Pioneer Surveyor." *West Texas Historical Association Year Book* 6 (1930): 80–94.

Connor, Seymour V. "Early Ranching Operations in the Panhandle: A Report on the Agricultural Schedules of the 1880 Census." *Panhandle-Plains Historical Review* 27 (1954): 47–69.

———. "The Mendoza-Lopez Expedition and the Location of San Clemente." *West Texas Historical Association Year Book* 45 (1969): 3–29.

Courtney, David. "The Texanist." *Texas Monthly*, January 2022, 142–43.

Crimmins, Col. M. L. "Captain Nolan's Lost Troop on the Staked Plain." *West Texas Historical Association Year Book* 10 (1934): 16–31.

———, ed. "Shafter's Explorations in Western Texas, 1875." *West Texas Historical Association Year Book* 9 (October 1933): 82–96.

Crudington, John W. "Old Time Amarillo." *Panhandle-Plains Historical Review* 30 (1957): 79–113.

Fleming, Elvis E. "Caprock Once Thriving." *Vision Magazine*, December 4, 1998, 4–5.

Flores, Dan. "Bison Ecology and Bison Diplomacy: The Southern Plains from 1800 to 1850." *Journal of American History* 78 (September 1991): 465–85.

Gracy, David B., II. "Selling the Future: A Biography of William Pulver Soash." *Panhandle- Plains Historical Review* 49 (1977): 1–75.

Griggs, William C. "The Battle of Yellowhouse Canyon." *West Texas Historical Association Year Book* 51 (1975): 37–50.

Haggard, Tiffany. "Rural Revolution: South Plains Cotton Farmers and Federal Farm Legislation, 1929–1936." *West Texas Historical Association Year Book* 76 (2000): 126–38.

Haines, Jared. "The Filthy '50s: The 1950–1957 Drought and Its Impact on Plainview, Texas." *West Texas Historical Review* 93 (2017): 70–78.

Hamilton, T. R. "Trends in the Sheep Industry in Texas." *Sheep and Goat Raiser Magazine* 25 (June 1945): 6–11, 46–47.

Hawkins, Arthur Stuart. "Bird Life in the Texas Panhandle." *Panhandle-Plains Historical Review* 18 (1945): 110–50.

Holden, W. C. "Coronado's Route across the Staked Plains." *West Texas Historical Association Year Book* 20 (1944): 3–20.

———. "Texas Tech Archaeological Expedition, Summer, 1930." *Texas Archaeological and Paleontological Society Bulletin* 3 (1931): 43–52.

Holliday, Vance T. "Middle Holocene Drought on the Southern High Plains." *Quaternary Research* 31 (1989): 74–82.

Hoover, D. Sandy. "W. F. Cummins' Repot on the Possible Origins of the Name, *Llano Estacado*." *West Texas Historical Association Year Book* 80 (2004): 184–89.

Hunt, Alex. "'Host and Hostage': Pantex and the Texas Panhandle." *Southwestern Historical Quarterly* 118, no. 4 (April 2015): 338–63.

Hutto, John R. "Mrs. Elizabeth (Aunt Hank) Smith." *West Texas Historical Association Year Book* 15 (1939): 40–47.

Inglis, G. Douglas. "The Men of Cibola: New Investigations on the Francisco Vazques de Coronado Expedition." *Panhandle-Plains Historical Review* 55 (1982): 1–24.

Johnson, William R. "Rural Rehabilitation in the New Deal: The Ropesville Project." *Southwestern Historical Quarterly* 79, no. 3 (January 1976): 279–95.

Jones, Arthur H. "The Story of William Davies: Texas Shepherd." *West Texas Historical Association Year Book* 58 (1982): 19–28.

Jordan, Terry G. "The German Settlement of Texas after 1865." *Southwestern Historical Quarterly* 73, no. 2 (1969): 193–212.

Kahlbau, Edna. "Ghostly Plazas Once Rang with Songs of Shepherds." *Amarillo News-Globe*, Golden Anniversary ed., August 14, 1938, sec. C, 4.

Kennedy, Kirby. "Harvesting History: The Ropesville Project." *The Plow* 14, no. 1 (May 2015): 1–2.

Kincaid, Naomi H. "Anniversary Celebrations of West Texas Towns." *West Texas Historical Association Year Book* 32 (1956): 135–48.

Leviton, Mark. "Our Fellow Americans: Paul Chaat Smith on the Complex Truth of Native American History." *The Sun*, no. 524 (August 2019): 4–13.

Lewis, Preston. "Bluster's Last Stand." *True West* 39, pt. I (April 1992): 14–18; pt. II (May 1992): 20–25.

Matthews, John F. "The Influence of the Texas Panhandle on Georgia O'Keeffe." *Panhandle-Plains Historical Review* 56 (January 1983): 107–36.

Matthiesen, Leroy T. "Statement on the Production and Stockpiling of the Neutron Bomb." *West Texas Catholic*, August 23, 1981, 2–3.

McClure, C. Boone. "History of the Manufacture of Barbed Wire." *Panhandle-Plains Historical Review* 31 (1958): 1–114.

McCullough, John W. "Pre-flights on Tech Campus: Texas Tech's World War II Pre-flight Pilots (1943–1944)." *West Texas Historical Association Year Book* 83 (2007): 19–34.

Miles, Susan. "Fort Concho in 1877." *West Texas Historical Association Year Book* 35 (1959): 29–49.

Mooar, J. Wright. "Frontier Experiences of J. Wright Mooar." *West Texas Historical Association Year Book* 4 (1929): 89–92.

Mosser, Dolores, and Sami Simpson. "*La Pista de Agua Vida*: The Portales Valley Trail." *West Texas Historical Association Year Book* 89 (2013): 45–58.

Mowrey, Daniel Patrick, and Paul H. Carlson. "The Native Grasslands of the High Plains of West Texas: Past-Present-Future." *West Texas Historical Association Year Book* 63 (1987): 24–41.

Murrah, David J. "Replacing the I-35 Bias with an I-20 Bias: The Landmark Work of Richardson, Holden, and Wallace." *West Texas Historical Review* 90 (2014): 47–56.

———. "'Round as Plates': Playas and the Exploration and Settlement of the Llano Estacado." In *Proceedings of the Playa Basin Symposium, 1994*, edited by Lloyd V. Urban and A. Wayne Wyatt, 15–22. Lubbock: Texas Tech University, 1994.

Nall, Garry L. "Dust Bowl Days: Panhandle Farming in the 1930s." *Panhandle-Plains Historical Review* 48 (1975): 43–64.

———. "Panhandle Farming in the 'Golden Age' of American Agriculture." *Panhandle-Plains Historical Review* 46 (1973): 68–93.

———. "Specialization and Expansion: Panhandle Farming in the 1920s." *Panhandle-Plains Historical Review* 47 (1974): 46–67.

Neugebauer, Janet McCreedy. "The Diary of William G. Deloach: A West Texas Farmer." *West Texas Historical Association Year Book* 59 (1983): 108–21.

Nolte, Elleta. "The Igo-Kokernot 06-Johnston Ranch." *West Texas Historical Association Year Book* (1998): 157–63.

Nunn, W. Curtis. "Eighty-Six Hours without Water on the Texas Plains." *Southwestern Historical Quarterly* 43 (January 1940): 360–64.

Olien, Diana Davids. "Rag Town Life in the West Texas Oil Fields." *West Texas Historical Association Year Book* 61 (1985): 15–29.

Parker, Mary E. "Frontier Experiments in Higher Education on the Llano Estacado." *West Texas Association Year Book* 78 (2002): 137–50.

———. "Hereford College: Soonover in Texas." *West Texas Historical Association Year Book* 70 (1994): 126–40.

Pate, J'Nell L. "Marjorie Rogers Morris and the Globe of the Great Southwest in Odessa, Texas." *West Texas Historical Association Year Book* 67 (1991): 18–30.

———. "A Syrian Immigrant in West Texas." *West Texas Historical Association Year Book* 82 (2006): 170–82.

Paxton, Jennifer L. "Silent Wings and Subtle Legacy: Lubbock's Forgotten Glider Base." *West Texas Historical Review* 92 (2016): 10–23.

Pope, Philip. "A Failed Plains Empire: W. P. Soash on the South Plains." *West Texas Historical Association Year Book* 84 (2008): 109–20.

Post, C. W. "Making Rain While the Sun Shines." *Harpers Weekly* 56 (February 24, 1912): 8.

Reeves, Brian O. K. "The Concept of an Altithermal Cultural Hiatus in Northern Plains Prehistory." *American Anthropologist* 75 (1973): 1221–53.

Sanchez, Jose Maria. "A Trip to Texas in 1828." Translated by Carlos E. Castañeda. *Southwestern Historical Quarterly* 29 (April 1926): 249–88.

Seibel, C. W. "The Government's New Helium Plant at Amarillo, Texas." *Journal of Chemical and Molecular Orbital Theory Engineering* 38, no. 9 (September 1938): 550–52.

Sheffy, L. F. "The Experimental Stage of Settlement in the Panhandle of Texas." *Panhandle-Plains Historical Review* 3 (1930): 78–103.

———, ed. "Letters and Reminiscences of General Theodore A. Baldwin: Scouting after Indians on the Plains of West Texas." *Panhandle-Plains Historical Review* 11 (1938): 7–30.

Sledge, Robert. "Girl Editor of the Plains: Cleffie Watson, the *Slatonite*, and the Ku Klux Klan." *West Texas Historical Review* 92 (2016): 24–40.

Smith, Paul Chaat. "Geronimo's Cadillac." *The Sun*, no. 524 (August 2019): 14–17.

Smith, Todd, and Paul H. Carlson. "Locating the Battle of Blanco Canyon." *West Texas Historical Review* 91 (December 2015): 99–118.

Sosebee, Scott. "Dashed Hopes and Gained Opportunities: Mexican American Educational Experiences in Lubbock, Texas from the 1920s through the 1960s." *West Texas Historical Association Year Book* 88 (2007): 67–86.

Starck, Michael, and Paul H. Carlson. "The Llano Estacado, Mexico and Gulf: West Texas' Phantom Railroad." *Permian Historical Annual* 11 (Winter 1975–76): 18–21.

———. "Shafter Lake: Boom Town Bust." *Llano Estacado Southwest Heritage* 5 (Winter 1974–75): 31–33, 38.

Stars, Margaret. "The LX Ranch of Texas." *Panhandle-Plains Historical Review* 6 (1938): 45– 51.

Steele, June M. "Mollie Abernathy: Rancher of the South Plains of West Texas, 1900–1919." *West Texas Historical Association Year Book* 75 (1999): 102–9.

Stephens, Christena. "'Thou Art a Priest Forever . . . ': The Early Priests That Shaped Nazareth, Texas." *West Texas Historical Review* 90 (2014): 103–12.

Strickland, Rex W., ed. "The Recollections of W. S. Glenn." *Panhandle-Plains Historical Review* 22 (1949): 15–64.

Stuntz, Jean. "The Early African American Community in Amarillo." *West Texas Historical Association Year Book* 87 (2011): 63–71.

Sweeney, Kevin. "The Ugly Mask of Vigilante Justice, or the Tragic Tar and Feathering of Father Joseph Keller." *West Texas Historical Review* 93 (2017): 24–34.

Taylor, A. A. "Medicine Lodge Peace Council." *Chronicles of Oklahoma* 2 (June 1924): 98–118.

Taylor, A. J. "New Mexican Pastores and Priests in the Texas Panhandle, 1876–1915." *Panhandle-Plains Historical Review* 56 (1984): 65–79.

————. "Pastores in the Texas Panhandle." Edited by Robert E. Simmons. *Hale County History* 10 (February 1980): 1–46.

Utley, Robert M. "'Pecos Bill' on the Texas Frontier." *American West* 6 (January 1969): 4–13.

Way, Sarah. "Bartonsite: The Passing of a Town." *West Texas Historical Association Year Book* 73 (1997): 83–95.

Weiner, Robert G. "A Brief 100 Year Personal History of the Lubbock and West Texas Musical Heritage." *West Texas Historical Association Year Book* 85 (2009): 175–92.

————. "West Texas and Lubbock Music in the Fifties." *West Texas Historical Association Year Book* 69 (1993): 7–17.

————. "West Texas and Lubbock Music in the Fifties, Part II." *West Texas Historical Association Year Book* 71 (1995): 118–26.

White, Benton R. "F. G. Oxsheer: The Forgotten Cattle King." *West Texas Historical Association Year Book* 61 (1985): 106–15.

Williams, Dennis. "East Invades West: The Salt Cedar Invasion of the Pecos River and Western Environmental Defense." *West Texas Historical Association Year Book* 64 (1988): 79–87.

Williams, J. W. "Coronado: From the Rio Grande to the Concho." *Southwestern Historical Quarterly* 43 (October 1959): 190–220.

Williams, O. W. "From Dallas to the Site of Lubbock in 1877." *West Texas Historical Association Year Book* 15 (1939): 3–21.

Williams, Stuart. "The South Plains and 'Southern-ness.'" *West Texas Historical Association Year Book* 88 (2012): 145–55.

"World War I's Impact on Wool and Lambs." *National Wool Grower* 55 (January 1965): 46–48.

Zeigler, Robert E. "Cowboy Strike of 1883: Its Causes and Meaning." *West Texas Historical Association Year Book* 47 (1971): 32–46.

Index